# DEBT RECOVERY IN EUROPE

# DEBT RECOVERY IN EUROPE

GENERAL EDITORS:
*Bermans, Liverpool*

CONSULTANT EDITOR:
*Andrew Bogle BA, Solicitor*

JORDANS
1995

Published by
Jordan Publishing Limited
21 St Thomas Street
Bristol BS1 6JS

British Library Cataloguing-in-Publication Data

A catalogue record for this book is available
from the British Library.

ISBN  0  85308  308  8

Typeset by Create Publishing Services Limited, Bath
Printed in Great Britain by Henry Ling Ltd, The Dorset Press, Dorchester

# PREFACE

The political debate on European unification may still be a live issue but the economic die has long since been cast. We are all Europeans. Trade between the countries of the European Union increases year by year. To do business successfully abroad, we need to understand the different cultures in which our trading partners operate, not least their legal systems. The aim of this book is to promote knowledge of those different legal systems. Although written by lawyers *Debt Recovery in Europe* is aimed at credit controllers and finance directors. Those reading on will find a refreshing absence of footnotes and references to statutes, save where these cannot be avoided. The style is direct; the message simple. How can a creditor best recover money owing to it in a particular jurisdiction and what is the likely timescale and cost.

Two initial chapters set the scene, providing advice on how to avoid debts going bad and the steps which should be taken to prepare any claim for legal action. The remainder of the text is devoted to a country-by-country survey. Each chapter includes consideration of the following matters: status of the debtor; sources of information; limitation periods; securities available; retention of title; letters before action; pre-litigation remedies; the court system; legal representation; costs and interest; issuing proceedings; obtaining judgment; enforcement options; and insolvency. There is scope to learn a great deal. I can vouch for that.

Thanks, as ever are due to many. There is a danger that the list could resemble an acceptance speech at the Academy Awards but I will attempt to be as brief as possible. The assistance of all involved in the project is greatly appreciated. Particular thanks are due to the contributors one and all. The grasp of abstract ideas by those for whom English is not the mother tongue would put many native speakers to shame. Special gratitude is due to Dennis Campbell at the Centre for International Legal Studies in Salzburg, who drove the project forward when it was in danger of stagnating. Thanks also to everyone at Jordans. On a personal note particular thanks for the tireless work of Mary Atkins, all the help from my wife Louise and, of course, David Orchard.

ANDREW BOGLE
Liverpool
*April 1995*

# CONTRIBUTOR FIRMS

Dr Herbert Matzunski,
Dr Gerald Hauska and
Dr Herbert Matzunski
Salurner Strasse 16/1
6020 Innsbruck
Austria
Tel: 0043 512 5827160
Fax: 0043 512 571467


Dr Elisabeth Hoffmann
Hoffmann & Jaspar
Avenue Franklin D. Roosevelt 96A
1050 Brussels
Belgium
Fax: 00332 640 27 79 040 50 53


Mr Ole Borch
Berning Schlüter Hald
Bredgade 6
1260 Copenhagen K
Denmark
Tel: 0045 33 14 33 33
Fax: 0045 33 32 43 33


Mr Andrew Bogle
Bermans
Pioneer Buildings
65/67 Dale Street
Liverpool
England
Tel: 0151 227 3351
Fax: 0151 236 2107


Mr Christer Ekman
Borenius & Kemppinen
Yrjönkatu 13 A
00120 Helsinki
Finland
Tel: 00358 0 615 333
Fax: 00358 0 615 33499


Mr Jean-Jacques Bertagna, Paris
Ms Lavinia Dugay, Paris
Mr Robert Stevenson, London
*In Paris as:*
Bertagna Gruia Dufaut
59 Avenue Marceau, 75116 Paris
Tel: 0033 1 47 23 05 09
Fax: 0033 1 47 23 04 09
*In London as:*
Berrymans, Salisbury House
London Wall, London EC2M 5QN
Tel: 0171 639 2811
Fax: 0171 920 0361


Dr Gernot Stenger
Alpers & Stenger
Ferdinandstrasse 67
20095 Hamburg
Germany
Tel: 0049 40 32 58 23 0
Fax: 0049 40 32 58 23 85


Mr Nicolas Anagnostopoulos
Lallis Voutsinos Anagnostopoulos
100, Kolokotroni Str.
185 35 Piraeus
Greece
Tel: 0030 1 4225631
Fax: 0030 1 4221543


Mr Frank Nowlan
Matheson Ormsby Prentice
3 Burlington Road
Dublin 4
Ireland
Tel: 00353 1 667 1666
Fax: 00353 1 676 0501

Mr Enrico Gilioli
Studio Legale Gilioli
Pizzale Principessa Clotilde
20121 Milan
Italy
Tel: 00392 29002932
Fax: 00392 6575969

Mr René Faltz
Faltz & Associés
B.P. 1147
1011 Luxembourg
Luxembourg
Tel: 00352 48 50 50
Fax: 00352 48 13 85

Ms Sandra A In't Veld
Van Schoonhoven In't Veld
PO Box 75999
1070 AZ Amsterdam
The Netherlands
Tel: 0031 20 6796969
Fax: 0031 20 6764339

Mr Brendan J Smyth
Bigger & Strahan
Belfast
Northern Ireland
Tel: 01247 270313
Fax: 01247 466939

Amaral Cabral – Advogados
Av. A. Augusto De Aguiar, 25
2° Esq
1000 Lisboa
Portugal
Tel: 003511 352 7255
Fax: 003511 353 3076

Mr Tony Deutsch
Bermans
1 Claremont Terrace
Glasgow
Scotland
Tel: 0141 248 1020
Fax: 0141 333 0318

Mr José A Rodríguez García and
Mr Juan Carlos Castro Rico
Castro, Sueiro & Varela
Claudio Coello, 46, 4°
28001 Madrid
Spain
Tel: 00341 577 50 20
Fax: 00341 431 59 31

Dr David Jenny
Gloor Schiess & Partner
Aeschenvorstadt 4
4010 Basel
Switzerland
Tel: 0041 61 279 33 00
Fax: 0041 61 279 33 10

# CONTENTS

## Chapter 1

# AVOIDING DEBTS GOING BAD

**Andrew Bogle**
**Bermans**
**Liverpool, England**

## 1.1  Introduction

Good credit control is the lifeblood of a healthy business. Before examining in greater detail the actions available to recover a bad debt, there follows an outline of the preventive measures available to a creditor, with advice on how to organise its business to minimise risk and be in a position to put forward a case in the best possible light. For convenience, reference is made to the supply of goods, but the principles set out apply equally if services are being provided to a customer.

Separate consideration should be given to home and export accounts. For those starting in domestic business, much assistance is available through banks, professional advisers, local chambers of commerce, regional development agencies, and the like.

For both domestic and foreign markets, companies need to establish effective credit control methods. Failure to do so means at best reduced profitability with the company acting in effect as its customer's bankers, and at worst the collapse of the business. There are many specialist works on credit procedures which repay study but, in outline, the principles a credit manager should consider are as follows.

### 1.1.1  People

Unless an organisation has motivated people with sufficient ability, any system it employs will be flawed.

### 1.1.2  Technology and training

A company is wise to invest in both technology and training to maximise results.

### 1.1.3  Planning

What are the credit control requirements of the business? Once these are identified, what procedures are to be followed to ensure these are implemented?

### 1.1.4  Administration

Who does what and when? In a small organisation, credit control may be only part of an individual's work. In such cases, it should be ensured that adequate time is set aside at specific junctures to see that credit control policy is implemented. Alternatively, it should be considered whether credit control should be devolved outside the organisation.

Where credit control is an individual's sole responsibility, he should schedule his working year as well as his working day so that priorities are maintained. Where a credit control department consists of several people, job descriptions and levels of responsibility should be established to maximise the human resources available.

### 1.1.5 Documentation

Documentation should be standardised and subject to regular review. The credit controller needs to satisfy himself that company procedures are implemented and that no short cuts arise.

### 1.1.6 Authorisation

All new accounts must be referred to credit control, as should any material change in the status of the customer, such as change in a partnership, a sole trader setting up a limited company, or a request for increased credit facilities.

### 1.1.7 Records

Accurate records of any particular customer and job should be retained and updated as appropriate.

### 1.1.8 Cash flow

Adequate cash flow must be secured. The profit element on each contract will be eaten away if payment is not made on the due date. Where complaints arise, these should be dealt with promptly. A creditor should protect its position as much as possible in the contract terms. Above all, the creditor should ensure that payment terms are adhered to. Where these are exceeded, procedures should be implemented to ensure that money is recovered sooner rather than later. Other methods of ensuring a satisfactory cash flow include credit insurance and factoring.

#### 1.1.8.1 Credit insurance

Insurance covering insolvency and continuing default in payment by a customer provides an additional safeguard. It should not be looked on, however, as a substitute for good credit control. Inevitably, when calculating the overall profitability of a business, allowance must be made for the premiums payable.

Credit control procedures will need to be acceptable to a company's credit insurers. Further information may be obtained from Trade Indemnity plc, Trade Indemnity House, 12/34 Great Eastern Street, London EC2A 3AX, telephone (0171) 739 4311.

*1.1.8.2 Factoring*

Factoring presents a further option. Factoring organisations provide a mix of related services. They administer the sales ledger, assess credit risks, give credit advice, arrange credit insurance, and make cash immediately available up to 80 per cent of the invoice value, the balance payable when a customer makes payment.

Like credit insurance, factoring is not a magic wand for a badly run business, but small to medium-sized companies especially can benefit from the factor's expertise and make savings in management time and administration costs. A variety of factoring companies operate, often tailored to the needs of particular retail sectors.

Factoring may be on a recourse or non-recourse basis, depending on whether the risk reverts on non-payment. In addition, there is the invoice discounting option, providing the cash injection but leaving administration of the ledger to the creditor. Further information regarding factors can be obtained from the Association of British Factors, 1 Northumberland Avenue, London WC2N 5BW, telephone (0171) 930 9112.

### 1.1.9 Other cash-flow finance

A company should attempt to arrange payment terms which will enhance its cash flow. Cash with order might be ideal, but most customers would not be prepared to deal on such terms.

One final option to consider is the employment of a professional debt collection agency. Like the factors, the larger of these tend to provide ancillary services, such as the provision of status reports and tracing missing debtors. The employment of a good collection agency should result in an improved cash flow. A company looks to their services to secure earlier payments.

Their performance should be monitored. If improvements in the rate of collection is insufficient, credit managers may consider it more appropriate to instruct a lawyer directly, once their own internal procedures have been exhausted. Further general information is available from the Small Firms Service, Department of Employment, Steel House, Tothill Street, London SW1H 9NF, telephone (0171) 210 3000, and the Institute of Credit Management, The Watermill, Station Road, South Luffenham, Oakham, Leicester LE15 8NB, telephone (01780) 721888.

## 1.2   Before entering the contract

### 1.2.1   In general

The best action is preventive. No one can eliminate the risk of bad debts, however, one can minimise that risk by taking prudent steps.

One category of risk is the debtor with whom a company has had dealings in the past and who has been associated with a failed business or has proved a bad payer. It is surprising that organisations are still prepared to deal with

such credit risks. Hope rarely triumphs over experience. Companies ignore the
warning signals at their peril.

If there have been no previous dealings with a business, contacts within the
trade and trade associations should be used to gather information regarding
the prospective customer. Again, if there are danger signals, goods should not
be supplied on credit.

A company must ensure that there is a credit management input and that all
new customers considered, or credit facilities offered to any existing customer,
are subject to review. Unless the new business presents a satisfactory credit
risk, a company should either not deal with it or deal only on a limited basis,
guaranteeing payment of cleared funds at or before the time of supply.

### 1.2.2   Bank and trade references

Credit control departments should, as a matter of course, obtain bank and
trade references for new customers. A reference should be requested from the
customer's bank up to a certain credit limit. Anything less than an unqualified
statement that the risk is good should put the enquirer on notice. The same
principles apply when obtaining trade references. If the reference provided is
not familiar, it should be verified that it is, indeed, bona fide. Any prospective
customer providing as a reference a company with which he or a colleague is
associated should be treated with suspicion.

### 1.2.3   Status reports on companies

Status reports on companies should be arranged when considering supply to a
new customer or extension of existing credit facilities. Information may be
obtained either directly from publicly available data lodged by a customer or
through status reports prepared by collection and data agencies. The extent of
the information revealed by the report is likely to be more detailed as the fee
increases.

Where obtaining information direct from a public source, such as accounts
from Companies Registry, the burden of interpreting that information will
fall more heavily on a credit controller. Notice should be taken of the date of
the information provided. Any accounting data will be for an earlier period.

Provided that, following investigation, a prospective customer presents a
good risk, a credit limit should be set for supplies to him and steps taken to
ensure this is adhered to.

## 1.3   Obtaining protection in the contract

### 1.3.1   In general

Further consideration of contractual terms and how these are incorporated
are contained in later chapters in the country-by-country guide. Certain basic
provisions apply wherever a customer does business. Companies should

ensure trading terms are reviewed on a regular basis to take into account any changes in the law or developments in a business. It should be remembered that the demands of individual contracts may make it appropriate to incorporate additional specific terms.

Representatives should ensure all material terms in the contract are agreed and that these are confirmed in writing. Where certain of these are standard terms, the contract must be clearly expressed to be subject to those trading terms. Standard terms will vary from industry to industry. Typically, a contract needs to include provision for the following items:

(1) general provision regarding the application of trading terms;
(2) variation (to be agreed in writing);
(3) price;
(4) description of goods or services;
(5) passing of property and risk;
(6) delivery (place and time);
(7) payment terms (including interest for late payment);
(8) customer's obligations;
(9) warranties;
(10) disclaimer of liabilities (placing a limit on the accepted liability); and
(11) English or Scots law, as appropriate, to apply.

By protecting itself in the contract, a company will have a greater degree of control in the transaction and be in an advantageous position should a dispute subsequently arise. It should be ensured that trading terms are incorporated in the contract. Standard contractual documentation should be expressed to be subject to those terms. A company should determine whether its customer is attempting to incorporate its own trading terms in the contract and agree only if those terms are acceptable and compatible with its own. Preferably, a customer should be persuaded to waive its terms. As a general rule, to be effective, trading terms must be brought to the attention of a customer prior to entry into the contract. They can only be incorporated subsequently with the agreement of all contracting parties.

### 1.3.2 Method of payment

A cheque may be dishonoured by a customer with insufficient funds or stopped, either through a reluctance to pay or a dispute regarding the goods supplied. Such problems can be circumvented by negotiating a guaranteed method of payment. Cash is only practical for smaller transactions. Where larger amounts are involved, the same result can be achieved by a bank draft or wiring funds into the creditor's bank account.

When will payment be made? From the seller's viewpoint, the ideal terms would be cash with order, a situation where no risk is incurred. Realistically, unless a company is dealing with a specialist product and unproven customers, the pressures of the market place are such that it is unlikely to be able to impose such a term. Other possibilities include cash before delivery of goods, usually with an initial down payment with final payment before completing delivery, or cash on delivery, ie, receiving payment before handover of the goods. Both terms create favourable cash flow, but the seller should be aware of the risk of non-acceptance of the goods.

Less satisfactory, but more commonplace, is payment after a specific period, usually net monthly or 30 days. If a customer can obtain supplies on equivalent terms elsewhere, a company may be obliged to deal on such a basis. In these circumstances, it is doubly important to be satisfied regarding a customer's creditworthiness. Terms of repayment of longer than 30 days are not unusual. It is suggested, however, that the longer the repayment term, the less this is in the creditor's interest. The longer the term is, the more it harms cash flow and the greater the risk of non-payment. For large contracts, a company may prefer progress payments, a down payment with scheduled payments when various stages of the contract are reached.

Generally, the earlier payment can be obtained, the better. Stage payments can provide a useful compromise where the customer is holding out for more time than is acceptable. A creditor should never agree to payment when its customer receives settlement himself. The position may be prejudiced through either a third party's inability to pay or a breach by the customer in his contract with that third party.

Obtaining a deposit will not, in itself, provide protection from a customer who subsequently refuses to accept goods or fails to make payment. However, it will provide improved cash flow and lessen any loss suffered.

### 1.3.3 Security

The provision of additional security can afford further protection. Typically, security will be provided by way of a guarantee or indemnity or a legal charge. A guarantee provides for a third party to make payment of money owing should a customer default. An indemnity is essentially similar, but entitles recovery from the indemnifier as a primary remedy, rather than when the customer defaults in payment.

A legal charge may be provided either by a customer or a third party. The debt is charged over the security, usually property, but this could be a life policy or shares. Another form of charge is a debenture over a customer's assets. In the United Kingdom, this is only available against a limited company. The debenture should be expressed to be either a fixed charge over specified company assets and/or a floating charge to take effect over all company assets once crystallised, that is on the occurrence of one of a given set of circumstances.

When are securities appropriate? The additional administration involved means they are inappropriate for routine transactions with tried and tested customers. Where extended credit is being sought or there is uncertainty regarding a new customer, they can provide an extra safeguard. Charges by way of debenture, since they attach to a customer's assets in such a fundamental manner, are only likely to be employed where a very substantial trading relationship exists. Ideally, protection should be by way of security when entering into the contract, but securities can be employed as readily when an existing customer hits financial difficulties.

Who, then, provides these securities? Often, a third-party security is provided by a relative, business associate, director, or another company within a group. Security by way of a legal charge can be furnished either by a third party or the customer. Security cannot be demanded. If, however, a creditor has a situation where the directors of an off-the-shelf limited company with a £2 issued share capital do not have the confidence to guarantee the debts of that company, why should its customers?

What form should securities take? A simple form of guarantee or indemnity will state that, in consideration of goods being supplied to the customer, the guarantor guarantees to pay the supplier on demand the sums owing by that customer, usually up to a specific figure. Legal advice should be sought regarding both the wording to be employed and arranging for the guarantee to be executed. This also applies in respect of charges and their registration. Securities can prove an efficient measure but, to avoid complications, a lawyer should be consulted.

### 1.3.4 Retention of title

The purpose of a retention-of-title provision is to protect a seller's title to goods supplied until such time as the buyer makes payment. Where payment is not made, this term may be invoked so that the goods are returned. The provision is of particular use where a customer becomes insolvent or ceases to trade. It should enable the creditor to receive an advantageous price on resale rather than relying on whatever sale value a receiver can negotiate for the benefit of all creditors in the insolvent estate. In certain circumstances, the retention-of-title clause can be invoked to attach to the proceeds of sale of the goods by the customer.

The country-by-country guide sets out the varying application of retention-of-title clauses. Many books are devoted to the wording and enforcement of such clauses. Decisions in this area have been made over a relatively short period, providing greater or lesser protection to the seller of the goods. Companies should seek legal advice regarding the wording of any retention-of-title provision and how it should be incorporated in their contractual documentation. Regular review of the clause should be made to keep it up to date with legal opinion.

### 1.3.5 Discount for prompt payment

Discount for prompt payment is usually shown on order and invoice documentation as a reduction by a certain percentage provided payment is made within a specified period, being the invoice due date or earlier.

This does create administrative problems, however, if payment is not received within the time specified. For the discount to be reclaimed, it is necessary to raise a further invoice each time payment is not received within the discount period.

### 1.3.6 Interest for late payment

It is surprising that every business does not demand interest for late payment. If a customer fails to make payment by the agreed due date, his cash flow benefits at the seller's expense, and interest on the debt should be allowed to compensate for this. A suitable provision should be incorporated in the seller's trading terms and clear reference be made to this in order and invoice documents.

Again, there are administrative complications if the interest rate is tied to a bank base rate. Far easier is to apply a fixed percentage rate across the board. Creditors should be aware, however, of fluctuating interest rates and keep the rate applied under review. If the rate is disproportionately high compared to those being charged in the marketplace, a claim for interest may be found to be a penalty at law and unenforceable. If the rate has lagged behind interest rate rises, it is affording insufficient protection.

A company's contract should be tailored to its needs. The temptation to cut corners by putting together what appear to be appropriate clauses from competitors' contracts should be avoided. The risk is that an unenforceable instrument may be created.

## 1.4 Monitoring the contract

### 1.4.1 Preventing breach of trade terms

Preventing breach of trade terms is a two-way process. A company must ensure not only compliance by its customer, but also internal implementation of its own policy. The procedures set for orders, new customers, and credit limits must be followed. If it proves necessary to vary the terms of a given contract, this should be confirmed in writing.

It may be that a customer attempts to alter unilaterally material terms of the contract. This may include anything from delaying an order, refusing to accept goods, or failure to make an agreed payment. The customer should be notified of the breach immediately and an explanation sought. There may be extenuating circumstances which mean that a supplier is still prepared to deal with its customer. If, however, a company can no longer deal with that customer in confidence, it can look to the customer for any damages suffered as a result of their actions. The decision and the reasons for it should be confirmed in writing.

### 1.4.2 Implementing repayment terms

Often, problems will only be encountered once the seller has performed its side of the bargain. Credit managers should ensure that an invoice is raised at the earliest opportunity once the contract is performed. Equally, where it proves necessary to raise a credit note, this should be done immediately so it cannot be used as an excuse for delaying payment. Statements of account should be sent out on a monthly basis.

Once an invoice is raised, the credit controller should employ a diary system to flag that particular invoice immediately if it becomes due for payment. Where repayment terms have been exceeded, the controller needs both an efficient procedure for pursuing payment and a policy decision regarding future dealings with that customer. Delay can turn late payments into a bad debt.

Where a customer is unable or unwilling to pay, the impetus must come from the seller. The first steps are internal:

(1)   statements;
(2)   reminder letters;
(3)   telephone calls; and
(4)   where appropriate, visits to the customer.

A contemporary record of discussions between the parties should be kept. If a customer states that he has cash-flow problems but will make payment in seven days, this should be noted and confirmed by fax or letter, indicating the action which will follow should the customer default.

Once internal chasing procedures are exhausted, the creditor should move promptly to the next stage. Where persuasion has failed, decisive legal action should be taken and, unless there exists a proven in-house system, it is at this stage that a lawyer should be instructed. Where a company employs factors or a collection agency, they will recommend appropriate courses of action. Where a company debt is insured, there will be requirements for notification of bad debts and procedures to be adopted.

It seems incredible that some companies are prepared to continue to trade with customers following an earlier default in payment. There may be commercial considerations which dictate that everything should be attempted to preserve the business relationship but, once this breaks down, the only sensible course is to cease all future dealings. In larger organisations, other trading divisions should be alerted. The situation of another depot continuing to supply a customer who has been placed on a credit blacklist is unlikely to appeal to any creditor's sense of humour.

A clear note of any delay or default in payment should be made on a customer's ledger. Checks should be made for any additional orders in the pipeline and halts placed on future work and deliveries. It should be considered whether it is appropriate to invoke a retention-of-title clause. It should be ascertained if there has been contra trading. If money is owing to the defaulting customer, settlement should be withheld. If the seller holds goods, plant, or designs owned by the customer, these should be retained pending settlement of the overdue account; in each instance, a letter should be sent to the customer confirming the action being taken.

Any debt is important, but priority should always be given to the larger sums outstanding whose impact on the health of a business will be proportionately greater.

## 1.5   Procedures checklist

The procedures to be followed when dealing with a new customer may be summarised as follows:

   (1)  Establish identity of customer.
   (2)  Obtain bank and trade references.
   (3)  Make status enquiries.
   (4)  Open customer file, setting credit limit.
   (5)  Enter into contract and:
      (a)  incorporate trade terms;
      (b)  consider steps to protect seller's position in contract;
      (c)  create written record of contract terms; and
      (d)  act immediately if terms breached.
   (6)  Supply goods on standard documents.
   (7)  Raise invoice immediately, with monthly statements.
   (8)  Monitor for payment by due date.
   (9)  On default, press for payment by:
      (a)  letter;
      (b)  telephone call;
      (c)  visit.
 (10)  Consider legal action immediately when internal procedures exhausted.
 (11)  Retain relevant documents.

## 1.6   Exports

### 1.6.1   In general

Even those familiar with the domestic market should be aware of the potential pitfalls when dealing in an unknown foreign market. A credit controller needs to be familiar with the regulations and customs of any given country, the ways of doing business and the documents required. The language in which to communicate and the political stability of those countries also should be considered. Practical assistance can be offered by a variety of organisations:

   (1)  British Export Houses Association, 16 Dartmouth Street, London SW1H 9BL, telephone (0171) 222 5419.
   (2)  British International Freight Corporation, Redfern House, Browells Lane, Feltham TW13 7ED, telephone (0181) 844 2266.
   (3)  International Chamber of Commerce, 14/15 Belgrave Square, London SW1X 8PS, telephone (0171) 823 2811.
   (4)  British Overseas Trade Board, Ashdown House, 123 Victoria Street, London SW1E 6RB, telephone (0171) 215 7877.

(5)  Export Credit Guarantee Department, 2 Exchange Tower, Harbour Exchange Square, London E14 9GS, telephone (0171) 512 7000.

### 1.6.2  Currency invoicing

The volatility of international currency markets presents an exporter with the dilemma of whether to invoice in sterling or the home currency of its customer. Until the advent of the European Currency Unit (ECU), businesses can only obtain limited protection by adopting the currency less likely to suffer from fluctuating exchange rates.

The Government's Export Credits Guarantee Department provides exporters with insurance cover and guarantees for repayment to banks for longer-term credit. Premiums payable are adjusted according to the creditworthiness of a given customer or country. Claims become payable on evidence of insolvency, following protracted default and for failure to take up goods resulting from delay in payment. Exporters also may wish to consider confirming house credits, where approximately 85 per cent of the contract price is paid on shipment by the confirming house (usually a division of a clearing or merchant bank).

### 1.6.3  Other cash-flow finance

Credit controllers will find many factoring companies that provide export assistance. When exporting, a company may prefer to liaise with its bank's operation in that country. Again, when exporting, consideration should be given to the possibility of using a confirming house. In such situations, the preferred method of dealing is likely to be by documentary credit where payment is made by a bank against documents on despatch of the goods. This may take one of several forms. The most satisfactory is an irrevocable credit issued or confirmed by a United Kingdom bank. This cannot be revoked without the vendor's consent, and it has the added advantage of a known financial institution rather than an unproven overseas bank.

When exporting, specific considerations are required before entering into the contract. References can prove more problematic. A company needs to be satisfied not only that trade references are authentic, but also regarding the standing of its customer's bank.

# Chapter 2

# PREPARING THE CASE

**Andrew Bogle**
**Bermans**
**Liverpool, England**

## 2.1   Introduction

A company has exhausted its credit control procedures, but has been unable to obtain payment from its debtor. Legal action is now required, and the steps to be taken are listed in subsequent chapters in the country-by-country guide. Before that happens, however, the credit manager needs to gather together all relevant documents and information.

A valid claim may fail because it has not been properly prepared. A well-presented case can make all the difference to an action where difficulties are likely to be encountered. This applies whether the credit manager is instructing lawyers, providing information to factors or a debt collection agency, or dealing with internal staff.

## 2.2   Identifying the debtor

Identifying the debtor is not always as straightforward as might be imagined. A contract is entered into by two legal entities. Is the seller really sure who it has contracted with? One potential problem here is that pressure to obtain sales can undermine successful credit management. The benefit of securing further business for a company and benefits for the individual sales person should never be at the expense of accurate information.

The credit manager needs to ensure that there are satisfactory procedures to correctly identify the debtor. The name and legal status of the party who is entering into the contract should be established. Does the customer trade in an individual capacity? Alternatively, is he a partner in a firm, in which case who are the other partners? Credit managers should obtain full names and home, as well as business, addresses if possible or, failing this, at least initials, surnames, and whether these individuals are male or female.

Is an individual contracting on behalf of a limited company or foreign body corporate? Again, the credit manager should establish the full, correct name, and its registered office or principal place of business. If an individual is contracting on behalf of a club, charity, or a body corporate, such as a local or health authority, it is necessary to establish its correct legal form. Where a party contracts as agent on behalf of a principal customer, credit procedures should ensure that full details of the principal against whom future action will follow are on file.

In addition to knowing the correct name and legal status of a debtor, a creditor must be able to prove it. The debtor may deny having entered into a contract with the creditor or may operate under a variety of legal entities, either for legitimate business reasons or to create confusion. The contract may be oral, in writing, or a combination of the two. In the United Kingdom, there is no particular magic attached to a written contract. Except for sale of land, an oral contract is valid. The difficulty can be in proving who said what. Where it is one person's word against another, the potential areas of dispute multiply and any contested action becomes that much more problematic. Therefore, whenever possible, the details of a contract agreed orally should be confirmed in writing immediately.

The contract documents should be retained. These will assist in identifying a debtor. There may be a request for an estimate, an order confirmation, letterheading, cheques, details on references, a calling card, or a signed proof of delivery. All can help in varying degrees. Sales representatives should not be satisfied with a trading name. If, for instance, a debtor is a limited company, trading as 'Law Books', it must be identified as such, preferably adding the trading name 'Law Limited t/a Law Books'.

Credit control departments should retain a customer profile comprising all essential information, including full name and legal status. This should be updated when any changes occur, for instance, when a customer previously trading as a firm sets up as a limited company.

Despite all best efforts, there may still be uncertainty regarding the correct identity of a debtor. In those circumstances, it is better to investigate further (see below) rather than guess. Where proceedings are issued in the wrong form, additional costs and delay are incurred. When a debtor is pursued using the wrong form, a creditor cannot oblige him to make payment. The creditor will incur irrecoverable costs and may be liable for costs incurred by the defendant. Vital time will be lost. Amendment or the issue of further proceedings will be required, with attendant further costs. In most jurisdictions, if a creditor issues proceedings in the wrong form and the principal debt is then paid, there is no entitlement to recover costs and interest.

## 2.3 Establishing the existence and credit status of the debtor

Knowing the correct identity of a debtor is irrelevant if the debtor's whereabouts cannot be established and the debtor has no ability to pay. A creditor who satisfies itself on these two points prior to issuing proceedings will reduce the risk of wasting money.

The creditor should physically check that the debtor is still at its last known address. A telephone call may suffice, but attendance at the premises will give a clearer picture of the debtor's assets. A disconnected telephone or mail returned undelivered are obvious danger signs. It would be foolhardy to do business with a customer only prepared to provide a post office box number. A trading address should always be required.

If the debtor has left its last known address, how can its current where-abouts be traced? Trade connections may provide useful information. Certain public information will be available (see the country-by-country guide). Cred-itors risk expending much time and effort attempting to track down a vanished debtor themselves. It is more efficient to instruct enquiry agents, placing a limit on their charges. They may have access to information not available to the general public. If they can trace the debtor, they may also be able to report on its financial status. Enquiry agents can be instructed directly. Solicitors, factoring companies, and debt collection agencies are likely to instruct enquiry agents with a proven track record and can arrange to instruct agents abroad.

Beyond physical inspection of the debtor's premises, further information will be available regarding its financial position. Individual countries will have their own laws regarding how much financial information must be filed centrally by businesses and provision for disclosure of this information. Such information, however, will often be of limited application. By definition, the information is likely to be out of date. A better, if more expensive, option would be to approach a credit reference agency. Such agencies provide a variety of reports, with additional information regarding the credit rating of a business.

## 2.4 Building the case file

### 2.4.1 In general

The importance of a well-documented case cannot be stressed too highly. The courts will not determine if a case is morally right. Each claimant must prove that his is a valid claim. Certain basic documentation is required for undis-puted claims. The value of being fully prepared will become apparent, however, when disputes arise. Credit controllers should ensure that the internal systems of their business are prepared for the possibility of future litigation and that essential documents are retained.

For lawyers to be effective, they should be provided with all relevant information about a given case. However, initially, a standard letter of instruction with full particulars of the debtor and the sum outstanding will be sufficient to enable the lawyer to issue a letter before action. If proceedings then follow, a statement of account should be furnished. Further require-ments are set out in the country-by-country guide. If there is a dispute, its nature should be outlined. If the lawyer needs more detail at this stage, he will contact his client. The following points also should be considered.

### 2.4.2 What is the nature of the claim?

A lawyer may not be familiar with the nature of the company's business. A claim may be for goods sold and delivered, services rendered, advertising, hire charges, and/or transport and may include various sundry items of expenses incurred.

This list is not exhaustive. Whatever constitutes the nature of the claim will need to be shown on the proceedings issued. For convenience, future references in this section are to goods sold, but the principles apply equally to other rights of action.

### 2.4.3    How much is owing?

If there has been a single transaction, an invoice will suffice to indicate how much is owing. Where there have been a series of transactions, there should be a clear statement of account listing the credit and debit entries. If a lawyer or collection agency is acting, the creditor should provide clear photocopies, retaining originals which may subsequently be required.

If, for ease of storage, the company reduces documents to microfiche, this is acceptable. An order only is not sufficient to pursue a money claim. There must also be an invoice.

### 2.4.4    Is contractual interest owing?

A creditor is only entitled to interest if such terms are incorporated in the contract. Details of the rate of interest applying should be provided and the total interest shown in the statement of account.

### 2.4.5    When is payment due?

A creditor will only be entitled to sue on an invoice if it is overdue for payment. A company may be in the situation where there have been a series of transactions and payments on earlier invoices have been exceeded, but more recent invoices are not yet due. The creditor may be able to sue on all invoices on the basis that the payment terms have been exceeded or may have to issue separate proceedings as and when the later invoices become due. Consideration as to which method should be used is given in the country-by-country guide. Where there is an entitlement to recover either statutory or contractual interest, its extent will be determined by the invoice due date.

### 2.4.6    Common defences

Where a debt is subject to dispute the possible defences should be considered. The most common defences encountered are as follows.

#### 2.4.6.1   'I never contracted with the creditor'

If a company has correctly identified its debtor, such an argument should be defeated.

#### 2.4.6.2   'I never received the goods'

A signed proof of delivery will counter this defence. Creditors should beware of unsigned proofs or a scrawled signature. The carrier or representative should insist on a clear signature from a person in authority. Where a customer is collecting goods, a signed receipt should be required.

### 2.4.6.3  *'That is not what we agreed'*

It should be verified that the contract is for the goods supplied. Clear details on estimates, orders, correspondence, and invoices can defeat a spurious defence. If the contract was by sample and the creditor has retained, for instance, proofs in artwork or fabric samples approved by its customer, these will strengthen the case.

### 2.4.6.4  *'The goods are defective'*

The nature of the dispute should be considered carefully. An inspection of the goods should be required. They are themselves evidence in the proceedings. If the goods have been tampered with, can the creditor prove this? It may be necessary to appoint an independent expert to determine the validity of such claims.

### 2.4.6.5  *'I rejected the goods'*

It must be for the debtor to provide evidence of valid rejection of the goods and his right to do so.

### 2.4.6.6  *'I want to return the goods'*

Not wanting or not being able to pay presents no defence, unless goods were supplied on a sale or return basis. A creditor should judge, however, the debtor's ability to pay and its own ability to resell.

In certain circumstances, it may make commercial sense to accept the return of goods, provided the debtor is responsible for carriage charges.

### 2.4.6.7  *'The goods arrived too late'*

The creditor should examine the contract terms. Was time of the essence? If so, were deadlines complied with? The contract documents and proof of delivery will be crucial here.

### 2.4.6.8  *'I have a claim to offset against the creditor'*

The debtor may be doing work for the creditor. In that case, he can offset valid claims against money owing to it.

### 2.4.6.9  *'I lost money because the creditor failed to perform the contract'*

A defence need not be restricted to a denial of liability. The debtor can look to the creditor for consequential loss he has suffered through any alleged breach of contract. Such counterclaims may include additional expense, loss of profits, and penalties incurred.

Again, it is for the debtor to satisfy the court that he has a valid counterclaim. Was the creditor aware or could it have reasonably foreseen the loss its customer would suffer?

### 2.4.7 Other factors

#### 2.4.7.1 Timing

Whatever the nature of the dispute, its timing will have a material bearing on its prospects for success. Certain defects may only become apparent some time after the date of supply but, as a general rule, one would expect disputes to be raised immediately.

Therefore, a creditor should keep copies of correspondence and accounts chasing late payment or, where these are in standard form, have the ability to reproduce them. If it can be shown that a dispute is only raised subsequent to reminders for payment, the debtor will face an uphill struggle convincing the court that his is a valid defence.

#### 2.4.7.2 Incorporation of terms

The need to incorporate the company's terms and conditions of trading into the contract has been discussed already. In disputed cases, a copy of those terms should be provided to the company's lawyer. The creditor should also identify how these have been brought to the attention of its customer. Price lists or brochures incorporating the terms and letterheadings and order confirmation with the terms on the reverse should be retained.

These terms may provide conclusive evidence of when payment was due. They should support a retention-of-title claim. They should be drafted to include a provision that any disputes must be notified to the supplier within a set number of days.

#### 2.4.7.3 What constitutes the contract?

Consideration should be given to what constitutes the contract. This may be a single document or several. Again, when a dispute arises, these will be required. Proving a claim is more difficult when all or part has been negotiated orally. Where practical, it is prudent to confirm oral terms in writing.

#### 2.4.7.4 Recording sales negotiations

Companies should encourage their sales departments to make a record of meetings and telephone attendances. When a dispute arises, a contemporaneous note will carry greater weight than someone attempting to recall events at a distance in time. Where there are subsequent variations in a contract, these should be noted.

When a dispute arises, signed and dated statements from those employees who had dealings with the contract should be obtained. There may be need for future clarification once full details of the defence are disclosed, but an initial statement will assist the creditor and its advisers in assessing the prospects for the claim.

### 2.4.7.5  Separate rights of action

Consideration also should be given to any separate rights of action which may be enjoyed. Dishonoured cheques are evidence of a debtor's inability to pay and will defeat a spurious defence. Immediately the creditor is advised the cheque has been rejected, notice of dishonour should be sent to the debtor (see Appendix to Chapter 6). In the English courts, a creditor will enjoy a separate right of action where it has given notice of dishonour on a cheque issued by a third party.

The creditor may have obtained a guarantee or charge. Where the debtor defaults, demand should be made on this third-party security and copies of the documents and correspondence provided.

### 2.4.7.6  Additional information

Finally, whether a debt has been disputed or not, creditors may possess additional information regarding their debtor's financial situation which would assist a recovery, and the company's lawyers should be advised of this. There may be alternative trading addresses, vehicles, assets held in store or in use on the site of a third party, money in a bank account, or property owned.

## 2.5   Evaluating the case

### 2.5.1   In general

The creditor should be aware of genuine weaknesses in a case. If there is a valid defence or counterclaim, time and money can be wasted pursuing a fruitless action.

Where the case is arguable or any dispute extends to only part of the claim, can a compromise be negotiated? Once a creditor decides to go ahead, however, the case should be pursued vigorously.

### 2.5.2   Checklist of documents

Before commencing litigation, consideration should be given to the following documents needed in support of the case:

(1) Terms and conditions of trading (and documents incorporating these).
(2) Estimates.
(3) Orders.

(4) Debtor's letterheading.
(5) Cheques.
(6) Bank and trade references.
(7) Proofs of delivery.
(8) Invoices.
(9) Statements.
(10) Reminder letters.
(11) Technical specifications.
(12) Product samples.
(13) Contemporary attendance notes.
(14) Correspondence between parties.
(15) Witness statements.
(16) Time sheets (or other proof of work done).
(17) Information regarding debtor's assets.
(18) Documents supporting action against third parties.

## Chapter 3

# AUSTRIA

**Herbert Matzunski**
**Dr Gerald Hauska and Dr Herbert Matzunski**
**Innsbruck, Austria**

## 3.1 Introduction

Under article 1 of the Federal Constitutional Act, Austria is a republic. It is a union and consists of nine states. Legislative and executive powers are distributed among the Federal Government and the states. The separation of powers between the Federal Government and the states is very complicated. The sources of law are constitutional law, ordinary statutes and regulations. The basic principles of the Constitution are the democratic, republican and federal principle and the principle of the rule of law.

The main sources of law for debt recovery are the Enforcement Code, the Code for Debt Recomposition, and the Bankruptcy Code, all statutes dating to 1914. Concerning debt recovery, all the statutes apply to the nine states ensuring uniformity in the legal system for debt recovery. All Austrian lawyers are entitled to represent parties in debt recovery throughout the whole of Austria.

## 3.2 Initial considerations

### 3.2.1 Status of the debtor

The status of the debtor should be established before business transactions are completed. Pursuing the wrong party will increase costs and incur delay, reducing the prospects of recovery. In the worst circumstances, demands are invalid and payment need not be made by the debtor. When beginning a business in Austria, attempts must be made to obtain relevant information about the business partner. The sources for obtaining such information in Austria are set out below.

### 3.2.2 Legal entities

The various legal entities which may be pursued in the Austrian courts are summarised as follows:

(1) an individual who may trade either in his own name or use a trading name;
(2) a firm, comprising two or more individual partners;[1]

---

1 The abbreviation GesBR, meaning *Gesellschaft bürgerlichen Rechts*, is used. All individual partners are fully liable, even if one partner makes a contract on his own behalf.

(3)   a limited company, either GesmbH or GmbH;[1]

(4)   a limited partnership, consisting of some limited partners and at least one general partner, who is fully liable;[2]

(5)   a company limited by shares;[3]

(6)   a charity;[4]

(7)   a club;[5] and

(8)   a body corporate.[6]

The Republic of Austria itself can be pursued and, in such case, letters before action should be sent to the *Finanzprokuratur*, Singerstrasse 17–19, A–1011 Vienna.

Minors under 19 years of age and individuals subject to mental health legislation who do not have the capacity to enter into contracts cannot be pursued. The same applies to an undischarged bankrupt. Where an individual debtor has died, a letter before action should be sent to the notary public who acts on behalf of the local probate court. Probate courts in Austria are exclusively district courts. If debts are disputed by the successors, legal action can be taken against these persons. Their liability for the debts of the deceased depends on their hereditary title and their declaration regarding the extent over which they claim the inheritance.

Where a person purports to contract on behalf of a company after it is placed in liquidation, a right of action will lie against that individual. Discharged bankrupts can be pursued if they commit an offence under the insolvency legislation; such claims should be prepared with care.

### 3.2.3 Sources of information

Generally, all relevant information should be at the creditor's disposal when business is commenced with a customer. If money remains owing, tracing a debtor can cause difficulties. First, one should consider using the telephone and trade directories. The Land Registry, the Commercial Register and the local Probate Register are also useful sources of information.

The Chambers of Commerce can also be a source of information. There are nine regional chambers and one Federal Chamber. Each are divided into six sections namely, commerce, trade, industry, banking and insurance, tourism

---

1 Limited companies are common in Austria. Limited companies are obliged on all their documents to show in which court they are registered at the Register of Companies.

2 Such companies are styled under the abbreviations GesmbH & Co KG, KG, or KEG.

3 The *Aktiengesellschaft*, or AG, is, compared to a GmbH, not common.

4 In a transaction with a charity, information and verification of status should be sought from the local authorities.

5 This type of entity is rare in business, although it can occur that an individual, a firm, or a limited company may trade as a club, which consists of at least two or more members. All clubs must register their details with the local authority, where there exists a special club register. Action is taken against either the club or against the officers of the club in their representative capacities. In such cases, careful investigation of the club register is required before pursuing a claim.

6 The range of such institutions is wide for historical reasons.

and traffic. All regional chambers maintain registers containing information about their members. The chambers of commerce provide such information at a minimal fee of up to ATS 100. However, such information may be out of date.

The cost for information from the Land Registry and the Commercial Register is ATS 100.

Information also is available from the two credit institutions in Austria, the *Kreditschutzverband* von 1870 (KSV), Zelinkagasse 10, A1010 Vienna, and the *Alpenländischer Kreditorenverband* (AKV), Schleifmühlgasse 2, 1040 Vienna. These two credit institutions provide excellent information on all debtors, especially in cases of moratorium, debt recomposition and bankruptcy.

Notice of winding-up petitions can be found in the Commercial Register, and bankruptcy orders and meetings of creditors are published in the *Amtsblatt der Viennaer Zeitung*, Rennweg 16, 1030 Vienna. Information regarding a debtor's ability to pay is available from the KSV and the AKV, as well as from D & B Schimmelpfeng GmbH, a well-regarded inquiries office at Opernring 3–5, 1010 Vienna.

### 3.2.4 Is the debt statute-barred?

For recovery cases in Austria, a creditor must issue proceedings within three years of the date on which the debt becomes due for payment. Otherwise, the debtor is entitled to apply to the court for the action to be struck out with costs. There is no other opportunity to bring the claim.

The claim must be brought to court no later than the last day of the three-year limitation period. The three-year period begins at the point when an initial invoice is issued. Letters before action do not affect the limitation period.

### 3.2.5 Security

Security can take various forms. Depending on the contract, security is obtained by fixed or floating charges, legal charges or guarantees. Holding security allows the creditor to choose whether to pursue the debtor for recovery, to enforce the security or to follow both options. Important contracts should entitle the creditor to encumber properties of the customer with a security mortgage. The cost for this is 1.1 per cent of the debt on mortgage.

The best security the creditor may hold is a guarantee. With bank guarantees, the creditor must make a formal demand for payment by registered letter. The remedies available to a creditor against a guarantor are the same as those against the principal debtor.

### 3.2.6 Retention of title

The customer cannot make payment. He is likely to go out of business or has already been declared insolvent. In this situation, if the customer continues to hold the goods and there is a retention-of-title clause in the contract, the creditor can at least attempt to obtain a return of those goods. A retention-of-title clause is part of the contract, and it must be agreed at the commencement of the contract. The retention-of-title clause is of no effect if it appears for the first time in a delivery note or in the invoice. Such clauses must be part of the initial order.

If the retention-of-title clause is valid, it must be enforced. The first step is to identify the goods, which requires that all goods be mentioned correctly in the order, the delivery note or the invoice. If this is not possible, the claim will fail. If the goods have been sold onward, the claim also will fail. The same applies where goods have been incorporated so that they are no longer identifiable.

If the retention-of-title clause is valid and the goods have not been sold onward, the creditor must notify the customer or the appointed receiver of the claim. Arrangements must be made for removal of the goods. The contract should include a clause which entitles the creditor to inspect the goods and to have them removed if there is a valid retention-of-title clause. If the customer refuses to give the goods back to the creditor, the creditor should immediately seek an injunction to protect his legal position.

Injunctions can be used to require deposit of goods in court until the end of the proceedings. When the court takes charge of the goods the plaintiff must put up security.

### 3.2.6.1  Simple retention of title

The above comments refer to a simple retention of title. Generally, retention of title must be agreed before the property is delivered to the buyer. Agreement on retention of title after the delivery of the property is invalid. Retention of title is extinguished by:

(1)   full settlement of the purchase price;
(2)   sale of property by the buyer when the original seller has agreed to this;
(3)   bona fide acquisition by a third party who either did not have knowledge of the retention of title or could not have been reasonably expected to have such knowledge;[1]
(4)   renunciation of the retention of title by the seller; or
(5)   loss or consumption of the property.[2]

### 3.2.6.2  Extended retention of title

'Simple' retention of title is sufficient security if the buyer intends to keep the property unaltered for himself. However, this is not always consistent with the

---

1   Bona fide acquisition can be prevented by marking the property in such a manner that everyone is informed of ownership by the original seller.
2   The courts have held that reworking of a property extinguished the retention of title under which such property was sold. However, the position now is that reworking such property brings about common ownership by both the manufacturer and the original owner of such property.

necessities of business. Reselling the property is often the normal course of action, thereby enabling the buyer to settle his debts with the seller. In order to maintain the maximum advantages of retention of title, special forms have developed, one being called 'extended retention of title'.

The buyer agreeing to extended retention of title assigns as security to the seller all receivables out of a future resale of the property and promises to deliver immediately to the seller all cash he will receive from such receivables. A third-party buyer must be informed of the obligations under such a retention of title.

### 3.2.6.3   *Enlarged retention of title*

Enlarged retention of title serves as security not only for the purchase price but also for other claims of the seller against the buyer. Such forms of retention of title are not valid in Austria.

## 3.3   Letters before action

### 3.3.1   Are they necessary?

It is usual, but not compulsory, for a lawyer's letter to be sent before action is commenced. Firms usually will have implemented a system of reminders by letter or telephone when an invoice becomes overdue. It is not necessary to send monthly statements to a debtor customer.

When the customer is in severe financial difficulties the creditor should issue proceedings immediately. In Austria, there is no general rule recommending that a lawyer's letter be sent, even if several reminder letters have been sent by the firm. Sometimes, receipt of a lawyer's letter can produce payment or can encourage debtors to put forward proposals, such as payment by instalments. Requests for payment for small sums are often made by collection agencies. Such agencies often charge a fixed fee and part of the interest paid by the debtor. The creditor, therefore, should make clear what costs will be deducted before authorising such agencies to pursue debt recovery.

It is recommended that a lawyer is given power of authority when the outstanding sums are ATS 50,000 or more or payment is overdue for more than six months. The practical consideration is to save time and to be successful in recovering debts. When letters before action are sent, a successful creditor is entitled to look to the debtor for payment of statutory interest. Interest rates are four per cent for customers, five per cent for merchants, and six per cent for drawn cheques. Higher interest rates can be charged as contractual interest or based on current bank rates.

As a general rule, letters before action should be sent, except where the invoice states the time of payment as a fixed date or a fixed period of time (usually 30 days). When the invoice is due for payment, the lawsuit can be taken immediately against the debtor.

### 3.3.2 What should they say?

The content of the letter depends on the needs of the creditor. A standard letter can be tailored to a client's particular needs. If additional information is incorporated into a standard letter or if multiple copies of the letter are faxed or posted, there may be additional costs. Creditors should avoid pre-printed forms incorporating typed-in debt details. Such letters have little influence on debtors. The following should be included in a letter before action:

(1) the full, correct name and address of the debtor;[1]
(2) the date of the letter and a copy, which should be retained;
(3) the full title of the creditor, including any trading name;[2]
(4) the amount due;[3]
(5) demand for payment within a specified period, usually 14 days or less; and
(6) the address to which payment is to be made.[4]

Letters before action should provide a clear indication that failure to make payment as specified will result in the issue of proceedings. It also should be noted that the debtor must pay all the costs of the proceedings if the lawsuit is won by the creditor. Judgment by Austrian courts entitles the creditor to execute for the costs of proceedings against the debtor in the same way that the initial debt can be executed. The creditor is also entitled to claim interest on costs at a rate of four per cent.

The letter should be clear and concise, avoiding legalisms. Experience has shown that the clear message 'proceedings will follow' often produces payment or at least a proposal to pay by instalments.

### 3.3.3 May they demand interest for late payment?

Interest for late payment may be demanded, from the date on which the invoice becomes due for payment. Lawyer's costs or the costs of collecting agencies are not always paid by the debtor, even if a letter before action by a lawyer was necessary and caused by the debtor. Over the last 20 years, Austrian courts have determined in various judgments that there is no compensation for the costs of the letter. Sometimes, however, the debtor can be persuaded to make payment for the costs of the letter.

Once the creditor gives a power of authority to a lawyer, negotiations should be through the lawyer. Confusion can arise if creditor and lawyer both negotiate with the debtor and there is no single line of communication. The creditor also runs the risk of reaching a less-than-satisfactory agreement with the debtor.

---

1 Where the debtor has several addresses, the payment section should be used, but it is also recommended to send the letter to the registered office of the debtor.
2 If the debtor is an individual, the date of birth should also be noted in order to avoid problems in enforcement procedures.
3 This will normally include invoices subject to dispute, invoices not yet due should be omitted.
4 In Austria, it is usual that payment is made to the lawyer rather than to the creditor directly.

## 3.4    Pre-action and non-judicial remedies

### 3.4.1    Court orders

Pre-action remedies in Austria are restricted to injunctions.[1] The costs for this remedy must be borne by the client. Thus, these remedies are expensive and risky. If the claim fails, the debtor may bring a claim for all the damages caused by an unjustified injunction.

Injunctions are a useful weapon in the legal armoury. They may be employed in the pre-action stage (preliminary injunctions), as well as in proceedings already commenced.

### 3.4.2    Injunctions

An application for an injunction must be a matter of urgency. The applicant must establish the likelihood of his claim and the potential prejudice to him which calls for immediate action against his adversary. The application is made to the court without notice first being given to the opposing party. The procedure has the advantage of speed and secrecy. Where the claim is of substance and there is an immediate risk of the debtor dissipating his assets, an injunction is the most useful weapon. An injunction can also be made to the court when proceedings have already started. Pre-action injunctions require the following conditions to be met:

(1)    there must be a serious question to be tried;[2]

(2)    the creditor is obliged to give a full and frank disclosure of all relevant facts, not merely those supporting his case;

(3)    the court aims to preserve the status quo and, therefore, will grant an injunction only if the creditor would not adequately be compensated by an award of damages;

(4)    the creditor must give evidence of the risk that a debtor will dissipate his assets, reducing the prospects for recovery; and

(5)    if evidence supporting the claim is weak, the court may direct the applicant to post security in cash, before issuing the injunction.[3]

In practice, providing evidence for the prospects of the claim is much easier than establishing potential prejudice. The ruling of the courts is very restrictive so that injunctions in Austria play a minor role when compared with the practice in other countries. In some areas, when potential prejudice need not be established, injunctions are common, ie, in unfair competition cases and some industrial property rights cases. However, preliminary injunctions in debt recovery cases are the exception.

---

1 Enforcement Code, Section 3.

2 The creditor must certify that his demand for payment is legal and admissible. The establishment of the claim is usually done by documents and affidavits and can be obtained by an affidavit declaration. The last monthly statement of account should be enclosed. The court may hear a witness if the witness can be immediately presented to the court by the applicant.

3 The deposit should cover any damages which the debtor would be likely to suffer as a result of an unjustified injunction.

When issuing an injunction, the court must order the applicant to file a lawsuit within a given period of time, usually two to four weeks. Consequently, applicants normally combine the lawsuit and the application for the injunction in one brief.

## 3.5  The court system

### 3.5.1  Structure of the courts

There are ordinary courts and special courts for civil disputes, for example the Cartel Court. Ordinary courts have jurisdiction over all civil disputes unless these are referred to special courts or other authorities. Furthermore, ordinary courts take jurisdiction over criminal cases. There are ordinary courts on four levels, namely:

(1)  district courts (*Bezirksgerichte*);
(2)  state courts (*Landesgerichte*);
(3)  courts of appeal (*Oberlandesgerichte*); and
(4)  the Supreme Court (*Oberster Gerichtshof*).

Civil cases must be filed either in a district court or in a state court, depending on the nature of the case and its value. Complicated rules distinguish the competence of the district courts and the state courts.

Appeals from the judgments of district courts are decided by the state courts. If the state court is the court of first instance, then an appeal from their decision is decided by the courts of appeal. An appeal from a decision by the court of second instance is brought before the Supreme Court. However, there are restrictions on the right of appeal so that the Supreme Court only accepts jurisdiction in major cases.

In the district courts, jurisdiction is exercised by a single career judge. In the state courts, jurisdiction is exercised either by a single career judge (in lawsuits up to a value of ATS 500,000) or by tribunals of three judges (in lawsuits exceeding this value). There are only four courts of appeal in Austria (in Vienna, Graz, Linz and Innsbruck). Judgment in appellate matters is exercised by a tribunal of three professional judges. The Supreme Court acts as court of last instance for final appeals. Judgments of the Supreme Court are exercised by tribunals of five professional judges. The Supreme Court allows arguments on points of law only and does not hear evidence. If the Supreme Court deals with a question of substantial importance which has not been settled adequately by the lower courts, or if the Supreme Court intends to deviate from its established jurisdiction, a panel of 11 judges considers the matter.

Commercial matters fall within the area of competence of the ordinary courts. If a tribunal of a state court or a court of appeal must decide a commercial matter, one of the judges must be an experienced business person appointed as a non-professional (lay) judge. At the Supreme Court level, no lay judge is necessary since the Supreme Court hears only points of law.

Commercial matters are defined in procedural law. Such matters consist of lawsuits against business persons or commercial companies based on business transactions, disputes over the use of trading names, disputes concerning the legal relationship of shareholders of a commercial company to one another or between a commercial company and its officers, disputes in matters concerning stock corporations or limited liability companies, disputes concerning bills of exchange and cheques, unfair competition and copyright.

When the demand for payment is expressed for a certain amount of money owing, these matters fall within the competence of ordinary courts. This also applies to labour courts where all civil law disputes of employers and employees resulting from employment, inclusive of questions of the existence of an employment relationship, and civil law disputes among employees in connection with their joint work for one employer, are handled. Labour courts consist of a tribunal of three judges; the chairperson is a professional judge, and the two other judges are lay judges. One is appointed by the representatives of the employee and one is appointed by the representatives of the employer.

### 3.5.2 Rules of jurisdiction

Actions can be begun in the district courts up to the value of ATS 100,000. Proceedings must be commenced at the defendant's home district court, unless the parties have agreed in the contract on another district court. The parties cannot agree in the contract to a state court having jurisdiction when the value is under ATS 100,000. On the other hand, it is possible to agree in the contract to a district court having jurisdiction when the value is more than ATS 100,000 and the action normally should be begun at a state court.

When the value exceeds more than ATS 500,000, the plaintiff can bring a petition that jurisdiction be exercised by a tribunal instead of by a single professional judge. Jurisdiction exercised by tribunals in the state court is usually seen in matters of unfair competition and disputes over the use of trading names. In debt recovery cases, jurisdiction exercised by tribunals in the state courts is the exception. In both district and state courts, the party bringing the action is known as the plaintiff (*Kläger*) and the party against whom proceedings are brought is the defendant (*Beklagter*). The value of the lawsuit is determined by the amount of the main claim, exclusive of default interest. If the matter in dispute is not a specified sum of money, the value of the suit is determined by the plaintiff. There are guidelines for setting the litigation value in some actions so that a pre-determined value can be ascertained. The litigation value serves as a basis for the calculation of the lawyer's fees and court fees.

### 3.5.3 Appeals

The lawsuit is either brought to the district court (value up to ATS 100,000) or to the state court (value over ATS 100,000). Appeals from the judgments of the district court are decided by the state court, those of the state court by the courts of appeal. An appeal from a decision by the court of second instance (state court or court of appeal) can be brought before the Supreme Court. As mentioned above, the Supreme Court accepts only jurisdiction in major cases (value more than ATS 50,000) and deals only with questions of substantial importance, mostly concerning legal problems. The Supreme Court does not hear evidence.

Lawsuits below the value of ATS 50,000 cannot be brought to the Supreme Court. In general, appeal with respect to debt recovery cases is the exception to the rule. It is costly and results in inevitable delay.

### 3.5.4 Status of the foreign creditor

#### 3.5.4.1 In general

When a foreign creditor brings a claim to court in Austria, the Civil Procedure Code states that the court may direct the plaintiff to make a deposit for costs on application by the defendant. The court can direct the plaintiff to make such a deposit only in cases where enforcement of the judgment in the country of the foreign plaintiff would be inadmissible.

There is no such court order in cases where bilateral treaties in respect of the enforcement of judgments are applicable. In all other respects, there is no difference between a foreign or a domestic creditor.

#### 3.5.4.2 Enforcement of foreign judgments[1]

Foreign judgments and foreign awards are enforced by ordinary courts in Austria. The Enforcement Act stipulates that reciprocity provided for in treaties must be established before enforcement of the judgment can take place. Enforcement, therefore, is subject to multilateral or bilateral treaties. Austria has entered into numerous treaties which effect enforcement; treaties concerning the enforcement of foreign judgments exist with Belgium, Germany, France, the United Kingdom, Italy, The Netherlands, Switzerland, and Sweden.

#### 3.5.4.3 Applicable law

If the facts of a particular case cross jurisdictional boundaries, the determination of the applicable body of law must be solved. The Conflict of Laws Act is governed by a number of basic principles which are applicable to all types of conflict issues. The Act follows the principle of the most significant relationship, which means that facts which have connections with more than one country are governed by the law to which the facts have the most significant

---

1 At present, preparations for a Bill changing the Enforcement Code in questions of foreign judgments recognition are made by the Austrian Parliament. The Bill is aimed to come into force by 1 July 1995.

relationship. This principle is followed by most of the European countries. Austrian conflict rules in the Conflict of Laws Act can also refer a case to foreign law. In such cases, the foreign forum's conflict rules either accept the referral of the matter to them, refer the case back to Austrian law, or transmit the matter to the law of a third state.

It also is possible that foreign law is applied. This means that an Austrian court has the duty to investigate and interpret the foreign provisions in the same manner as a foreign court would do. The parties have the right to assist the court in such an investigation. The court may also appoint an expert or may send official interrogatories to a foreign authority. These interrogatories are presented to the Federal Ministry of Justice, which then submits them to the foreign authority according to the provisions of applicable international treaties.

Parties to a contract often have the document interpreted under a given national law. For this purpose, they insert choice-of-law clauses into the contract. The Conflict of Laws Act recognises choice-of-law clauses.

The personal status of an individual is governed by his nationality. If a person has more than one nationality, the law of that state to which the individual has the most significant relationship prevails. When one of the nationalities is Austrian, this nationality prevails. If a person is stateless or if the nationality is unclear, habitual residence is the determining factor. The personal status of a legal entity is governed by the law of the principal office or main location of the administration of that entity.

## 3.6   Legal representation

### 3.6.1   Nature of legal representation

Attorneys and notaries make up the legal profession in Austria. Apart from these, persons with a legal background are employed in private enterprise on a large scale. However, such persons are usually not members of the bar. They are not admitted to courts, and they enjoy no professional privilege.

The Austrian attorney must be a member of the local bar and, without bar membership, he is prohibited from representing a client in court or rendering out-of-court legal advice. No distinction between barristers and solicitors exists in Austria. Attorneys act under a professional oath. An Austrian attorney who is admitted to any of the local bars is allowed to represent clients in any Austrian court, including any appellate courts, the Supreme Court, the Administrative Court, and the Constitutional Court. His representative authority extends to all civil and penal matters and to acting before administrative agencies, ministries, and tax offices.

At the district court level, a party can act on his own behalf if the litigation value does not exceed ATS 30,000. If the value of the claim is more than ATS 30,000, legal representation by an attorney is compulsory. A party involved in a state court action must be represented by an attorney; this rule also applies to appeals in the courts of appeal and in the Supreme Court.

### 3.6.2 Mode of payment for legal representation

As a rule, a party instructing an attorney is responsible for payment of his costs including any expenses in the conduct of the action. The basis of the charge should be agreed when initial instructions are given. The fees for attorneys' services are established in the Official Tariff of Attorneys' Fees (*Rechtsanwaltstarif*) and the Autonomous Guidelines for Fees and Disbursements (*Autonome Honorarrichtlinien*). Such tariff rates are binding. They are based on the time spent, the effort and difficulty of work, and the value of the matter. Attorneys are obliged to provide clients with full information regarding their charging rates.

Apart from the tariff rates, an hourly rate may be agreed between client and attorney. This is frequently done if a steady business relationship exists. It is generally prohibited for lawyers in Austria to accept a matter on a mere contingency fee basis, as this violates the Code of Ethics for attorneys and the Autonomous Rules of the National Bar Association. Attorneys may not accept instructions from clients on a fee basis computed on a commission or a brokerage basis or where there is a fixed charge plus an additional percentage where a recovery is effected.

Where a party is registered for value added tax (VAT), that element of any costs paid can be reclaimed from the Austrian tax offices. Legal costs in Austria are business expenses, and they can be offset against profits for tax purposes. The VAT rate for legal costs in Austria is 20 per cent. There are proposals to reduce the VAT rate for legal costs to the comparable VAT level in Germany when Austria enters the European Union in 1995.

## 3.7 Costs

### 3.7.1 Current fees

With respect to trial costs, a distinction must be made between court fees and an attorney's fees. The fees for an attorney's services are established in the Official Tariff of Attorney's Fees and the Autonomous Guideline for Fees and Disbursements. The fee largely depends on the number of written statements of the parties, the number of hearings, and the time involved in the lawsuit.

Therefore, rarely, if ever, can estimates of fees be given to clients. The value of a lawsuit is an important determining factor for both the graduated scale of court fees and the attorney's fees. In litigation, the attorney's fee reflects the type of services rendered. For the submission of each written statement, including the complaint and an appeal, the attorney earns a fee determined by the value of the lawsuit, irrespective of the amount of time expended. Hearing fees depend both on the litigation value and on the duration of the hearing.

### 3.7.2   Availability of legal aid

In contrast to the rules in England and Wales, legal aid in Austria is not limited to individuals. Limited companies and clubs may qualify for legal aid. The determining factors are:

(1)   the merit of the claim, as determined by the judge; and
(2)   the party's financial circumstances;[1]

For individuals, rights to pay or receive alimony are carefully examined. Company shareholders and members of clubs can be required to provide financial statements. Anyone who wishes to qualify for legal aid is obliged to make a statement of liabilities. Legal aid is not retrospective, and any work undertaken prior to the completion of the statement of 'resources and liabilities' must be paid for by the individual. A copy of the statement is available to the opposing party.

When qualifying for legal aid, the creditor should immediately contact an attorney. Legal aid is not available to a creditor who is not represented by an attorney. Legal aid means that the creditor need not pay court costs or the attorney's fees. On the other hand, the creditor must pay the costs of the opposing party if he loses the claim. Therefore, such costs can be enforced against the party who received legal aid. If a party with legal aid recovers money within the next three years, the court can decide that such money must be utilised for discharging the costs of the party's attorney.[2]

### 3.7.3   Liability for and recovery of costs

Primary responsibility for payment of costs rests with the party instructing the attorney, subject to legal aid entitlement. An attorney is entitled to charge his clients based on either the Official Tariff of Attorney's Fees or the Autonomous Guidelines for Fees and Disbursements. The losing party is compelled to reimburse the successful party for court fees and attorney's fees. Care must be taken since such reimbursement does not usually cover all the attorney's costs. The attorney has a right to demand his fee directly from his client, and it is only the client who has a right to recover from the losing party. Since such recoverable costs are part of the judgment, enforcement under the Enforcement Code is possible. In the judgment the court can require the losing party to pay attorney's fees only on the basis of the Official Tariff of Attorney's Fees. This principle applies to all levels of courts.

If the defendant is legally aided or otherwise unable to pay, the creditor must bear all of the attorney's costs. It can occur that the creditor is not completely successful. If the creditor wins only 80 per cent of the claim, for

---

1   Persons with a net income of more than ATS 10,000 to ATS 12,000 monthly and who have no severe financial hardship will not qualify for legal aid, except when several aspects of the proceeding are expected to be very complicated and costly.

2   In legal aid cases, Austrian attorneys do not receive money in the form of direct payment; the fee amount, excluding VAT, is paid to the pension fund of the attorney's local bar, with a percentage negotiated each year between the National Bar and the Ministry of Justice.

example, the defendant must pay only 80 per cent of the costs, and the creditor is liable for 20 per cent of the costs of the defendant's attorney. Consequently, the creditor only obtains 60 per cent (80 per cent minus 20 per cent) of the attorney's costs from the opposing party.

If the court orders against the claim, costs will follow fully against the creditor. If the creditor discontinues proceedings or fails to prosecute, a defendant can apply to have costs ordered against the creditor. Creditor plaintiffs also are entitled to recover interest out of legal costs when the judgment fixes the liability of the opposing party for such costs. A creditor plaintiff must claim expressly for such interest.

## 3.8 Civil procedure

A lawsuit commences when the plaintiff submits the complaint to the competent court. Service of legal process is not made by the plaintiff by way of personal service on the defendant. The court undertakes to serve the action on the defendant.

If it is possible to accomplish service of the legal process, then a formal first hearing may be held at the court. Usually, this is followed by a written answer (*Klagebeantwortung*) to the complaint, submitted by the defendant within a prescribed period no longer than four weeks. If no formal first hearing is held, the judge orders the defendant by written procedural order to submit a written answer to the complaint.

In lawsuits not exceeding ATS 100,000 in value, there is no formal first hearing. The court undertakes to serve the action on the defendant stating that the judgment will be valid unless the defendant disputes the debt within two weeks by a written answer.

It is a particular provision of Austrian civil procedure that all opposing arguments and all evidence in support of the case must be stated in the answer to the complaint. In exceptional cases, the parties are allowed to present subsequent preparatory writs. Supplementary oral contentions also are possible and occur frequently in court proceedings. It can cause problems for foreign clients before Austrian courts when parties are obliged at the outset of the proceedings to submit all their contentions and evidence. Foreign clients rarely understand that they must provide their lawyer with full information at the very beginning of the proceedings. Apart from some exceptions, there is no later possibility of submitting contentions and evidence.

Once the complaint is filed with the court, the court deals with service of the documents. The court fixes the hearings, hears the evidence, records the evidence heard, and closes the hearing in order to issue its written decision, normally in the form of a judgment. Pre-trial depositions are unknown. It is up to the parties to support their respective positions in litigation and to submit the necessary evidence to the court. The court itself has discretionary power to investigate.

As a rule, proceedings at the court of first instance are public. In certain cases, the public can be excluded. In proceedings before the state court, as well as before the courts of appeal and the Supreme Court, the parties must be represented by a lawyer.

### 3.8.1    Duration of the procedure

The time needed to resolve the matter does not vary greatly when dealing with civil, commercial, or labour lawsuits. Generally, Austrian courts promptly accept any new action that is filed. The complaint will immediately receive a file number, and the matter will be put on the court calendar.

The court will normally start to take evidence within the first six months after the commencement of a lawsuit. The trial in the court of first instance is frequently interrupted. Court sessions are held mostly for taking part of the evidence, such as hearing one or several witnesses or accepting documents as means of proof. The courts do not sit from 24 December to 6 January and from 15 July to 25 August. Depending on the volume of evidence submitted to the court, a proceeding in the court of first instance may take between six months and three years to complete. More complicated cases can take five years or more.

With appellate procedures it is difficult to estimate their duration. Oral hearings at the appellate level are held only on demand by a party. Revision of the evidence gathered during the trial in the court of first instance is unusual. This means that, at the appellate level, the court rarely takes new evidence or supplementary evidence. An appellate proceeding, therefore, takes between three and six months if no supplementary evidence is taken.

## 3.9    Procedure to judgment

### 3.9.1    The debtor pays the debt

If the debtor pays, the matter is concluded. An agreement is usually confirmed in writing, although a formal notice of discontinuance can be lodged with the court. If this is not done, the matter is concluded by the court when both parties fail to appear at the next session. If payment does not include fixed costs and interest, the plaintiff may continue the trial.

### 3.9.2    The debtor admits the debt

The plaintiff should enter judgment immediately to protect his position. If the defendant does nothing more, the plaintiff can proceed to enforcement. In Austria, there is no possibility for the defendant to apply for time to pay. This can only be reached when the creditor accepts it and the court makes an order to this effect. If the creditor rejects the proposal, the proceedings continue, usually by hearing evidence. If the defendant does not appear, the court can pronounce judgment by default. The debtor then has four weeks to pay the debt, or the plaintiff can proceed to enforcement.

This procedure applies to all civil courts. The debtor has no right to apply for a stay of execution because execution takes place only in district courts before a judge, competent only for executional matters.

### 3.9.3    The debtor disputes the debt

In the district court, the defendant may dispute the debt by submitting a pre-printed form or a separate defence to the court. It is sufficient to say, 'I dispute the debt'. The defendant is not obliged to give a full disclosure of the facts. This dispute of the debt (*Einspruch*) must be sent to the court within 14 days. When the debt is disputed, the judge must order a term for proceedings. If the debtor appears, the judge examines all the matters in dispute and usually orders the debtor to bring a writ within 14 days to 4 weeks.

In the state court, a formal first hearing is usually held. This is followed by a written answer to the complaint, submitted by the defendant within four weeks. If no formal first hearing is held, the judge orders the defendant to submit a written answer to the complaint.

A disputed debt proceeding results in a judgment by the court. This usually is done in written form; in a few cases, the judgments are oral. The losing party has four weeks to bring an appeal, either to the state court or to the court of appeal.

### 3.9.4    The debtor disputes part of the debt

When the debtor disputes part of the debt, the undisputed part of the debt may be enforced; for the disputed part of the debt, the proceedings continue.

### 3.9.5    The debtor neither admits nor disputes the debt

When the debtor neither admits nor disputes the debt, the creditor may proceed to default judgment and enforce action.

### 3.9.6    The debtor is declared insolvent

Where the defendant is declared insolvent, further steps in the proceedings differ, depending on the nature of the insolvency. If the debtor requests a respite with court assistance, the trial continues, and further steps in the proceedings can be taken.

If the debtor applies to the court for the opening of a moratorium or a debt recomposition proceeding, a receiver is appointed by the court. Further steps in the proceedings against the debtor are possible, but not common. If a bankruptcy proceeding is opened, no further steps in the debt recovery proceedings are possible. In insolvency cases, an application to the insolvency court, consisting of debt, interest, and all costs, should be made, although the prospects for an unsecured creditor are, at best, a low dividend. Payment in insolvency cases is first made to secured creditors; since 1983, Austrian law has not recognised the legal position of preferential creditors.

# 3.10   Enforcing judgment

Once judgment is obtained, a variety of enforcement procedures is available. Except for insolvency, all enforcement procedures are called execution. All remedies are available only in the district courts.

## 3.10.1   Execution on immovable property

Execution on immovable property requires that the debtor be in possession of land or property. Execution on immovable property takes three forms.

### 3.10.1.1   *Public sale of the property*

The success of a public sale of the property depends on the value of the property and the mortgage debts. Proceedings begin with an order of attachment and result in the public sale of the property. The remedy is costly and risky.

### 3.10.1.2   *Forced administration of the property*

Proceedings begin with an order of attachment, and a receiver is appointed. His duty is to officially administer the property and to deposit all the money realised out of the forced administration of the property.

The appointed receiver obtains payment for his efforts, which is deducted from the realised money. The money is distributed to the creditors by the court by a written order. Not all property is suitable for forced administration. Forced administration is done normally by renting the property.

### 3.10.1.3   *Forced incorporation of a mortgage*

Proceedings begin with an order of attachment, and the local land registry office incorporates the mortgage. An incorporation fee of 1.1 per cent must be paid. This remedy should be taken if the creditor is unsure of an application for forced sale or forced administration. This remedy protects a creditor's position in the short term, but money remains still owing to the creditor until the property is realised.

## 3.10.2   Execution on personal property[1]

Execution on personal property and attachment of earnings are the most common remedies in execution. Execution on personal property begins with an order of attachment. This order of attachment is given to the competent

---

1 A draft of a Bill for a change of the Enforcement Code provides that the court bailiff is enabled, within a maximum period of 4 to 6 months, to handle all the proceedings of an execution on personal property on his own, until success or failure has become clear. The bill should pass into law by 1 July 1996.

court bailiff, with directions to attend the defendant's premises and to seize any available goods. This process takes, depending on the court, from 2 to 10 weeks.

At this stage, the goods are not generally removed from the defendant. From that point, the defendant is not allowed to dispose of or partition the goods. Within three weeks from seizing the goods, the court bailiff fixes a date for sale by auction. Usually, the goods are removed two or three days before the auction sale. The debtor, therefore, has very little time from the seizing of the goods to make payment.

The defendant will not always be in a position to clear his liability immediately. If he offers to pay by instalments, it is at the creditor's discretion whether to accept this. If the instalment proposal is acceptable, goods are not removed for auction sale but remain seized. The creditor can instruct the court bailiff to remove the goods if the debtor defaults on the instalments. There is no right for the defendant to make an application to the court for a stay of execution if the creditor does not agree to an instalment arrangement.

The defendant may have goods, but there may be prior executions applicable to them. Any money collected by the court bailiff will be paid to execution creditors in chronological order. It may be that the defendant has goods but that these are subject to third-party claims. Such claims can be identified immediately, such as a hire-purchase agreement for a vehicle supported by an appropriate documentation. Other claims can be more difficult to assess, such as a supplier claiming goods pursuant to retention of title. 'Twilight claims' are usually unsupported by documents and are the most difficult to assess.

It is up to the third party to claim rights on seized goods and it is up to the creditor to admit or dispute such third-party claims. If the claim is admitted, the court bailiff cannot proceed against those goods. If the creditor disputes the claim, the third party must bring a lawsuit, and proceedings follow where a judge competent for execution cases determines whether the defendant or the third party owns the goods. If the third party succeeds, the creditor also is liable for the costs of the proceedings. Third-party proceedings can be expensive. They should only be contemplated if the goods in question are of significant value. If the creditor does not know what evidence the third party may produce in the proceedings and the risk of proceeding to trial is too high, the creditor should admit the third-party claim and pursue an alternative enforcement action.

### 3.10.3 Attachment of earnings

An attachment of earnings order can be obtained where a defendant is in employment, but it does not apply where he is self-employed. As in all execution cases, application is made to a district court. The creditor must identify the employer. Where this is not possible, the court takes the date of birth of the debtor (the date can be obtained by the local authority when a copy of the judgment is enclosed with the enquiry) and makes an inquiry at the

National Federation for Social Insurance. If this certifies any employment of the debtor, the employer must make monthly payments to the plaintiff's lawyer. It is notable that the court does not calculate a protected earnings level; payments are made directly to the plaintiff's lawyer and not to the court.

The protected earnings level is ATS 8,500 per month for a single person. Further reduction is made if the debtor is required to pay alimony. The employer is liable for all damages caused if he fails to deduct the correct amount from the earnings or fails to pay it directly to the plaintiff's lawyer.

Attachment of earnings is an effective remedy, but it can become less attractive because of the time involved where a debt is large or where the defendant's unprotected earnings are low. In such circumstances the practical course is to pursue an alternative enforcement action.

### 3.10.4  Garnishee

The aim of garnishee proceedings is to obtain payment for the benefit of the plaintiff of money owing to the defendant by another person or company within the jurisdiction. Apart from the attachment of earnings, in practice, nearly all the debts may be attached. The most usual are trade debtors of the defendant and bank or building society accounts of the defendant.

The procedure begins with an attachment order where the creditor must identify the third party, its legal title, and the amount owing. No notice is given at this stage to the defendant or third parties. Within days, the court will attach the money held or owed by the third party. The order of attachment is then served on the defendant and the garnishee. From that point, the court is no longer concerned with the case. The third party must declare to the creditor's lawyer whether he admits the debt or disputes the debt. If he admits the debt, payment to the creditor's lawyer is the next step. If he does not pay or if he disputes the debt, legal action can be taken against the third party.

This remedy is a useful weapon, but relevant information must be to hand. Sometimes, inquiry and detective offices are instructed to obtain the relevant information, especially when other execution remedies have failed. Garnishee proceedings are the most creative part of enforcement. All rights of a debtor resulting from his various contracts with third parties can be attached. The contract rights must be realised. In complicated cases, the court can set a hearing on how to realise such rights of a debtor.

### 3.10.5  Oral examination

Oral examination forms part of the remedies previously mentioned. If the debtor is unable to pay, he or an officer of a limited defendant company is obliged to attend court to give evidence on oath about the defendant's financial position. The defendant must disclose relevant documents. The costs of this examination can be recovered.

The examination also can be done by the court bailiff at the defendant's premises. Such an examination usually only results in a statement of information about the financial situation of the debtor. It can be a useful device to obtain information for an alternative enforcement action. Against an obstructive defendant, however, it usually proves a blunt instrument.

If the defendant lies on oath, he is guilty of forgery, since he must sign the document at the examination. A further application for his committal to prison can be made but, usually, this does not lead to payment of the debt, and it is questionable whether the additional time and cost are worthwhile.

### 3.10.6  Insolvency

The courts frown upon insolvency proceedings being used for debt collection purposes. Sometimes, practitioners consider them the ultimate sanction they can apply. In Austria, these proceedings are inexpensive compared to other proceedings. Consequently, this remedy is often utilised. Lawyers use these proceedings when they believe the extra pressure may result in payment. When insolvency proceedings are commenced, the creditor must start a separate action by writ in the competent insolvency court. Insolvency proceedings by a creditor are possible only in bankruptcy. In all other insolvency proceedings, only the debtor can commence proceedings.

Bankruptcy proceedings are appropriate only for undisputed debts. When a debtor disputes the debt and he can satisfy the court, the creditor's application will be rejected. The application for bankruptcy proceedings will also be refused by the court if the available assets of the debtor are not sufficient to cover the costs of the proceedings. In Austria, there are three types of insolvency proceedings.

#### 3.10.6.1  *Moratorium*

The moratorium proceedings was introduced into Austrian insolvency law in 1984. The purpose of the moratorium proceedings is to enable such businesses that are only in temporary financial difficulties, but are basically fit and healthy to stay in business, to continue to carry on their activities. Only the debtor can apply for the opening of these proceedings. On application to the insolvency court, a temporary receiver is appointed by the court to supervise the proceedings. The debtor must submit a detailed proposal for the reorganisation of his business, together with the application for the opening of the proceedings.

The temporary receiver examines the reorganisation plan with experts appointed by the court, the creditors, and any institutions interested in the continuation of the debtor's business. Inquiries are made into whether any banking and financing institutions are willing to provide new funds to the debtor or will provide guarantees to the creditors in case the reorganisation fails. The temporary receiver also must inquire into the attitude of the employees of the debtor regarding the proposed continuation of the business, whether third parties are interested in carrying on the business, and whether or not the carrying on of the business will increase the creditor's losses.

On application by the debtor, the court can also decide on the validity of any claims raised against the debtor. Recognition of a claim in these proceedings confers a legal title to a creditor for subsequent enforcement proceedings without first having to obtain a court judgment. A further important aspect is that any claims that come into existence after the opening of these temporary proceedings have priority over other prior claims in subsequent insolvency proceedings, should the reorganisation fail.

At the end of the period given by law, the court will satisfy itself that the temporary incapacity of the debtor to meet his financial obligations is remedied (the proceedings will be terminated and the debtor will be free to continue its business activities). Otherwise, the court will decide, on application of the debtor, to open formal settlement proceedings or, if no such application has been filed, whether bankruptcy proceedings should be opened.

Moratorium proceedings are costly, and the time given by law to reorganise businesses is too short. Nearly all the moratorium proceedings opened in Austria have ended in debt recomposition and bankruptcy proceedings.

### 3.10.6.2 *Bankruptcy proceedings*

Bankruptcy proceedings commence when it has been established that the debtor is incapable of meeting his financial obligations, ie, that outstanding receivables cannot be settled within the due time. Legal entities, such as corporations or associations, are subject to an even stricter requirement. In their case, bankruptcy proceedings must commence if there is 'over-indebtedness', ie, when liabilities exceed assets.

An application for bankruptcy proceedings will be refused by the court if the available assets of the debtor are not likely to be sufficient to cover the costs of the court proceedings, unless a creditor makes a deposit in an amount to be determined by the court, usually ATS 20,000 to ATS 50,000 or more.

The application for bankruptcy proceedings must be filed by the debtor or by a creditor. The debtor is under a statutory obligation to file an application without delay, at the latest 60 days after the debtor became incapable of meeting its financial obligations. In the case of an individual business, this obligation rests on the owner; in the case of a partnership or limited partnership, it rests on the partners with unlimited liability; in the case of a legal entity, it rests on each individual with statutory representative power for the legal entity, ie, the managing directors or the members of the board of management. Failure to meet this obligation exposes such representatives to personal liability towards creditors and to criminal prosecution.

A creditor applying for bankruptcy proceedings must establish that at least one other creditor with claims against the debtor exists and that the debtor is incapable of meeting his financial obligations or is 'overindebted'. In the case of an application by the debtor, bankruptcy proceedings are opened without delay. In the case of an application by a creditor, a formal hearing must be conducted, with both the creditor and the debtor being given the opportunity to appeal the decision of the court.

With the opening of bankruptcy proceedings, the debtor is placed in the position of an 'infant'; he is deprived of all rights to make any dispositions with respect to his property. Any transactions carried on by the debtor after the opening of bankruptcy proceedings are void with respect to his creditors. Legal proceedings can no longer be instituted against the creditor once bankruptcy proceedings begin. Pending litigation is temporarily suspended. The conditions for its resumption are determined by law, and the decision on resumption depends on how the receiver evaluates the merits of a pending case.

When the court decides on bankruptcy proceedings, it will also appoint a receiver (*Masseverwalter*), in most instances an attorney. In addition, the court will appoint a creditor's committee if it deems this necessary in view of the size of the debtor's business. Under the supervision of the court and the creditor's committee, the receiver is in charge of the bankrupt's estate. If the receiver cannot continue to trade because of the bad financial situation of the debtor's business, he is obliged to sell off all assets and distribute proceeds to the creditors.

Under Austrian law, distribution of the debtor's assets need not discharge the debtor of his debts. The debtor remains liable for all unsettled debts for the 30-year period of the statute of limitations.

Any claims against the debtor must be notified to the court within a period set by the court when it decides on bankruptcy proceedings. In a formal court hearing, the receiver is then required to state whether each claim is recognised. Recognition of a claim takes the form of a court judgment and entitles the creditor to attempt enforcement of the claim for 30 years, to the extent that the claim is not settled in the course of the bankruptcy proceedings.

If the receiver objects to a claim, the court will set a date by which the creditor must institute legal proceedings in order to have a court decide on the validity of the claim against the bankrupt's estate represented by the receiver. If the creditor is successful in its litigation, the claim is officially recognised and settled to the same extent as all other claims are settled, following the distribution of the debtor's assets. If the creditor does not file a court action by the set day, the creditor will not be able to participate in the distribution of the debtor's assets. Priority in the settlement is now granted only to a limited number of claims, including:

(1)   the costs of the proceedings;
(2)   the costs of maintaining and administering the bankrupt's estate; and
(3)   such claims of employees that originate after the opening of the bankruptcy proceedings (ie, where the business has been carried on by the receiver).

Secured creditors in whose favour a mortgage, lien, encumbrance, or any other security was constituted (by way of contract or by way of seizure in enforcement proceedings) have priority in the settlement of their claims with respect to the assets in which they hold a security right. Should such a security not be sufficient to cover all of a secured creditor's claims, such creditors must file for the unsettled balance of claims in the proceedings, such balance being treated like other unsecured claims.

As a general rule, security interest contracted within 60 days preceding the bankruptcy proceedings will not be recognised. Clearly, the purpose of this provision is to avoid preferential treatment of certain creditors at a time when bankruptcy is imminent. The law also provides for the possibility of having certain transactions undertaken by the debtor during specified periods preceding the bankruptcy declared null and void.

With respect to third-party rights, objects in the possession of the debtor at the time of bankruptcy proceedings can be claimed by the third party. This applies in particular to any supplier that delivered goods under retention of title.

Secured creditors are barred from exercising their rights for 90 days after the opening of bankruptcy proceedings if the exercise of such rights would endanger the carrying on of the business and provided the bar does not constitute severe personal or economic damage to a particular secured creditor. In this respect, the 90-day waiting period also applies to suppliers who delivered goods under retention of title.

Bankruptcy proceedings are terminated when all assets of the debtor have been sold and distributed to the creditors and all litigation, if any, in this connection is terminated. As explained above, creditors are free for a further period of 30 years to attempt collection of the unsettled portion of claims, should the debtor come into possession of any assets. In the case of a legal entity, proceedings for the dissolution of that entity are instituted ex officio after the close of the bankruptcy proceedings.

### 3.10.6.3   *Debt recomposition*

Whereas bankruptcy proceedings ultimately lead to the distribution of the debtor's assets, with the debtor remaining liable for unsettled debts, debt recomposition proceedings (*Ausgleich*) are aimed at enabling the debtor to continue his activities and to be discharged from a part of his debts.

An application for debt recomposition proceedings can be filed by the debtor only when the debtor is unable to meet his financial obligations. The application cannot be filed if bankruptcy proceedings have already begun, although an application by a creditor to open bankruptcy proceedings does not prevent a debtor from trying to institute debt recomposition proceedings. The application must include a correct and complete description of the debtor's financial status and a proposal stating the share of debts that the debtor is willing to settle, the period of time during which this share is to be settled, and the way in which the debtor proposes to raise the necessary funds.

Debt recomposition proceedings do not deprive the debtor of his ability to carry on transactions with respect to his assets. The court-appointed receiver has a right of veto over any ordinary transaction of the debtor and must expressly agree to any transaction of the debtor beyond the ordinary course of business. Any acts of the debtor in violation of these provisions are deemed to be of no effect towards the creditors if the third party involved knew or should have known that approval was required.

The court will also schedule a meeting of creditors and will notify all creditors of the debt recomposition proceedings. The creditors are given time to file their claims with the court. Within 90 days of the opening of debt recomposition proceedings,[1] the creditors must decide on whether to accept the debtor's offer.

The statutory minimum requirements for the offer provide for a settlement of 40 per cent of the claims within two years. A positive vote by the creditors requires either an absolute majority of the creditors present and voting and/or a majority of three-fourths of the sum total of all claims filed. Only creditors who have filed their claims in time and had their claims recognised are authorised to participate in the vote. If a debtor's offer is accepted by the creditors, the court will issue an order approving the agreement reached between the parties. The effect of such order is that the debtor must repay only such quota of his debts as is specified in the order. If the debtor's proposal is not accepted by the creditors, the court must decide whether bankruptcy proceedings should immediately be instituted. In practice, this is almost always the case.

When the debtor's proposal is accepted and the court order approving the agreement is issued, the debtor will be discharged of part of his debts when the proposal is fulfilled. Any claim not settled at maturity is revived in full, provided the creditor has granted the debtor a 14-day grace period in writing. The acceptance of the debtor's proposal does not influence the rights of secured creditors or third parties that hold title to any assets in the possession of the debtor. However, the 90-day waiting period, as in bankruptcy proceedings, applies to debt-recomposition proceedings.

The approval of creditors can be made subject to the appointment by the court of a supervisor (*Sachwalter*) for the period granted to the debtor for the settlement of the approved quota of its debts. The supervisor is normally the same individual who serves as a receiver. The supervisor acts as trustee of the creditors and oversees the debtor carrying on its business in a way that enables him to meet his obligations under the agreement reached with creditors. The supervisor has the same rights as the receiver and can be entrusted with the administration and sale of the debtor's assets.

A special form of debt recomposition proceedings is provided in the course of bankruptcy proceedings. A bankrupt is thereby given the possibility to turn the bankruptcy proceedings into a 'forced debt recomposition' (*Zwangsausgleich*). The offer during bankruptcy proceedings must provide for the settlement of at least 20 per cent of the debtor's obligations within two years. Creditor approval of the proposal is subject to the same majority requirements as apply to debt recomposition proceedings. Creditors normally will agree to such a proposal only if, otherwise, the chances for recovery would be virtually nil. If the debtor's proposal for 'forced debt recomposition' is

---

1 This period can be extended only for important reasons.

approved by the creditors, bankruptcy proceedings are terminated, pending the debtor's fulfilment of the terms of the agreement reached with the creditors.

### 3.10.6.4 *Bankruptcy proceedings for individuals*

In 1994, a major amendment to the Austrian Bankruptcy Code was passed by the Austrian Parliament to come into force by 1 January 1995. The main purpose of this amendment to the Bankruptcy Code is to enable individuals to obtain discharge of unsettled debts when a certain amount of the debt is being paid within certain periods. Contrary to other bankruptcy proceedings, the competent courts for bankruptcy proceedings of individuals will be the district courts. These cases will be handled by judicial administrators.

It is estimated that 80,000 to 120,000 individuals will choose this form of private bankruptcy over the next three years. As a general rule, these bankruptcy proceedings for individuals are comparable to 'normal' bankruptcy proceedings, with the following major distinctions:

(1)  the debtor, an individual is prohibited from opening business relations or from doing business;
(2)  the debtor must prove that he attempted pre-court arrangements with his creditors, and he must certify that these arrangements failed;
(3)  the debtor must make full and frank disclosure through a statement of his resources and liabilities, signed before the court; and
(4)  the debtor must make an admissible proposal to the creditors regarding the amount of debts he will pay within a given period.

To obtain relief from unsettled debts, the debtor has various possibilities in bankruptcy proceedings for individuals. First, as far as assets exist, all must be sold. Then, an attachment of earnings order is made by the court. At this stage, the debtor's legal position is comparable to that when attachment of earnings is enforced by execution. Thereafter, the debtor has five possibilities:

(1)  to pay a minimum quota of 20 per cent of all debts within two years;
(2)  to pay 30 per cent of all debts within five years;
(3)  to make payment by instalment within seven years, where the maximum quota must exceed 10 per cent of all debts and the maximum quota could reach 100 per cent of all debts;
(4)  to pay a quota of 50 per cent within three years; or
(5)  to pay 10 per cent of all debts within seven years.

The attachment of earnings continues until the end of the maximum period. If the debtor fails to pay the minimum quotas within the given period, he remains liable for all unsettled debts for the 30-year period of the statute of limitations.

### 3.10.7  The 'bankruptcy court'

All insolvency proceedings as outlined above are conducted under the supervision of the 'bankruptcy court'. Bankruptcy proceedings for individuals are to be dealt with by the district courts from 1 January 1995. 'Bankruptcy courts' are not organised as separate courts in their own right. Despite their name, they are specialised departments within each court of first instance, entrusted exclusively with the conduct of insolvency proceedings. For practical purposes, the role of the bankruptcy court is limited to that of supervising the giving formal approval to any decisions reached by the receiver and the creditors. They are the more active parties in any insolvency proceedings.

In this connection, it should be noted that the law provides for the existence of so-called 'associations for the protection of creditors' interests' that professionally represent creditors in insolvency proceedings and often play a decisive role in such proceedings and in attempts for the re-organisation or restructuring of a business. In Austria, two such organisations exist and are called preferential creditor institutions (the *Kreditschutzverband von* 1870 and the *Alpenländischer Kreditorenverband*). There is no statutory requirement for a creditor to have his interests in insolvency proceedings represented by such associations. A creditor can file his claim on his own or appoint an attorney as his representative. Foreign creditors must appoint an Austrian-based agent for the service of process.

## 3.11  Conclusion

Austria provides a wide range of legal provisions for the recovery of debt. Experience shows that all creditors should have an implemented system of reminders by letter and telephone once an invoice becomes overdue. The case then should be handed to a lawyer, without delay and with all relevant information about the debtor, to commence action.

Unnecessary and useless letters before action should be avoided. The more information the lawyer obtains about the debtor, the greater the prospects of a successful recovery. In general, legal matters about which the creditor is unsure should be examined by the lawyer. Debt recovery in a foreign country may be one of these matters.

*Chapter 4*

# BELGIUM

**Elisabeth Hoffmann**
**Hoffmann & Jaspar**
**Brussels, Belgium**

## 4.1  Introduction

Belgium is a small country placed in the middle of the European Union (EU), at the crossroads of several trading routes. In consequence, many transactions conducted in Belgium have non-Belgian aspects.

This, in turn, raises questions regarding the application of Belgian law to such transactions. The laws of another country must be taken into account when there are transactions or legal acts which do not have a purely Belgian character and potential conflict of laws must be resolved. Thus, the applicability of Belgian law must be ascertained. This may be established by the law chosen by the parties to the contract or the circumstances of the case. Alternatively, if the parties have not made a definite choice regarding the law applicable, this will be determined on the basis that the contract is most closely connected with the country of residence or principal place of business of the performing party in the contract.

Contracts for international sale of goods will normally be governed by the law of the country in which the vendor has his habitual residence at the time he receives the order. If the order is received by the seller, his agent, or his representative in the country where the buyer has his habitual residence, the law of the country of the buyer's habitual residence will apply.

However, if the international sale requires the supply of goods or services to a person for a purpose which can be regarded as being unconnected to his trade or profession, ie, a consumer contract, the choice of law made by the parties will not deprive the consumer of the protection afforded to him by the laws of his own country. Moreover, in default of declaration as to the law applicable by the parties, the consumer contract will usually be governed by the law of the country where the consumer resides.

In debt collection actions, when a non-Belgian party has fulfilled all his obligations but money remains owing from a Belgium resident or a company having its central administration in Belgium, proceedings should be initiated and conducted from Belgium. This will avoid the delay and costs linked with the required to recognise procedure and enforce foreign judgments in Belgium.

## 4.2 Initial considerations

### 4.2.1 Status of the debtor

Before action can be commenced, all relevant information and evidence for the case should be gathered, ie for a commercial debt:

(1) a copy of the order form signed by the debtor;
(2) a copy of completed delivery forms;
(3) a copy of the shipping document;
(4) a copy of the invoice; and
(5) especially if the general conditions of the vendor are printed on the back of order forms and invoices, an original exemplar of the wording used for that purpose.

Copies of all written reminders for payment should also be gathered, together with the debtor's responses.

#### 4.2.1.1 *Legal entities*

The various legal entities which may be pursued in the Belgian courts are summarised as follows:

(1) an individual, trading in his own name or using a trading denomination or logo; and
(2) a large number of companies, the most common of which are identified by the following abbreviations:

Associations without legal personality can only be pursued by proceedings against their individual members, eg, with *associations de fait* or *feitelijke vereniging* and *associations momentanées* or *tijdelijke vereniging*. The state of Belgium can be pursued through the relevant Ministry and the different decentralised authorities through their executive bodies. Individuals under the age of 18, as well as those individuals covered by a mental health registration can be pursued only through their responsible parent, tutor, or administrator appointed by law or by court order.

#### 4.2.1.2 *Information on the debtor*

Current information on the whereabouts of an individual cannot readily be obtained at the local Town Hall; indeed, this is privileged information. However, when starting proceedings against an individual, the court citation must be processed by the *Huissier de Justice* or *Gerechtsdeurwaarder* who has access to the national register of Belgian citizens and who will verify the information given to him and provide confirmation of current address and marital status.

Current information on the status of a firm, company, or corporation can be obtained through the *Greffe du Tribunal de Commerce* or *Griffie van de Rechtbank van Koophandel du chef-lieu du canton judiciaire*. Its localisation can be identified through the company's registration number which must be preceded by the terms of *Registre de Commerce* and the name of the city. For example, 'RCB' or 'HRB' will stand for *Registre de Commerce de Bruxelles* or *Handelsregister* Brussel. Indeed, all companies or corporations are required by law to identify themselves with information concerning their corporate name and corporate status, registered office, registration number, and value added tax (VAT) registration number on all their documents.

### 4.2.1.3 *Financial status of the debtor*

No current and exact information on the solvency status of a debtor is readily obtainable in Belgium. Companies or corporations are obliged to file annual accounts, copies of which are available from the *Greffe du Tribunal de Commerce* or *Griffie van de rechtbank van Koophandel* at a small cost. Because they are often filed late and drawn up for tax purposes, they may not offer a real picture of the debtor's financial situation and certainly no conclusive warning of a future or imminent bankruptcy.

The *Greffe du Tribunal de Commerce* or *Griffie van de rechtbank van Koophandel* receives information on the protested payments (*protêts* or *protesten*) drawn up by the *Huissier de Justice* or *Gerechtsdeurwaarder* after presentation of letters of credit. These payments are published on a daily basis in a weekly bulletin, but this information is not processed in alphabetical order until a year later, so that it is quite time-consuming to check. In cases of insolvency, this source of information is often inadequate or too slow to serve as a warning.

Only when judged and pronounced will bankruptcy orders be filed at the *Greffe du Tribunal de Commerce* or *Griffie van de rechtbank van Koophandel* and become information available to the public.

### 4.2.3 Is the debt statute-barred?

Generally, a creditor must issue proceedings within a period of 30 years from the date on which the money becomes due, ie, on the date of delivery of the goods. Unless otherwise provided for by the invoice, this period is the common law limitation period.

However, for debt collection, various other and shorter limitation periods apply, eg in civil law, five years for all annually or periodically payable debts such as rents and one year for fees from members of the medical profession or for fees from the *Huissier de Justice* or *Gerechtsdeurwaarder*.

In the field of commercial law, the limitation periods are, eg: three years for all actions resulting from a letter of credit against the acceptor; two years for all liability actions in cases of transport by air and in some cases for actions related to the international transport of goods by railway or by sea and for all actions related to a travel contract when these actions are based on the death or injury of the traveller; one year for actions by businesses for goods sold to a buyer who is not a business, for actions related to the international transport of goods or persons by railway, for actions related to the international transport of goods by way-bill, and for actions from the carrier of a letter of credit against its endorsers or drawers and all other actions related to a travel contract; and six months for actions derived from a postal cheque or a bank cheque, for actions related to the national transport of goods, and for actions based on a letter of credit between the endorsers or drawers against each other.

These limitation periods do not apply in cases related to taxation, social law, or criminal law. However, these specific issues will not be dealt with here as they fall outside the scope of the present chapter.

### 4.2.4 Security

#### 4.2.4.1 Privileges

Under Belgian law, as a form of specific security, privileges (*privilège du vendeur* or *voorrecht van de verkoper*) in general are rights conferred on a creditor because of the particular nature of his claim. Such privileges give the creditor the right to be preferred above other creditors; so that, for instance, in bankruptcy or attachment cases, he should be paid before the other creditors.

The law governing privileges determines which creditors are preferred creditors and in what order.

However, the privilege of the vendor of movable goods (*privilège du vendeur* or *voorrecht van de verkoper*), which should have been one of the most important and useful privileges in the business world, has been forfeited by the legislature in cases of bankruptcy. It thus has little or no usefulness in respect of a bankrupt debtor.

The reasoning behind this legislation is that a vendor who has delivered goods without demanding immediate payment has created in the buyer's mind the appearance of wealth which may induce third parties, and especially other creditors, to misjudge the debtor's wealth. In consequence, the seller-creditor will receive only his share of the distributed proceeds of the realisation of the estate assets of the bankrupt trader, along with the other unprivileged creditors on a pro rata basis.

#### 4.2.4.2 Retention of title

An unpaid vendor or manufacturer still in possession of goods may refrain, however, under certain circumstances and in good faith, from delivering the goods that he sold, manufactured, or repaired until complete payment of the price. This form of security (*droit de rétention* or *Retentierecht*), although incomplete as it offers the vendor no title or preference, does place the unpaid vendor in an improved position should the buyer be made bankrupt. Indeed, retention of the goods will give the unpaid vendor a very good negotiating position against the trustee in bankruptcy.

As the trustee in bankruptcy cannot demand delivery without paying the price of the goods first, he will often agree to termination of the sales contract to avoid deadlock, thus saving the vendor from taking proceedings to obtain release from the contract.

Where the sales contract is terminated, the vendor will not have made either a profit, or a severe loss. The goods retained will still be available for another sale.

### 4.2.4.3  *Privilège industriel*

Where equipment is sold and subsequently becomes a fixture or fitting attached to the buyer's property, creditors enjoy a specific security or privilege. This will apply even in cases of bankruptcy.

In order to enjoy this privilege, the vendor must register his invoice at the Tribunal of Commerce for the buyer's residence or registered office within 15 days of delivery of the goods. After accomplishing this formality, the vendor will enjoy this privileged position for a period of five years.

### 4.2.5  Retention of title

Under Belgian law, which favours a consensus approach, a sale is concluded as soon as both parties agree on the object to be sold and the sale price. At that moment, title to the goods is normally transferred to the buyer. However, nothing prevents the parties from deciding that transfer of title is delayed until complete payment.

The sales contract or the general sales conditions printed on the back of both order forms and invoices should include such a clause.

However, since a decision from the Supreme Court (*Cour de Cassation* or *Hof van Cassatie*) of 9 February 1933, such a retention of title (*clause de réserve de propriété* or *beding van eigendomsvoorbehoud*) cannot be raised against the other creditors as soon as a concurrence of creditors exists, eg, in cases of attachment or bankruptcy of the debtor.

In order to be enforceable, retention of title must be claimed before the concurrence of creditors exists, preferably through a registered letter addressed to the debtor, and the recovery of the goods must be put into effect.

## 4.3  Letters before action

### 4.3.1  Are they necessary?

Letters before action (*Mise en Demeure* or *Ingebrekestelling*) are recommended for several reasons, among them the following:

(1)  once the creditor's invoice becomes overdue, they allow the debtor a final term of payment and warn him of impending proceedings that will follow if he continues to; and

(2)  interest will normally not be due for the period of time preceding the dispatch of such letter.

However, well-written conditions of sale will incorporate the payment of interest at a set rate 'without preliminary reminders or letters before action'.

Here again, the wording of the general conditions of sale are very important. Indeed, the interest rates required by such clauses are usually higher than the statutory rate of eight per cent. The rate should be no higher than 12 per cent which is generally accepted by the courts. The courts may reduce higher interest rates to what they consider proper and reasonable in the given circumstances.

The existence and/or acceptance of general conditions of sale will not render the sending of a letter before action superfluous. Letters sent by a lawyer (*avocat* or *advokaat*) are recommended. Their receipt will often induce a debtor to pay or at least put forward a settlement proposal.

### 4.3.2   What should they say?

*4.3.2.1   Drafting requirements*

An appropriately worded letter before action should include:

(1)   the full and correct name and address of the debtor;
(2)   the exact date;
(3)   the full title of the creditor;
(4)   the amount due and claim details (ie, all information on the invoice, such as date, amount, and interest);
(5)   a demand for payment within a specified period, usually 8 to 15 days;
(6)   the account to which payment is to be made; and
(7)   a clear indication that failure to make payment as specified will result in the issue of proceedings.

*4.3.2.2   Interest for late payment*

As mentioned above, interest for late payment will be due as soon as the invoice becomes overdue, insofar as this is provided for by the general conditions of sale. In case interest for late payment was not contractually agreed, the letter before action should mention that the overdue payment will carry interest at the statutory rate (eight per cent) from the date of the letter; otherwise, no interest can be claimed prior to issuing the summons.

Such letters need not be sent exclusively by a lawyer. When they are not, however, it is advisable to send them by registered mail in order to have date and receipt confirmed. Even if a creditor has sent his own letter before action, a further letter will be sent by the lawyer for the reasons outlined above.

## 4.4   Pre-action and non-judicial remedies

### 4.4.1   In general

Non-judicial remedies, such as retention of goods and retention of title have been covered earlier in this chapter. The main pre-action remedies are attachments (*saisies conservatoires* or *bewarend beslag*) which will prevent the debtor from disposing of or selling the assets attached. These remedies may also be employed later in proceedings already commenced.

There are three forms of conservatory attachment, determined by the nature of the asset attached, ie, movable property (*saisie conservatoire mobilière* or *roerend bewarend beslag*), a sum owing to the debtor by a third party (*saisie-arrêt conservatoire* or *bewarend beslag onder derden*), and land and buildings (*saisie conservatoire immobilière* or *onroerend bewarend beslag*). Each requires action by both a lawyer and a bailiff (*huissier de justice* or *gerechtsdeurwaarder*) to be put into effect.

Several additional conditions must be fulfilled, and these include:

(1)   the matter must be urgent (ie, there must be serious risk that the debtor will become insolvent);
(2)   the claim must be certain (ie, the debt cannot be reasonably contested);
(3)   the debt must be due and liquidated (ie, the amount of the debt can be at least provisionally determined); and
(4)   unless provided otherwise by law, authorisation of the court.

### 4.4.2   Attachment

Two attachment procedures (*saisies conservatoire mobiliere et immobiliere* or *roerend en onroerend bewarend beslag*) require preliminary authorisation from the attachment judge (*Juge des Saisies* or *Beslagrechter*). However, this essential requirement does not affect the advantages of secrecy and speed which makes both procedures so effective.

Application for authority to attach is made by unilateral petition (*requête* or *verzoekschrift*) to the court, indicating the amount for which permission is sought. The attachment will be carried out by the bailiff without notice first being given to the opposing party. The attachment is valid for a period of three years.

These procedures create no right of preference for the creditor. However, the attached goods cannot be disposed of. In consequence, they bring pressure to bear on the debtor.

### 4.4.3   Attachment of movable property held by a third party

As explained above, with this procedure (*saisie-arrêt conservatoire* or *beslag onder derden*) the creditor will attach movable property that belongs to the debtor but is in the possession of a third party, himself debtor of the main debtor.

No preliminary authorisation from the court is required to execute this attachment. Only an authenticated title is required. Title may be evidenced by, eg, all accepted commercial invoices. A document unilaterally established by the creditor, such as retainer or other fees, will not suffice as evidence of title.

In the absence of sufficient title, this form of attachment will be possible only after authorisation from the court.

As a consequence of this attachment procedure, the attached third party is required to retain the assets attached and to declare all assets belonging to the debtor. In practice, this procedure is used to attach all accounts of a debtor at a bank or factoring company. As this usually creates enormous liquidity problems for the debtor, the pressure put to bear on him may result in at least partial payment on the debt.

### 4.4.4 Attachment with authorisation of the court

To enable the *droit de suite* or *volgrecht* to be exercised over movable property this procedure (*saisie-revendication* or *beslag tot terugvorddering*) always requires preliminary authorisation by the court. The movable property is placed under the authority of the court to ensure its conservation and restitution once the case has been decided by the court.

The procedure is especially useful for an unpaid vendor to ensure his privileged position against the debtor after having delivered the goods. Indeed, this attachment procedure prevents the debtor from disposing of the goods and allows the unpaid vendor to claim retention of the goods. The procedural aspects of this attachment are similar to those of the attachment for security purposes, mentioned above.

## 4.5 The court system

### 4.5.1 Structure of the courts

The Belgian court system has been territorially organised. Belgium is divided into more than 200 counties (*canton* or *kanton*), 26 districts (*arrondissement* or *arrondissementen*), and five judicial areas (*ressort judiciaire* or *rechtsgebied*).

#### 4.5.1.1 Courts at county level

At county level, the lowest level, a distinction is to be made between the Police Court (*tribunal de police* or *politierechtbank*) and the Justice of the Peace Court (*justice de paix* or *vredegerecht*). As both courts are presided over by a single magistrate, in smaller counties only one magistrate will be appointed to fulfil both functions.

The Justice of the Peace Court is empowered to hear all cases involving claims up to BEF 75,000. However, two exceptions exist to this general rule if the law expressly provides otherwise (ie, mainly when the subject matter of the case is specifically and expressly attributed to another court, eg the Labour Court) or when the parties have made an agreement to submit their dispute to arbitration and one of the parties relies in due time on the arbitration agreement to contest the jurisdiction of the Justice of the Peace Court.

In addition, the Justices of the Peace have exclusive jurisdiction over a variety of specific claims, regardless of the amount involved. These matters include disputes concerning real property, leases or joint ownership.

### 4.5.1.2 Courts at district level

In each of the 26 judicial districts of Belgium, there is a Court of First Instance (*tribunal de première instance* or *rechtbank van eerste aanleg*), a Commercial Court (*tribunal de commerce* or *rechtbank van koophandel*), a Labour Court (*tribunal du travail* or *arbeidsrechtbank*), and a District Court (*tribunal d'arrondissement* or *arrondissementsrechtbank*).

The Court of First Instance is composed of three divisions: one dealing with civil law, one dealing with criminal law, and one dealing with juvenile matters. Each division is composed of one of more chambers, each of which is composed of one or three judges.

Given the scope of this chapter, only the jurisdiction of the Civil Court will be examined here.

The Civil Court is empowered to decide on all claims which exceed BEF 75,000 and which do not fall within the specific jurisdiction of the Justice of the Peace Court, the Commercial Court, or the Labour Court. However, the Court of First Instance may not refuse to hear the case on its own initiative, having a right to contest jurisdiction at this level.

Apart from its general jurisdiction, the Civil Court also deals with a wide variety of matters, such as copyright claims and execution of foreign judgments in civil matters. This court also hears all cases involving disputes over the execution of judgments through the attachment judge (*juge des saisies* or *beslagrechter*).

The Commercial Court has special jurisdiction and is empowered to hear:

(1) all claims between traders (*commercants* or *handelaars*) relating to transactions which are deemed commercial by law and which do not fall within the general jurisdiction of the Justice of the Peace, ie, claims exceeding BEF 75,000;

(2) commercial claims between a claimant who is not a trader and a defendant who is a trader, if the amount involved is higher than BEF 75,000;

(3) claims arising from the law on commercial corporations or companies; and

(4) claims involving bankruptcy proceedings.

The Commercial Court is composed of one or more chambers, each consisting of three judges, of which only one is a professional judge. He is assisted by two lay judges (*juges consulaires* or *rechters in handelszaken*).

### 4.5.1.3 Courts at the level of the judicial area

In each of the five judicial areas, there is a Court of Appeal (*cour d'appel* or *hof van beroep*), composed of one or more civil chambers, criminal chambers, and juvenile chambers, each consisting of one or three judges.

The main function of the civil chambers of the Court of Appeal is to hear appeals lodged against the judgments of the Court of First Instance and of the Commercial Court.

### 4.5.1.4   The Supreme Court

Located in Brussels, the Supreme Court consists of three chambers, the first of these hearing all civil and commercial cases. The principal task of the Supreme Court is to review judgments against which no ordinary appeal rights are available. This review is limited to issues of law, as the Supreme Court only verifies whether the judgment which is being reviewed has applied the law correctly and has respected mandatory procedural rules. No factual issue will be reviewed by the Supreme Court.

The procedure before the Supreme Court is governed by specific rules, and only 16 attorneys admitted to the Supreme Court may appear and file briefs before the court.

### 4.5.2   Rules of jurisdiction

The Belgian Judicial Code distinguishes between subject-matter jurisdiction (*compétence d'attribution* or *volstrekte bevoegdheid*) and territorial jurisdiction.

Subject-matter jurisdiction determines the type of court which has authority to hear a given action. It is based on the object and the value of the claim and, as the case may be, the urgency of the claim or the nature of the parties. The principles governing subject-matter jurisdiction are those of public policy and may not be modified by agreement between the parties unless specifically provided otherwise by the law. Arbitration is one example where the law authorises the parties to derogate from the principles of subject-matter jurisdiction.

Territorial jurisdiction determines the venue where a given lawsuit must be tried. It is the authority of a court to hear actions within a certain geographical area. Unless provided otherwise by law, the claimant may institute proceedings before a court which has territorial jurisdiction over the area where the defendant is domiciled or where the legal obligations which are in dispute have arisen or have been or should have been performed.

### 4.5.3   Appeals

Appeals against decisions of the Justices of the Peace, depending on the subject matter, are heard by the Court of First Instance or the Commercial Court of the district in which the Justice of the Peace is located. However, in collection cases, no appeal is possible for claims with a value of BEF 50,000 or less.

As mentioned above, appeals against the judgments of the Court of First Instance or judgments of the Commercial Court will be heard by the Court of Appeal.

# 4.6   Legal representation

### 4.6.1   Nature of legal representation

The parties may appear in court in person or represented by a lawyer. Only for specified matters before the Justice of the Peace Court, the Commercial Court, or the Labour Court has it been allowed that a next of kin (spouse, parent, or relation by marriage) represent an individual. In such cases, the representative must have a written mandate or proxy and the appearance must be agreed by the court.

Companies must be represented by their board of administrators or directors. Unless one or two members have been authorised to represent the company in legal matters, the entire board must attend the court in person.

Thus, while an individual may be represented by his next of kin under certain conditions and circumstances, a company can only be present as set out above or if represented by a lawyer.

Without making the intervention of a member of the Bar compulsory in all cases, only lawyers have the right to plead, the right to present to court the defence of third parties, and the right to represent a party before the court. Additionally, provisions of the Judicial Code set out that, save in a few exceptional cases, only a lawyer may file unilateral petitions on behalf of a party.

Except for the few cases mentioned above, representation of parties at court rests with lawyers. Before the court, a lawyer justifies the existence of his mandate with a simple oral declaration. He need not carry a written proxy.

### 4.6.2   Mode of payment for legal representation

#### 4.6.2.1   Lawyers' fees

The party instructing a lawyer will be responsible for payment of the lawyer's fees and expenses incurred in the conduct of his case. The basis of the charge for fees is not set by law but rather is freely determined, usually on the basis of an hourly rate, according to the value of the claim, or as a fixed fee.

Members of the Bar are free to determine the basis of their charge, but their code of practice requires that the client receive preliminary information regarding charges during the initial contact. No payment in kind is allowed.

The code of practice also provides several compulsory minimum amounts for each of the charging bases. These amounts will be adapted, taking into consideration, eg, the services offered by the firm, the complexity of the case, and the expertise of the lawyer. Lawyers are forbidden by their code of practice to accept instructions on a contingency-fee basis.

When regular use is being made of the services of a firm, it may be advisable to negotiate a written contract of 'subscription' or retainer, determining the services to be rendered, the charges for the incurred expenses, the subscription-fee, and the applying rules if the agreement is terminated.

### 4.6.2.2 *Liability of other party*

Lawyer's fees borne by the parties are not recoverable, apart from a small amount which is called the procedural indemnity (*indemnité de procédure* or *rechtsplegingsvergoeding*).

The amount of the procedural indemnity is a lump sum established by law, and it depends on the type of court before which the case is brought and on the amount claimed. The procedural indemnity currently ranges from BEF 1,140 to BEF 11,400 (the latter for claims of BEF 100,000 and more), and it is periodically adjusted to reflect the cost of living.

### 4.6.2.3 *Value added tax element*

The European Union Directive foreseeing the application of VAT to lawyer's charges remains at the proposal stage. While it is possible that the fees of lawyers in Belgium will be subjected to VAT in early 1995, no certain date has been established.

## 4.7 Costs

### 4.7.1 Liability for and recovery of costs

The amounts of legal costs in Belgium are set by Decree and are periodically adjusted to reflect the cost of living. Legal costs, depending on a variety of factors, may range from approximately BEF 3,500 to issue proceedings before the Justice of the Peace to approximately BEF 8,500 to issue proceedings before the Court of Appeal. These amounts do not include disbursements, such as travel or translation expenses or other services to be rendered by the bailiff.

In principle, all legal costs linked to the issue of proceedings and execution of a judgment must be borne by the claimant until they are recovered from the losing party. Indeed, any final judgment must order the losing party to bear the legal costs. However, as the court sees fit, costs may be compensated when parties fail on certain aspects of their claims.

The costs of execution of a judgment must be borne by the party against whom execution is sought. Legal costs which may be recovered from the losing party include:

(1) stamp duties;
(2) registration fees and registration rights;
(3) costs and fees related to legal documents (eg, the legal fees of a bailiff for a writ of summons);
(4) cost of authenticated copies of the judgment;
(5) costs of investigative measures (witness testimonies and court-appointed experts);
(6) travel costs of magistrates, registrars, and parties, if these journeys are ordered by the court; and
(7) the procedural indemnity (see above).

Registration duties on judgments, currently amounting to 2.5 per cent of the sum which a party is ordered to pay, are payable by the losing party. The sums representing these duties have priority over all other privileges eventually granted to the winning party.

### 4.7.2   Legal aid

*4.7.2.1   For legal representation*

The Judicial Code provides legal assistance and representation for those persons with insufficient income. Such persons will be assigned a young lawyer to handle their case.

The effective organisation of such assistance and representation is ensured by a specific service called the *Bureau de Consultation et de Défense* or *Bureau van Consultatie en Verdediging*. The service is under the supervision of the Bar in each judicial district.

To qualify for legal aid, consideration will be given to the party's financial situation and to the merit of the claim. Cases with little prospects of success will not be dealt with, and no recourse is possible against the decisions of the Bureau.

Persons suffering severe financial hardship (with an annual income of BEF 19,000 or less) will receive the services of a lawyer without charge. Those with a greater income (up to BEF 33,000, or more depending on the circumstances) will be expected to pay a small contribution. In addition, these persons may apply for legal aid to cover the costs of proceedings, as explained below.

*4.7.2.2   For legal costs*

The Judicial Code provides for legal aid for those having insufficient income to be able to afford bearing the costs of proceedings, stamp duties, registration fees and rights (*assistance judiciaire* or *rechtsbijstand*). When granted, this legal aid provides for exemption from all costs for acts taken by judicial officers, including the bailiff.

This exemption does not result in free proceedings, as it is not a definitive exemption. The exemption concerns only the advance of those legal costs which eventually must be borne by the losing party when the judgment is executed.

Legal aid is to be granted on petition to the court before which proceedings will be issued. The petition must contain a short statement concerning the claim and must be accompanied by an official proof of identity and insolvency of claimant, which document is provided by the Administration of the city or town of domicile. The court will verify the financial situation and the apparent merit of the principal claim. Decisions refusing legal aid may be appealed to the Court of Appeal.

### 4.7.3 Interest

For entitlement to claim interest, see **4.3.2.2** above.

## 4.8 Issuing proceedings

### 4.8.1 Writ of summons

Unless the use of a petition (*requête* or *verzoekschrift*) is specifically provided for, all claims must be commenced by a writ of summons (*citation* or *dagvaarding*). The text of the writ must be prepared by a lawyer, setting out the basis of the action and a brief summary of the facts, the amount claimed including all costs and interest, the full name and address of both parties, and the judge before whom the case will be brought.

The actual summons can be served only by the bailiff, who will turn the draft prepared by the lawyer into a legally binding writ, having added, among other formalities, the place, day, and hour of the hearing.

The writ of summons will be served at the domicile of the defendant if an individual. In the case of a legal person (eg, a company or a corporation), process will be deemed served on that organisation if the writ is handed over to a body or agent who is entitled to represent that organisation in court. In practice, it will be handed over to an individual at the registered or administrative office of the organisation.

For defendants who do not have a known domicile or residence in Belgium, process will be served by the bailiff at the Public Prosecutor's Office (*Procureur du Roi* or *Procureur des Konings*) of the legal district in which the court hearing the case is located. For defendants domiciled abroad, the above rules are without prejudice to any other rules contained in international treaties.

The service of the writ of summons is followed by an introductory hearing. The minimum period of time between the service of the writ and the hearing is eight days, with the possibility of extension for defendants domiciled abroad.

### 4.8.2 Injunction of payment

For undisputed claims whose value is less than BEF 75,000, the Judicial Code provides a 'fast', unilateral, and written procedure, the injunction of payment (*procédure sommaire en injonction de payer* or *summiere rechtspleging om betaling te bekomen*). Several conditions must be met by the application:

(1) the defendant must have a domicile in Belgium;
(2) the object of the claim must be a sum of money, the amount of which may not exceed BEF 75,000; and
(3) the claim must be justified by a written document established by the debtor, which supports the presumption that the claim is not disputed. This document need not be an acknowledgment of indebtedness as such, a signed order or delivery note sufficing.

For this procedure, the letter before action (*mise en demeure* or *ingebrekestelling*) is a necessity. The debtor must be aware of the impeding proceedings to be taken against him. The content of the letter is determined by law. It must reproduce the various provisions of the Judicial Code concerning the procedure, as well as indicating the amount claimed and the court before which the case will be brought.

The debtor will be given a compulsory period of 15 days within which to pay his debt. In default of payment, a petition will be drafted and brought to the court within 15 days of the expiration of the 15-day payment period. This unilateral petition must be drafted and signed by a lawyer in order to be considered by the court.

The Justice of the Peace before whom the matter is brought may either:

(1)  summon the parties to appear at a hearing;
(2)  reject the petition; or
(3)  grant the petition.

If the petition is granted, the claimant will receive notification of the ruling of the Justice of the Peace, possibly allowing the debtor terms of payment. This order has the same effect as a judgment by default, which means that, after notification to the defendant by the bailiff, the order can be appealed.

If the judge rejects the petition, no appeal is possible, but the claimant can always issue proceedings by way of a writ of summons. The procedure does have several advantages. Although it requires the intervention of a lawyer, it is faster and greatly reduces judicial costs.

### 4.8.3  Court appearance

Parties may appear in court either in person or represented by their attorneys. The judge may refuse parties the right to appear personally if their inexperience or other factors would prevent them from presenting their arguments with sufficient clarity and dignity.

The attorneys who appear before the court on behalf of their clients must justify their appearance by presenting a proxy or mandate from the client.

## 4.9  Procedure to judgment

### 4.9.1  Introductory hearing

If the defendant fails to appear at the initial hearing of the writ of summons, under certain circumstances, the claimant will be allowed to obtain a default judgment. In cases where only short pleadings will suffice, procedural rules require notice in the writ of summons of the intent to use an accelerated procedure.

If both parties attend, the case can be referred to a subsequent hearing. In all other circumstances, the case will be referred to the general docket (*rôle général* or *algemene rol*) in order to allow the parties to exchange exhibits and briefs.

### 4.9.2 Further proceedings

Belgium's Judicial Code provides quite formal procedural rules, making it necessary to consult an attorney. In short, however, further proceedings consist of an exchange of briefs and, after a joint request to the court to set a date for oral arguments, the presentation by the parties of their views to the court in oral pleadings. Following these, the court will declare proceedings closed and take the case into deliberation and render judgment. In principle, the judgment must be rendered within one month of the case being taken into deliberation. In practice, the judge presiding over the court will indicate a date at which the judgment can be expected; in complex cases, this may be several weeks or months.

## 4.10    Enforcing judgment

Judgments may be executed only on the basis of an authenticated copy (*expedition* or *uitgifte*), to which the executory formula has been added after it has been notified by the bailiff on the application of one of the parties, usually the winning party. The executory formula contains the order of the King to all judicial officers to assist in the execution of the judgment.

Appeal proceedings or filing opposition to a judgment by default must be instituted within one month of notification of the judgment. This period is extended if the losing party has no domicile in Belgium, and this will suspend enforcement of the judgment.

The Judicial Code provides for several exceptions to the above process and, under certain circumstances and only if requested by the claimant, the court will render a judgment allowing provisional enforcement (*exécution provisoire* or *voorlopige tenuitvoerlegging*), notwithstanding opposition or the filing of an appeal. Any enforcement of a judgment pending opposition or appellate proceedings is done at the risk of the party seeking enforcement.

All acts of enforcement, including attachment, will be performed by the bailiff in his capacity as judicial officer, the costs of which will be borne by the party against whom execution is sought. All these costs, however, must be advanced by the party seeking enforcement and may not be recovered if the debtor appears to be insolvent or goes bankrupt during the course of enforcement proceedings.

## 4.11    Conclusion

In order to prevent major difficulties in the collection of a claim in Belgium, special attention should be given to the wording of the general conditions of sale agreements in the first instance. They should at least provide for a rate of interest due on late payments and for retention of title.

In addition, the period before taking action when facing a failure of payment should be reduced to the minimum commercially acceptable, especially in bankruptcy-sensitive fields or in cases related to the transport of goods.

Finally, when responding to non-payment, professional advice sought immediately will ensure fast and effective action, while reducing the number of intermediaries.

*Chapter 5*

# DENMARK

**Ole Borch**
**Berning Schlüter Hald**
**Copenhagen, Denmark**

## 5.1   Introduction

This chapter covers the main points of debt collection in Denmark. Danish law contains a variety of exceptions to the usual rules on debt collection, however, only those issues of general interest to the creditor are discussed here. Legal advice should be sought on issues of specific interest.

It should be emphasised that, although there are no short cuts to be taken in debt recovery cases,[1] they are usually regarded as uncomplicated and are normally settled within a short period of time.

It should also be noted that if a foreign creditor takes legal action in Denmark, the court may, on the request of the defendant, decide that the foreign creditor must provide security for possible costs accrued in the proceedings. However, this rule only applies if the same conditions apply to Danish creditors in the foreign country in question.

## 5.2   Initial considerations

### 5.2.1   In general

Debt collection in Denmark is regarded as a straightforward process. However, the decisions to be made by the creditor and his legal advisors before initiating debt collection proceedings do not vary substantially from the decisions necessary before initiating every legal action.

### 5.2.2   Status of the debtor

*5.2.2.1   Legal entities*

It is important to establish the identity of the debtor in order to avoid objections at a later stage. The different legal entities appearing in the Danish economy in its widest sense are listed below. It must be emphasised that the list is not complete:

(1)   Individuals, eg conducting business as a sole proprietorship or as firms
  – The significant point regarding sole proprietorship and firms is that the estate of the business and that of the owner are not separated.

---

1 Debt recovery actions, in principle, are conducted as normal court cases.

(2) Partnerships and co-ownerships – In these forms of legal entities, the estate of partnership or co-ownership is separate from that of the owners, but the owners are personally liable for debts incurred in connection with the partnership or co-ownership.

(3) Limited companies (*Aktieselskab* (A/S)) – The minimum share capital for an A/S is DKK 500,000, and there are approximately 30,000 limited companies registered in Denmark. Registration takes place in the Commerce and Companies Agency, situated in Copenhagen, eg the size of the share capital, the names and addresses of the members of the board of directors, the managing director and the auditor(s) and the annual accounts of the company. All this information is accessible to the public for a small fee.

(4) Limited companies (*Anpartsselskab* (ApS)) – The minimum invested capital for an ApS is DKK 200,000. Approximately 65,000 ApSs are listed in the Commerce and Companies Agency register and the same rules as apply to the A/S regarding the public's access to information apply to the ApS.

(5) Limited partnerships (*Kommanditselskab* (K/S)) – The owners of these entities are one general partner, directly liable for the debt of the partnership, and a number of limited partners.

(6) Associations and societies – These legal entities appear in a variety of different forms, and it is not possible to enumerate firm guidelines applying to associations and societies, as these depend primarily on the rules for the particular entity.

All of the above listed entities have the capacity to sue and be sued and, usually, every entity in possession of a legal personality has the capacity to sue and be sued. For individuals there exist almost no limitations in their legal personality. Every individual has a legal personality, regardless of nationality, domicile or age. The same applies to legal entities. The legal personality of companies and similar legal entities consists of the officers of the company, eg, the board of directors or the managing director. However, limited companies not yet registered with the Commerce and Companies Agency are deprived of their legal capacity. International organisations with extraterritorial rights, foreign heads of state, diplomats, and members of the latter's household cannot be sued.

A question distinct from that of legal personality is that of legal capacity, the ability to acquire rights and incur obligations. Individuals under the age of majority (18) cannot enter into commitments in regard to property without the approval of their parent or guardian. The same applies to individuals deprived of control over their estates in accordance with the Custody of Minors Act and to companies not yet registered with the Commerce and Companies Agency. The latter cannot acquire rights and incur obligations at all, and claims against a company about to be established must be directed against the original subscribers personally. Usually, these exceptions to legal personality also apply to the capability to present evidence in court.

### 5.2.2.2 Information

After having stated the correct identity of the debtor, which is essential to avoid unnecessary costs for suing the wrong party, the financial status of the debtor should be examined if possible. By doing this, unfortunate surprises regarding the debtor's solvency may be avoided and, in case of the debtor's insolvency, the debt-recovery procedure stopped in order to avoid unnecessary costs. The weak financial status of the debtor might also encourage the parties to reach an agreement, eg, to pay by instalment or a composition.

A creditor wishing to investigate the financial status of the debtor before initiating debt-collection proceedings may acquire information from several sources. The primary source to be consulted is, of course, the debtor himself. For individuals, the last annual settlement from the taxation authorities, and for companies and firms, the latest annual accounts may provide valuable information. However, debtors are often unwilling to provide their creditors with information regarding their financial situation and, in that case, the creditor may have to turn to other sources of information.

For limited companies, an obvious solution is to order the last annual accounts from the Commerce and Commercial Agency. Partnerships, co-ownerships, and firms are not bound to make their annual accounts public. For such legal entities and individuals, including sole proprietors, there are no simple methods to gather information about their finances.

Some Enforcement Courts maintain a register of insolvency declarations given in the court, but the practice of the courts varies from district to district. However, on request, the bankruptcy courts throughout Denmark will advise if a debtor has been declared bankrupt. Another possibility is to request a credit report from the debtor's bank, but the bank may have to refuse this request as it requires approval from the debtor to reveal such information. The bank normally charges a fee for procuring a bank report.

Finally, there is the possibility of contacting a credit enquiry agency. There are several of these agencies in Denmark, of which the largest and most well known is RKI-Information. The major drawback of these agencies is that registration of a delinquent payer is only done on request from a creditor. In general, a preliminary stage to a debt collection procedure should always include investigations of the financial status of the debtor. Whilst cost and delay will be involved, the investment is worthwhile as the report may reinforce the need for immediate legal action.

### 5.2.3 Is the debt statute-barred

A pre-condition for recovery of a debt is, of course, that the debt is not statute-barred. Under a Danish law a debt is statute-barred in five years from the time when the creditor was entitled to demand payment from the debtor. The period of limitation can be suspended only by obtaining acknowledgement from the debtor regarding the debt, by taking legal action or, if the creditor has been unable to advance his demand towards the debtor due to the latter's disappearance or if the creditor has been ignorant of his claim and such ignorance is not attributable to him. However, if the creditor has obtained a special legal basis, eg a judgment, an instrument of debt, or a written voluntary settlement, the period of limitation is extended to 20 years from the date of issue of the document.

### 5.2.4  Security

#### 5.2.4.1  *In general*

If possible, a creditor should attempt to secure his position in the best possible manner. The financial status of a debtor may change substantially within a short period of time, and the creditor who has initially taken security is normally in a good position compared to unsecured creditors. A company which is asked to supply on a credit basis or to give a loan to a company or another legal entity will normally always make certain reservations in order to carry out in-depth investigations.

Suppliers, as well as banks, should always be provided with extra security. Only the most common forms of security are described below, these being mortgage and pledge, retention of title, and transfer of claims.

#### 5.2.4.2  *Mortgage and pledge*

A creditor may seek security through a mortgage and pledge of assets belonging to the debtor. Generally, almost any asset in a commercial business may be mortgaged, but different rules apply to the various kinds of assets. For example, property and operating equipment are mortgaged by way of official registration of a mortgage deed.

It is very important that the creditor makes sure that the appropriate formalities are complied with. As mentioned above, the supplier should preferably require that security is provided by way of a banker's guarantee against the mortgage being placed at the disposal of the bank.

#### 5.2.4.3  *Retention of title*

Retention of title with respect to goods is recognised under Danish law, but foreign creditors should be especially aware that a number of requirements must be complied with. In order for a retention of title to be valid, it is required that the following conditions exist:

(1)  there must be a clear agreement;
(2)  it must be made not later than at the delivery of the goods; and
(3)  it must concern specified and identifiable objects.

Special note should be made of the claim for specification and identification of the goods supplied. Supply of a stock of goods in the form of products which cannot be identified individually once they are in the receiver's stock will not be a valid retention of title according to Danish law, and the stock will be included as a free asset in the event of a subsequent bankruptcy. A valid retention-of-title claim is only effective regarding individual, identifiable objects, eg, machines and equipment.

It also should be noted that retention of title may not be used to cover an old debt. Retention of title will be valid only to the extent that it is made as a condition for payment of the service supplied. In the case of supplies of operating equipment, there may be a further risk. According to the Danish Registration Act, building elements and fittings which are built-in by the owner in property to be used, eg, by a company, will be comprised by the mortgage on the property, with the result that the property right of a third party in this equipment lapses. Examples of these building elements and fittings are: hard, white goods, wall-to-wall carpeting, ventilating plants, etc.

A supplier of machines installed in premises owned by the company runs the risk that an otherwise valid retention-of-title clause will be unenforceable. If, on the other hand, the operating equipment is installed in a property where the company is merely a lessee, the retention of title is valid.

### 5.2.4.4  *The debtors of the debtor*

Another way for a debtor to procure security to his creditor is to mortgage the debtor's claims on his debtors. According to Danish law, the mortgaging of debtor loans is, in principle, a simple procedure. The act of giving security is the debtor's receipt of notice that the original creditor has transferred the right to payment to the new creditor (the lending or supplying company, ie, the creditor). When the debtor has received this information, the debtor is under an obligation to follow the instruction, and the debtor's possible failure to do so will have the result that the debtor may be held liable to pay the claim again to the new creditor.

Although the system is easy to handle, it is not recommended that (particularly foreign) creditors themselves receive claims, either as security or as payment. If there are or there will be free claims at disposal, it is recommended that the suppliers demand that the debtor himself use the claims for financing, ie, that a bank, against having the claims concerned assigned to it, provide a guarantee to the supplier.

In all of the above situations, creditors supplying against additional security must be aware that the Bankruptcy Act provides that such security must be granted not later than simultaneously with the contracting of the debt, and the security act must be performed without delay. Delay could mean that the right of security is made voidable in the event of a subsequent bankruptcy, with the effect that the security provided will fall to the estate and that the creditor then must be satisfied with his position as ordinary creditor.

## 5.3  Letters before action

### 5.3.1  Are they necessary?

It is not necessary to issue a letter to the debtor when the debt is due in order to initiate legal proceedings. The debtor is expected to know of the debt, the amount owed, and the due date, and he is obliged to pay in the way determined by the creditor, unless otherwise agreed.

However, there are substantial advantages in issuing a letter of demand before further action is taken. This is the course usually followed. Issuing a letter to the debtor will clarify whether the debtor will dispute the debt or part of it. In that case, the creditor will be aware of reasonable objections from the debtor and will be able to act accordingly. Disputed proceedings may result in considerable costs for the creditor and, in that situation, it is often an advantage for the creditor to attempt to reach an agreement with the debtor without involving the legal system.

In any case, issuing a letter will often persuade the debtor to contact the creditor. If the debtor has temporary difficulty in meeting his payments, a letter of demand from the creditor might encourage the debtor to offer to pay by instalments or to sign a voluntary settlement or an instrument of debt. The two latter documents can be used to proceed directly to the Enforcement Court without having to obtain a judgment, and this will normally speed enforcement.

It is always an advantage to know the financial status of the debtor. If the debtor is insolvent, further action may be withheld. If an initial letter from the creditor fails to provide a positive result, a formal demand should be sent to the creditor's lawyer.

Receiving a letter from a law firm often results in a reaction from the debtor. The creditor is liable to pay the lawyer's collection fee but usually he can recover collection charges from the debtor. The lawyer's formal demand will require payment within, say, three to eight days. However, as the chances of a reply from the debtor increase considerably, this minor delay will normally be worthwhile.

### 5.3.2  What should they say?

There are no fixed conditions regarding the contents of a letter of demand. They may be standard letters or individual letters drafted in accordance with the creditor's specific wishes or demands. However, the following are some items which should be included in these letters:

(1)  the correct name and address of the debtor;[1]
(2)  the date of dispatch of the letter;
(3)  the full name and address of the creditor;

---

1  By this, the creditor avoids objections over whether the debtor has received the letter and the debtor is, therefore, liable for the collection charges. Furthermore, disputes about the identity of the debtor can be avoided.

(4)  the amount due;[1]
(5)  interest on overdue payments;
(6)  if the letter of demand is issued by a lawyer, his collection fee for which the debtor is liable;[2]
(7)  the address to which payment should be made;[3] and
(8)  notice that failure to adhere to the time-limit specified in the letter will cause immediate action and thereby further costs without further notice.

It is not necessary to forward the letter of demand by registered mail, but often this is an advantage as objections regarding whether the debtor has received the letter and is liable for the collection charges can be avoided. It is rather expensive to register a letter in Denmark (DKK 27) and, therefore, the creditor may instead request the postal services to issue a certificate of receipt when the letter is delivered.

In summary, the letter of demand should be clear and concise in order to avoid all possible misunderstandings. A letter of demand issued by a lawyer may not include threats to report the debtor to bad debt registers. In addition, threats to file a petition in bankruptcy against the debtor are regarded as a violation of the regulations of the Danish Bar Association save in exceptional circumstances.

The lawyer can claim collection fees from the date he receives the case from the creditor, regardless of whether the debtor has already paid or pays before the lawyer forwards the letter of demand. As long as the amount is due when instructions are submitted to the lawyer, the debtor is liable to pay the collection fee, irrespective of whether the letter of demand has been received prior to his payment.

### 5.3.3  May interest for late payment be demanded?

Generally, interest for late payment must be agreed, eg, in a contract, in order to be obtained by the creditor. A note on an invoice that payment overdue will cause interest for late payment is not sufficient. However, there are some exceptions to the usual rule.

If the parties have had business relations for a long period of time and interest for late payment has been a firm part of the business relationship, the creditor can demand interest for late payment. This also applies if the payment due date has been fixed in advance. In addition, a letter of demand may

---

1  If, for example, the debt includes several overdue invoices, the amount, number and date of each invoice should appear in order that the debtor is able to identify the full amount. A statement of account would be sufficient.

2  A creditor issuing a letter of demand himself cannot claim a collection fee unless otherwise agreed between the parties. Prior notice that a formal letter of demand, including a claim for a collection fee, will be issued if the amount due is not paid within a specified time is a pre-condition to claiming the collection fee from the debtor.

3  Normally, the lawyer directs the debtor to make payment to his office.

include a provision for interest for late payment starting 30 days after the date of the letter, but it must be mentioned explicitly in the letter.

If not otherwise agreed, the rate of interest is always the bank rate of the Danish Central Bank plus five per cent. It is always recommended to make provision for interest on late payment in the contract. In those circumstances, the rate of interest can be fixed at a higher level than the bank rate, but the rate cannot be exorbitant.

## 5.4   Pre-action and non-judicial remedies

Security provided before the commencement of a business relationship or in connection with specific deliveries of goods has been dealt with above. In addition, one further pre-action remedy is available, pre-trial attachment. This procedure is dealt with below. At this stage, it should be mentioned that the pre-conditions for satisfying the Enforcement Court to levy attachment are very limited, and the costs are normally considerable. In addition, an attachment does not prevent other creditors already in possession of a judgment from enforcing against the asset seized by the attachment.

However, attachment also can be used as a remedy to establish venue in Denmark, eg, for later proceedings against a foreign debtor. In such a situation, the pre-conditions for levying attachment are not as limited. Injunctions are not used for debt collection, and other remedies are not available. Collection by the creditor of the debtor's assets without following the statutory procedure is a criminal offence according to the Danish Criminal Code.

## 5.5   The court system

### 5.5.1   Structure of the courts

Denmark is divided into 82 City (County) Court districts. Each City Court has its own judge or, depending on the size of the district, several judges and departments.

The jurisdiction of the courts is limited to that district. Each City Court also has its own division for enforcing judgments, called the Enforcement Court, and a Probate Court, which also is used as a bankruptcy court. Normally, proceedings for recovery of debts are initially submitted to the City Courts in order to obtain a judgment against the debtor.

However, under certain circumstances, actions can be submitted directly to the Enforcement Court, a step which will reduce the time to enforce the debt and make the debt collection more efficient. Depending on the size of the amount owed, proceedings can also be brought before the High Court, also known as the Court of Appeal. There are two High Courts in Denmark, the Eastern High Court, situated in Copenhagen and having jurisdiction for the Islands, and the Western High Court, situated in Viborg in Mid-Jutland with jurisdiction for Jutland. The two High Courts also function as Courts of Appeal for judgments from the City Courts and, as a rule, any legal action can go through two stages, either the City Court as the court of first instance and then the High Court, or the High Court and then the Supreme Court.

The Supreme Court in Copenhagen is used only for appeals. In proceedings before the City Court, the High Court, and the Supreme Court, the parties are known as the plaintiff and the defendant. In the Enforcement Courts the parties are known as, respectively, the claimant and the debtor. The structure of the courts mentioned above relates primarily to individual proceedings by creditors. If a creditor wishes to initiate compulsory universal proceedings against the debtor, the procedure is to file a petition in bankruptcy directly with the division of the City Court known as the Probate (Bankruptcy) Court. Finally, the Maritime and Commercial Court should be mentioned. This court, which also is domiciled in Copenhagen, normally deals with complicated commercial and maritime disputes.

### 5.5.2 Rules of jurisdiction

The rules of jurisdiction are determined by both the local and the factual authority of the courts.

#### 5.5.2.1 *Local authority*

A legal action must be brought before the court in the court district in which the defendant has his permanent address or his principal place of business. This rule applies no matter whether the proceedings are brought before the City Court or the High Court as court of first instance. However, the Danish Act of Administration of Justice contains several provisions which can be applied if the defendant has no permanent address.

#### 5.5.2.2 *Factual authority*

If the amount owed does not exceed DKK 500,000, the plaintiff must bring the action before the City Court. If the debt or the value of the action exceeds DKK 500,000, or the case raises fundamental legal questions, proceedings can be brought directly to the High Court but, in such cases, the parties can also agree to bring the proceedings to the City Court.

If the claim for DKK 500,000 or more is initially brought before the City Court by the plaintiff, the defendant can demand that the proceedings be referred to the High Court and, in that case, neither the plaintiff nor the City Court judge have a choice, the proceedings must continue before the High Court.

### 5.5.3 Procedures of the courts

In principle, the procedure is the same whether the case is submitted to the City Court or to the High Court at first instance. However, there are some differences which might influence the decision whether to submit the case to the City Court or the High Court, where a plaintiff has the choice.

At least three judges are involved in High Court cases, whereas only one judge takes part in cases before the City Courts. Therefore, some lawyers, if possible, prefer to take action in the High Court, as they consider the chance of obtaining a correct decision to be better. The appeal of the decisions of the High Court lies to the Supreme Court, where at least five judges attend the proceedings.

The cases decided by the City Courts are appealed to the High Court and, as Danish legislation is based on a two-instance principle, the decision of the High Court as Court of Appeal can be appealed only to the Supreme Court with permission from the Danish Ministry of Justice. The permission is granted only, eg, if the case raises questions of legal principle or if the decision of the court of first instance is obviously wrong. However, it is the exception rather than the rule that such permission is granted.

The disadvantage of taking action in High Court instead of the City Court is the time required for the preparation of the cases. Usually, it takes approximately 12 months to prepare a case for a City Court. Before the High Court, it is usually 18 months. Apart from these fundamental distinctions between the two courts, there are no substantial differences. The costs are almost the same but, if the plaintiff, the defendant, or their lawyers are not domiciled in the immediate vicinity of one of the two High Courts, it is of course more convenient to bring the action before the City Court situated in the court district.

### 5.5.4 Appeals

Cases initially heard in the City Court are appealed to the High Court and cases first heard in the High Court are appealed to the Supreme Court. Decisions from the Enforcement Courts and the Probate (Bankruptcy) Court are appealed to the High Court.

The normal time for appeals is four weeks after the court's decision, and a failure to meet that deadline will result in an order of dismissal from the appeal court. If the claim does not exceed DKK 10,000, it cannot be appealed, unless permission is granted by the Ministry of Justice.

## 5.6  Legal representation

### 5.6.1  Status of the foreign creditor

The Danish Act of Administration of Justice does not require the litigant to be represented by a lawyer in court unless the court decides otherwise in the actual case. However, a foreign creditor who seeks to collect his debt in Denmark is advised to seek legal representation. Ordinary debt collection cases are normally regarded as simple cases, and almost all law firms in Denmark can undertake such work.

However, some firms specialise in debt collection. A foreign creditor would be well-advised to instruct a specialist firm to ensure rapid and efficient conduct of the action. Such firms normally employ a computerised collection system.

### 5.6.2  Lawyer's fees

The current lawyer's fees for debt collection cases are provided in a set of rules fixed by the Danish Bar Association jointly with the Danish Association of Judges. These comprise collection fees, fees for obtaining a judgment without a hearing, fees for carrying through oral pleadings, and attendance fees for hearings in the Enforcement Court.

The fee for obtaining a judgment without a hearing is DKK 1,665 for a claim of DKK 25,000, and 1.5 per cent of the amount exceeding DKK 25,000. The fee for carrying through oral pleadings is DKK 6,100 for a claim of DKK 25,000, and seven per cent of the amount exceeding 25,000, up to DKK 270,000, and then three per cent of the amount above DKK 270,000. Contingency fee agreements are not generally approved and may be unethical. However, it should be mentioned that these rules are only intended as a guideline, and the lawyer's fees may well be higher, depending on the case. Many lawyers would charge extra if the correspondence were to take place in other languages than Danish.

## 5.7  Costs and interest

### 5.7.1  In general

Debt collection costs comprise chiefly court fees and lawyer's fees, but additional costs may be incurred. Fortunately, the approximate costs incurred by an ordinary debt collection procedure can be foreseen quite accurately.

### 5.7.2  Court fees

The most common court fees connected to debt recovery are as follows. Fees for the City Court (County Court) are a basic fee of DKK 500 and an additional one per cent of the amount at issue exceeding DKK 6,000. If a hearing is necessary, an additional fee of one-fifth of the fee paid initially is imposed. This amount also applies to cases submitted directly to the High Court.

If proceedings for enforcement of judgment are necessary, the fees for the Enforcement Court are DKK 300, plus a half per cent of the amount exceeding DKK 3,000. An additional fee of DKK 400 must be paid to the Enforcement Court if the enforcement procedure is to be continued.

### 5.7.3  Availability of legal aid

#### 5.7.3.1  *For the creditor*

The availability of legal aid is described in the Danish Act of Administration of Justice. In principle, only individuals of limited means can obtain legal aid. The rules also apply to foreign citizens. The limitations on the maximum income are fixed in regulations. In addition to these income limits, a precondition for obtaining legal aid is that reasonable grounds to litigate can be adduced and that the creditor is considered unable to pay the necessary costs attached to the proceedings.

However, in practice, legal aid is not usually available in debt collection cases, as these are regarded as ordinary business matters and the debt as a business expense. In general, only individuals can receive legal aid but, in special circumstances, eg, cases raising a fundamental legal question or having a substantial impact on the social or commercial status of the creditor, legal aid may also be provided to legal entities other than individuals. The same practice regarding the granting of legal aid in debt collection cases applies. In summary, the availability of legal aid for the creditor must be regarded as severely limited.

*5.7.3.2   For the debtor*

The same rules as described for the creditor apply for a debtor seeking legal aid. However, another possibility of obtaining legal aid for the debtor exists, as the court can assign a lawyer to a debtor who otherwise would be without legal representation. This is the exception rather than the rule. In addition, the Enforcement Court can assign a lawyer to the debtor.

### 5.7.4   Liability for recovery of costs

Whatever the outcome, the creditor is liable for the costs incurred in connection with the proceedings. For example, the debtor's insolvency does not release the creditor's liabilities regarding payment of court fees and lawyer's fees. The greater part of the costs, however, are recoverable, if the debtor pays the debt, whether this happens voluntarily or compulsorily through proceedings before the Enforcement Court.

Normally, judgment costs are equal to costs incurred. However, the lawyer is entitled to fix his fee regardless of the judgment. Debt collection cases which have included meetings with the debtor, comprehensive correspondence, and complicated issues may cause the lawyer's fee to exceed the usual level, and these additional expenses are not recoverable. If the debtor seeks legal assistance, he is liable for these costs, and these expenses are not recoverable unless the creditor loses the case.

### 5.7.5   Interest

Whether a creditor is entitled to interest is determined by the Danish Interest Act which covers the date from which the creditor can demand interest and the rate of interest applying.

The Danish Interest Act provides that, unless otherwise agreed between the parties, a creditor can always demand interest from the day on which proceedings are instituted. However, for the creditor to be entitled to interest, it must be claimed in the writ. If a letter of demand has previously been sent, the creditor is entitled to interest on the claim from 30 days after the letter provided that the claim for interest together with the rate of interest is specifically mentioned in the letter. The creditor may claim interest from an even earlier stage, namely if the creditor has fixed a due date in advance, ie before the delivery of goods. Under very special circumstances, the Court may decide that interest shall run from an earlier or from a later stage.

According to the Danish Interest Act, the interest rate is the bank rate of the Danish Central Bank plus five per cent. The parties may have agreed otherwise and, in that case, a higher interest rate can be demanded by the creditor. This, however, normally requires a contract or a business relationship between the parties. Accordingly, the claim for a higher interest rate than the legal rate is generally only of interest in cases regarding contractual obligations. If the agreed interest rate is exorbitant, the Court may reduce it.

## 5.8 Proceedings

There are only small differences between the procedure in the City Courts compared to that of the High Courts. That of the Supreme Court varies a great deal as it is solely a court of appeal, and the same applies to the divisions of the City Courts designated the Enforcement Court and the Bankruptcy Court.

### 5.8.1 Issuing proceedings

To obtain a judgment the following procedure is employed. If the plaintiff decides to institute proceedings before the City Court or the High Court, a writ of summons will be drawn up. In addition to the sum claimed, the writ must include a detailed statement of claim and the petitions made in support of the claim. In addition, the documents on which the plaintiff relies in the proceedings must be enclosed. The court arranges service of the writ and the enclosed documents on the defendant and sets a hearing date at which the defendant must produce his reply. This pleading must include the same elements as the writ.

Usually, a case will be presented by submission of two written pleadings from each party, including the writ and the reply. When both parties have submitted these pleadings, the preparation of the case is considered concluded and a date for the trial is set. Before this stage, both parties must state the names of the witnesses to testify at the trial. The proceedings will be oral.

Exceptionally, evidence may be given abroad through the forwarding of a commission rogatory by the Danish court to a local foreign court, requesting an examination in court of the witness or witnesses concerned.

## 5.9 Procedure to judgment

### 5.9.1 The debtor pays the debt

At what stage of the action the debtor pays the debt is important. If the creditor receives payment after instructing his lawyer, the debtor must also pay the lawyer's collection fee. If proceedings have already commenced, the debtor also must pay the court fees and additional costs.

The plaintiff determines expenses incurred and interest accrued at the time of payment. If the payment does not include these the plaintiff may continue proceedings for expenses and interest. The debtor is not entitled to a receipt for payment, but normally this is confirmed in correspondence. The plaintiff is obliged to discontinue the action if the case has already been brought before the court.

### 5.9.2   The debtor admits the debt

Again, the time at which the debtor admits the debt is important. If the creditor has not already obtained judgment, he should proceed in order to strengthen his position relative to other creditors. However, if the debtor is virtually insolvent and there is no chance of the debtor regaining his financial strength within the foreseeable future, the only solution may be to shelve the matter.

If the defendant acknowledges the claim, the court will normally enter judgment at the first court hearing, and the plaintiff can proceed to enforcement. The same applies when the defendant fails to appear in court. His absence is regarded as an acknowledgement of the claim. Only if the formal provisions in the Danish Act of Administration of Justice are not observed (eg, if the legal action is brought before the wrong City Court) or if it is evident that the claim is incorrect or untrue (eg, if it is obvious that the debt is statute-barred) will the court not pass judgment. When this happens the case will be dismissed.

Reaching an agreement, eg, an instalment-payment agreement with the defendant avoiding the necessity to proceed at the enforcement court is possible. However, the Danish Act of Administration of Justice only imposes an obligation on the plaintiff to accept an instalment-payment agreement which does not exceed 10 months. If the defendant's proposal to pay by instalments exceeds this period, the plaintiff may prefer to proceed in the Enforcement Court. Once the plaintiff has accepted the debtor's proposal, he is bound by the agreement. Should the defendant default, the plaintiff can then proceed to enforcement.

### 5.9.3   The debtor disputes the debt

When the debtor disputes the debt, proceedings must take their course, with the issue of a writ of summons, exchange of written pleadings, production of documents, and the final oral hearing with examination of witnesses and oral pleadings by the lawyers. In such a case, the foreign creditor should consider his situation thoroughly. First, he and his lawyer must consider the character of the debtor's objections and the chances of successfully carrying through the collection action. In addition, the amount disputed must be taken into consideration. It is costly to conduct a defended case, and it may be that the costs, even if successful, will exceed the amount collected. This is because the costs imposed on the defendant do not always cover the costs paid by the plaintiff.

If the debt is substantively disputed, eg, if the parties disagree about the facts, the creditor should consider the possibility of negotiating with the debtor in order to reach a compromise before legal action is taken. This might benefit both parties. In Denmark it is normal to propose such a settlement. Even after proceedings are instituted the parties are free to initiate or carry on negotiations. The parties normally request adjournment of the case and the court usually accepts such requests.

The Danish Act of Administration of Justice confers an obligation on the judge in the court of first instance and, sometimes on the judge in the Court of Appeal, to mediate between the parties. This mediation is normally carried out during the preparation of the case. After the oral proceedings and when the trial is over, the court will usually ask the parties if they are interested in receiving a compromise proposal and the court will then indicate its decision on the matter. If both parties agree to conclude the case on this basis, usually no actual judgment will be pronounced, but the parties will make a settlement in court having the same binding effect as a judgment. Such a settlement cannot be appealed. If one of the parties does not accept the decision of the court, a written judgment must be requested. This requires an additional one to three months and provides a possibility to appeal the case to a higher court.

If a negotiated settlement is reached during the pending court case, it is important to determine whether the settlement should be contracted before the court or outside the court. If the defendant breaches an agreement reached before the court, the plaintiff can proceed directly to the Enforcement Court. Agreements reached outside court will be enforceable only under certain circumstances.

As indicated, the Danish legal system and tradition in many ways urges the parties to reach a settlement. In addition, the rules stipulated by the Danish Bar Association (*Advokatrådet*) require the lawyers representing the parties to investigate the possibilities of reaching a settlement before proceedings are instituted. A breach of this rule could result in penalties imposed by the Bar Association.

### 5.9.4 The debtor disputes part of the debt

In this situation, the same procedures as described above relating to the debtor's admission or denial of the full debt apply.

### 5.9.5 The debtor neither admits nor disputes the debt

This normally occurs when the creditor has been unable to contact the debtor or the latter has not responded to the approaches of the creditor. In order to secure his position against other possible creditors, he should then follow the procedure described above relating to the debtor's admission of the debt. As noted, the court will normally pass judgment in accordance with the claim on the defendant who fails to appear in court.

The plaintiff can proceed to enforcement. Approximately 90 per cent of the cases brought before the City Courts and the High Courts are concluded after the first court hearing by judgment on the claim because the defendant fails to appear in court.

### 5.9.6   The debtor is declared insolvent

A declaration of insolvency can be made in several ways. The debtor can inform the creditor that he is unable to pay the debt. This, of course, need not prevent the creditor from proceeding but it might influence initial investigations regarding the financial status of the debtor before further costly action is taken. In addition to an informal declaration of insolvency, the debtor might be declared or declare himself insolvent in connection with individual and universal proceedings by (other) creditors.

Individual proceedings normally take place in the City Courts and the Enforcement Courts. Normally, the debtor declares himself insolvent in the Enforcement Court, but this can also take place in the court of first instance. The legal effect is that no requests for enforcement can be brought before the court until six months after the declaration of insolvency. The creditors must wait for this period to expire and requests brought before the Enforcement Court during that period will automatically be dismissed.

Unfortunately, no official central register for declarations of insolvency submitted in the Enforcement Courts throughout the country exists, and the different courts have different procedures. Some Enforcement Courts maintain an insolvency register and some do not. The time for a creditor's acknowledgement of an insolvency declaration of the debtor, therefore, varies from court district to court district.

Universal proceedings are discussed in the text below relating to insolvency.

## 5.10   Enforcing judgment

### 5.10.1   In general

If the debtor, despite a judgment obtained by the creditor, does not fulfil the creditor's claim, the next step is to proceed with enforcement or execution. The procedure under Danish law is the same whether the target for the enforcement is the debtor's property, other assets belonging to him or claims against third parties.

The creditor requests that the execution court levy execution on some of the debtor's assets. By the levied execution, the creditor is entitled to demand that part of the debtor's assets be sold by a forced sale to settle the amount owed, including incurred expenses and accrued interest. At the same time, the creditor obtains a mortgage on the assets concerned.

### 5.10.2   Basic document

A pre-condition for execution proceedings is that the creditor be in possession of a so-called basic document. A judgment constitutes a basic document, but the Act of Administration of Justice enumerates several other types of documents which can be used. All these other documents allow the creditor to proceed directly to the Enforcement Court without having to obtain a judgment.

Therefore, these documents are attractive to the creditor as he can speed the debt collection by several months and make the procedure more efficient. In addition, the debtor's signature on one of these other basic documents will normally prevent him from disputing the debt mentioned in the document, as his signature is regarded as an acknowledgement of the debt.

Apart from a judgment, the following documents can be used as basic documents:

(1) negotiated settlements contracted in court;
(2) voluntary settlements;
(3) instruments of debt;
(4) mortgage deeds;
(5) bills of exchange; and
(6) cheques.

In addition, the creditor, pledging in a claim, can proceed directly with enforcement. Settlements contracted in court, voluntary settlements and instruments of debt must be provided with the following endorsement: '*Nærværende fundament kan danne grundlag for tvangsinddrivelse, jf. Retsplejelovens* Section 478'. Otherwise, the request for execution will be dismissed. It is also recommended to have the document signed before two witnesses.

Voluntary settlements and instruments of debt issued in Denmark must be stamped with 0.3 per cent of the principal debt and, if the creditor retains a Danish lawyer to have the document issued, expenses incurred in that connection will usually be between 1 to 2.5 per cent of the claim. These amounts will also be added to the debt and appear in the document. Normally, an instalment-payment agreement is contained in a voluntary settlement or in an instrument of debt, and only if the debtor breaches this agreement can the creditor proceed in the Enforcement Court. The same applies to settlements contracted in court and to mortgage deeds. For bills of exchange and cheques a rather complex set of rules apply and these documents will not be mentioned further in this chapter.

### 5.10.3 Procedure

As mentioned above, the creditor requests the Enforcement Court in the district of the debtor's residence or where he carries on his business to levy execution on some of the debtor's assets. A judgment from a Danish court allows the debtor a fortnight to settle the judgment, and a request will not be tried before the expiry of this deadline. The fee for the Enforcement Court is DKK 300, plus a half per cent of the claim exceeding DKK 3,000. Normally, the debtor will then be summoned to the Enforcement Court to a hearing at which the creditor or his representative must attend approximately one month after receipt of the request for execution.

During the hearing, the debtor will be questioned by a deputy judge or, in simple cases, by a clerk. Initially, he will be informed that false statements before the court will constitute a violation of the Danish Criminal Code and he will be asked to verify his identity. After these opening remarks the oral examination will take place. The debtor will usually be questioned about his financial status, whether he is able to pay the debt or enter into an instalment-payment agreement and, if so, the conditions for this.

In addition, the creditor will normally ask the debtor about his assets and perhaps his liabilities. This hearing may result in the following: the debtor either pays the debt, offers to pay by instalment or declares himself insolvent. The two latter possibilities can be combined with the Enforcement Court levying execution on some of the debtor's assets.

Under the Act of Administration of Justice the creditor must accept an instalment-payment proposal from the debtor which does not exceed 10 months, but he is entitled to accept any proposal put forward by the debtor. However, if he accepts an instalment-payment agreement taking longer than 10 months he is bound by that acceptance. If the debtor fails to appear in the Enforcement Court, the creditor has three options. He can decide not to proceed because further proceedings will result in further costs. If the creditor decides to proceed, he can either request the court to continue the execution at the debtor's address or, under certain circumstances, he can request the court to have the debtor arrested by the police and be presented in court.

These further proceedings cause additional court fees of DKK 400. On the creditor's request and under special circumstances, the court may decide to convene at the debtor's home or place of business without previous notice to the debtor. This procedure improves the chances of obtaining settlement for the creditor where there is a risk that the debtor will give false statements in court or hide his assets before the execution. Where execution is undertaken based on a mortgage deed securing the debtor's property as a basic document, the levy of execution does not require the debtor's presence in court. Execution can be levied and the debtor's property sold by a forced sale. A creditor who is to have execution levied should expect, in addition to the court fee, costs amounting to approximately two per cent of the amount due.

### 5.10.4  Assets

Execution may be levied on practically all tangible assets. However, the Act of Administration of Justice provides that a number of assets are exempt from execution. Execution cannot be levied on the necessities of life of the private debtor. A business debtor has almost no protection for assets attached to his business. With the exception of real property and cash, the debtor has the right to identify which of his assets will be subject to execution and the creditor must accept the choice of the debtor if the judge deems this to be sufficient security.

Execution can be levied only on such part of the assets that will secure the claim of the creditor. Depending on the nature of the matter, including whether it is anticipated the debtor will fulfil his obligation to pay, the

Enforcement Court may decide that the assets on which execution is levied will be removed immediately and kept until an auction can take place.

### 5.10.5 Execution

Execution is levied for the purpose of selling the asset in question within a certain period of time at an auction. The term of limitation of execution differs, depending on the nature of the asset. A creditor who has obtained execution on chattels of the debtor, therefore, is forced to proceed with an auction within one year. Execution on land is time-barred after 20 years.

The legal effect of the execution is that the debtor has no authority to sell, pledge, or lend the asset without observing the creditor's rights. If he does so, he infringes the Danish Criminal Code and risks conviction for embezzlement.

### 5.10.6 Forced sales

Except for pledged assets, levied execution is a pre-condition for a forced sale of the asset. Different procedures apply regarding how a forced sale is implemented, depending on the nature of the asset. Sales of land usually occur at a forced sale. The time required for a forced sale can vary. A forced sale of plant, machinery and other chattels may be carried out immediately when it is established that the debtor is no longer able to pay and cannot offer an instalment agreement satisfactory to the creditor. In view of delays in the courts because of the number of forced-sale cases, six to nine months will be required to carry out a forced sale of land.

It is important to note that it is relatively expensive to carry out a forced sale. First, significant costs, especially for forced sales of land, are incurred by way of fees in connection with the procedure. Secondly, the prices obtained at a forced sale are usually substantially lower than in a sale on the open market. If at all possible, it often pays to attempt to obtain an agreement with the debtor for a voluntary sale. Such agreements may be made, eg, by the creditor's lawyer obtaining a power of attorney from the debtor to realise the assets in question on condition he settles sums due to execution creditors or other mortgages. It is important to determine whether a forced sale is the most effective means of proceeding.

### 5.10.7 Pre-trial attachment

A creditor who has reason to fear that a debtor is about to evade his payment obligations may ask the Enforcement Court to levy attachment. Attachment is an interlocutory seizure of part of the debtor's assets and it remains in force until the time when the creditor has obtained a basic document.

It is difficult to have the Enforcement Court carry through attachment. The effect of the attachment is that the debtor is deprived of the possibility of disposing of the asset(s) on which attachment is levied. Attachment may be effected by removing the assets from the debtor, but usually it is done solely by the Enforcement Court giving notification that the attachment has been levied and that the debtor will commit a criminal act if he acts contrary to the attachment. The weakness of the attachment is that any other creditor who already has obtained a basic document has priority over the creditor who has only an attachment.

In the event of the debtor's bankruptcy, an attachment is without legal effect with the result that the estate can dispose of the assets for the benefit of all the creditors. An attachment requires that a special legal action be instituted to confirm its validity within a week after the attachment has been levied. If not, the attachment will lapse. If it is later found that the attachment is not justified because the asserted claim appears not to exist in whole or in part, the applicant for the attachment becomes liable to pay compensation for the losses the debtor may have suffered in connection with the attachment.

Although the compensation awarded in this respect is usually limited, the Enforcement Courts almost always request that an applicant for an attachment provide a bank guarantee in favour of the debtor, covering an amount corresponding to the creditor's claim. Expenses incurred in connection with attachment proceedings will usually be 2.5 to 4 per cent of the claim, plus expenses incurred in connection with a bank guarantee.

## 5.11   Insolvency

### 5.11.1   In general

The term 'insolvency' is used both in connection with individual proceedings by creditors and in connection with universal proceedings. The insolvency of a debtor during individual proceedings normally leads to postponement of enforcement proceedings and, in such a situation, the creditor must often recognise that further action is futile; the debtor is simply not able to pay the amount owed, at least not at present. Had the insolvency of the debtor come to the knowledge of the creditor at an earlier stage, he probably would not have instituted proceedings.

Where there are universal proceedings the situation is different. Insolvency is a pre-condition for instituting universal proceedings and a creditor filing a petition in bankruptcy against the debtor has acknowledged the insolvency of his debtor. There are four kinds of universal proceedings, all described in the Danish Bankruptcy Act:

(1)   suspension of payments;
(2)   bankruptcy;
(3)   enforced composition and enforced moratorium; and
(4)   discharge of debts.

Suspension of payments, bankruptcy, and enforced composition and enforced moratorium apply to all legal entities. Discharge of debts applies only to individuals. The only type of universal proceedings that can be forced on the debtor against his will is bankruptcy. The other types of universal proceedings require an initiative from the debtor. This section focuses on bankruptcy and with a brief mention of the other kinds of universal proceedings.

The purpose and the result of a bankruptcy is a termination of the debtor's business, whereas the aim of the other kinds of universal proceedings is a reconstruction of the debtor's business or financial status. A creditor may file a petition in bankruptcy against a debtor for several reasons. The primary purpose of the bankruptcy is to satisfy the claims of the creditors by an equal distribution of the debtor's assets amongst them. Suspecting that the debtor may avoid seizure of his assets through concealed sales, the creditor may file a petition in bankruptcy in order to strengthen his position.

Additionally, the creditor might suspect the debtor of favouring some of his creditors over others or making unusual realisations of his assets. If the debtor is declared bankrupt, transactions made in favour of one or several specific creditors and carried out within a short time before the bankruptcy may be declared invalid. The invalidation of such transactions might transfer considerable assets to the estate in bankruptcy and thus improve the standing of the creditors.

Finally, it should be emphasised that instituting bankruptcy proceedings should not be used for individual debt-collection purposes. Bankruptcy proceedings should be considered carefully and be applied by the creditor only as a last resort. Threatening a debtor or filing a petition in bankruptcy against the debtor as part of individual debt-collection proceedings is regarded as an infringement of the rules of the Danish Bar Association and might result in penalties for the lawyer.

### 5.11.2 Winding up of limited companies

#### 5.11.2.1 *Universal proceedings*

Voluntary universal proceedings normally take place either by the debtor contacting his creditors directly in order to obtain a voluntary settlement (a 'quiet' suspension of payments) or by the debtor himself, through a notice to the local Bankruptcy Court, stating that he is entering into suspension of payments. A notice of suspension of payments is usually filed by the local Bankruptcy Court if the debtor expects to reach agreement on a deed of arrangement with a majority of his creditors.

The period of suspension of payments is used to 'protect' the debtor against individual proceedings while he and his advisors are preparing his proposal to the creditors in order to continue his business after financial reconstruction. As this protection does not apply in an unofficial suspension of payments, this method will almost never be recommended by the debtor's legal advisors. If the debtor realises that an arrangement with his creditors can be reached, the step leading to suspension of payments is an enforced deed of arrangement, an enforced moratorium, or a combination of these.

The pre-condition for enforced deeds of arrangement and moratoriums is that, at minimum, 60 per cent of the debtor's creditors, determined by number and size of debt, agree to write down their respective accounts receivables by up to 75 per cent of the total debt. An enforced composition or moratorium binds the minority of creditors who have voted against the composition or who have abstained from voting.

### 5.11.2.2 Liquidation

One way of winding up a Danish limited company is by the shareholders passing a resolution for liquidation of the company at a general meeting. The company's solvency is a prerequisite for this termination procedure. If the company is insolvent, the sole winding-up procedure available to the company is bankruptcy. If the appointed liquidator ascertains that the company was insolvent from the beginning or has become insolvent at a later stage, the winding up of the company must be continued by the filing of a petition in bankruptcy against the company.

The Danish Commercial and Companies Agency may demand a compulsory liquidation if the company has not presented its annual accounts according to the time-limit determined in the legislation or if an auditor or the board is not elected in accordance with the legislation. Whether the compulsory liquidation will be carried out as a solvent liquidation or as a bankruptcy depends on the financial status of the company.

### 5.11.2.3 Bankruptcy

Bankruptcy proceedings are identical whether the debtor is an individual or a legal entity. Thus, the procedures mentioned below apply to limited companies, individuals, partnerships and proprietors, with certain exceptions resulting from the different characteristics of these entities. Compulsory universal proceedings are established by a creditor requesting the court to issue a bankruptcy order against the debtor.

In addition, the debtor can himself file a petition in bankruptcy. It should be noted that, contrary to the rules applying to execution in the case of individual proceedings by creditors, no formalities are required with respect to the creditor's claim. Thus, the creditor need not document his claim in the form of a judgment, an instrument of debt, or a voluntary settlement signed by the debtor; nor is documentary evidence as to due date on the debtor's payment required. The creditor need only convince the court that:

(1)  the debtor owes money to the creditor; and
(2)  the debtor is unable to pay his creditors in general (including the creditor in question) when their respective claims fall due.

A creditor who has filed a bankruptcy petition may request that a bankruptcy order be made even though the debtor offers to pay the claim. This is due to the fact that, if the debtor is insolvent, the creditor may be subject to the risk that the payment offered by the debtor will be voidable in a subsequent bankruptcy. The rules providing that a creditor's claim need not be documented by a judgment or a settlement, or that the claim need not be due, respectively, do not mean that the Bankruptcy Court will rule arbitrarily. They allow the court to disregard groundless objections by a debtor attempting to prevent or delay universal proceedings.

Conversely, it must be emphasised that a severe financial liability in damages is imposed on the creditor if it subsequently appears that his claim was not justified and the debtor's objections accordingly were valid. Once the bankruptcy order has been pronounced, usually within a short period of time after filing of the bankruptcy petition, the debtor is deprived of management of his estate. A trustee is then appointed by the creditors. The trustee's task is to realise all assets of the debtor and to distribute the proceeds to the creditors. The order of priority for distributions is as follows:

(1) expenses incurred in connection with estate proceedings by way of remuneration to the trustee and other expenses incurred by the estate;
(2) expenses, if any, validly incurred during a preceding suspension of payments;
(3) wages and salaries; and
(4) ordinary creditors.

It usually takes between one and two years to finalise proceedings in bankruptcy. Bankruptcy proceedings do not mean that the debtor is discharged from any part of the debt not covered by these proceedings. There may be further claims by creditors. However, as the company declared bankrupt ceases to exist, such further claims may well prove futile. One of the more significant effects of bankruptcy may be the possibility of invalidating transactions performed by the debtor within a specific time, normally three or six months before the declaration of bankruptcy. It is for the trustee to investigate whether such transactions may have taken place and, if so, to restore the assets to the bankrupt estate.

Such transactions may include large gifts granted within six months before the bankruptcy, the waiving of an inheritance due and salary contributed to closely-related persons. Unusual payments and granting of mortgages after the debt incurred can be voidable if the transactions have taken place within three months prior to the bankruptcy.

Execution levied within the same time-limit is automatically set aside and all payments after the bankruptcy will usually be automatically declared voidable. There are several other forms of transactions which may be declared invalid. However, the specific transactions mentioned above are the most common. The Danish Bankruptcy Act contains a general provision which may apply if none of the listed provisions are applicable.

Under this provision, transactions may be set aside if the debtor was insolvent or, by the transaction, became insolvent and the creditor may have acknowledged the insolvency. The transaction must also be one not authorised by the legislation. It is important to note that the bankruptcy petitioner is personally liable for the bankruptcy costs. The debtor's assets are used, inter alia, to cover these expenses but, if the debtor does not possess sufficient assets or the debtor's assets are encumbered by a third party's priority claim (eg, by way of non-voidable and valid mortgages), the expenses will be borne by the bankruptcy petitioner.

There is no ceiling in principle to these expenses, but usually the court will request that the petitioner provide security of DKK 20,000 to pay for preliminary examinations and establish whether the debtor has any assets to be sold and provide payment to the creditors. The court fee for a bankruptcy petition is DKK 750 and this must be paid by the petitioner.

### 5.11.3 Bankruptcy of individuals

The procedure described for limited companies also applies to individuals, with some minor differences.

### 5.11.4 Insolvency of partnerships and proprietors

Many firms in Denmark are organised as partnerships or proprietorships. The owners are liable for costs incurred in connection with the firm or the business, and thus they will also be regarded as liable if the firm cannot fulfil its obligations to make payments. Therefore, a creditor contracting with a partnership or proprietorship may seek recovery from the individual or the business.

Individual proceedings may be instituted against the firm represented by the owners, the owners alone, or both the owners and the firm. There can be problems regarding universal proceedings. A petition cannot be filed against the partnership or proprietorship alone. The creditor wanting to institute bankruptcy proceedings must file a petition against both the partnership or proprietorship and each of the partners or proprietors. Thus, it is usually costly to request bankruptcy against a partnership or a proprietorship. When commencing bankruptcy proceedings the creditor must present a security of approximately DKK 20,000 for each bankruptcy estate and the costs incurred in the proceedings will usually be considerable.

Apart from these considerations regarding the special rules applying to partnerships and proprietors, there are no further differences in bankruptcy proceedings.

### 5.11.5 International bankruptcy

The five Nordic countries (Denmark, Sweden, Norway, Finland, and Iceland) have a common convention in which the countries mutually respect suspension of payments and compositions in bankruptcy proceedings. Denmark has no such conventions with other countries. For corporate bankruptcy estates, this problem is usually solved by the Danish authorities and courts furnishing the trustee with the required official documents confirming that the trustee is authorised to deal with assets which may be held abroad.

The trustee's ability to include the assets in the estate depends on this ability to convince either the foreign authorities in question or the bankrupt of the expediency of co-operation. Conversely, Denmark does not generally recognise bankruptcy orders pronounced by other countries.

## 5.12 Recognition of foreign court decisions

### 5.12.1 In general

Generally, only Danish court decisions will be recognised. However, Denmark has acceded to a number of conventions with the result that decisions made by a number of countries will also be respected. Foremost of these conventions are the following.

### 5.12.2 The Brussels Convention

The Brussels Convention guarantees mutual recognition of the participating Member States, including the United Kingdom, with regard to all judgments and other court decisions made by the courts of the States comprised by the convention, notwithstanding who the parties are, the basis of venue, whether the decision is a judgment by default, or whether the case may be appealed. In such cases, the substance of the decision cannot be tried. Only the competence of the foreign court of law, by exception, may be examined.

On this basis, if a creditor makes a request for attachment to be levied, he will be free to choose whether he wants the attachment levied by a Danish Enforcement Court according to Danish rules or by the court of another EU Member State where the dispute is pending or will be pending. The Convention also provides that a compromise made before the court of the Member State will have the same status as an actual court decision.

### 5.12.3 The Nordic Judgment Convention

The Nordic Judgment Convention corresponds in a number of areas to the Brussels Convention but does differ in certain aspects, such as not recognising judgments by default.

### 5.12.4 Outside the Conventions

Legal decisions of countries that are not signatories to either of the above Conventions may not be recognised immediately in Denmark. However, the Ministry of Justice is authorised to recognise the judgments of selected countries. The fact that a court decision of a country is not recognised does not mean that no importance is attached to it. The evidence from testimony of parties and witnesses presented before the foreign court, the evaluation of evidence made by the court, and often its legal application will provide the foundation of the Danish court's decision, unless information provided by the parties suggests that the foreign judgment may be erroneous.

However, the decision cannot be enforced immediately but must be tried through ordinary legal action. It is of no importance whether the court decision is based on an agreement between the parties regarding the venue. The decision must still be tried by a Danish court to form the basis for enforcement.

*Chapter 6*

# ENGLAND AND WALES

**Andrew Bogle**
**Bermans**
**Liverpool, England**

## 6.1 Introduction

This chapter deals with actions commenced in England and Wales. The legal system in the British Isles has evolved over centuries. Therefore, not only the Republic of Ireland, but also Scotland and Northern Ireland, have separate legal systems.

In addition, the Isle of Man and the individual Channel Islands each have their own independent courts. Once it becomes necessary to issue proceedings, an English lawyer must instruct a counterpart in that jurisdiction to act as his agent.

## 6.2 Initial considerations

### 6.2.1 Status of the debtor

Money remains owing to the creditor. Its own efforts to obtain payment have failed. Relevant information and evidence has been offered. There are some further considerations before action is commenced.

The need to establish the status of the debtor is dealt with in Chapter 2. Its importance cannot be overstated. Pursuing the wrong party will increase cost and delay and reduce the prospects of recovery. Full names and descriptions should be employed where possible.

### 6.2.2 Legal entities

The various legal entities which may be pursued in the English courts are summarised as follows:

(1) an individual, who may either trade in his own name or use a trading name;
(2) a firm, comprising two or more individual partners;
(3) a limited company, styled either 'Limited', 'Company Limited', 'Ltd, Co', or 'Ltd', or a 'Public Limited Company', 'plc';[1]

---

1 The vast majority of companies in England and Wales are limited by shares, a few being limited by guarantee. Foreign companies can be pursued where they have a principal place of business in England and Wales.

(4)    an unlimited company, although this type of entity is rare;
(5)    a charity;[1]
(6)    a club;[2] and
(7)    a body corporate.[3]

Those entities which cannot be pursued in the English courts include:

(1)    minors under 18 years of age and individuals covered by the mental health legislation who do not have the capacity to enter into contracts; and
(2)    an undischarged bankrupt.[4]

The circumstances in which a creditor may and why a creditor would want to pursue a company in liquidation are discussed below.[5] Where a person purports to contract on behalf of a company after it is placed in liquidation, a right of action will lie against that individual.

Where an individual with whom a creditor contracts, either on his own behalf or as a partner in a firm, then dies, a claim should be lodged with his estate and, if necessary, proceedings may be instituted against his executors or administrators. Searching and lodging caveats at the local Probate Registry may assist in identifying these individuals. Reference should be made to the telephone directory.

### 6.2.3   Sources of information

When attempting to trace a debtor, consideration should be given to telephone and trade directories, trade federations, the Land Registry, the voters' roll, and searches at Companies House for details of directors. Such information may be out of date. The Drivers and Vehicle Licensing Centre in Swansea should not divulge information, and the same applies to financial institutions and professional advisers.

In England and Wales, limited companies are obliged to file annual accounts. These, together with information including the officers of a company, its registered office, share capital, appointment of liquidators and receivers, and debentures taken are available from Companies House. Company agents will provide such information at a fee. A telephone search available to subscribers at the Land Charges Department in Plymouth (telephone (01752)

---

1   Details should be sought from the Charity Commission, St Albans House, 57 Haymarket, London SW1Y 4QX, telephone (0171) 210 3000.
2   An individual, firm, or limited company may trade in this form. There are also members' clubs which must lodge details with the local authority. Action is taken against the officers of the club in their representative capacity. Careful investigation may be required.
3   This range of institutions includes local, health, and education authorities. Again, care needs to be taken here.
4   However, such a party will have committed an offence under the insolvency legislation.
5   'Receiver' is used throughout this chapter as an all-purpose term, encompassing nominees and supervisors under individual voluntary arrangements, trustees in bankruptcy, administrators, administrative receivers, and liquidators.

701171) will reveal if a bankruptcy petition has been issued against an individual.

A register of county court judgments is kept by the Registry Trust Limited, 173/175 Cleveland Street, London W1P 5PE. Postal searches cost £4.50. Advertisements of winding-up petitions, as well as publication of winding-up and bankruptcy orders and meetings of creditors, appear in the *London Gazette*, published daily. A central registry of winding-up petitions issued is kept at the Royal Courts of Justice (telephone (0171) 936 7328).

### 6.2.4  Is the debt statute-barred?

Various other limitation periods apply in personal injury and actions relating to land but, for recovery cases, a creditor must issue proceedings within six years of the date on which the money becomes due for payment. Otherwise, the debtor is entitled to apply to the court for the action to be struck out with costs, and there is no second opportunity to issue proceedings.

### 6.2.5  Security

In Chapter 1, reference is made to the possibility of obtaining security to afford further protection in the contract. Security can take various forms, the most likely being fixed and/or floating charges, legal charges, and guarantees. If security is also held, there is a choice whether to pursue the debtor for recovery, enforce that security or follow both options. Where either a fixed or floating charge is held, a receiver is appointed to enforce its powers.

Possession proceedings may be instituted to realise the security covered by the legal charge or, where there are tenanted properties, a receiver for rents can be appointed. The most likely security held will be a guarantee. Once formal demand for payment has been made, the remedies available to a creditor against a guarantor will be the same as those against the principal debtor discussed later in this chapter.

### 6.2.6  Retention of title

A customer is in financial difficulties. He cannot make payment, and the creditor fears that recovery through court action will be too late, as the customer is about to go out of business. Alternatively, the customer has already been declared insolvent. It is too late to obtain payment but, if the customer continues to hold goods, and there is a retention-of-title clause incorporated in the creditor's contract, return of those goods can be sought.

The importance of ensuring that a valid clause has been incorporated into the contract is discussed in Chapter 1. Consideration will now be given to its enforcement.

First, can the goods be identified? If not the claim will fail. This will also be the case where goods have been sold onwards, unless the sale proceeds can be identified. Have the goods been incorporated so that they are no longer identifiable, such as resin incorporated in furniture? If so, again, the claim will fail.

Assuming, however, these various tests can be satisfied, a creditor should notify its customers or the appointed receiver immediately of its claim and make arrangements for removal of the goods. The person having control of the goods should be put on notice that, if the goods are disposed of, an action for damages for conversion will be made against them personally. If access to inspect the goods or for removal is refused, force should not be employed but consideration should be given to seeking an injunction to protect the creditor's position (see **6.4**, below).

## 6.3    Letters before action

### 6.3.1    Are they necessary?

It is usual, but not compulsory, for a solicitor's letter to be sent before action is commenced. A well-versed credit controller will have implemented a system of reminders by letter and telephone to suit his business once an invoice becomes overdue. A suggested specimen solicitor's letter appears in the Appendix to this chapter. The wording can be tailored to the client's needs. In addition, monthly statements should be sent out to a customer.

Once a creditor perceives it is necessary to issue proceedings to recover payments, can a solicitor's letter be dispensed with or should immediate proceedings follow? There may be overriding considerations which determine immediate issue, such as reliable indications within the trade that a creditor is in severe financial difficulties. However, these are the exceptions and, as a general rule, a solicitor's letter is recommended.

Receipt of such a letter often produces payment or causes many debtors to put forward proposals. 'Professional' debtors may recognise the letterheading of a firm of solicitors who have pursued them previously. The short delay in sending a solicitor's letter is likely to be more than compensated by the response rate.

There is another practical consideration. As will be seen, a successful creditor is entitled to look to the debtor for payment of statutory interest and the fixed costs of proceedings. Where payment of the principal debt is made after issue and service of proceedings, the debtor may argue that he received no notification of an intention to issue proceedings and, therefore, should not pay those costs and interest. If a suitably worded solicitor's letter has been sent, that argument must fail.

Otherwise, the conduct of the debtor and the notification given to him needs to be examined. Was there, for instance, a failure to maintain a previously agreed schedule of repayments or a dishonoured cheque? Reminders may have been given by the creditor, but did these constitute sufficient notice to the debtor that proceedings would follow if payment was not made? Failure to give sufficient notice increases litigation costs. As a general rule, letters before action should be sent.

### 6.3.2 What do they say?

Letters prior to winding-up proceedings are dealt with in connection with insolvency, see **6.11**, below. The solicitor will be able to tailor a standard letter to a client's particular needs. There may always be a need for additional information to be incorporated into a non-standard letter. It must be appreciated, however, that the creditor is likely to pay significantly more for this service. Equally, there is likely to be an additional cost if further copies of the letter are faxed or sent to other individuals representing the debtor. Whatever the letter, to maximise its impact, pre-printed forms incorporating typed-in debt details should be avoided. The following should be included:

(1)   the full and correct name and address of the debtor;[1]
(2)   the date;[2]
(3)   the creditor's full title, including any trading name;
(4)   the amount owing;[3]
(5)   requirement of payment within a specified period, usually seven days or less; and
(6)   the address to which payment is to be made.[4] There should be a clear indication that failure to make payment as specified will result in the issue of proceedings. Even where there is an earlier breach in payment terms, only overdue invoices should be pursued by letter and action.

The letter should be clear and concise, avoiding legalisms. The message should be unmistakable: pay or proceedings will follow. A dated confirmation of the letter sent should be required from the company's solicitors so that this may be noted for appropriate action if there is no satisfactory response within the period specified.

### 6.3.3 What else can be included in the letter?

The costs of the letter will be borne by the client unless, unusually, the debtor can be persuaded to make payment. Interest for late payment will be recoverable only if that is incorporated as a term of the contract.

It is considered inappropriate for letters before action to threaten credit blacklisting. The use of threats, harassment, and defamatory remarks is to be avoided.

Once solicitors are instructed, should negotiations be conducted through them or directly by the creditor? It will be cheaper for the creditor to monitor responses to letters before action. Once proceedings are issued, however, a single line of communication should be established through the company's solicitors. If both the lawyer and client are dealing with the debtor, confusion

---

1   This may include the reference or be marked for the attention of a particular individual. Where the debtor has several addresses, the payments section should be used.

2   A copy should be retained or another means of recalling that text should be employed.

3   This will normally include invoices subject to dispute but omit invoices not yet due.

4   For administrative convenience, it is preferable that payment be made to the company rather than to its solicitor.

can arise, and the debtor may seek to play off one against the other. Where a creditor deals direct, he runs the risk of reaching an agreement prejudicial to his position. This can apply especially to costs and interest once execution is underway.

At the letter-before-action stage, consideration should be given to any additional remedies available. Where a third-party security is held, a formal demand should be sent incorporated in a letter before action. Where a third party has dishonoured a cheque, notice of dishonour should be incorporated in the letter before action.

## 6.4    Pre-action and non-judicial remedies

### 6.4.1    In general

In England and Wales the pre-action remedies, apart from retention of title, are restricted to *Anton Piller* orders and *Mareva* injunctions. These remedies share two features: they are very much the exception rather than the rule, and they are expensive.

### 6.4.2    Anton Piller orders

*Anton Piller* orders are much the rarer of the two pre-action remedies and are increasingly out of favour with practitioners and the legal establishment alike. The order enables a creditor to enter a debtor's premises, in what would otherwise be an act of trespass, to search for and seize specified goods. It is an extreme and unusual order and is most likely to be found in intellectual property and fraud disputes.

### 6.4.3    Mareva injunctions

*Mareva* injunctions, by contrast, form a useful weapon in the legal armoury. They may also be employed in proceedings already commenced. The particular advantage of a *Mareva* injunction is that it acts to prevent a debtor from disposing of or selling assets either within or outside the country.

Application is made to the court without notice first being given to the opposing party. The procedure has the advantage of speed and secrecy. It should be actively considered where the claim is of substance and there is an immediate risk the debtor will dissipate his assets. In such a situation, creditors should contact their solicitor. The matter must be one of urgency. There are further tests required, and these are:

(1)   there must be a serious question to be tried;
(2)   the court will aim to preserve the status quo before the alleged wrong took place;
(3)   the court will grant an injunction only if the creditor would not be adequately compensated by an award for damages;
(4)   the creditor is obliged to give a full and frank disclosure of all relevant facts, not merely those supporting his case; and

(5)   the creditor must provide an undertaking for damages suffered as a result of the injunction by the debtor or a third party.

Obtaining an injunction is not the end of the matter. It is a stage pending the final determination of the case. It must be kept in mind that, ultimately, the injunction may have preserved assets only for the benefit of preferential creditors.

## 6.5   The court system

### 6.5.1   In general

There are two courts in which proceedings can be brought for recovery of debts owing, the county court and the High Court. There are county courts throughout England and Wales, each with its own local jurisdiction. There is a tendency to associate the High Court with the Royal Courts of Justice in London. While this is the principal office of the High Court, it also has various District Registries nationwide, invariably under the same roof as the local county court. These District Registries perform the vast majority of the functions available at the Royal Courts of Justice.

In both courts, the party bringing the action is known as the plaintiff and the party against whom those proceedings are brought is the defendant. The majority of interlocutory applications, ie, applications prior to the final hearing, will be heard by district judges. In the High Court in London, such applications are heard by a Master. For convenience, future references to a 'district judge' include 'Master'.

Larger trials will be heard by a judge, but smaller trials and arbitrations will be heard by district judges. Generally, at the hearings discussed, there will be no need for a party to attend in person. His solicitor attends on his behalf. Although the two court systems have developed separately, their functions are converging increasingly. As a rule, smaller actions are dealt with in the county court, larger actions in the High Court. However, there is a considerable area of overlap. In which court then should proceedings be brought?

### 6.5.2   County court

#### 6.5.2.1   Jurisdiction

Actions can be begun in the county court up to an amount of £50,000. Over recent years, the upper limit has tended to increase. Recent changes in the County Court Rules mean that proceedings can be commenced in any county court, although there is an automatic transfer to the defendant's home county court if a defence is filed.

#### 6.5.2.2   Advantages and disadvantages for a creditor

There are certain circumstances in which a creditor must pursue an action in the county court:

(1)   when suing on an agreement pursuant to the Consumer Credit Act;
(2)   where a creditor is a limited company acting in person; and
(3)   where the debt owing is less than £600.[1]

When the claim exceeds £50,000, a creditor must issue proceedings in the High Court. When the claim comes to between £600 and £50,000, the creditor can weigh the relative advantages of the two systems.

The county court system is administered by civil servants who are paid irrespective of results. During a period when the amount of work they have been obliged to deal with has spiralled upwards, the courts have been under a tight financial rein. The courts are overworked which must harm their efficiency. From a plaintiff's standpoint, the standard forms accompanying a county court summons and warrant of execution encourage a defendant, unable or unwilling to make immediate payment, to enter a defence or make application to pay by instalments. The inherent problems in the county court system create delay, the creditor's worst enemy.

For these reasons, many lawyers favour taking action in the High Court. The county court should not, however, be disregarded. The cost of litigating in the county court remains slightly lower than in the High Court. One of the major advantages of issuing in the High Court is that execution is pursued by the Sheriff's Officer as opposed to his equivalent, the county court bailiff. A county court judgment of more than £2,000, however, can be enforced in the High Court. County court judgments of more than £5,000, unless governed by the Consumer Credit Act, must be enforced in the High Court. A certificate of judgment needs to be obtained from the county court before this can be done. The delay is minimal and more than justified by the greater efficiency of High Court execution.

A recent innovation which has improved the efficiency of the county courts is the centralised Summons Production Centre, which guarantees prompt issue of proceedings and has proved especially helpful to large users.

County court judgments are registered. All the major collection and data agencies carry this information. Paradoxically, no similar registration applies for the usually larger High Court judgments. A county court judgment, therefore, can hamper a defendant's credit rating and make him more anxious to avoid having such a judgment entered.

There are county court software packages on the market, both for the creditor considering 'in-house' collection and on offer from solicitors. Whether in-house collection is viable will depend on the size and nature of each business. Its success will depend on the quality of the personnel handling the work and the training given to them. Such computerised packages mean that solicitors can undertake collection work at competitive rates.

A cautionary word is in order, however. The creditor should ensure that a quality service, as well as a competitive price, is obtained. Many firms latterly moved into debt collection as their usual work diminished during the

---

1 If proceedings are issued in the High Court for less than £600, there is no entitlement to costs and interest.

recession. The creditor should ensure that the firm approached knows debt collection procedure and practice. More advanced software packages are increasingly available, especially among practices which have gathered expertise in the field over years, offering combinations of both High and county court actions and on-line reporting.

### 6.5.3  High Court

#### 6.5.3.1  Jurisdiction

For practical purposes, the threshold for determining whether it is worthwhile to issue proceedings in the High Court is £600 since, below this figure, costs are not recoverable. There is no upper limit.

There are specialist courts operating within the High Court which may assist a creditor's case. The Official Referee's Court is an appropriate venue for building litigation. The Commercial Court in London and the equivalent Mercantile Lists, operating initially in Liverpool and Manchester, deal with complex commercial disputes. In both instances, a judge specially assigned to that court deals with the case from application to trial, ensuring that it is handled throughout by someone with an expertise in the particular field. Where a claim is relatively small, it may, once a defendant indicates an intention to defend, be transferred to his home county court. More rarely, county court actions can be transferred to the High Court.

#### 6.5.3.2  Advantages and disadvantages for a creditor

The main advantages gained from taking action in the High Court stem from control resting with the solicitors. They can prepare and serve proceedings and should be in a position to do this immediately. Similar speed is available when judgment and execution are taken. The incentive to the solicitors is that a job well done will result in successful, loyal clients.

The High Court Sheriff's Officer, unlike his equivalent, the county court bailiff, is paid by results. If the execution is unsuccessful, he will recover only a basic fee but, if the plaintiff recovers payment after he has been instructed, the Sheriff's Officer is entitled to recovery poundage, a percentage of that recovery.

Costs in the High Court are higher than those of the county court but, in uncontested actions, the difference is marginal, save in circumstances where the Sheriff's Officer builds up substantial fees on an ultimately abortive execution. Given the choice, the greater speed and control afforded by the High Court make it preferable to commence proceedings there rather than in the county court.

### 6.5.4  Appeals

Any order made by the courts during an action is subject to appeal to a higher level of the judiciary, ranging through a judge, the Court of Appeal, the

House of Lords and, indeed, the European Court of Justice. Appeal is on points of law rather than findings of fact. Appeals are very much the exception to the rule. They are costly and result in inevitable delay to an action. It should be considered only where a bad decision is materially prejudicial to an important claim.

## 6.6   Legal representation

### 6.6.1   Nature of legal representation

A party either acts on his own behalf or instructs someone else to represent him in proceedings. There is nothing to prevent an individual or the partners in a firm from representing themselves in person. There are no restrictions on a company acting for itself in county court proceedings. The legislation governing companies provides, however, that a company involved in a High Court action must be represented by a solicitor. If a company has its own 'in-house' legal department including a solicitor or barrister, this does not apply.

If the creditor does act in person, the court officials are usually helpful regarding the forms to be completed and the procedures to follow. The idea of reducing the bill for legal costs is attractive. The real cost of self-representation, however, may be higher than instructing an expert. It includes much administrative time and visits to court when the creditor should be pursuing new, profitable work. Lack of familiarity with court procedures may operate against a non-lawyer so that he does not secure the best possible result.

Where a party is not acting on his own behalf, legal representation should be by a solicitor. When selecting a firm, it should be verified that it has expertise in debt recovery. A solicitor, during the course of an action, may instruct a barrister, eg, to draft papers, advise on the merits of the case or for representation at a hearing. Barristers cannot be instructed directly by lay clients. Where a debt collection agency or factoring company is assisting in the recovery of debts, unless they have an in-house legal department, when proceedings are issued, they will act as agents and instruct solicitors on their client's behalf.

Clients should ensure that their solicitor keeps them advised regarding the progress of the action and the options available. It should be remembered, however, that the solicitor's time costs money. Unnecessary calls should be avoided. If dissatisfied regarding the service provided, it is always open for a client to instruct another solicitor. If this happens, the new solicitor will be able to advance matters only when the solicitor originally instructed has released the papers, invariably after he has been paid. The usual result of changing instructions is delay and additional cost. Clients should not need to take such an unusual step if they originally chose wisely.

### 6.6.2   Mode of payment for legal representation

A party instructing a solicitor is responsible for payment of his costs, including any outgoings incurred by the solicitor in the conduct of the action.

The basis of the charge should be agreed when initial instructions are given. Under Rule 15 of the Law Society Solicitors' Conduct Rules, as amended, solicitors are now obliged to provide clients with information regarding their charging rates. Work will be undertaken usually based on an hourly rate or on a fixed-fee.

Solicitors cannot accept instructions on a contingency fee basis, ie, no charge if no recovery and payment of a percentage of money recovered where successful. Solicitors may accept instructions from foreign clients where there is a fixed charge plus an additional percentage where a recovery is effected. The liability of the other party to pay a party's costs is discussed below. Where a party is registered for value added tax (VAT), that element of any costs paid can be reclaimed from HM Customs & Excise.

## 6.7   Costs and interest

### 6.7.1   Liability for and recovery of costs

Primary responsibility for payment of costs rests with the party instructing his solicitor, subject to legal aid entitlement. A party may be entitled to recover an element of costs from the opposing party where successful. Recoverable costs are fixed fees in uncontested actions or costs on a standard basis where an action or application is contested.

Fixed costs are a set sum, depending on the size of the action. They do not represent the full costs, and standard costs may be typically 65 per cent of overall costs. The difference is payable by the plaintiff.

If the defendant is legally aided or otherwise unable to pay, the plaintiff still must bear all the costs. In certain instances, costs will not be recoverable in any event. These include oral examination applications, letters before action, and statutory demands prior to a bankruptcy petition being issued. If a plaintiff is successful in a court action but the court finds insufficient notice of proceedings was given to the debtor, it may make no order as to costs.

While a party may attempt to incorporate a contractual provision providing that its customer be responsible for any legal costs incurred, it is questionable whether that party would be able to enforce such a provision. Costs are not recoverable in the High Court under £600 and are usually not recoverable in the county court under £25.

A party may be liable for part of the other party's costs. If he counterclaims against the creditor, the provisions set out above apply. If the court orders against the claim, costs will usually follow against the unsuccessful party. If proceedings are discontinued or a claim is not prosecuted, a defendant can apply for a costs order.

A party acting on its own behalf will be entitled to recover from the other side disbursements incurred and reduced costs. A third party, other than a solicitor acting, is not entitled to seek costs from the opposing party. This rule is to be relaxed so that collection agencies will be entitled to costs in actions commenced by them.

### 6.7.2  Legal aid

Taking proceedings against a legally aided defendant presents special difficulties. Only individuals, not a limited company, may qualify for legal aid. Limited initial advice is available on a green form. Qualification depends on income and expenditure. While those in greatest need make no payment, a contribution on a sliding scale operates for those with greater income. Increasingly, legal aid is available only to those in severe financial hardship.

For proceedings, a legal aid certificate is required. There are two tests here, the party's financial circumstances and the merits of the claim.

Legal aid is not retrospective.

Notice of the issue of a legal aid certificate must be given to the opposing party. Details of any contribution by the assisted party need not be provided. The certificate may contain a limitation for review once a certain stage in the proceedings has been reached.

Where a party believes he may be entitled to legal aid, he should advise his solicitor immediately. Legal aid is not available to parties acting on their own behalf. An assisted party enjoys two advantages. First, he does not bear all or part of his legal costs. Secondly, save in exceptional circumstances, costs will not be enforced against that party. Clearly, this gives the opposing party an incentive to settle on more favourable terms. There is one further aspect to consider: if he has legal aid, what is his ability to pay?

It also should be considered that The Law Society's statutory charge operates against property recovered or retained on behalf of an assisted party. If a legally aided party recovers money, this will be utilised first in discharging his legal costs.

### 6.7.3  Interest

A creditor is entitled to recover interest only if he claims for it. This may be either contractual or statutory interest.

#### 6.7.3.1  *Contractual interest*

Contractual interest is available only where there has been incorporated into the contract a provision for payment by a customer of interest at the given rate on overdue invoices.

It may be difficult to satisfy the court that this term has been incorporated in the contract. Alternatively, if interest sought is excessive, the defendant may claim the provision operates as a penalty at law and should not apply. Therefore, unless a creditor is confident such arguments can be defeated and the difference in rates claimed is significant, it may be preferable to claim statutory interest.

#### 6.7.3.2  *Statutory interest*

Statutory interest is available on all claims. Where the claim is for a liquidated sum, interest is claimed from the invoice due date. The rate of interest applying is eight per cent per annum. As with costs, the defendant may seek to avoid liability for interest if insufficient notice of proceedings has been given.

While statutory interest to issue of proceedings and to judgment can be claimed in both the High Court and county court, there is no entitlement to statutory interest in the county court subsequent to a county court judgment unless the judgment is £5,000 or more.

## 6.8 Issuing proceedings

### 6.8.1 County court

The plaintiff's solicitor prepares particulars of claim, setting out the basis of the action, the amount owing, and claiming interest, and a summons showing the figures claimed and costs, setting out the name and address of the defendant. These are forwarded to the county court for issue, with the fee on a sliding scale up to £60 if issue is via the Summons Production Centre; otherwise, the fee is up to £80. The court arranges for service by first class post. Where the defendant is a limited company, service is at its registered office or place of business. The summons is deemed served on a limited company after two days; in other instances, it is deemed served after seven days.

In addition to the summons and particulars of claim, the defendant will receive from the court a pre-printed form where he can indicate if he intends to admit or dispute the proceedings in whole or in part, the grounds for any dispute and, if the debt is admitted, how much he can afford to pay. If the defendant does not respond to the court within 14 days after service, the plaintiff may apply to the court for judgment.

### 6.8.2 High Court

In straightforward actions, the plaintiff's solicitors prepare a writ of summons incorporating a statement of claim providing information similar to that in the county court summons and particulars of claim. On payment of the fee, currently £100, the writ is issued immediately by the court staff. The plaintiff's solicitors serve the writ together with a form of acknowledgement of service.

The same periods for service apply as in the county court. Where appropriate, the plaintiff may opt for personal service by an enquiry agent on, eg, an evasive defendant. The writ must be served within four months from issue, or six months where a party outside the jurisdiction is to be served. The same periods apply for county court summonses. If the defendant fails within 14 days to either file the acknowledgement with the court or serve a defence on the plaintiff's solicitors, judgment can be entered.

## 6.9 Procedure to judgment

### 6.9.1 The debtor pays the debt

When the debtor pays the debt, the matter is concluded. Agreement is usually confirmed in correspondence, but a formal notice of discontinuance can be lodged with the court. If payment does not include fixed costs and interest, the plaintiff may continue proceedings for these.

### 6.9.2   The debtor admits the debt

When the debtor admits the debt, the plaintiff should enter judgment immediately to protect his position. If the defendant does nothing more, the plaintiff can proceed to enforcement (see below).

The defendant, on the pre-printed county court form, may apply for time to pay, a stay of execution. He should disclose information regarding his capital and liabilities and income and outgoings and indicate the monthly repayments he proposes. If the plaintiff accepts this, the court will make an order to this effect. If the plaintiff rejects the proposal, there will be a hearing to determine whether the defendant should be allowed more time and, if so, the appropriate rate of repayments.

In the High Court, the defendant may complete the acknowledgement indicating that he will apply for a stay of execution. He has a further 14 days beyond the date on which judgment would have been originally due to issue a summons supported by details of his financial position on affidavit. In default of agreement, the application again will be determined at a hearing.

In either court, should the defendant default in the repayments ordered, the plaintiff can proceed to enforcement.

### 6.9.3   The debtor disputes the debt

In the county court, the defendant may dispute the debt either on the pre-printed form or in a separate defence. In the High Court, he may indicate on the acknowledgement his intention to contest proceedings. He then has a further 14 days beyond the date on which judgment was originally due in which to serve a defence on the plaintiff's solicitors.

The creditor is prevented from applying for default judgment or enforcement. Each fully defended action will involve an exchange of pleadings in which the parties set out their respective claims, exchange of witness statements, and disclosure of relevant documents, leading to a full trial in open court where witnesses give evidence and are subject to cross-examination. In claims below £1,000 in the county court, a more informal arbitration replaces the trial.

Each fully defended action is different and needs to be considered in detail. By definition, all are costly and protracted, taking many months, perhaps years, before they are determined. The economics of pursuing such actions requires careful consideration. Negotiated settlements are common and should be considered at an early stage. Defended actions begun in the High Court for less than £50,000 may be transferred to the county court for trial, and this is likely to occur where the claim is less than £25,000.

### 6.9.4  Summary judgment

The defence, however, may not be bona fide or may apply only to part of the claim. In such cases, application for summary judgment should be made, provided this is for an amount greater than £500. The procedure in both courts is similar. A summons is issued supported by affidavit evidence. At the hearing, the court must be satisfied there is no defence or real triable issue. Relevant documents will strengthen the application. A dishonoured cheque is conclusive evidence of entitlement to summary judgment. Where there is conflicting oral evidence between the parties, the action is unlikely to be resolved by summary judgment.

The court may order summary judgment for the whole debt or part of it, allowing the defendant leave to defend as to the balance. Where the position is less clear, conditional orders can be made, such as leave to defend conditional on payment into court of the claim.

### 6.9.5  The debtor disputes part of the debt

In such cases, the provisions discussed at **6.9.2** apply to the admitted part of the debt and at **6.9.3** and **6.9.4** to the disputed part of the debt.

### 6.9.6  The debtor neither admits nor disputes the debt

Where the debtor neither admits nor disputes the debt, the plaintiff may proceed to default judgment and enforcement action on the first available date.

### 6.9.7  The debtor is declared insolvent

What constitutes insolvency? For a limited company, this will be the appointment of a liquidator, either after a meeting of creditors or following a winding-up order of the court. For individuals, a bankruptcy order by the local county court or, in London, the High Court, is made and a trustee in bankruptcy appointed. Where there is a certificate for summary administration, the bankrupt obtains automatic discharge after two years; otherwise, discharge normally is after three years.

Where the defendant is declared insolvent, further steps in the proceedings can be taken only in exceptional circumstances with the consent of the court. Unless security is held, a creditor proves in the estate as an unsecured creditor. Payment is made in order to secured creditors, insolvency costs, preferential creditors (PAYE and National Insurance, VAT, and employees' wages, with ceilings placed on each), creditors having a floating charge, and unsecured creditors.

As such, an unsecured creditor's prospects are at best for a low dividend. If he has obtained judgment, the creditor will also be entitled to include fixed costs and interest in his claim. Otherwise, he is restricted to the debt only. VAT on the debt is reclaimable. If a creditor believes the insolvency appointment is irregular or the insolvency practitioner's conduct is unsatisfactory, he should seek legal advice.

More rarely, a creditor may come across an administration order. This is made against a company and also prevents steps from being taken in court proceedings. A receiver may be appointed over specific assets of the company or an administrative receiver over the whole of the company's property. Appointment is by a debenture holder, typically a financial institution, or the court. Such appointments do not prevent steps from being taken in proceedings, but their worth is questionable since title to company assets will be claimed by the receiver.

An individual owing not more than £5,000 may apply to the court for an administration order. Where such an order is made, creditors will receive pro rata payments from the court on a periodic basis. An individual may attempt to come to an arrangement with his creditors through a voluntary arrangement. If he obtains an interim order from the court, all proceedings are stayed until the creditors consider his proposal at a meeting. If the creditors' meeting rejects the proposal, court action may continue. When the proposal is upheld, the creditors will receive payments under the terms of the proposal.

## 6.10 Enforcing judgment

### 6.10.1 In general

Once judgment is obtained, a variety of enforcement procedures is available:

(1) execution;
(2) garnishee;
(3) charging order;
(4) attachment of earnings;
(5) oral examination; and
(6) insolvency.

### 6.10.2 Execution

Execution is by far the most common remedy. As such, it is considered here in some detail. In the High Court, execution is taken by the Sheriff's Officer under a writ of *fieri facias* (known as *fi fa*); a largely similar procedure in the county court is undertaken by the county court bailiff under a warrant of execution. In this section, for convenience, references to the Sheriff's Officer also apply to the bailiff, unless otherwise stated.

Execution may be obtained at any time from the date on which judgment is taken and is very often sought on the same day. A fixed fee, currently £20, is payable for the writ of *fi fa*. The fee for the warrant operates on a sliding scale increasing with the size of the debt.

The writ of *fi fa* directs the Sheriff of the county in which the defendant resides or carries on business to seize and sell the defendant's goods. The company's solicitor will arrange for the *fi fa* to be sealed at the court and, on the same day, should arrange for it to be posted to the relevant Under-Sheriff. He, in turn, instructs his Officer for a given locality, who will attend at the defendant's premises and seize any available goods, often within a day or two.

At this stage, the goods are not generally removed from the defendant. He will be asked to enter into a walking possession agreement in which he promises not to dispose of or part with those goods and to allow the Sheriff's Officer to re-enter. The defendant may arrange for payment to the Under-Sheriff. If that is not done, the goods may be removed for auction sale. The procedures in the county court are largely similar.

As indicated earlier, practitioners recognise the advantages of effecting execution in the High Court. There are greater incentives for the Sheriff's Officer to ensure a positive outcome. In addition, the county court bailiff is obliged to furnish a pre-printed form to the defendant, advising him of his entitlement to apply to the court for a stay of execution, ie, payment by instalments. Reporting time and speed of recovery are quicker in the High Court, important considerations where the defendant is likely to be in financial difficulties.

The initial fee for a *fi fa* is lower than the county court warrant. This presumably reflects lower administration costs, since dealings are between the solicitor and Sheriff's Officer directly rather than through the court. If execution of the *fi fa* is successful, the Sheriff's Officer also will recover fixed costs, including execution costs, interest, and his own charges. If execution is unsuccessful, the plaintiff will be obliged to pay his abortive fees. These are generally limited, unless he has been in possession of goods of substantial value or incurred a significant outlay, such as the hire of a removal van.

Where there is a successful county court warrant, interest to judgment and fixed costs are also recoverable. Interest after judgment is recoverable where judgment was for £5,000 or more. Those costs include fairly minimal execution costs as well as the warrant fee. Save in exceptional circumstances, which the court will advise in advance, the plaintiff will not incur any obligation for further costs.

A defendant will not always be in a position to clear his liability immediately. He may offer to pay by instalments. It is for the plaintiff to determine if that is acceptable. If the proposal is accepted, it is preferable, where possible, for collection to be by the Sheriff's Officer. The defendant will be aware that, should he default, the plaintiff can instruct the Sheriff's Officer to remove goods. In addition, the plaintiff maintains its priority should any subsequent creditor issue a *fi fa*. Where agreement for instalment payments is reached, in the county court, instalments will be paid direct to the solicitors.

If the plaintiff does not agree to an instalment arrangement, the defendant may make application to the court for a stay of execution, as discussed earlier.

The defendant may have goods, but there may be prior executions. The plaintiff can still require a forced sale of the goods, but that will only be worthwhile if sale proceeds will be available to clear all or part of its debt after the prior creditors have been settled.

Again, where there are prior executions on which repayment is being made by instalments, the plaintiff has a choice. Any money collected by the Sheriff's Officer will be paid to execution creditors in strict chronological order. The plaintiff must assess what the prospects are if it waits in line or if it withdraws the Sheriff's Officer and attempts alternative enforcement action or direct negotiation.

It may be that the defendant has goods but that these are subject to third-party claims. The plaintiff may be able to immediately identify these as genuine, eg, a hire-purchase agreement for a vehicle supported by appropriate documentation. Other claims may be more difficult to assess, such as a supplier claiming goods pursuant to retention of title. At worst, there is a variety of twilight claims usually unsupported by documents.

It is for the plaintiff to admit or dispute such third-party claims. If the claim is admitted, the Sheriff's Officer cannot proceed against those goods. If the plaintiff disputes the claim, a separate set of interpleader proceedings will be instituted by the Under-Sheriff to determine whether the defendant or third party owns the goods. If the court finds that the defendant owned the goods, the execution may proceed but, where the third party succeeds, that avenue of enforcement will be blocked, and the plaintiff will pay three sets of costs, those of its solicitor, the successful third party and the Under-Sheriff.

Third-party proceedings can be protracted and expensive. They should be contemplated only if the goods in question are of sufficient value. Even then, they are a gamble. The defendant may be declared insolvent. While the plaintiff may well be right to treat the third-party claim with suspicion, he does not know what evidence the third party may produce. The practical course then is often to admit the third-party claim and pursue alternative enforcement action.

If the defendant has goods but fails to pay, the goods may be removed for a forced sale. It should be borne in mind that, at a forced sale, goods are likely to realise significantly less than their true worth. Any removal and auctioneer's charges will be included in the fees of the Sheriff's Officer, and these are deducted from the sale proceeds before payment is made to the company's solicitor.

Where the Sheriff's Officer has been unable to effect a full recovery for whatever reason, he will make a return of *nulla bona* (no goods), and alternative enforcement action may be considered.

### 6.10.3 Garnishee

Garnishee proceedings are available in both the High Court and the county court. While there are some procedural differences, the same principles apply. The aim of garnishee proceedings is to obtain payment for the benefit of the plaintiff of money owing to the defendant by another person or company within the jurisdiction. There are rules setting out which debts may be attached. The most usual are trade debtors of the defendant and bank or building society accounts of the defendant. In the latter case, details of the branch in question will be needed.

The procedure is for an affidavit to be sworn, reciting the facts and the grounds of belief for the third-party indebtedness, including the amount owing. No notice is given at this stage to the defendant or third party. Provided the court is satisfied, within a number of days, it will make an order nisi, attaching the moneys held or owed by the third party (the garnishee). This is served on the defendant and garnishee, together with details of the hearing when the court will give further consideration to the matter.

Only when the order nisi is served on the garnishee does it bind him. Therefore, timing can be crucial. For instance, the creditor may know that, under a particular contract, money is paid into a defendant's bank account on a given day of the month. Service should be arranged immediately after this. The garnishee should be served before the defendant so that he does not himself obtain payment or withdraw funds and defeat the application.

At the hearing, provided the court is satisfied that the money is owing by the garnishee, it will make an order absolute, directing payment to the plaintiff of the whole debt or so much as to satisfy the judgment, including fixed costs of the application. If, as a result of representations made by it or the defendant, the court is not satisfied the money is owing by the garnishee, the order nisi will be dismissed, and the plaintiff may be obliged to pay the costs of the other parties.

Provided the relevant information is to hand, garnishee forms a very useful enforcement weapon.

### 6.10.4 Charging orders

Charging orders are available in both the High Court and county court. Where the sum owing is below £5,000, the plaintiff must proceed in the county court. If the plaintiff has a High Court judgment for less than £5,000, the plaintiff must transfer to the county court to issue the application. Charging orders may be obtained against a defendant's shares or government stock but most usually against his interest in land. A charging order is obtained without the agreement of the owner of the property. The protection offered by a mortgage is greater and, if one is volunteered, it should be sought in preference.

Charging orders, like garnishee and divorce, come in two stages, the order nisi and order absolute. Application is made to the court by affidavit. Details of the amount outstanding are recited and evidence provided to show the defendant is the owner of or has a part interest in the land. Provided the court is satisfied on these points, it may make an order nisi.

A charging order is, however, a discretionary remedy. The plaintiff is also obliged to disclose details of any other creditors of whom it is aware. The court may refuse to grant the application on the grounds that the plaintiff would be gaining an unfair advantage over other creditors. This is particularly galling if those creditors are taking no action themselves.

Assuming the application is successful, the order nisi will be granted within a few days. The order nisi, endorsed with a hearing date, will be served on the defendant and any co-owner or creditor directed to be served by the court. Of equal importance is registration of the order nisi at HM Land Registry or the Land Charges Department to put prospective purchasers or lending institutions on notice. Any subsequent attempts to sell or mortgage the land are notified to the creditor. It may be appropriate to object if the creditor's position would be prejudiced by such action.

At the hearing, the court may make the charging order absolute, in which case the security conferred on the plaintiff will continue. However, on representations by the defendant or other creditors, it may refuse to make the order and discharge the earlier order nisi.

A charging order differs from both execution and garnishee in that its main aim is not to recover payment but to secure the debt. As such, it holds a greater appeal for financial institutions than for trade creditors, who are less likely to take this longer view. Despite this, charging orders are a useful weapon, either on their own or in conjunction with a subsequent agreement for instalment payments. As with a mortgage, a further set of proceedings would be required if it was desired to enforce sale of the property.

The open search facility offered by HM Land Registry means it is now relatively easy to establish ownership details for the majority of properties. Plaintiffs must assess what the value of the defendant's interest in the property is likely to be. Mortgage holders will disclose how much is owing to them only once the order absolute is obtained. It should be considered, therefore, that there is a risk that the charging order may prove valueless.

### 6.10.5   Attachment of earnings

Attachment of earnings is available only in the county court. Where a High Court judgment is obtained, it is necessary to transfer to the county court for enforcement. Such an order can be obtained where a defendant is in employment, but it does not apply where he is self-employed. Application is made, and the court requires the defendant to provide details of income and expenditure. After prescribed deductions, the court calculates a protected earnings level. Any balance available over this figure is paid by the defendant to the court or, if he defaults, by his employer, and monthly payments made by the court to the plaintiff's solicitor.

Attachment is worthwhile for relatively small debts, especially where the defendant has a good salary, but it is less attractive because of the time taken where a debt is larger or the defendant's unprotected earnings are small. Plaintiffs also should consider the problems which arise when a defendant changes or loses employment.

### 6.10.6   Oral examination

Oral examination is available in both the High Court and county court. Under this procedure, the defendant or an officer of a limited company defendant is obliged to attend at court to give evidence on oath about the defendant's financial position. He is also required to disclose relevant documents. Costs of the examination are not usually recoverable.

At best, the procedure can be a useful device to obtain further information for alternative enforcement action. Against an obstructive defendant, it can prove a blunt instrument. Weeks may be lost before the defendant either fails to attend or provides no useful information. If he fails to attend or lies on oath, he is guilty of contempt and a further application for his committal to prison can be made. It is questionable whether the additional time and cost is worthwhile.

## 6.11 Insolvency

### 6.11.1 In general

Courts frown on insolvency proceedings being used for collection purposes. Practitioners consider them the ultimate sanction they can apply. The proceedings are expensive but should be given serious consideration where the sum owing is sufficiently high and the creditor believes the extra pressure may result in payment. They may be commenced either at the outset or subsequent to judgment when, perhaps, other remedies have failed.

If initial action is by insolvency proceedings, and a creditor should subsequently decide to adopt a different enforcement strategy, it must start a separate action by writ or summons and will have wasted time and money.

Insolvency proceedings are appropriate only for undisputed debts. Where the debtor satisfies the court that there is a genuine dispute, the proceedings will be dismissed, with costs awarded against the creditor, and there is a potential for a further claim in damages if the debtor can satisfy the court that he suffered loss through the creditor's action.

The aim of insolvency proceedings is to induce payment. If, however, payment is made by the debtor of all or part of the debt after presentation of the petition, but before the making of a winding-up or bankruptcy order, that payment will be subject to claw-back for the benefit of all creditors. This may encourage dismissal of proceedings to safeguard partial payments.

### 6.11.2 Winding up of limited companies

A winding-up petition against a limited company may be presented based on a statutory demand, proof that the company is insolvent and unable to pay its debts, or a Sheriff's return of *nulla bona*. The statutory demand is prepared by the creditor's solicitors and is personally served on the company. The company has 18 days in which to apply to set aside the demand. If it fails to do so within 21 days after service, the creditor may issue a petition. A petition should normally be issued within four months of service of the statutory demand.

Section 122(1)(f) of the Insolvency Act 1986 provides that it is just and equitable for a company to be wound up where there is evidence of its insolvency. Proof of insolvency and inability to pay debts may arise from failures to respond to earlier requirements for payment or dishonoured cheques. A letter before action in this context need not be restricted to a 21-day period, and the petition can be issued earlier.

The above two options can be employed whether or not judgment has been first obtained. A petition based on a Sheriff's return of *nulla bona* can only follow judgment.

The petition may be issued in the High Court or county court. Typically, a hearing date will be fixed six weeks hence. The creditor's solicitors arrange for personal service on the company's registered office. This presents the ideal time to negotiate since it is unlikely that other creditors will be aware of the existence of the petition. If no progress can be made and a creditor wishes to obtain a winding-up order, he must first advertise the petition in the *London Gazette*. Advertisement will alert other interested creditors and so should be delayed and the hearing adjourned if necessary to assist negotiations.

From seven days after service of the petition, the creditor may serve the company's bank account, an action which will freeze any money held in that account.

Unless judgment is obtained prior to the insolvency proceedings, the creditor will not be entitled to costs and interest, subject to any contractual provision, if payment is made prior to the issue of the petition. Where the petition post-dates judgment, costs and interest will be provided for in the petition. In addition, after service of the petition, the petitioning creditor is further entitled to winding-up costs, and the creditor can require these as a condition of withdrawal of the petition.

If a winding-up order is made, the petitioner proves in the insolvent estate as an unsecured creditor, save for the winding-up costs which have priority. Any liquidator appointed should be advised of any matters requiring investigation.

If a party becomes aware that another creditor has issued a winding-up petition, it may support or oppose that petition and, if the petitioning creditor withdraws, apply to be substituted and have conduct of the action.

### 6.11.3 Bankruptcy of individuals

A bankruptcy petition issued against an individual can be presented based on either a statutory demand or return of *nulla bona*, as set out above. The petition is issued in the debtor's local county court or, in London, in the High Court. Typically, a hearing date approximately six weeks hence will be fixed. The rules require personal service of the petition. If that proves impossible, further application, supported by affidavit evidence, can be made for substituted service, by post at a given address or by newspaper advertisement.

On the hearing, a bankruptcy order may be made or the petition withdrawn or adjourned. If a bankruptcy order is made, the amount claimed in the petition will rank as an unsecured claim in the bankrupt's estate. Recoverable bankruptcy costs will have priority. As indicated, the courts frown on insolvency as a collection procedure. Therefore, they will grant only a small number of adjournments for limited periods where, eg, a creditor is negotiating with the debtor.

If the debtor makes payment, the creditor may also require recoverable bankruptcy costs. If, through payment or otherwise, the creditor wishes to dismiss the petition, this can be done only with the approval of the court. Affidavit evidence needs to be filed to satisfy the court that arrangements have been reached with the petitioner and other known creditors.

As with winding-up petitions, there is provision for other creditors to support and be substituted on the petition. In cases where there is a chance the debtor may dissipate his property, application for an expedited petition may be made before the end of the 21-day period in the statutory demand.

### 6.11.4 Insolvency of partnerships and proprietors

A creditor may be faced with a situation where he wishes to take insolvency proceedings against two or more partners trading as a firm. In those circumstances, the creditor should correctly proceed by way of a winding-up petition against the firm and bankruptcy petitions against the individuals following service of statutory demands in both instances.

The need for multiple petitions considerably increases costs, and consideration should be given to proceeding against one or more individuals in the first instance to make such action more economic. The procedure for issuing winding-up petitions against partnerships and proprietors is similar to that against limited companies.

## 6.12 Other jurisdictions

Sometimes, where a debtor is resident out of the jurisdiction, the creditor will face a choice of whether to issue proceedings in that jurisdiction or in England and Wales. If the creditor can show that he has a right of action in England and Wales, eg, if the contract was made in England, proceedings can be issued in the English courts and served out of the jurisdiction.

This is advantageous where the defendant has assets in the jurisdiction against which the plaintiff can enforce. There are reciprocal rights of enforcement of judgments with European Union (EU) countries. Therefore, the plaintiff can apply to enforce an English judgment in another EU country. A speedier and more cost-effective route, however, is often to issue proceedings in the first instance in that country where the debtor is resident and has assets.

# APPENDIX

## Notice of dishonour

Dear Sirs

Account Reference 5479

TAKE NOTICE that the cheque drawn on account number 113333 of Jason Associates at Golden Fleece Bank of 123 Helen Street, Troy, dated 28 February 1995, in favour of Argonauts Limited for £5,000.00 has been dishonoured on presentation. Unless, within seven days from the date of this letter, we receive from you a replacement Bank Draft for £5,000.00, High Court proceedings will be issued against you without further warning or notice.

Yours faithfully

*Note:* To ensure that the notice of dishonour provides a further valid right of action, it must be sent immediately the creditor becomes aware the cheque has been dishonoured.

## Letter before action

Dear Sirs

Argonauts Limited £6,500.00

Unless you pay the sum of £6,500.00 which you owe to our above-named clients within seven days from the date of this letter, High Court proceedings will be issued against you without further warning or notice.

Payment should be made directly to our clients Argonauts Limited at Unit 5, Ulysses Trading Estate, Olympia.

Under no circumstances whatsoever will we discuss this matter with you personally or by telephone, and any correspondence from you must quote the name of our clients, your own name, and the reference number set out above. If any of these details is omitted, it may be that your correspondence cannot be dealt with and the proceedings referred to above will automatically follow.

Yours faithfully

# Debt recovery procedure

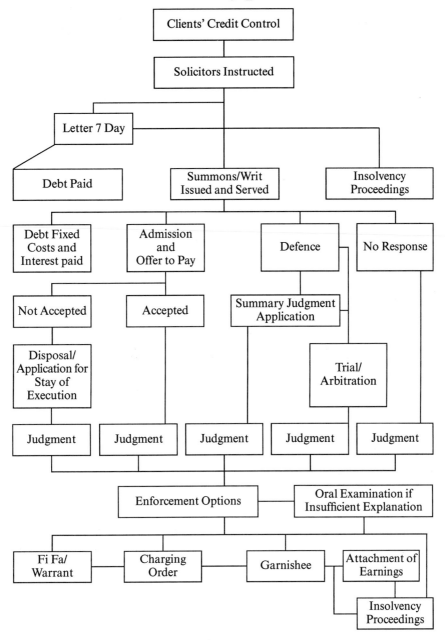

*Note:* In the High Court or County Court the judgment in default can be entered 14 days after service of the summons or writ. In the High Court: if acknowledgement is entered indicating an intention to defend, there is a further 14 days before entry of judgment; if acknowledgement is entered indicating an intention to apply for a stay of execution, there is a further 14 days in which to make application, in default enter judgment.

*Chapter 7*

# FINLAND

**Christer Ekman**
**Borenius & Kemppinen**
**Helsinki, Finland**

## 7.1    Introduction

The following survey reviews the requirements for recovery of debts in Finland.

## 7.2    Initial considerations

### 7.2.1    Status of the debtor

#### *7.2.1.1    Legal entities*

The various legal entities which may be pursued in the Finnish courts are summarised as follows:

(1)    an individual or natural person;
(2)    a partnership (unlimited or limited), the responsible partners in such companies are also personally liable for the commitments of the partnership;
(3)    a limited company;
(4)    an association;
(5)    a co-operative society; and
(6)    a foundation.

A shareholder of a limited company is not liable for the company's commitments. The exception is that the owner of a lawyer's office which is a limited company is also personally responsible for all liabilities arising from work commissioned.

#### *7.2.1.2    Sources of information*

Contact information for private individuals can be obtained from the national address service, telephone 9700–7700. Company addresses, domiciles, and similar information can be obtained from the Trade Register and the population register in the district registry office. Data on associations is available from the association register and on foundations from the foundation register.

Larger companies (turnover in excess of FIM 4 million with a balance sheet total of more than FIM 2 million) must supply the Trade Register with their annual accounts. The parent companies of groups must supply such information as well. Small companies must supply a copy of their annual accounts on request to anyone who is willing to pay for the copy.

A company known as Suomen Asiakastieto Oy provides credit information. Credit data on individual firms can be requested via telephone number 9600–7323 (at the rate of FIM 17.70 per minute). Credit information is also provided by the co-operative society known as Suomen Luottotieto-osuuskunta.

### 7.2.2 Is the debt statute-barred?

A debt becomes statute-barred 10 years from the date of signing the debt instrument. The limitation is terminated when the debt is installed or interest is paid on it, or when the creditor gives notice to the debtor. In the notice, it is said: 'In order to interrupt the period of limitation, we remind you of the promissory note, 100.000 FIM, signed 15.6.1985'. This interruption starts a new 10-year period.

A guarantee is also statute-barred 10 years from the date of signing, but is affected by a special one-year limitation period which begins when the debt falls due. This special limitation period is interrupted only if an application for a summons on the guaranteed debt is made to a court. New legislation on the statute of limitations is under preparation.

### 7.2.3 Security

If the creditor holds security, he can choose whether to recover the sum concerned from the security or to apply to a court for a demand for payment. Realising payment on property is usually a slower and more complicated procedure than realising payment on pledges comprising movable assets. If the security given is owned by someone other than the debtor or is owned by both the debtor and some other person, however, good collection procedure requires the creditor to attempt to obtain payment first from the debtor or from security owned by the debtor.

If, for example, the security is a bank deposit, the creditor should obtain a commitment from the bank in which it engages not to exercise its set-off right, while also confirming that it is aware that the deposit has been pledged.

### 7.2.4 Retention of title

It is possible for the parties to agree on retention of title in the contract or deed. The retention of title must be written into the contract; neither an oral agreement nor, generally, a simple reference to general contract terms containing a reference to retention of title is sufficient.

A hire-purchase agreement (ie contracts in which the selling price for goods or services are paid in several instalments) must always be made in a specified form. The law provides more detailed instructions on this point.

### 7.2.5    Debt maturity in special cases

The consumer is protected in the case of hire-purchase agreements and housing or study loans which are paid off by several instalments. In such contracts, the creditor cannot call in instalments due in the future on the grounds that an instalment has not been paid, unless the payment is at least a month late and represents at least 10 per cent of the credit price. However, in cases where the debtor's payment difficulties have social causes such as unemployment, sickness, or other reason beyond the consumer's control, the creditor is not entitled to call in the debt.

## 7.3    Letters before action

### 7.3.1    Are they necessary?

Although new legislation on collection procedures is under preparation in Finland, the law does not as yet require the sending of letters before action. However, with consumers, good debt collection procedure requires both the creditor and the party handling the actual collection to send a letter to the debtor. The term 'consumer' means a private individual (ie not a merchant) who has a contractual relationship with the creditor.

### 7.3.2    What should they say?

A letter before action should clearly explain the demand made of the debtor by:

(1)  naming those party to the debt relationship, ie the debtor, the party ordering the collection, and the collection office;
(2)  clearly explaining the legal grounds for the demand;
(3)  itemising the principal sum demanded, the rates of interest and penalty interest, the sums of interest and penalty interest and, if the debtor so requests, a detailed account of how the interest has been calculated, and the collection costs; and
(4)  clearly stating the total sum demanded.

### 7.3.3    May they demand interest for late payment?

By law, the amount of penalty interest applicable in Finland is 16 per cent, even if the agreement or contract makes no mention of this. However, it is possible to agree on a different figure, ie a higher rate of penalty interest. If the due date of the debt has already been agreed on, the penalty interest can be collected as of that date. Otherwise, penalty interest can be collected one month after the letter before action is sent.

## 7.4 Pre-action and non-judicial remedies

### 7.4.1 Court orders

#### 7.4.1.1 Attachment

The particular advantage of an attachment is that it prevents a debtor from disposing of or selling assets either within or outside the country. Application is made to the court without notice first being given to the opposing party. The procedure has the advantage of speed and secrecy.

A creditor seeking an attachment may be required to put up security for the losses that the debtor may suffer if it proves that the attachment has been sought without good reason. A guarantee by two persons is also acceptable security.

#### 7.4.1.2 Action on draft

With the exceptions mentioned below, it is possible to order a draft on an ordinary claim. The draft procedure has evolved out of practical needs and, as yet, there are no provisions concerning it in law. In the draft procedure, the creditor usually takes the invoice to be collected to the creditor's bank, which sends a letter before action to the debtor, threatening to protest the draft. If the claim is not paid within the prescribed time, which can be for example three weeks, the bank protests the draft, ie sends it to a notary public. The notary public informs the business newspaper *Kauppalehti* of all drafts protested, and the paper publishes a list. The bank charges the creditor FIM 200 per draft. However, the procedure does not apply to consumer credit, ie a loan that a business grants a consumer.

## 7.5 The court system

The usual court of first instance is the district court.

### 7.5.1 Structure of the courts

In criminal cases and cases concerning family law and tenancies, the court comprises a magistrate and three lay members. In other civil cases, ie cases of debt, the court comprises three magistrates, although a single magistrate deals with preliminary hearings or main processes held in connection with preliminary hearings (see **7.8**, below).

### 7.5.2 Rules of jurisdiction

The debtor is usually summoned to appear before a court in his place of domicile. If there are several debtors, or a debtor and guarantor, responsible for the same debt, the suit is raised in the district court within whose jurisdiction one or other of them is domiciled.

If the security is land, the suit is raised in the district court of the locality where this is located. The promissory note or contract can elect a specific court for this purpose.

### 7.5.3   Appeals

District court decisions can be appealed to a court of appeal. To retain this right of appeal, dissatisfaction with the district court decision must be expressed within seven days of the lower court's judgment being pronounced. The appeal must be lodged within 30 days of the same date. Because of the backlog of cases, obtaining a decision may take approximately one year. The cost to file an appeal is FIM 800.

An appeal court decision can be appealed to the Supreme Court only if the latter grants permission. The appeal and the application for permission to appeal must be made within 60 days of judgment being pronounced. Permission for appeal is granted if the case could result in a precedent, the decision diverges from normal legal practice, or some processing or other error has been made. The appeal to the Supreme Court costs FIM 1,000.

### 7.5.4   Status of the foreign creditor

In principle, a foreign creditor can seek a court decision on a debt with the same rights as a Finnish creditor.

## 7.6.   Legal representation

### 7.6.1   Nature of legal representation

A party either acts on his own behalf or instructs someone to represent him in proceedings. There is nothing to prevent an individual or the partners in a firm from representing themselves in person. If the creditor does act in person, the court officials are not usually very helpful in advising him regarding the procedures to follow because they consider that the court must be impartial. This approach may be changing. The real cost of self-representation may, however, ultimately be higher than instructing a lawyer.

Where a party is not acting on his own behalf, he can be legally represented by anyone. There is no obligation to employ a lawyer. However, the creditor should ensure that he selects a representative who is an expert in debt collection.

### 7.6.2   Mode of payment for legal representation

#### 7.6.2.1   Contractual agreement on costs

In Finland, the work of lawyers is usually undertaken on the basis of an hourly rate or on a fixed-fee basis. A fee-fixing system based on the total assets involved used to be employed for the management of bankruptcy estates but, in 1993, the profession changed to a system of charging according to the work done.

### 7.6.2.2  Contingency fee basis

Although it is unusual, lawyers in Finland can also accept instructions on a contingency fee basis, ie 'no recovery, no charge' with payment of a percentage of the award when recovery is successful.

### 7.6.2.3  Deduction of value added tax

In Finland, lawyers have been required to add value added tax (VAT) to their bills since the beginning of June 1994. Under certain conditions, the client can recover the tax paid from the government. The application must be made in writing to the Uusimaa provincial tax authority. Legal costs are a business expense, and they can be offset against profits for tax purposes.

## 7.7  Costs and interest

### 7.7.1  Current fees

The general fee for district court proceedings is FIM 300 in cases settled after a short hearing and FIM 750 in cases that take a longer hearing. A further charge of approximately FIM 2,000 may be made for publishing the summons in the *Official Gazette* when the debtor's whereabouts are unknown. The fees in the higher courts have been dealt with above.

Stamp duty of 1.5 per cent of the principal is charged on promissory notes presented to the court. The law does not require all kinds of promissory notes to be placed before the court, although this is mandatory in the case of bills of exchange, cheques, and negotiable bonds. It may be necessary to place some other types of promissory note before the court if the debtor disputes the debt; if so, stamp duty must be paid.

### 7.7.2  Availability of legal aid

The various municipalities' legal aid offices provide general legal aid. It is also possible for the needy to be granted free legal process and, if necessary, counsel whose fee is paid out of government funds. Only individuals, whether a creditor or debtor, may qualify for legal aid. Such assistance is not available to limited companies. Whether the individual creditor qualifies for aid depends on the creditor's income and expenditures.

### 7.7.3  Liability for and recovery of costs

The general rule in Finland is that the losing party is required to pay the other party's legal costs. In one case, the debtor paid the debt but declined to pay the collection costs claimed by the collection office in its letter before action. The collection office was entitled to seek a court decision on the collection costs alone, and the debtor also was ordered to pay the office's legal costs.

Interest can also be demanded on legal costs from one month after the court decision. If one party or the other has unjustifiably drawn out the court proceedings, this can be taken into account in determining liability to compensate for legal costs. A creditor who has not given the debtor an opportunity to pay a due debt and goes directly to the courts may find himself required to pay the debtor's legal costs. This is why anyone seeking to collect a debt should send a letter before action.

### 7.7.4   Interest

See **7.3.3**, above.

## 7.8   Proceedings

The court gives notice of the summons to the defendant. The defendant is asked to answer in writing within 14 to 30 days (the court decides the time). There are no pre-printed forms.

### 7.8.1   The Court of Appeal

Appeal is made to the Court of Appeal. There are six Courts of Appeal in Finland.

### 7.8.2   The Supreme Court

The appeal and the application for permission to appeal must be made within 60 days of judgment being pronounced.

## 7.9   Procedure to judgment

Procedure to judgment in a debt case at a district court falls into two stages:

    (1)   a preliminary hearing; and
    (2)   a main hearing.

If the case is settled in the preliminary hearing, the decision is usually called a default judgment. If the case is settled in the main hearing, the decision is called a court judgment. The preliminary hearing is divided into written and oral parts. The written documents needed for the proceedings must be presented, the witnesses and the subject of the evidence stated and the aspects of the matter in dispute identified. The preliminary hearing also must establish whether the parties can agree on the matter. In the oral hearing no process documents may be read out and counsel must be sufficiently familiar with the case that he can present his argument orally. The idea is that the preliminary hearing is a less formal process than the main hearing. In practice, the preliminary hearing may take place in a courtroom different from that used for the main hearing. Preliminary hearings are also open to the public.

Witnesses are heard in the main hearing. Unless special grounds can be demonstrated, no evidence may be offered in the main hearing unless it has been presented in the preliminary hearing. The intention is that there will be no surprises with regard to the substance of the case.

If the case is a major one the court hearing may take several days. To ensure that the hearing is not protracted through long adjournments, the law requires the case to be considered on at least three days in a week. There is a legal ruling that all material must be completely reprocessed if the main hearing is protracted beyond 45 days after its commencement, this is designed to prevent hearings being drawn out.

### 7.9.1   The debtor pays the debt

If a summons has already been applied for, it is advisable to inform the court that the matter has been settled.

### 7.9.2   The debtor admits the debt

If the debtor admits the debt, the matter is concluded with a default judgment in the preliminary hearing. A default judgment can be sent directly for debt recovery without notifying the debtor.

### 7.9.3   The debtor disputes the debt or part of it

It should be mentioned that there are no particular forms for disputing a debt. If the debt is obviously being contested without grounds, the district court none the less issues a default judgment and the case is concluded in the preliminary hearing. If substantive grounds are put forward for disputing the debt, the case will go on to the oral hearing and then to the main hearing.

### 7.9.4   The debtor neither admits nor disputes the debt

If the debtor offers no reply, the case is settled in the preliminary hearing with a default judgment. The debtor is entitled to appeal against the judgment within 30 days. The case will then once more come before the same district court.

### 7.9.5   The debtor is declared insolvent

Even if the debtor has been declared insolvent in a debt-recovery process at the application of some other creditor, a creditor can none the less seek a court judgment on his own claim against the debtor.

If the debtor is declared bankrupt in the middle of the court proceedings, the court does not issue a binding decision and the claim must be secured in the bankruptcy proceedings.

If debt rescheduling commences in mid-proceedings in the case of a private debtor, or corporate restructuring in the case of a corporate debtor, the court none the less issues a decision. However, debt recovery under this decision cannot proceed whilst the debt rescheduling or corporate restructuring is in effect.

## 7.10    Enforcing judgment

### 7.10.1    Execution

When a decision has been issued and it has taken on legal effect, either once the seven-day period for expressing dissatisfaction with the judgment is over or when a higher court decision takes legal effect, the debt recovery process can be initiated. Appeal by the defendant against a default judgment does not prevent debt recovery. Similarly, no other appeal application prevents debt recovery, but the distraint officer cannot sell assets before the decision has taken on legal force.

The rural police chief or, in the older towns, the bailiff is asked to recover the debt. The system is currently being revised. All municipalities will eventually have the same debt recovery organisation, with the district bailiff acting as the distraint officer.

The creditor can ask the distraint officer to make a debt-recovery survey providing a detailed account of the debtor's assets, income, and any assignments of property. Minutes are made of this survey. If the debtor lies during this procedure, he is guilty of fraud. Unfortunately, such fraud is usually lightly punished, mainly through fines.

Debt-recovery proceedings are requested from the distraint authority in the debtor's place of residence. If one and the same judgment requires several persons to pay the debt, the decision can be passed for debt-recovery proceedings to the distraint authority in the locality where any one of the debtors lives. The authority then uses executive assistance to recover the debt from the debtors living elsewhere.

If the creditor has a judgment against the debtor and gives notice in a newspaper or the *Official Gazette* (eg, that land owned by the debtor is to be auctioned at the application of some other creditor), he can request debt recovery by virtue of his own judgment. This is worthwhile if the property is not so highly mortgaged that its entire value will go to preferential creditors.

It is also worthwhile for the creditors to institute debt-recovery proceedings in late autumn, when the debtor may receive a tax rebate that can be distrained.

When movable assets are distrained, the distraint officer takes official possession of the assets or attaches a notice stating that they have been taken in execution. This latter procedure can be used in the case of large machines, for instance. In the case of immovable assets, the distraint officer sends a notice to the land register maintained by the district court. Every careful financial institution obtains an abstract from the register on any land put up as security before granting a loan. This abstract also will reveal any levy of execution.

### 7.10.2 Charging order

If the debtor receives rent revenues from a property or flat, this income can be seized by the distraint officer, who orders the tenant to pay his rent to the distraint office.

If the debtor owns property, its attachment is entered in a register kept by the district court, as noted earlier. This register covers the whole of Finland and nearly all its property data are now on computer. Anyone can obtain information from this register against a charge. Larger companies can have a paid computer link with the register.

By checking with the register as to how many mortgages there are on the property, it is possible to judge whether the debtor has any unencumbered assets or whether the property is already fully mortgaged as security for the claims of other creditors.

The district courts also keep a register of ownership data on property. This register does not provide a completely up-to-date picture of ownership, however, because a new owner has up to six months to report his ownership to the register, and sales of parcels of land are not always entered in the register.

### 7.10.3 Garnishee

It is possible to attach a debtor's claims on others. The garnishee is then forbidden to pay back the debt to anyone other than the distraint officer and does so when the debt falls due. If he pays the debtor, he is not released from his debt.

If the debtor has bank deposits, the funds also can be attached. The attachment affects the funds in the account at the time concerned. If the aim is to attach funds entering the account at a later date, the attachment must be carried out again. The distraint officer can either forbid the bank to pay any funds to the debtor, leaving the money in the account (when the bank freezes it) or, if the deposit can be raised immediately, to transfer the funds to the distraint officer at once.

If the bank has a due claim on the debtor, however, it exercises its set-off right to the money in the account, thereby preventing attachment.

### 7.10.4 Attachment of earnings

Any pay, fee, unemployment allowance or pension received by the debtor can be attached. The general rule is that one-third of the net sum of such payments can be attached. However, child benefit and housing allowance are not attachable.

# 7.11   Insolvency

## 7.11.1   Winding up of limited companies

### 7.11.1.1   Liquidation

If the board of a limited company finds that the company's equity is less than one-third of the share capital, it must convene a shareholders' meeting to consider placing the company in liquidation. This must take place unless the ordinary shareholders' meeting dealing with the annual accounts for the next financial period, at the latest, finds that equity represents at least half of the share capital.

### 7.11.1.2   Bankruptcy

As a general rule, bankruptcy proceedings take place where the company is mainly administered. One or more persons, usually with legal training, are appointed as receivers following representations by the creditors. The larger a creditor's claim, the more voting power he has. The court proceedings comprise a hearing of creditors, at which the debtor swears to a debt inventory. During this session the creditors still have an opportunity to replace a receiver with a person of their choice. It is also possible at this stage for the bankruptcy to be dismissed because of lack of funds. In general, the property must comprise approximately FIM 50,000 in free, ie, unpledged, funds or claims if it is to suffice to cover the receivers' costs and for proceedings to continue. If there is less than FIM 50,000, and none of the creditors are willing to answer for the costs, the bankruptcy proceedings are dropped.

In every case of bankruptcy the claims are secured, ie, are reported to a receiver or the court (whichever is stated in the court decision). A copy of the debt instrument or invoice, for instance, must be attached to each notice made to secure a claim. If claims are not properly secured, the creditor forfeits his right to payment from the remaining funds. Even so, a creditor is entitled to payment when, for instance, a property has been pledged as security for the debt or through set-off, or in a limited or unlimited partnership he can seek a decision against the responsible partner.

From 1 December 1993 it is possible to make written notice of a claim in a language other than Finnish or Swedish (Finland's official languages). The receiver must then have the notice translated and the translation costs are deducted from the creditor's future share.

### 7.11.1.3   Corporate restructuring

Since 8 February 1993, there has been a Finnish law on corporate restructuring as an alternative to bankruptcy, and this procedure can be used to allow viable enterprises to continue operating. The pre-condition is that it is possible to eliminate the company's insolvency through restructuring.

Some companies may attempt to use restructuring as a delaying tactic. If such attempts are made, the law states that restructuring may not be embarked on if the debtor's application is designed to delay recovery procedures by a creditor.

Once corporate restructuring begins, the debtor may not pay off his debts and penalty interest may not be charged. A creditor may seek a demand for payment order in court but he cannot proceed to distraint. Obtaining a court decision may be necessary if the creditor suspects that the restructuring will not be successful.

Once restructuring begins, no assets put up as debt security may be realised; nor can the creditor exercise his right of set-off. He can only demand payment from certain guarantors, such as banks or another company in the same group.

One or more administrators are appointed to supervise the restructuring. The creditors can form a committee to supervise the administrator(s) and issue instructions.

A creditor must also secure his claim in a restructuring process, ie, give notice on a specified day. In corporate restructuring this notice is always made to an administrator and cannot be made to a court. A creditor who does not do so forfeits his rights to payment from the company's funds, unless the debt was already demonstrably known to the administrator(s).

The administrator makes a proposal for a restructuring programme. The creditors are also entitled to suggest changes in this proposal, or to make a proposal of their own. The programme must explain how the company's operations will be restructured, any realisation of funds, and proposals concerning personnel and debts. Debts can be dealt with in four ways:

(1)  by changing the repayment schedule;
(2)  by ordering payments to concern firstly the principal and only then interest;
(3)  by reducing the interest percentage; or
(4)  by reducing the principal.

Debts with security are in a better position than unsecured debts, in that their principal cannot be waived.

### 7.11.2   Bankruptcy and debt rescheduling of private persons

#### 7.11.2.1   *Bankruptcy of a private person*

In the case of a private person, bankruptcy proceedings take place in the district court of his place of residence. Such bankruptcy does not cancel his debts and they are never waived in such proceedings but remain in force even after the legal process is over.

#### 7.11.2.2   *Debt rescheduling of a private person*

As a result of legislation enacted in 1993, debt rescheduling may be accorded to private persons. Debt rescheduling is not granted under the law if the person concerned has got into debt thoughtlessly or his debts arose from speculative business operations (investment in securities or property speculation), or if the debtor is guilty of financial crimes.

If a debtor does not retain the home he owns, he is usually given a five-year schedule during which his income is used to pay his debts. After this, his remaining debts are waived. If the debtor retains his home the schedule may take 10 years.

The same four approaches as are listed above for corporate restructuring are used in debt rescheduling of private persons (including lowering the interest rate). In exceptional cases, it is also possible to waive the debt completely.

### 7.11.3   Insolvency of partnerships and proprietors

For partnerships the rules pertaining to companies will apply. For proprietors the rules pertaining to private individuals will apply.

## 7.12   Conclusion

The recession has led to higher credit losses among companies and banks in Finland. The number of demand-for-payment cases before the district courts has also grown. New legislation is to be passed on debt recovery to prevent irregularities and, for instance, to limit the use of general securities.

It should be noted that this chapter is intended only as a general survey of the laws and procedures of debt recovery in Finland and a creditor is well advised to engage a lawyer for collection purposes.

## Chapter 8

# FRANCE

**Jean-Jacques Bertagna, Lavinia Dugay and Robert Stevenson**
**Paris: Bertagna Gruia Dufaut**
**London: Berrymans**

## 8.1   Introduction

Much is made of the fact that France is a civil-law country with a codified system of law which those used to a common-law jurisdiction will find difficult to understand. Whilst of course the origins of a codified system are different, the objectives of the law, particularly in the field of commerce, are the same. Similar solutions to particular problems are often arrived at from different starting points. Our aim in this chapter will be to draw parallels with the similarities between common- and civil-law systems and explain the differences which can be minimised or exploited as the case may be.

French terms and expressions (in italics) have been retained where necessary and useful. Their meaning is explained.

## 8.2   Initial considerations

The first consideration is to establish whether court proceedings have to be brought, and where. The basic rule is that the defendant is sued in the country in which he is domiciled.

### 8.2.1   The exceptions

(i)    if the contract gives jurisdiction to a particular country;
(ii)   if the performance of the contract is to be undertaken in a particular country;
(iii)  in the case of a harmful event causing damage, the person responsible can be sued in the country where the damage occurred.

### 8.2.2   France

This includes not only France on the continent of Europe, but also departments of France (*DOM*) and overseas territories (*TOM*). The overseas departments are Guadeloupe, Guyane, Martinique and Réunion, whilst the overseas territories are Wallis and Futuna, Saint-Pierre and Miquelon, Polynésie française and Nouvelle Calédonie. The same legal rules and procedures apply in *DOM* and *TOM* as they do in Metropolitan France.

### 8.2.3 The status of the debtor

In any court proceedings, the debtor needs to be correctly identified. A failure to do so can cause delay, prevent a quick judgment or, indeed, judgment at all and may frustrate measures to preserve or enforce the debt. The principal types of legal entity can be summarised as follows:

(a) individuals acting as sole traders either in their own names or under a trading name;

(b) limited liability company (*Société à Responsabilité Limitée* (SARL)), a very widely used form, similar to a limited company;

(c) a joint-stock limited liability company (*Société Anonyme* (SA)) – most well-known French companies are SAs, equivalent to an English PLC;

(d) *Société par Action Simplifiée* (SAS). A company similar in structure to an SA but with a greater freedom in its contractual arrangements;

(e) a general partnership (*société en nom collectif*) equivalent to a partnership in England and Wales. All the parties have joint and several liability for each other's acts undertaken in the course of the business;

(f) limited partnership (*société en commandite simple*). There are two types of member of such partnerships: partners, and those who only contribute capital (*commandité*). The latter are responsible to the extent that they have contributed capital to the partnership, ie if they have contributed 10,000 FF, this is the limit of their liability to third parties. There is another less common type of limited partnership called a *société en commandite par actions*, which can be quoted on The Stock Exchange;

(g) An Economic Interest Grouping (*Groupement d'Intérêt Economique* (GIE)), a form of joint venture between companies or individuals which, when registered, acquires its own legal personality. This form has been adopted by the European Union and is called a European Economic Interest Grouping (EEIG) (*Groupement Européen d'Intérêt Economique*). An example is the EEIG between Aérospatiale SA and British Aerospace;

(h) Associations (*Associations*). As an association, it acquires a separate legal personality. The members of such an association are not responsible for its debts.

When an individual debtor dies and his heirs inherit, they also adopt responsibility for his debts, given there is sufficient money in the estate.

### 8.2.4 Sources of information

If precise details of the debtor's address, etc are not available and the creditor does not know whether he has sufficient assets to meet the debt, certain enquiries may need to be made.

France has a system of electronic information which can be accessed by anyone with a telephone line and with the correct equipment (*Minitel*). This service provides an up-to-date record of all registered companies in France, their registered office and whether or not they are in liquidation. For detailed information on their accounts, reference may be made to the Commercial Court which is closest to the company's registered office. It is possible to search for the name of an individual on *Minitel*, although an individual can request to be made ex-directory. To ascertain whether an individual owns land and whether it is mortgaged, a request can be made to the local keeper of mortgages (*Conservation des Hypothèques*), the equivalent of a local land registry.

It is also possible to ask specialist detectives or companies to make enquiries about the debtor, details of bank accounts, addresses, etc.

### 8.2.5   Limitation (*Prescription*)

Although the fundamental principle is that the period during which proceedings should be commenced is 30 years, there are numerous exceptions to this.

The most important exceptions are:

- commercial contracts: between either two commercial entities or one commercial entity and an ordinary individual, the period is 10 years from the breach of contract;
- for actions to recover rent or payments under a lease for buildings or land, 5 years from the date when payment was due;
- to recover unpaid wages or salary due in France, the period is 5 years.

These are only a few of the exceptions to the general rule and great care must be taken to commence proceedings in sufficient time.

### 8.2.6   Retention of title

A retention-of-title clause can be included in any sale contract for goods. It has to be written to be valid.

As there has been no transfer of title the creditor can reclaim the goods in the event of non-payment in the following cases:

when the debtor is solvent;
when the goods are still under the debtor's control.

When the goods are no longer in the debtor's control but have been sold to a third party in 'bad faith', they can still be reclaimed by the creditor.

If, however, the goods were bought in good faith, the French law principle that possession equates title will apply, and it will be much more difficult for the creditor to reclaim his goods. In addition, the creditor is not a party to the contract for the resale of the goods.

In an attempt to avoid this problem, any contract for the sale of goods with a retention clause should require the purchaser to inform any purchasers from him of the existence of the retention-of-title clause.

When the debtor is declared bankrupt, goods can be reclaimed within three months. Equally the creditor can also claim repayment of the price of the goods within four months of the publication of the judgment of insolvency in the BODACC.

## 8.3 Letters before action (*Mise en demeure*)

### 8.3.1 Are they necessary?

The sending of a registered letter before action is not obligatory but it does have the effect of starting interest running on the debt. If proceedings are issued, then interest can be claimed from the date of notification and not simply from the date of issue of the proceedings. The moral is to send out the letter before action as soon as possible.

Once a letter before action is sent, proceedings can be issued for the interest even if the principal sum has been paid. In cases where the contract itself provides for interest on late payment, interest will run according to the terms of the contract and will not depend upon the sending of a letter before action.

### 8.3.2 Contents and method of service

Whether or not the letter before action should be sent by a firm of lawyers is a matter of choice and circumstances. Whilst early involvement of lawyers may demonstrate a firm approach, it may, in certain circumstances, preclude the amicable settlement of the debt. On the other hand, it is important to send the letter as early as possible to start interest running. Any such letter must:

(a) give correct details of the debt and the creditor;
(b) be dated;
(c) give a brief description of what is claimed and why;
(d) state the amount that is due;
(e) make a clear demand for payment within a specified time, otherwise proceedings will follow and the matter be referred to lawyers;
(f) make mention of article 1153 of the Civil Code, which permits interest to be claimed.

The letter must be sent by registered delivery, otherwise it will be only considered as a reminder, quite apart from the risk of the debtor denying receipt.

It is preferable that the letter should be written in French and the expression *mise en demeure* employed so all doubt is avoided.

## 8.4 Securing the sum in dispute at the outset of proceedings

French law enables a creditor who is claiming a definitive sum of money (rather than damages to be calculated by the court) to ask the court to require the debtor to give security for that sum.

The creditor will not need to ask for the court's authorisation if he has what is called executory title, ie an enforceable judgment, a letter of exchange, an unpaid cheque or an unpaid rent.

The creditor is required to show to the court some imminent danger that the sum in dispute will be dissipated but, in practice, this is fairly easy to demonstrate.

Security over money, goods and other material objects is called *'saisie conservatoire'*. Security over real property is termed *'inscription provisoire d'hypothèque'*. An initial search against the property at the local keeper of mortgages will reveal whether the property is already mortgaged and whether any equity remains.

The court is requested to authorise the placing of a charge over the property for a 3-year period. This period can be extended.

Once security over goods or property has been obtained the debtor must be informed.

## 8.5 The court system

8.5.1 There are three types of civil court in which proceedings can be brought:

### (a) Tribunal d'Instance
This court is for sums up to 30,000 FF. It is presided over by one judge and has certain specific jurisdiction and remedies. The use of an *Avocat* is not obligatory, but a knowledge of the procedure is nevertheless helpful. In principle, there is a *Tribunal d'Instance* in each *arrondissement* (sub-division of a *département*) usually close to or actually in the local Town Hall.

### (b) Tribunal de Grande Instance
This court has monetary jurisdiction from 30,000 FF upwards and is presided over by three judges (one president and two assessors). Each *Département* has at least one *Tribunal de Grande Instance*. Use of lawyers is obligatory and the procedure is highly formalised.

### (c) Tribunal de Commerce
This court has unlimited monetary jurisdiction.

An individual can commence proceedings against a commercial entity but not vice-versa.

It is a court specially established for settling disputes between commercial entities. One company suing another must use this court. It has jurisdiction for matters involving an *Acte de commerce*, ie letters of exchange, etc.

The procedure is much less formal than the *Tribunal de Grande Instance*. Use of a lawyer, although not obligatory, is recommended.

The judges in the *Tribunaux d'Instance* and *Grande Instance* are lawyers who have chosen at the outset of their careers to become judges. The three judges who preside over the *Tribunal de Commerce* are not lawyers; they work part time and are unpaid, and in most instances they are local businessmen.

### 8.5.2   Appeal

Appeals on facts and law can be made from all three of the above tribunals to the *Cour d'Appel* (Court of Appeal). There is one exception for judgment of less than 13,000 FF, where no appeal is possible. The period for making an appeal is one month from the date that the winning party formally notifies the losing party of the court's decision. In cases of summary judgment, the period is 15 days. Execution may not normally be commenced until one month has expired. Once an appeal is lodged, in most cases execution must await the decision of the *Cour d'Appel*. An exception is made for summary judgments.

#### 8.5.2.1   Cour de Cassation
In most cases, appeals to this court, on points of law only, are made from the *Cour d'Appel*. Execution is not suspended during an appeal to the *Cour de Cassation* (Final Court of Appeal). .

### 8.5.3   Status of foreign creditors

The Brussels Convention, to which France, along with other member states of the European Union, is a signatory, places all residents of these countries on an equal footing so far as commercial and civil proceedings are concerned.

## 8.6   Legal representation

### 8.6.1   Nature of legal representation

There are now two main types of lawyers in France, *Avocats* and *Notaires*. The latter do not have rights of audience before the courts. The profession of *Conseil Juridique* was merged with that of the *Avocat* in 1991. As has been explained, the use of an *Avocat* is only obligatory before the *Tribunal de Grande Instance*, *Cour d'Appel* and *Cour de Cassation*.

### 8.6.2   Payment for legal representation

The client is responsible for the fees of his lawyer. There is no scale of fees and therefore the basis and rate at which the *Avocat* will charge his client should be agreed at the outset. It is possible, but unusual, to arrange contingency fees but they must be additional to a fixed sum payable to the *Avocat* in any event. There is a procedure for the *Avocat*'s costs to be examined by the *Bâtonnier*, who is the head of the local Bar Association.

## 8.7   Costs and interest

### 8.7.1   Costs

The sums payable to initiate proceedings in any of the three courts (*frais de timbres*, literally stamping costs) are relatively low, between 100 FF and

150 FF. There are then the costs of the court bailiff (*Huissier*), who serves the defendant with the proceedings (300–400 FF). After the court has rendered its decision, a further 300–400 FF is payable to the *Huissier* to serve the judgment.

If an appeal is launched, then specialist lawyers called *Avoués* have to be employed alongside an *Avocat* to prepare the proceedings. Their fees are fixed, unlike those of the *Avocat*, and will include any additional costs required by the *Cour d'Appel* or the *Cour de Cassation*.

### 8.7.2   Legal aid

This is only available to individuals and the levels of entitlement according to income are set very low. To obtain full legal aid, an individual must earn less than 4,400 FF per month.

For those who earn less than 6,000 FF per month, partial legal aid is available. A change in the circumstances of the legally aided person may result in that aid being withdrawn.

### 8.7.3   Liability for and recovery of costs

The client is primarily responsible for the *Avocat*'s fees. If he wins his case, he can ask the court to require the losing party to pay all or some of those fees.

These are divided into two parts: (i) the expenses, ie costs incurred in running the case, such as payments to bailiffs to the court and to their public officials; and (ii) the fees of the *Avocat*.

The court orders the losing party to pay the winning party's expenses in their totality. However, the court usually only orders that a small part of the *Avocat*'s fees be paid by the losing party.

### 8.7.4   Interest

This has largely been dealt with in the section on letters before action. There are essentially two types of interest:

(i)   contractual interest, provided for in the contract in the event of late payment – such interest can be compound;

(ii)   simple interest, which starts to run upon service of the letter before action. The rate is set by the French National Bank, close to the current bank base rate. For interest of either sort to be recoverable, it must be claimed in the document which commences the proceedings (the *Assignation*).

## 8.8   Issuing proceedings

The plaintiff creditor files his *assignation* with the court. This document gives a detailed description of the facts of the claim and, where necessary by law, the amount of the claim including interest. The document must be stamped by the court.

In the *Tribunal d'Instance*, it is possible to adopt a less formal procedure called a *declaration*. This is a printed form supplied by the court upon which the plaintiff enters details of his claim.

The defendant must be served with the *assignation* at least 15 days before the hearing in the *Tribunal d'Instance*, *Tribunal de Grande Instance*, or *Tribunal de Commerce*.

### 8.8.1   Summary judgments (*Ordonnance de référé*)

In cases before all three courts where there is no real defence to the claim, the plaintiff can apply for summary judgment (*référé provision*). The date for the hearing is marked on the *assignation* and is then served by the court bailiff on the defendant.

Once the *assignation* has been served, the court is then notified and the date of audience is then formalised. At the hearing, the plaintiff obtains an immediate judgment which can be executed there and then without awaiting the usual one month for an appeal. It is of course possible for the defendant to appeal but he may be compelled to pay the amount of the judgment (as a condition of his appeal).

If at the first hearing the defendant appears and seriously contests the proceedings, the judge will rule that he cannot continue and the matter will have to be dealt with under the full procedure.

## 8.9   Procedure to judgment

If the service of the *assignation* results in payment by the debtor including the costs of the bailiff, then the action is at an end. However, if part of the sum claimed is not paid then the action continues.

### 8.9.1   Procedure before the *Tribunal d'Instance*

Three types of action can be brought before the *Tribunal d'Instance*:

- in the case of small contractual debts a creditor can request the court to issue an 'order to pay' (*injunction de payer*) without the formalities required under the full procedure. If, however, a defence is raised then the mater reverts to being dealt with under the full procedure. If a defence of some sort is anticipated, the use of this procedure is not advised as it simply wastes time;
- summary judgment (see **8.8.2**);
- full procedure.

At the first hearing, the defendant will probably arrive with his documentary evidence and the judge will then give a new date for a hearing. The judge can come to a decision immediately and give judgment. This will depend upon the weight and complexity of the proceedings and the defendant's documents in particular. If the defendant does not come to the first hearing, the judge can give judgment for the plaintiff. Between the first and second hearing, the parties will exchange documents and in the case where the *Avocat* is used, the defendant will serve a document called *conclusions* setting out his defence. This, however, is not obligatory. At the second hearing, the judge will make the decision based on the documents presented to him, his questions to the parties and the arguments of the *Avocats*. No witnesses are called; their evidence is in written form for all cases where the sum in issue exceeds 5,000 FF.

### 8.9.2   Procedure before the *Tribunal de Grande Instance*

The options are:

– summary judgment (see **8.8.2**);
– full procedure.

As the use of *Avocats* is obligatory, the procedure is more formal. The *Avocat* for the defendant is obliged to inform the plaintiff's lawyer and the court of the fact that he is acting for the defendant within 15 days of the service of the *assignation*.

The court will then fix a date for a hearing at which procedural directions are given. There will be several of these during which pleadings and documents are exchanged. The judge will decide when this exchange should end and fix a date for a hearing when the two *Avocats* will present their arguments, which will have previously been served on the court and the opposing party. The courts of France do not recognise the common-law concept of discovery of documents, by which a party is obliged to disclose all documents relevant to an action. The only documents which the parties are obliged to disclose are those upon which they wish to rely. It is possible to request specific disclosure of particular documents (*injonction de communiquer*) but this relates only to specific documents known to be in the possession of the party.

After hearing the arguments of the *Avocats*, the judge will then deliberate for an indeterminate period, usually one month, and will the deliver a written judgment.

### 8.9.3   Procedure before the *Tribunal de Commerce*

Three types of procedure can be employed before the *Tribunal de Commerce*:

– *injonction de payer* (see **8.9.1**);
– summary judgment (see **8.8.2**);
– full procedure.

The defendant must be served with the *assignation* at least 15 days before the hearing.

The jurisdiction of the court can also be invoked by a written joint request or an appearance in person by both parties before the court.

If the defendant individual or company is placed in receivership (*redressement judiciaire*), the proceedings are suspended except where the claim is not for a liquidated sum and an action has already been commenced. A request for payment is then addressed to the court which is handling the bankruptcy proceedings.

## 8.10    Enforcing judgment

If at the outset the sums in dispute have been secured (see **8.2.3**) then once an enforceable judgment has been obtained, the next step is to obtain executory title (*titre exécutoire*), which will convert a *saisie conservatoire*, and the *inscription provisoire d'hypothèque* into respectively *saisie execution* and *inscription définitive d'hypothèque* or attachment and charging orders. This must be done within 2 months of the date of the enforceable judgment.

In addition to enforceable judgment, executory title may also be obtained directly in the following instances:

– in case of non-payment under a notarised document (such as a lease);
– non-payment of judgments of the administrative courts or of other state bodies such as the Social Security;
– foreign judgments and arbitral awards;
– a bailiff's certificate that a valid cheque has not been paid.

### 8.10.1    Execution on chattels

A copy of the enforceable judgment is given to a court bailiff, who is the appropriate person to execute court judgments.

The court bailiff then sends the debtor an order to pay (*commandement de payer*) which contains the following information:

– notice of the judgment;
– the amount due;
– a formal demand for payment; and
– an indication where execution is to take place.

The court bailiff proceeds to the place where the chattels are located. If he is denied entry then he can and must request police assistance to enter. A request can be made to the *Commissaire de Police*, the Mayor, or a member of the local council (*conseil municipal*).

After entry, the bailiff draws up a schedule of the goods seized. They then become 'unavailable' to the debtor, although in most cases they are left on the premises in the safekeeping of the debtor.

A copy of the bailiff's schedule is then served on the debtor.

The public auction will take place at least 8 days after the notification of the *saisie* to the debtor. The auction is normally conducted by an auctioneer (*commissaire priseur*) but a notary or a bailiff can equally well conduct the proceedings.

For a debtor to release his goods from seizure and avoid their sale at auction he must pay the full amount claimed, plus the costs of the execution.

### 8.10.2   Execution on land

To execute on property, one must have an executory title (see **8.10**).

The court bailiff then serves on the debtor an order to seize (*commandement valant saisie*) which contains the following required information:

- an order to pay a certain sum;
- the judgment to be enforced;
- a description of the property including its detail; and
- details of the bailiff's powers, together with a warning that if payment is not made it will be lodged with and become enforceable at the office of mortgages (*bureau des hypothèques*).

The document must also indicate the court before which the seizure order will be made. If this court is not the local court of the creditor's lawyers, he is obliged to instruct another lawyer as his agent. This agent's details must also be entered on the document.

The order to seize must be registered at the mortgage office within 90 days of its notification to the debtor.

A document called a *cahier des charges* is then compiled, containing:

- the executory title (enforceable judgment or other);
- order to seize and date of registration with the mortgage office;
- description of the property; and
- conditions of the auction (payment of the price, delay and interests, and rights to which the property is subject).

This document must then be deposited within 40 days with the *Tribunal de Grande Instance* from the registration of the order to seize.

Before a hearing before the *Tribunal de Grande Instance*, the following steps must be taken and time periods observed:

- within 8 days of the *cahier des charges* being deposited at the *Tribunal de Grande Instance* the bailiff must notify the debtors, the principal creditor and all other creditors who have registered an interest at the *bureau des hypothèques*.

All the persons to which orders have been served can give their opinion on the *cahier des charges* by written statement deposited with the court clerk and noted on the *cahier des charges*. This must be done at least 3 days before the hearing.

At the hearing, the judge takes a decision regarding the disputes.

The *cahier des charges* is published in the official journal at least 15 days before the sale by auction, which takes place in the court and which is called an *ajudication*.

### 8.10.3   Execution on a third party – garnishee orders

When a creditor has acquired executory title, he can seize money owed to the debtor by a third party or garnishee.

When a bank account is garnisheed, the bank is obliged to give the balance of the account at the date it receives the order *saisie*. Fifteen days must then elapse, during which time bank transactions effected before the *saisie* can be debited/credited to the account.

### 8.10.4   Execution on motor vehicles

This can be done in two ways:

(1)   A declaration is lodged with the *prefecture*. This must indicate the name and address of the debtor, the make of the care, the executory title and the amount of the money owed (principal and interest); the vehicle cannot then be sold. A bailiff must notify the debtor of the declaration within 8 days of the lodging of the declaration;

(2)   The immobilisation of the vehicle by the bailiff fixing a wheel clamp. Then the bailiff delivers an order to pay; failure to comply within 8 days will lead to the car being auctioned.

### 8.10.5   Execution on salary

It is also possible to seize part of the debtor's salary. The exact amount depends upon how much he receives, his outgoings, family commitments, etc.

The *Tribunal d'Instance* has exclusive jurisdiction to deal with the execution on salaries.

## 8.11   Insolvency

### 8.11.1   In general

Bankruptcy proceedings may be instituted against a business, whether an individual or a body corporate, where it is impossible to pay the debts due from the assets of the business.

Bankruptcy proceedings aim to effect the liquidation of the property of a business and its distribution to the various creditors in settlement of their claims.

### 8.11.2   Requirements for declaring a business bankrupt

As mentioned above, a business may be declared bankrupt if it has suspended payments in a general and permanent way.

### 8.11.3   Who may be declared bankrupt

(1)   Individuals in business;
(2)   General partnerships of both limited and unlimited liability;
(3)   Limited liability companies and joint-stock limited liability companies.

### 8.11.4   Procedure

As soon as bankruptcy proceedings are instituted, all the actions against the debtor are suspended. The creditors must lodge a formal demand within 4 months from the date the judgment of insolvency is published in an official publication called *Bulletin Officiel des Annonces Civiles et Commerciales* (BODACC).

The creditors' claims cease to earn interest from the issue of the bankruptcy proceedings.

The bankruptcy administrator proceeds to accept and accord precedence to the creditors' claims.

The bankruptcy may be terminated either by the settlement of the creditors' claims or by the liquidation of the debtor's property.

*Chapter 9*

# GERMANY

**Gernot Stenger**
**Alpers & Stenger**
**Hamburg, Germany**

## 9.1   Introduction

The following survey reviews debt-collection procedures available in Germany and the legal and practical considerations relevant to securing the creditor's rights.

## 9.2   Initial considerations

### 9.2.1   In general

Debt collection, litigation in order to obtain legal title and enforcement of legal title in Germany are all part of the Federal law. This also holds for the various states (*Länder*) and the five new states of the former German Democratic Republic which joined the Federal Republic of Germany in 1990.

In German courts the German language must be used. All documents submitted to courts must be filed in a proper German translation.

### 9.2.2   Status of the debtor

As a first step, any creditor must clearly identify the target of his claim. Naming an incorrect defendant in a letter before action or in any kind of lawsuit will usually produce negative consequences, such as a rejection of entitlement to interest or the claim as a whole.

If the creditor is unaware of the present name of a legal entity, the address, its legal status or any other information needed to file a lawsuit information should be sought from the trade registers (*Handelsregister*) which are all located and operated by the municipal courts (*Amtsgerichte*), the Industry and Trade Chamber (*Industrie- und Handelskammer*) and the administrative agencies which are in charge of controlling and supervising trade and trade conduct (*Gewerbeaufsichtsamt*). For individuals, it may be worth seeking information from the municipal citizens register (*Einwohnermeldeamt*). The various legal entities which may be sued in German courts are summarised as follows:

(1)   an individual, who may either trade in his own name or use a trade name (*Firma*);

(2)   several individuals, if acting in the form of a simple partnership, as

defined by the Civil Code (*Gesellschaft bürgerlichen Rechts*), who must always be sued collectively, ie, each single partner must be named as a defendant in the lawsuit;

(3) a partnership, comprising two or more partners who, in turn, may act in the form of limited liability companies, partnerships, or as individual persons;[1]

(4) a limited liability company, usually designed as GmbH;[2]

(5) a stock corporation, usually displaying its legal status by the suffix AG (*Aktiengesellschaft*);[3]

(6) non-profit organisations acting in the form of a so-called registered association (eV, meaning *eingetragener Verein*) or as a non-registered association;[4]

(7) foundations (*Stiftung*);[5]

(8) the government, sub-departments of the government, states, districts, and cities;[6] and

(9) minors under the age of 18 years.[7]

Should the target of the claim be an individual who happens to die before action is commenced, then the action must be brought against the heirs. If the heirs declare vis-à-vis the competent authorities that they do not wish to succeed to the deceased's estate, then the creditor's claim is lost.

### 9.2.3 Is the debt statute-barred?

The German Civil Code provides a range of limitation periods for various claims. The creditor's claim may be statute-barred between three months (for the purchase of cattle) and 30 years (for all claims that are not specifically listed in the Civil Code).

---

1 Such partnerships may operate under the names OHG (*offene Handelsgesellschaft*), KG (*Kommanditgesellschaft*) or various forms of legal entities that combine legal persons and partnerships in order to avoid unrestricted liability, such as AG & Co KG (a stock corporation acting as a general partner within a *Kommanditgesellschaft*) or GmbH & Co KG (limited liability company acting as a general partner within a *Kommanditgesellschaft*).

2 The share capital of a GmbH (under law, the share capital must be at least DM 50,000) indicates the amount which must at any time be available to cover liabilities of the company. This liability capital (*Haftkapital* or *Haftsumme*) is expressly shown on the extract obtained from the commercial register.

3 The share capital must be at least DM 100,000.

4 Both forms may participate in trade and business but not for the purpose of making profits.

5 Foundations are also registered in a special register with the municipal courts; they are not seen very frequently in Germany and may, but usually do not, participate in trade and business. By law, they are not allowed to work with the intention of making profits if they operate for the common interest.

6 If any of these entities participates in trade and commerce (eg, a city purchasing its annual demand of stationary supplies), then the entity may be sued in court according to normal rules and procedures.

7 While minors under the age of 18 years may be sued in court, such actions are not likely to succeed because, under civil law, minors are not entitled to enter into any contract unless that contract proves to be advantageous only for them, or if they have received permission from their legal representatives (parents), or if they have purchased goods by using their own funds.

Generally, most civil and/or commercial claims are statute-barred after a period of two years or four years. If the claim arises out of ordinary business between merchants, then usually the two-year period will apply. It is important to note that two years normally does not mean two years after the claim first became due but two years starting with the first calendar day of the year that follows the maturity of the claim. One important further limitation is the six-month warranty rule for all ordinary purchases, ie, beyond six months after the sale the seller can be held liable or be obliged to reduce the purchase price only in exceptional circumstances (such as fraud).

### 9.2.4   Security

Depending on the nature of the business, charges, liens and transfer of ownership as security on a debt may be recommended with respect to the item or the goods sold. Personal guarantees are recognised by German law and are a recommended additional security when dealing, eg, with a limited liability company. Bank guarantees are usually still more advantageous, but they will involve costs for the debtor ranging between 0.5 per cent and 1.5 per cent of the guaranteed capital.

A potential debtor may also be asked to submit himself in a notarial deed to 'immediate execution levied against one's entire personal property' (*Unterwerfung unter die Zwangsvollstreckung*) which, from the view point of the creditor, will avoid the often lengthy and cumbersome procedure required to obtain legal title against the debtor. With the notarial deed the creditor may instruct a bailiff to collect the monies owing at any time. In such a case no further legal action is required.

### 9.2.5   Retention of title

German law recognises and allows various forms of retention of title and also has developed mechanisms for ensuring that the legal title will fall into the hands of the creditor if there is a default in payment.

Frequently, sellers of movable goods will provide in their general terms of trading that the property title will remain with the seller until the entire purchase price has been paid. In addition, the seller should stipulate that the purchaser will be allowed to sell the products in question in the ordinary course of business, provided that the purchaser assigns any claims against third parties resulting from his sale to the original seller. Thus, the title in the product sold may be converted into a valid claim for payment against a third party.

Furthermore, especially for expensive items such as capital goods (cars, machinery, and equipment), most sales contracts provide that the purchaser of the item in question retransfers the property title to the seller without making the retransfer public. The retransfer will be terminated on full payment of the purchase price. This contractual mechanism allows the purchaser of the item to use the item fully and work with the so-called 'economic property' which will only appear on the user's own balance sheet. The seller (creditor) will retain the legal title until his claim is completely satisfied.

## 9.3 Letters before action

### 9.3.1 Are they necessary?

Although not strictly necessary, letters before action are recommended unless they may lead to a situation where the debtor will try to hide assets or conceal valuable information. Unless the terms and time of performance are clearly fixed on a certain date within the contract, the claim of the creditor will not start to bear interest until the creditor has announced in written form to the debtor that he is in default.

Further, if legal action is commenced immediately without notice, the debtor may appear in court, claim not to be responsible for the delay in payment and recognise the claim of the creditor as valid. In such a case the court may decide to allocate the costs of the proceedings to the creditor (plaintiff) because the debtor (defendant) has not caused the legal action.

### 9.3.2 What should they say?

Letters before action should clearly indicate that a failure to effect payment, as specified in the letter before action or as defined in the underlying contract, will result in the issue of legal proceedings.

The letter should not be ambivalent or offer options or alternatives. The letter should always set a certain date for payment and declare that, if payment has not been received by that date, legal action will follow. All legal rights should be expressly reserved.

If payment is already due and the debtor has received a reminder and the letter before action is sent out by the creditor's attorney, then the attorney's costs for writing the letter may be claimed from the debtor within the same letter.

### 9.3.3 May they demand interest for late payment?

Letters before action may and should demand interest for late payment. Unless there is an express agreement between the parties for another rate, all monetary claims will bear interest at a rate of four per cent or, in the case of liabilities under the Commercial Code, five per cent. However, the letter should indicate that, if payment is not effected by the date set out in the letter, then the creditor will borrow money from his own bank and rightfully claim the interest rate payable to the bank from the debtor.

## 9.4 Pre-action and non-judicial remedies

### 9.4.1 In general

Two traditional sets of procedures may be distinguished. There are facilitated procedures to obtain a title against the debtor through court action, which may then be enforced in due course. Additionally, to ensure that assets or funds do not disappear or that the debtor will not conceal funds or engage in secret activities, interim injunction and arrest procedures may be initiated. Non-judicial remedies other than those described above are not available. Bailiffs will act only on behalf of the creditor on the basis of court documents.

### 9.4.2   Court orders

Obtaining legal title for collecting money may be realised through a single-page document which should identify the creditor, the debtor, the amount the creditor is asking for and, in a short description, the legal nature of the claim. The document will be served on the debtor. If the debtor objects to the claim (in writing), the creditor may ask the court for regular legal proceedings to be opened.

The deadline for the debtor's response is two weeks after service. If the debtor does not object in time, the creditor may proceed and obtain an enforcement document, which again must be served on the debtor. If the debtor objects to the enforcement procedure (the deadline for reply is again two weeks), the creditor may ask for regular court proceedings. If the debtor fails to object, the creditor will obtain the legal title which may then be enforced.

### 9.4.3   Injunctions and arrests

A broad range of injunctions and arrests is generally available to the creditor.

The creditor must file a petition at court, seeking either a court order that the debtor refrain from activities which must be specified by the creditor or seeking the attachment of assets. In exceptional cases, the debtor himself may be arrested.

The petition must be filed with the court. Affidavit evidence attached to the petition is sufficient support for the creditor's claim. The creditor must show that there is a legal basis for the claim (in substantive law) and that an immediate court order is necessary because the creditor would otherwise lose a certain position or a chance to collect the amount owed. If the creditor can successfully demonstrate that the claim would otherwise be seriously jeopardised, the court can be petitioned to issue the order without the attendance of, or prior notice to, the debtor. The court order must be served on the debtor by a bailiff.

Courts will generally refuse interim orders and arrests if issuing such an order would mean that it will be impossible for the debtor to establish a position in subsequent regular proceedings. Therefore, if the creditor seeks to repossess goods, the petition necessarily must ask for a court order to hand over the goods to a third person, usually a bailiff.

Non-compliance with the court order by the debtor will usually result in fines (up to DM 500,000) or jail (up to six months).

## 9.5   The court system

Unless otherwise stipulated in the agreement between the parties or contained in the general conditions of one of the parties, all court proceedings must be brought before the competent courts at the place of residence of the debtor or the registered office of a legal entity. Some exceptions apply, eg for actions based on torts, which may always be initiated within the venue where the tort has happened.

There are two courts which may hear civil claims, the Municipal Court (*Amtsgericht*) and the District Court (*Landgericht*). Municipal courts will always have jurisdiction if the amount at stake does not exceed DM 10,000. Should the claim be higher, then action must be taken in the District Court.

Depending on the entry court the next higher level will exercise the functions of a court of appeal. However, claims not exceeding DM 1,500 cannot be appealed. Any decision on a claim higher than DM 1,500 may be appealed to the District Court, and all decisions of the District Courts may be appealed to the Court of Appeal in the respective state. Within the District Courts special chambers have been established in order to settle claims between businesses.

Claims brought before the Municipal Courts will always be handled by a single judge. Claims filed with the District Court may be handled by a full chamber of three judges (qualified lawyers), by one of these designated judges or, in the case of disputes between businesses, by one judge assisted by two laymen.

Cases that were first decided by the District Court and then by the Court of Appeal may be brought before the Federal Civil Court. This court will not decide on the facts but only on legal issues. The Federal Civil Court will only consider cases if either the Court of Appeal has decided that the matter is of material legal interest and has allowed the plaintiff to present the case to the Federal Civil Court or if the value of the dispute does exceed DM 60,000. Also, the Court of Appeal will admit the further appeal if the Court of Appeal itself has rendered a decision which is not in line with a decision of the Federal Civil Court.

Foreign creditors are not at any disadvantage compared to German creditors. They (in case of the Municipal Courts) and their legal representatives (in all other cases) have full standing before German courts. They may call on and instruct bailiffs to enforce their legal titles.

## 9.6   Legal representation

### 9.6.1   Nature of legal representation

No restrictions apply to legal proceedings commenced in Municipal Courts. Individuals and legal entities are fully authorised to act on their own behalf or to represent that legal entity and/or partnerships. They may also issue powers of attorney to any other person, so long as such person has reached legal majority.

Private persons may use the services of the Municipal Court and orally dictate to court stenographers their claims and motions. In simple cases private persons will act on their own behalf and thus avoid attorney's fees.

All legal proceedings before the District Court and any other higher court, including all motions and actions before those courts, must be filed by attorneys admitted to the respective bar. Attorneys may practise only in one bar district, which coincides with the court district. Thus, an attorney can be admitted to only one District Court. However, every attorney is allowed to act before any Municipal Court in Germany.

### 9.6.2 Mode of payment for legal representation

#### 9.6.2.1 Application of fixed tariff

German law provides a fixed tariff which sets out in different schedules the fees that attorneys and courts will collect. Court fees are lower than attorney's fees.

The fees that an attorney will collect depend on the value of the claim and the course of the legal proceedings. In normal legal proceedings, the attorney will be entitled to collect two fees. If, for example, the creditor asked for payment of DM 100,000 by the debtor, the applicable tariff awards the attorney a fee of DM 2,125, plus value added tax (VAT).

For any proceedings filed in court and ending with a judgment by the court, the attorney will be entitled to claim two times DM 2,125 (exceptions apply for unilateral injunctions). Should the court rule that evidence must be taken, the attorney will be entitled to a further fee of DM 2,125. Another fee of DM 2,125 will be due if the proceedings are terminated by a settlement agreement between the parties. Individual agreements deviating from the tariff are allowed (see below).

#### 9.6.2.2 Contractual agreement for costs

In recent years, it has become more common to stipulate fixed fees for legal representation or to have attorneys work on an hourly basis. Both would be allowed under German law but such arrangements require clear and precise rules of agreement.

#### 9.6.2.3 Contingency fee basis

German law, ie, the Ethics Code for attorneys, does not allow contingency fee agreements.

#### 9.6.2.4 Liability of other party

Generally, the losing party will have to pay all legal costs involved including court fees and the fees of the attorney of the winning party.

*9.6.2.5  Deduction of value added tax*

Attorneys issue invoices to their clients adding to any fees VAT in the amount of 15 per cent. However, if the client resides outside Germany or has its registered office outside Germany, invoices will be zero-rated for VAT.

## 9.7  Costs and interest

### 9.7.1  Current fees

Reference to the German statutory tariff has been made above. This tariff will provide the applicable fees for any given amount. A single attorney's fee for a claim having a value of DM 5 million would amount to DM 18,225. The law provides that any claim in excess of DM 5 million will generate a fee of DM 300 per DM 100,000. Therefore, every DM 1 million in value beyond DM 5 million will trigger another DM 3,000 in attorney's fees.

In legal activities preceding court action attorneys may ask for, from a quarter of a fee, up to two full fees, depending on the complexity of the case and on whether the attorney would have to negotiate with the debtor or simply send out a letter claiming money. There is great discretion for the attorney and, within a given range, the fee basis may be negotiated.

Court fees are generally lower than attorney's fees. In a normal action before the District Court, a claim having a value of, eg, DM 100,000 will cost three court fees, each amounting to DM 955, or of a value of DM 5 million, each amounting to DM 17,905.

### 9.7.2  Availability of legal aid

Creditors and debtors may file petitions seeking legal aid with the court where proceedings are pending or even before proceedings begin.

Under the current system, the approval of legal aid releases the party from making down payments for court fees and would include the party's attorney's fees. However, legal aid is granted generally only on a loan basis and must be repaid in up to 48 instalments.

The decision to grant legal aid rests solely with the court having jurisdiction. The court will approve the application if it appears the plaintiff or defendant applicant will be successful.

Any party seeking legal aid must demonstrate that it is not, or only partly, able to pay its own legal costs. Again, there is a statutory tariff, setting out the net monthly income limit in order to be considered in need of legal aid.

National legal entities may be granted legal aid under exceptional rules, ie, if they can demonstrate that if they were not allowed to present their case this would run counter to the common (public) interest. Foreign legal entities are excluded from legal aid.

### 9.7.3  Liability for and recovery of costs

The general concept is that the losing party must bear all costs. That includes court and attorney's fees, both based on the statutory tariffs, but never on individual agreements, as well as costs of witnesses and experts. If a party is partly successful, costs must be borne in proportion to the amount won. The court sentence will always include a precise declaration regarding the costs to be borne by either party.

After obtaining a judgment which allows a party to claim part or all of its costs from its opponent, a motion must be filed with the court register, seeking a legal title which will fix the exact amount of money to be collected from the opponent. This legal title can be served on the opposing party and enforced in exactly the same way as any judgment or other legal title.

### 9.7.4   Interest

Once the debtor has defaulted, interest will accrue on the outstanding debt. In the absence of a written agreement between the parties, a law provides for an interest rate of 4 or 5 per cent. In court action, creditors may also claim that they have incurred a higher interest rate versus their own lender and thus be entitled to collect their respective interest from the debtor. Alternatively, creditors may claim that they would have invested the monies due to them at a certain interest rate. If found to be correct, the court will award such an interest rate in addition to the principal sum.

## 9.8   Issuing proceedings

After a lawsuit seeking payment has been filed, the court will serve a copy of the suit to the debtor respectively – in case of legal entities – to the legal representatives. Normally the court will also require the debtor (defendant) to formally declare within a short period of time (2–4 weeks) whether the defendant will actually raise objections against the suit. The court may order the defendant to furnish any and all objections that may be raised against the suit and present any evidence available within another period of several weeks. If the defendant meets the deadlines, the court will hold an oral (public) hearing during which the parties or, if necessary, their attorneys will present their motions. Depending on the complexity of a law suit, proceedings may last in one court instance anywhere between 6 months up to several years. However, for a lawsuit, concerning the collection of debt, which has been properly prepared, legal proceedings, in order to obtain an enforceable title, should normally not take more than one year. The time-frame may also depend on individual courts in the various districts.

## 9.9   Procedure to judgment

### 9.9.1   The debtor pays the debt

In this case, the creditor must lodge a declaration with the court that the claim has been settled and ask the court to render a judgment stating who will bear the costs. If the debtor was in default, the court will render a judgment in favour of the creditor.

### 9.9.2 The debtor admits the debt

The creditor must bring a motion seeking a judgment by consent, imposing responsibility for costs on the debtor.

### 9.9.3 The debtor disputes the debt

The creditor must produce all necessary documents and proper evidence to demonstrate that the debtor owes money. The court will decide on the basis of such evidence and, in addition, may hear witnesses and collect other evidence which has been offered by the creditor. Depending on the quality and credibility of the evidence, the court will render a judgment.

### 9.9.4 The debtor disputes part of the debt

If a large amount of money is at stake and part of it is undisputed while the rest may require lengthy proceedings gathering evidence, the court may render a partial judgment in favour of the creditor on the undisputed part of the debt. The creditor also may be awarded a favourable judgment, at least with respect to an undisputed part of a lawsuit, if the claim of the creditor is based on more than one factual situation.

### 9.9.5 The debtor neither admits nor disputes the debt

If the debtor does not dispute the debt and the facts presented by the creditor are conclusive, the court will decide in favour of the creditor. If the debtor does not appear in court or is not represented, judgment in default will be ordered.

### 9.9.6 The debtor is declared insolvent

If, during collection proceedings the creditor becomes aware that the debtor is insolvent, the creditor may petition the appropriate Municipal Court to commence bankruptcy proceedings. If awarded a favourable judgment within the debt collection proceedings, the creditor presents the legal title to the debtor's trustee in bankruptcy. If there is money to be paid out, the creditor will be compensated according to the quota.

## 9.10 Enforcing judgment

### 9.10.1 Execution

If the debtor does not pay within seven days after legal title has been served on him, the creditor may instruct the competent bailiff to enforce the judgment.

The bailiff will attend at the place of residence or business of the debtor and ask for payment. If no liquid funds are available, the bailiff will seize assets by attaching a seal to movable property.

All movable property seized may be auctioned to the general public according to procedures established in the Civil Procedure Code. After deduction of costs of the auction, the surplus will go to the creditor and any remaining monies will be repaid to the debtor.

### 9.10.2   Charging order

If the debtor owns immovable property, the creditor may ask the court where the land or house is registered with the land register to issue a charging order (forced mortgage). This order will be registered immediately in the land register and, thus, prevent the debtor from disposing of the property or otherwise obtaining personal mortgages preferential to those of the creditor.

Once the charging order on the property has been registered, it is at the creditor's discretion whether to force its sale or to continue to demand payment from the debtor.

Depending on the nature of the property and the amount already secured by mortgages on it, a charging order on immovable property can be a powerful means of securing the debt. No general information is available regarding ownership from what is provided in the land register maintained by the court. Notary publics are authorised to examine the land registers. However, the registers are far too voluminous to be searched generally for assets of a specific debtor.

### 9.10.3   Garnishee and attachment of earnings

The creditor may file a motion with the court which made the judgment to issue a garnishee order, which may then be served on any known debtor of the debtor or, in the case of expected earnings, the debtor's employer. Once the order is properly served, any further payment by the third party debtor will not indemnify them vis-à-vis the creditor who obtained the garnishee order. The garnishee must pay the creditor.

For earnings, a tariff exists, setting out that minimum wages for personal needs of the debtor will be barred from being confiscated in favour of the creditor.

### 9.10.4   Oral examination

If the debtor is an individual and does not have any obvious monetary funds or movable or immovable property, then the creditor may file a motion requiring the debtor to appear before court and declare that he does not have any assets or sufficient income. The order to appear before court may be enforced by personal arrest.

Once the debtor has sworn by affidavit that he does not possess money or assets, the debtor may be exposed to criminal prosecution if any of his

statements are found to be incorrect. The debtor may object to the requirement to declare and disclose his financial status. The court will decide whether
to reject or uphold the objection. If the motion is rejected, the debtor who
refuses to declare will be arrested.

### 9.10.5 Insolvency

If the debtor is not an individual but a legal entity, or at least a partnership
consisting of a general and a limited partner, then normal insolvency proceedings may be initiated on the creditor's request (see below).

## 9.11 Insolvency

### 9.11.1 Winding up limited companies

Limited companies will generally have only a fixed liability (in the case of a
limited liability company or GmbH, DM 50,000 or more; in the case of a stock
corporation or AG, DM 100,000 or more) which may serve as a basis to repay
any debts. If a limited company is found to be in a state of over-indebtedness
or in a position where it cannot meet due payments, then its managing director
must file for bankruptcy with the Municipal Court of Registration.

The judge will consider the facts presented and appoint a preliminary
receiver or a trustee to present an expert opinion on whether there are
sufficient funds to meet the costs of the bankruptcy proceedings and examine
whether a quota may be fixed and later paid out to the creditors.

Most bankruptcy proceedings do not actually go to the next stage, but
simply end with the expert opinion, since most limited companies are found
not to have funds to cover even the costs of the proceedings. Thus, most
bankruptcy proceedings will not be formally commenced. However, if bankruptcy proceedings are formally begun by the court and a trustee is appointed,
then the trustee will have all necessary powers to act on behalf of the company
and dispose of assets or sue other parties in order to collect outstanding debts.

If bankruptcy proceedings have been commenced, then any creditor must
present his claim to the trustee in written form, frequently having to meet
deadlines that are published in the relevant gazettes. If there are assets
available, the creditor may obtain a decision in the form of a quota in which
the trustee will indicate what percentage of claims will be met.

Certain creditors, such as the Internal Revenue, social security insurance
and similar institutions have preferential rights. In addition, certain assets
may have been pledged or transferred as security to banks and other similar
creditors and will not be available to unsecured creditors. Often normal trade
creditors will find themselves among the unsecured creditors being granted a
low dividend or learning that there will not be a dividend.

### 9.11.2 Bankruptcy of individuals

Individuals may be declared bankrupt under similar terms and conditions as
limited companies. However, bankruptcy proceedings against an individual

will be considered only if the individual has substantial business interests and business relationships. Otherwise an individual need only swear by affidavit that he does not possess sufficient funds and assets.

### 9.11.3 Insolvency of partnerships and proprietors

Regular partnerships registered with the trade register and composed of at least one limited and one general partner may be subject to insolvency proceedings in the same way as limited companies. German law does allow partnerships that are composed of a limited partner and a general partner which is a limited liability company (GmbH & Co KG). Such a corporate entity may enjoy tax privileges while none of its partners is exposed to full liability.

Even though concepts such as piercing the corporate veil and unlimited liability because of insufficient capitalisation exist, it is extremely difficult to successfully collect outstanding debts in court based on those concepts. More often than not an insolvent partnership will not have full liability or sufficient funds to meet creditor's claims.

Builders and property developers often act under a common umbrella in the name of an entity or partnership in civil law (*Gesellschaft bürgerlichen Rechts*, GbR). This concept is used especially in site development and for properties where more than one person owns a specific site, mostly for tax purposes. Such partnerships cannot be declared insolvent and cannot be part of any bankruptcy proceedings. If the creditor has a valid claim against such a partnership, all of its partners may be individually and without limitation held liable for any of the debts of the partnership.

## 9.12 Conclusion

The range of legal measures and procedures to obtain title and enforce debt collection in Germany is comprehensive. The fact that, in court proceedings, the losing party must bear all costs, including those of its opponent, encourages the initiation of formal procedures before court.

However, in stark contrast to the availability of legal means, the reality of insufficient funds or assets poses a severe problem for creditors seeking to collect a debt. In numerous cases, debtors escape payment by hiding behind the impenetrable walls of limited companies. No solution is in sight to change this ongoing tendency.

The lesson to be learned is to secure payment through proper mechanisms, employ retention of title and to ask for collateral security if the title to goods sold must be passed over and payment has not yet been collected.

*Chapter 10*

# GREECE

**Nicolas Anagnostopoulos**
**Lallis Voutsinos Anagnostopoulos**
**Piraeus, Greece**

## 10.1   Introduction

This chapter deals with debt collection actions taken in Greece. The legal system in Greece is highly and extensively codified, and it has been greatly influenced by German and French law. Successful attempts are being made so that the procedures relating both to obtaining a final judgment and to its enforcement result in a simple and speedy recovery exercise.

## 10.2   Initial considerations

### 10.2.1   Status of the debtor

Should the need arise to take court action to recover money, then the need to establish the status of the debtor is of paramount importance. To avoid defects in the court action, which may entail additional costs and delay and, in some instances, elimination of the prospects of recovery, the status of the debtor must be clearly and unambiguously described in the writ. This should also contain a full description of the debtor's name and address, so that the writ may be properly served. The various legal entities, which may be pursued in the Greek courts, are summarised as follows:

(1) an individual, who may either trade in his own name or use a trading name;
(2) a general partnership (*societe en nom collectif* or OE), in which the partners have unlimited, joint and several personal liability;
(3) a limited partnership (*societe en commandite* or EE), which is a general partnership with one or more partners being liable only to the extent of their contribution;[1]
(4) a silent partnership (*societe en participation*), which is an extremely rare type of entity;
(5) a limited liability company (*societe a responsabilite limitee* or EPE or LTD);[2]
(6) a joint stock, limited liability company (*societe anonyme*, AE or SA);[3]

---

1 General and limited partnerships are often used as corporate vehicles for small businesses.
2 This type of company is very often used for medium businesses.
3 This type of company is used for most business enterprises of some substance.

(7) a society, which is a non-profit union of at least 20 individuals;

(8) an institution, which is a body corporate having certain assets for serving a specific purpose;

(9) a maritime limited liability company (NE), usually used as the owner of small and medium Greek-flag vessels; and

(10) a partnership which owns and commercially exploits a vessel (*societe navalis*).[1]

When an individual debtor dies, then a claim may be pursued against his heirs, unless, of course, the heirs deny the inheritance.

### 10.2.2   Sources of information

If a debtor needs to be traced, then various searches may be made. In respect of general partnerships, limited partnerships, limited liability companies and societies reliable and updated information may be obtained from the relevant Registries maintained in the competent High Court. In respect of a *societe anonyme* or an institution, information may be obtained from the Registry maintained in the competent Prefecture. In respect of maritime companies, information may be obtained from the relevant Registry maintained in Piraeus.

Information may also be obtained, of course, from the telephone and trade directories and Chambers of Commerce and from data banks at a fee. In respect of the bankruptcy of individual merchants or corporations, information may be obtained from the relevant Registry maintained in the competent High Court.

### 10.2.3   Is the debt statute-barred?

Greek law does not provide for a single time-limit applicable to all recovery cases. The limitation period depends on the nature of the claim to be pursued. There is a general provision in Greek law, stating that, 'unless otherwise provided, the claims are subject to a 20-year time-limit'. However, the exceptions are so extensive that specific advice should be sought from a lawyer in respect to the limitation period applicable in each particular case. It may be said that certain recovery claims are subject to a five-year time-limit and others to a two-year or a one-year time-limit (such as maritime claims). The time-limit commences from the time the money becomes due and the debt could be pursued by court action.

### 10.2.4   Security

A creditor may have been provided with security by his debtor for further protection in the contract. Security may take various forms, the most usual being:

---

1 This is a rare and old-fashioned type of ownership and use of vessels.

(1) the registration of a charging order on land or property of the debtor or a third party, known as prenotation of hypothec;[1]
(2) bills of exchange or post-dated cheques; and
(3) guarantees.

If the creditor holds security, then (subject, of course, to any agreement to the contrary) he may be able either to pursue the debtor for recovery or to enforce the security provided. In the case of a charging order, auction proceedings may be instituted against the land or property. In the case of protested bills of exchange or unpaid cheques, summary judgment may be quickly obtained against the defendant (with dishonoured cheques there are also criminal implications). With guarantees the guarantor is normally equally answerable to the creditor as the principal debtor, if the principal debtor ignores the demand for payment.

## 10.3 Letters before action

### 10.3.1 Are they necessary?

It is not compulsory under law for a letter to be sent to the debtor before the issue of proceedings. However, the sending of a letter to the debtor before action is taken may be advisable for two reasons:

(1) receipt of a letter may sometimes produce payment or cause the debtor to put forward proposals for the settlement of the dispute; and
(2) once the debtor has been notified about the claim and has been asked to settle it, then interest starts running and, therefore, if proceedings follow, interest will be awarded from the time of notification and not from the issue of proceedings.

### 10.3.2 Contents and mode of service

Whether or not a letter should be sent by a lawyer depends on the peculiarities of the particular case. The involvement of a law firm, of course, is indicative that the claim is approaching a legal recovery process and this may sometimes be taken into serious consideration by the debtor. The exact wording of a letter depends on many factors. However, it is advisable that such letters should be clear and concise without legalisms and should include the following:

(1) correct details of the debtor and the creditor;
(2) date of the letter;
(3) a clear and brief description of the dispute or claim;
(4) the amount due; and

---

1 Such registration may be made with the consent of the debtor or of a third party, and it provides security similar to the mortgage.

(5)    a clear demand for payment within a specified period of time, with the threat that unless payment is made as requested, legal proceedings will follow.

The demand may be sent either by post, telefax or telex. If the creditor wishes to be absolutely certain that the debtor will not dispute receipt of the message, then a letter may be sent through a court bailiff, in which case the bailiff's report is conclusive evidence of service of the letter.

## 10.4    Pre-action remedies and security

### 10.4.1    In general

It is most important for a creditor, before embarking on the main court proceedings, to obtain security for his claim to be able to enforce a judgment on the merits of the case. Therefore, a creditor frequently applies to the court requesting security (interim relief) for his claim. For a creditor to apply to the Greek courts for security for his claim, he must satisfy two basic requirements:

(1)    he must establish an arguable case on the merits; and
(2)    he must show that there is an imminent risk that his claim may not be satisfied or an urgent need justifying the granting of the interim relief requested.

The application for interim relief is heard by the court in a very short period of time (one to five days), and the hearing takes place with notice being given to the debtor. In some exceptional cases, the court may provide interim relief without notice to the debtor. The courts deliver their orders for interim relief shortly after the hearing, and these orders are immediately enforceable. Greek law provides for seven specific security measures, which may provide interim relief in respect to the claim of the creditor, and these are the following:

(1)    conservative attachment;
(2)    charging order on land or property, known as prenotation of hypothec;
(3)    judicial sequestration;
(4)    lodging of guarantee;
(5)    provisional regulation of a transaction or relationship;
(6)    provisional adjudication of a debt; and
(7)    seal, unseal, inventory or public deposit.

In respect to the security of a claim of a pecuniary nature (debt collection), the creditor normally seeks from the court the measure of conservative attachment of the debtor's property or the prenotation of hypothec of the debtor's immovable property. These two security measures provide good security to a creditor for the eventual satisfaction of the judgment to be issued on the merits.

### 10.4.2 Conservative attachment

A conservative attachment aims at the 'preservation' of the attached property until the issue of final judgment in the main proceedings. Once the conservative attachment is effected on any assets of the debtor, he is deprived of the administration of these assets and he is further prohibited from disposing of the attached property. Particular mention should be made regarding the attachment (freezing) of bank accounts. According to the established view of the Greek judiciary, the attachment of bank accounts maintained in any Greek or foreign bank organisation in Greece is not possible.

### 10.4.3 Prenotation of hypothec

Prenotation of hypothec is a legal charge registered on an immovable property of the debtor, and it provides security to the creditor in the sense that the charge attaches to the property and the creditor enjoys a preferential right in the charged property as a mortgagee. If a creditor seeks security for his claim and it is found that his debtor owns land or property, then the prenotation of hypothec provides a very good security.

It should be noted that the debtor has the right, at any time, to defeat an application for interim relief or to lift any measure already ordered and/or attached on his property, by providing a bank guarantee to his creditor. As will be appreciated, the issue of obtaining security for a claim is equally as important as obtaining a favourable judgment on the main action. A solicitor should be in a position to advise which would be the more appropriate action in the circumstances.

## 10.5 The court system

### 10.5.1 Structure of the courts

There are three types of civil courts in which proceedings can be brought for recovery of debts, namely magistrate's courts, one-member High Courts, and three-member High Courts.

#### 10.5.1.1 *Magistrates' courts*

Magistrates' courts are divided among approximately 300 districts throughout Greece and they are competent to hear cases in which the amount claimed is up to Drs 600.000.

#### 10.5.1.2 *High Courts of first instance*

There are 63 High Courts in Greece, in jurisdictional areas which roughly coincide with the boundaries of the respective Prefectures within Greece. The High Courts hear civil cases either as one-member High Courts or three-member High Courts.

The one-member High Courts are able to hear cases in which the amount claimed is from Drs 600.001 to Drs 5 million. The three-member High Courts are able to hear all cases in which the amount claimed is more than Drs 5 million.

Greek judges are professional judges who, having first obtained a lawyer's licence from the competent Bar, pass special examinations and are admitted as judges. There is no jury or other lay element in the Greek civil courts.

### 10.5.2 Appeals

All judgments rendered by the magistrates' courts (with few exceptions) and the High Courts of first instance (sitting either as one-member or three-member courts) are subject to appeal. In other words, the right of appeal is not left to the discretion of the court. Appeals filed against judgments of the magistrates' courts are heard by the three-member High Courts, which sit, for this purpose only, as appeal courts.

Appeals filed against judgments issued by the High Courts of first instance (either a one-member or a three-member court) are heard by the Court of Appeal. There are twelve Courts of Appeal in Greece, and they sit in the largest cities of the country and hear appeals against the judgments of the High Courts. The Courts of Appeal always sit in panels of three judges.

Apart from the High Courts and the appellate courts, there is also the Supreme Court (*Cour de Cassation*). The Supreme Court is competent to hear applications filed against the decisions of the Courts of Appeal, but its jurisdiction is strictly confined to examining legal errors of appellate court judgments and not findings of fact which cannot be re-examined and reversed.

### 10.5.3 Status of a foreign creditor

It is a basic provision of the Greek Constitution that 'foreigners enjoy the same civil rights as the Greek citizens do'. Therefore, a foreign creditor may apply to the Greek courts and institute debt recovery proceedings, or request interim relief for his claim, in the same way as a Greek national.

## 10.6 Legal representation

### 10.6.1 Nature of legal representation

Any individual or body corporate wishing to apply to the Greek courts should instruct a lawyer to appear before the court. The parties are not allowed to represent themselves in the courts except in two instances, namely in proceedings before the magistrates' courts and when interim relief is requested in security-measures proceedings. In all other cases, a lawyer should be instructed. If the party is not represented by a lawyer, then the action taken is inadmissible.

It should be noted, in this respect, that self-representation sometimes may be more expensive than instructing a lawyer and, more important, may be prejudicial, given the unfamiliarity with the law provisions and the court procedures.

### 10.6.2 Mode of payment for legal representation

The party who instructs a lawyer is responsible for the payment of his fees, including any expenses, which have been incurred in the conduct of the action. Normally, the costs of legal representation should be discussed and agreed between the client and the lawyer in advance. The basis for the payment of the costs may be one of the following:

(1)  the charge may be based on an hourly rate;
(2)  the charge may be agreed on a fixed-fee basis; or
(3)  the charge may be agreed on a contingency fee basis.[1]

## 10.7 Costs and interest

### 10.7.1 Costs

For pursuing a recovery action in Greece, the following amounts should be paid:

(1)  an amount of Drs 10,000 to Drs 20,000 for filing the writ of action with the court and for serving the proceedings on the opponent;
(2)  at the hearing date, approximately one per cent of the amount claimed (comprising the capital and interest calculated up to the hearing date) as stamp duty and approximately Drs 20,000 for petty expenses;
(3)  if case witness examination follows the hearing of the case, Drs 50,000 to Drs 70,000 as additional costs;
(4)  once a final judgment is issued, then for obtaining an enforceable copy of the final judgment, two per cent on the capital awarded, plus interest, and, in respect of unpaid invoices, only two per cent of the interest;
(5)  if an appeal is filed, Drs 40,000 to Drs 60,000 for various expenses in respect to the appeal proceedings; and
(6)  if the matter is taken to the Supreme Court, a further amount of Drs 40,000 to Drs 60,000.

The above amounts do not include the lawyers' fees and expenses.

### 10.7.2 Legal aid

Only individuals and companies of unlimited liability may qualify for legal aid. The court which will try the case also decides the legal aid issue. The two basic requirements which are considered by the court are:

(1)  the severe financial hardship of the applicant; and
(2)  the merits of the claim.

A party who has qualified for legal aid is released from the obligation to pay

---

1 According to the Code on Legal Profession, the relevant contingency rate should not exceed 20 per cent of the amount recovered.

legal costs, including his lawyer's fees. The issue of legal aid may be reviewed once it appears that there has been a change in the conditions on the basis of which legal aid was provided. Given that legal costs in Greece are not very high and that the conditions and procedure for providing legal aid are not simple, legal aid is only exceptionally sought by the parties.

### 10.7.3  Liability for and recovery of costs

Primarily, the obligation for payment of costs rests with the party who instructs his lawyer. However, the issue as to which party will ultimately bear the legal costs of the proceedings is decided by the final judgment on the basis of the so-called 'defeat principle', which provides that the losing party pays the legal costs of the winning party.

If the debtor has not caused the institution of the proceedings and, once the proceedings were commenced, the debtor admitted the claim, then the legal costs are borne by the creditor. If the proceedings are partially successful, it might be decided that each party bears his own costs. If the losing party had reasonable doubts regarding the outcome of the case, then the court may reduce the costs of the winning party, payable by the losing party, or it may order that each party bears his own costs.

### 10.7.4  Interest

Interest is recoverable only if it has been claimed. Interest in respect of commercial debts between merchants runs from the agreed due date for the debt. In all other cases, to start interest running the debtor should be notified about the claim, with a request to pay it. Such notification is made either by a letter before action or by service of the writ.

## 10.8  Issuing proceedings

The plaintiff's solicitor prepares a writ, which should contain full particulars of the litigants, a detailed description of the facts of the claim, and the amount claimed including interest. The writ is filed with the Registrar of the appropriate court (magistrates' court, one-member or three-member High Court) and is registered in the appropriate court lists.

When the writ is filed, the hearing date is fixed. Next, through a court bailiff, the plaintiff serves on the defendant an official copy of the writ. Service should be effected at least 30 days prior to the hearing date. The proceedings are considered as having been instituted from the date they were filed with the court, provided service followed.

## 10.9  Procedure to judgment

If the debtor pays the debt in full after the issue of proceedings, then the matter is concluded, and a formal writ of discontinuance is filed with the court before which the proceedings have been pending. If part of the debt was paid or payment did not include interest and costs, the proceedings may be pursued for the unrecovered part of the debt. If the debt is not paid, then the procedure to judgment may be outlined as follows.

### 10.9.1   Procedure before the magistrates' court

At the hearing date, the parties enter an appearance before the court and submit their points of claim and defence respectively, along with available supporting documents. In addition, at the hearing, the parties produce their witnesses, who are examined-in-chief and cross-examined. Three working days after the hearing the parties must file with the court further submissions referring mainly to the oral hearing. Within approximately two to four months judgment is issued. It is subject to appeal to the three-member High Court.

### 10.9.2   Attempt for an out of Court settlement

It is a condition precedent that for recovery actions to be heard before the one-member and three-member High Court, the litigants must first attempt to find an out of Court settlement of the case. The hearing of the action can only take place if the attempt for an out of Court settlement has failed.

### 10.9.3   Procedure before the one-member High Court

The litigants should file with the court their respective points of claim and defence three working days prior to the hearing date and their relevant replies to the points of claim and defence one day before. At the hearing, the parties produce their witnesses, who are examined-in-chief and cross-examined. Three working days after the hearing date the parties may file with the court a memorandum commenting on the witnesses' evidence. The judgment is issued in two to four months and is subject to appeal to the Court of Appeal.

### 10.9.4   Procedure before the three-member High Court

When a writ is filed with the three-member High Court, the judge decides in chambers whether such a writ may be tried in accordance with the rules applicable to the writs filed before the one-member High Court described above. This normally applies if the claim appears to be straightforward and the witnesses are not likely to add much to the case. If the judge does not decide to follow the rules of procedure of the one-member High Court, then the procedure is as follows.

On the hearing date, the parties enter an appearance before the court and submit their respective points of claim and defence, together with available supporting documents. A reply to these points must be submitted to the court three working days after the hearing date. In two to four months, the court issues a preliminary judgment, directing the parties to prove the disputed issues by examination of witnesses. Once examination of the witnesses is concluded, the court confers again and issues its final judgment, which is subject to appeal.

### 10.9.5   Admission or denial of the claim

The above procedures are followed irrespective of whether the claim is admitted or denied. However, where a claim is admitted the court will not call for further evidence and will proceed to issue judgment.

### 10.9.6   Summary procedure in special cases

In respect of unpaid cheques, bills of exchange or other negotiable instruments and, in certain instances, of unpaid invoices where the amount due and the legal basis is sufficiently proved by the document itself, a plaintiff may apply to the court for the issue of a payment order. This is provided by the court ex parte and is fully enforceable against the debtor's assets. The time taken to obtain this order is one to two weeks. However, the debtor is entitled to file opposition to the payment order and to ask for a stay of execution of the order pending judgment on his opposition.

### 10.9.7   The debtor is declared insolvent

Where the debtor, either an individual or a company, is declared bankrupt, court proceedings cannot be pursued against the debtor. Instead, the plaintiff should participate in the bankruptcy proceedings to recover his claim. If bankruptcy is ordered during recovery proceedings, these are automatically suspended, and the plaintiff should also participate in the bankruptcy proceedings to effect recovery.

If a company is put into liquidation following a decision of the partners or shareholders of the company, then a creditor may pursue his claim against the company which, in this case, is represented by the liquidator(s).

If the company is put into 'compulsory administration' and an administrator is appointed, then the creditor should submit his claim to the administrator for satisfaction. Every three months the administrator is obliged to draw up a list for the distribution of the company's income to the creditors. In the event of disputes, the creditor may apply to the court for correction of the list.

## 10.10   Enforcing judgment

Once a judgment is obtained, then it may be executed in any of the following ways, as provided for by Greek Procedure Law.

### 10.10.1  Execution on chattels

The plaintiff/creditor obtains an enforceable copy of the judgment. A copy of it, with relevant written instructions, are given to a court bailiff, who is the appropriate person to execute court judgments.

The court bailiff proceeds to the place where the chattels are situated, removes them from the possession of the debtor and hands them over to a third party, called a trustee. At the same time the court bailiff draws up a report in which he enters a full description of the seized chattels, an estimate of their value, notes the date and place of the auction which shall follow, the amount of the first bid and other relevant information. A copy of the bailiff's report is served on the debtor and the magistrates' court in which the execution took place.

If the goods have already been executed, then the law does not permit a second execution. In such a case the plaintiff should attend and participate in the auction proceedings which follow the first execution. If there is a delay in the auction proceedings by the first seizing creditor, then a second creditor may enforce the auction proceedings.

The seized chattels should be auctioned in public within 15 days from the date of their execution. The public auction takes place before a notary public who is in charge of the auction. For a debtor to release his goods from seizure and, thus, avoid the auction, he must pay the full amount claimed, plus the execution costs. However, it is possible for the creditor and the debtor to ask for an adjournment of the auction, pending settlement of the claim.

### 10.10.2  Execution on land, property, vessels and aircraft

Like the execution on chattels, the court bailiff is provided with a copy of the enforceable judgment and written instructions to proceed to execute the judgment.

Next, the bailiff visits the property, vessel or aircraft and drafts a report in which the same particulars are entered as in the execution on chattels. A copy of the report is served on the debtor as well as on the appropriate Estate Registry (or Ships or Aircraft Registry). The possessor of the property at the time the execution was made is appointed as trustee of the seized property.

No execution may be made on these assets if already seized by another creditor. As with chattels, the new creditor should attend and participate in the auction proceedings to recover his claim and, in case of delay, the second creditor may enforce the auction proceedings.

The seized property should be publicly auctioned within 40 days after the seizure was made. The debtor is entitled to ask the court to adjourn the auction for up to six months (three months for vessels) if he can show to the court that he may pay the debt or that higher auction proceeds may be realised within the period of the adjournment. The court may grant such an adjournment under conditions, normally that the debtor, in the meantime, must satisfy part of the debt.

### 10.10.3   Execution on a third party (garnishee)

The law provides that a plaintiff may execute the judgment on chattels which belong to the defendant but which are in the possession of a third party or on claims of the defendant against third parties. The relevant procedure is as follows.

The plaintiff serves on the garnishee a document containing details of the judgment issued and a request to him not to deliver the goods or pay the claim to the defendant. A copy of this document also is served on the defendant. Once the garnishee is served with the document, he becomes a trustee of the goods or the money. Within eight days from service of the document the garnishee has a duty to make a 'declaration' to the magistrates' court of his residence stating clearly whether he possesses the goods or owes the debt to the defendant and whether other attachment has been effected.

A garnishee responding positively must deliver the goods or pay the money to the plaintiff. Where there is a 'negative declaration' or a failure to declare by the garnishee, the matter comes to an end. However, the plaintiff has the right to dispute the negative, absent or untrue declaration of the garnishee and may also have a claim for damages against him in tort. Provided that relevant information is available to the plaintiff, the garnishee procedure provides a very useful enforcement weapon.

### 10.10.4   Compulsory administration

One of the means of enforcement of civil judgments is the compulsory administration of a business or property of the debtor. A plaintiff who has obtained a final judgment may apply to the court to put his debtor's property or business into compulsory administration. The court considers the circumstances of the particular case (the extent of the claim, the value of the business or property and possible prejudice to the business operation) and delivers its judgment.

The administrator is appointed by the court. The administrator conducts the affairs of the enterprise with a view to distributing the profits to the plaintiff, having first paid the obligations of the business or property. If there is more than one creditor, the administrator issues every three months a list of payments to the creditors who have announced their claims to him. The administration is terminated if all the creditors' claims have been satisfied or where the court, on re-examining the case, decides that the administration procedure is no longer advisable.

### 10.10.5   Personal detainment of the debtor

Greek law provides that one of the means of enforcement of civil judgments against individuals is the personal detainment of the debtor. The following conditions should be satisfied before the court orders the personal detainment of a debtor:

(1)  the debtor must be in business;
(2)  the claim should be of a commercial nature;
(3)  the debtor must not be over 65 years of age; and
(4)  a final judgment must have been issued on the merits of the case.

The period of personal detainment is up to 12 months. Although personal detainment is criticised by commentators as a means of enforcement which violates the Greek Constitution, it is a very useful weapon in the practitioner's armoury. A debtor threatened by personal detainment often settle the claim or come to terms with the creditors.

### 10.10.6  Oral examination

Greek law provides that a creditor who has obtained an enforceable judgment may request that the debtor appear at court to give evidence on oath regarding his assets (property, other assets and claims against third parties). If the debtor fails to appear or refuses to take the oath, then he is guilty of contempt and an application for his committal to prison may be made. Oral examination is sometimes useful because the creditor may obtain information for an alternative enforcement action. However, in most cases, the procedure is not a rewarding court exercise.

## 10.11   Insolvency

### 10.11.1  In general

Bankruptcy proceedings may be instituted against a merchant, whether an individual or a body corporate, provided he has suspended his payments generally and permanently.

Bankruptcy proceedings aim at the liquidation of the property of a merchant and its distribution to the various creditors for settlement of their claims. However, practitioners often use bankruptcy proceedings in order to induce payment of the debt. The debtor, under the threat of being declared bankrupt, may settle the claim or otherwise come to terms with his creditor.

### 10.11.2  Requirements for declaring a merchant bankrupt

As mentioned above, a merchant may be declared bankrupt if he has suspended his payments in a general and permanent way. In other words, a temporary inability to pay or the non-payment of a specific debt, while other debts are paid, is not sufficient to declare a merchant bankrupt.

### 10.11.3  Who may be declared bankrupt

The following may be declared bankrupt:

(1)  individual merchants;
(2)  general partnerships of both limited and unlimited liability;

(3)    limited liability companies, joint stock limited liability companies, and
       maritime companies.

### 10.11.4    Procedure

An application is filed with the three-member High Court, and a copy of the
application is served on the debtor. The hearing is normally fixed in three to six
weeks' time. At the hearing both parties present their cases to the court and
submit their written memoranda with all supporting documents. In addition,
any witnesses are orally examined before the court at the hearing. The court
normally issues its judgment in two to four months. The judgment, although
subject to appeal, is immediately enforceable. A receiver is also appointed by
the judgment and he will administer the bankruptcy procedure.

### 10.11.5    Results of a bankruptcy judgment

Once the court's judgment is issued declaring a merchant bankrupt, then:

(1)    the creditors are not allowed to pursue their claims directly against the
       debtor outside the bankruptcy proceedings. Instead, they can satisfy
       the claims only by participation in the bankruptcy proceedings and
       through the bankruptcy property;
(2)    all creditors' claims against the debtor become due at the time the
       court declares the debtor bankrupt;
(3)    the creditors' claims cease earning interest from the issue of the court's
       judgment; and
(4)    the receiver is obliged to register a mortgage against any land or
       property of the debtor in favour of the creditors.

Following the issue of the court's judgment, the receiver takes all necessary
steps to trace the debtor's assets and he proceeds with the verification and
admission of the creditors' claims. The bankruptcy procedure may be terminated either by the settlement of the creditors' claims or by the liquidation of
the debtor's property and its distribution among the creditors. If there are
insufficient assets, the court may decide that the bankruptcy proceedings are
terminated. In such a case, the creditors may re-pursue their claims against the
debtor.

A new bankruptcy code is under preparation aiming to bring Greek bankruptcy provisions into line with bankruptcy law within the European Union.

*Chapter 11*

# IRELAND (REPUBLIC OF)

**Frank Nowlan**
**Matheson Ormsby Prentice**
**Dublin, Ireland**

## 11.1   Introduction

Ireland has inherited a great deal of its legal system from the English common law system. This has been extensively added to by national legislation, as well as legislative measures implemented through membership of the European Union (EU), of which Ireland has been a member since 1973. The currency is the Irish Pound or Punt and is denoted as IEP, IRP, or IR£.

It should be noted that the six counties of Northern Ireland comprise a separate jurisdiction and are not dealt with in this chapter.

## 11.2   Initial considerations

The principal method by which any debt arises is as result of a contract, be it a contract for supply of goods or services on credit or a loan. While debts can arise under certain other headings, such as tax or levies, this chapter is primarily concerned with the question of debts arising under contract or, to be more precise, the failure of a party to a contract to comply with its obligation to pay under that contract.

The first question which will be asked in relation to any such contract is who are the parties to the contract. Usually, there is little doubt who the creditor is, but sometimes it is necessary, particularly where a group of companies is concerned, to clarify exactly who the creditor is. This rarely causes difficulty, but it is necessary before pursuing a debt to be sure as to whom it is due.

### 11.2.1   Status of the debtor

A far greater concern and difficulty is likely to be the status of the debtor. For debt collection purposes, the status of the debtor has two aspects. These are, first, the legal status or identity of the debtor and, secondly, his creditworthiness or, perhaps more specifically when it comes to debt recovery, whether or not he is worth suing. If, in the first instance, action is taken against a debtor without specifically identifying the individual or company concerned, then that action is likely to be pointless. Irish law insists that a defendant be specifically identified in any action taken against him in any respect, debt or otherwise. If a debtor-defendant is not adequately identified, then any proceedings are likely to be invalid and pointless. Equally, actions taken against a defendant debtor who has no assets can also be pointless.

## 11.2.2   Legal entities

Business is often carried on in Ireland using trading names, business names or styles, logos, or brand names. Anyone who deals with such an entity should ensure that they are aware of the exact identity of the person, people or company behind the name. The principal legal entities with which the creditor might trade would be as follows.

### 11.2.2.1   An individual

An individual may trade either under his own name or under a business name or trading style and, where he does so, he will have personal liability for debts incurred. In order to sue him successfully, it is important that the creditor know not just his surname but also his first name. Small businesses are often conducted by individuals operating under a business name.

### 11.2.2.2   A partnership

A partnership consists of several other entities, probably individuals, joining together for a common purpose. Usually, each will be individually responsible for all the debts of the business and usually each is entitled to bind the partnership. Again, a partnership can trade under the names of the partners or under a trading style or business name. Partnerships exist in Ireland mainly in the area of professional services such as lawyers, accountants, and architects, but there is no reason why they should not operate in any area. If action is to be taken against a partnership, then the names, including first names, of all the partners should be included in that action.

### 11.2.2.3   An Irish incorporated company

Companies incorporated in Ireland under the Companies Acts, usually with limited liability, are divided into two categories: private limited companies which have the word 'Limited' or 'Ltd' and public limited companies which are designated as 'Plc' or 'Public Limited Company'. Private limited companies can be of varying sizes from very small to large, while public limited companies tend to be large. All companies are required to carry details of the company name, place of incorporation, registered number, registered office and names of officers on their note paper and all official documentation. Unfortunately, this is not always adhered to. Information on all incorporated companies is available from the Register of Companies. All companies are required to file certain information with the Register, which is available for public inspection.

### 11.2.2.4   Government departments and statutory bodies

The government assumes responsibilities directly through the government departments. These have various, different titles but would be typically, eg the

Department of Finance headed by the Minister for Finance. Statutory bodies would be various state-backed organisations set up under a specific statute or charter to perform a particular function. They might include local authority or health boards. There is no state immunity and, therefore, any of these organisations can be sued.

### 11.2.2.5 *A foreign incorporated company*

A foreign incorporated company is required to register in Ireland with the Register of External Companies, also monitored by the Register of Companies, before it can establish a place of business. Such companies are referred to as external companies.

### 11.2.2.6 *Other bodies*

There is a variety of other bodies which can be encountered from time to time. These are organisations such as sports clubs, unlimited companies, and charities. Care needs to be taken when dealing with these organisations to establish clearly who is contractually responsible.

### 11.2.3 Immunity from suit

Those who cannot be sued include:

(1) an individual under 18 years of age (except in certain circumstances);
(2) an undischarged bankrupt;
(3) a company which is in liquidation or examinership (under the protection of the court), unless court permission is obtained; and
(4) a debtor whose identity is not adequately specified.

### 11.2.4 Sources of information

There are several types of information that may be required before taking action to pursue a debtor. Having considered the question of legal entities outlined above, the creditor may wish to clarify who exactly it is the creditor should be pursuing. To do this, enquiries can be made through various indexes and registers, in some cases by the creditor directly or, alternatively, by the creditor's local or Irish lawyers or enquiry agents.

Apart from obvious reference points, such as correspondence with the debtor, which should disclose his identity, the telephone or other directories may be helpful. If necessary, searches can be carried out simply and easily in the Companies Registration Office to check for the identity of companies registered there. All companies, whether private or public, will be registered there, including external companies. The Companies Registration Office also maintains a Register of Business Names or trading styles but, as registration is not compulsory, the register is by no means complete.

Almost all companies are required to file annual returns which include accounts. These are usually readily available from the Companies Registration Office. The Companies Registration Office is a public office, and its information is available to personal callers to Dublin Castle, Dublin 2, or to searchers or enquiry agents as well as the creditor's Irish lawyers. If the creditor's debtor is not a limited company, then other enquiries can be carried out to establish its identity. All of these enquiries, to a degree, can be helpful in establishing the debtor's financial strength. Unfortunately, reports of financial strength are naturally subjective, and their accuracy cannot be wholly relied on. Enquiry agents and searchers, referred to above, can also assist in tracing debtors who may have moved address.

### 11.2.5   Is the debt statute-barred?

While various limitation periods apply to different actions, generally, a six-year period applies to issuing proceedings relating to debt recovery. This period runs from the date on which the debtor defaulted, ie the date on which the cause of action arose. This period is extended by either the debtor formally acknowledging the existence of the liability or by the issue of proceedings relating to the debt within the six-year period.

It should be noted that shorter periods can apply in certain limited circumstances. These would typically be where a debtor company goes into liquidation or where an individual debtor dies. In each of these cases, prompt action should be taken immediately the creditor becomes aware of the situation.

### 11.2.6   Security

*11.2.6.1   Guarantees*

The benefits of guarantees as security are discussed in Chapter 1. In Ireland, such guarantees must be in writing and must be signed by the guarantor. While it is possible to take guarantees from parties other than those individuals directly involved in the operation of the customer/debtor company, care should be taken about relying on those guarantees. If the guarantee is issued by an associated company, it could be void in certain circumstances. Further, if the guarantee is issued by a third party who may be influenced by the customer, perhaps the customer's husband or wife, caution should exercised, as Irish courts have held that such guarantees can be ineffective in certain circumstances. Despite this, personal guarantees can be of value.

*11.2.6.2   Retention of title*

For retention of title to apply, it must be specifically incorporated into the contract, ie the customer must be aware of the terms before concluding the agreement to purchase. While he need not be aware of the specific terms, he must be aware that there are terms and have the opportunity of familiarising himself with them. Where difficulties arise and a creditor seeks to rely on retention-of-title terms, the most usual problem results from the debtor being able to show that he was not aware that retention of title applied.

A further difficulty can arise where the creditor sells in accordance with his terms and conditions of trading but the purchaser or customer purports to buy in accordance with his own terms and conditions of trading. It is important for a creditor to ensure that his terms and conditions apply and that they are not superseded by those of the customer.

Retention-of-title terms, and indeed terms and conditions of trading, must be carefully drafted. The terms must be broad enough to give full cover to the creditor and must be appropriate to his type of business. However, they may not go so far as to create a charge on the customer company's assets, as this could render the terms void. They should clearly state that, while title is retained by the seller until payment is received, they cover the point at which responsibility for the goods passes to the buyer.

## 11.3 Letters before action

### 11.3.1 Are they necessary?

There is no formal requirement stating that a letter before action should issue in any particular form, but it makes good practical sense that a final demand letter should be issued. Most credit controllers will have in place an existing plan for dealing with outstanding accounts.

Ultimately, a point arrives where the credit controller must decide to abandon the debt or to seek outside assistance. At this stage, a formal letter should be written to the debtor, advising him that the matter is being transferred to solicitors for action. Whether that letter comes from the solicitors threatening proceedings or comes from the creditor is of little consequence, as long as it makes the situation clear. It is generally thought that a letter coming from solicitors will have greater impact than if it comes from the credit controller.

In reality, if it is likely that proceedings will be pursued in respect of the account, then solicitors might as well send the letter, as they will rarely be in a position to issue proceedings the same day as instructions are issued. A demand letter, on the other hand, will normally issue from solicitors the same day they receive instructions. A reply might well be received to the formal demand letter issued by the solicitors before they are able to issue and serve the proceedings.

There can, of course, be circumstances where it is desirable to issue proceedings immediately or where other urgent action is required. The issue of a demand letter can affect the creditor's right to recover legal costs. If proceedings are issued and served without a formal demand letter having been issued and the debtor responds with a query relating to the account, he may be successful in arguing that he should not bear the costs of the proceedings as he would have responded to an initial letter. This is a tenuous argument, but it can be hard to deal with. It must also be remembered that the resolution of outstanding queries by correspondence before the commencement of proceedings can be quicker and cheaper for the creditor.

### 11.3.2    What should a letter before action say?

A letter before action should be clear and concise. It should provide all necessary information to enable the debtor to identify the creditor, the debt, and the person or people within the debtor's organisation who might have been involved. The more questions that the letter answers before they are asked, the better.

At the same time, the letter must be concise and leave the debtor in absolutely no doubt that this letter is his last opportunity to discharge the account before he becomes involved in legal proceedings. It should identify the invoice(s) or alternatively refer to a statement of account and the date on which the account or accounts became overdue. It should set a last day for payment, typically seven days, after which it should be clear that proceedings will be commenced. If interest is included, the amount and its manner of calculation should be specified.

Where the debtor is a limited company and the debt is more than £1,000, it may be possible to threaten liquidation by issuing a 21-day notice. This is a form of initial demand. In certain circumstances, a particular creditor may have a need for a special type of initial demand letter. Most solicitors who engage in debt recovery will understand and respond to this need. It is important that such letters only threaten legitimate procedures. To make threats or suggestions which could amount to harassment could cause the solicitor issuing it and the creditor to be embroiled in an action brought by the debtor seeking damages!

It is not essential that the solicitor have full information relating to the claim or the exact identity of the debtor at the time of issuing an initial letter. It can be issued while searches are being carried out to establish the exact identity of the debtor or the exact amount due is being clarified, or indeed while enquiries are being made as to the debtor's credit worthiness. It is important that a creditor, when instructing a solicitor to issue an initial demand letter, gives him any other relevant information, such as that he holds a guarantee, that cheques have been received and returned by the bank marked 'refer to drawer', or that there is a dispute in relation to the liability. Any contract on special terms should also be brought to the solicitor's attention.

### 11.3.3    Claiming of interest

A creditor is entitled to be paid interest if either his contract with the debtor provides for it or if a court considers that interest should be awarded. From this, it can be seen that there is no automatic right to interest on late payments.

If interest is to be claimed on overdue accounts, an appropriate term or provision must be included in the contract relating to the sale. Ideally, such a provision should be included in the creditor's terms and conditions of trading. Where a term relating to interest is only set out on an invoice, which comes after the contract, the right to include it in a claim is questionable.

If there is a right in terms and conditions of trading, then letters before action should demand payment of that interest and should set out the total amount due inclusive of interest, pointing out that interest is continuing to accrue. Where the terms applicable to the sale do not provide for the charging of interest, interest can nevertheless be included but not as a matter of right. Irish courts have a discretion to award interest in claims where it is considered appropriate, even though the parties did not agree that interest should be charged. In practice, it is unusual for such interest to be pursued as it can complicate a claim.

If a judgment is issued, interest will automatically accrue on the judgment debt from the date of the judgment at the standard court rate (currently 8 per cent per annum), unless the judge otherwise directs.

### 11.3.4   21-day letters threatening liquidation

The Companies Act 1963 provides that, where a creditor is owed a debt in excess of £1,000, it may serve a notice, called a 21-day notice, requiring a debtor company to discharge the debt within 21 days. Should the debtor fail to do so, it may be deemed to be unable to pay its debts and be the subject of a High Court petition for winding up and appointment of a liquidator. These notices are sometimes used to frighten a debtor company and can be effective. However, proceeding to liquidate on the basis of such a notice can be problematic unless the debtor has acknowledged the liability in some way or a judgment has first been obtained.

Therefore, a 21-day notice, unless it is accompanied by a judgment, must be an acknowledgment of debt in some form regarded as a mere threatening action in many cases.

## 11.4   Pre-action and non-judicial remedies

In regard to pre-action and non-judicial remedies, it is assumed that a creditor has already encountered problems regarding a debtor. He either has a retention of title and goods supplied or he has not. A creditor is not able to incorporate new terms or conditions into the sale agreement, as that has long since been concluded.

A creditor may wish to enforce rights or provisions, such as retention of title, but these are initially a matter for direct action by the creditor with lawyers becoming involved only if the debtor fails to comply. There are other remedies, however, which could be beneficial.

### 11.4.1   Assignment of debt

The debt owed to the creditor is an asset of the creditor and can usually be assigned. If the creditor becomes aware of a third party who is indebted to the debtor, then it may be possible for the creditor and the third party to collaborate by the creditor assigning his assets (the debt that is due to him by the debtor) to the third party for valuable consideration, and the third party may then be in a position to set off the debt which is due to the creditor against the debt which he owes to the debtor. However, certain criteria must be met before an assignment and set-off can be effected.

### 11.4.2 Injunctions

In certain circumstances, injunctions can be sought from the court, seeking immediate relief. These injunctions can be sought speedily but are issued by the court only in certain, special circumstances. The principal form of injunction which would be sought in relation to a debt matter would typically be a *Mareva* injunction. The purpose of a *Mareva* injunction is to prevent a defendant from dissipating his assets so as to frustrate the creditor's efforts at recovery of debts due.

Such an injunction may be sought before or after the issue of proceedings and its effect, if granted, will be to freeze all or part of the debtor's assets and prevent him from disposing of or selling them for a period. If an injunction order is granted by the court, the court will also usually give instructions on how the order is to be served and to what it applies in terms of assets and territory. An injunction could also be sought in Ireland, supporting a similar order made in another jurisdiction but relating to assets in Ireland.

A *Mareva* injunction is an extremely useful tool, but it is not appropriate to all circumstances. Courts are reluctant to make orders where issues have not been tried, and there are strict rules which apply relating to the issue of injunctions.

The court will not grant injunctions in trivial matters or those where it feels that an action for damages would provide a satisfactory remedy. The creditor seeking the injunction must be prepared to give an undertaking to the court to be responsible for damages to the debtor in the event that his claim is not supported and the granting of the injunction causes loss to the debtor. Finally, the creditor must disclose all facts which it considers may be relevant to the application and not just those which are helpful to its cause.

Obtaining an injunction to freeze all or part of the defendant's assets does not, of itself, give the creditor who obtains the injunction any priority over other creditors should the debtor become bankrupt or go into liquidation. The obtaining of an injunction, it should be pointed out, simply freezes the position and it is usually necessary to pursue proceedings to justify the creditor's entitlement to payment. Naturally, a debtor whose assets are frozen is likely to make some effort at resolving the dispute with the creditor, so as to enable his assets to be released from the injunction.

While a *Mareva* injunction has the objective of freezing assets, it may also be possible to seek an *Anton Piller* order. With such an order, a creditor might seize goods or papers on a debtor's premises to prevent them from being destroyed. Such orders are rare.

A lien might be exercised by a creditor where he is in possession of goods owned by the debtor and where money is owed to the creditor arising typically out of work done to those goods. The circumstances in which a lien would apply are limited, and there are restrictions to its use, eg it cannot be used against a liquidator or an examiner where the company is under court protection.

## 11.5 The court system

### 11.5.1 In general

Debt recovery in Ireland falls within the jurisdiction of the civil courts. The civil courts deal with all personal and commercial matters which are not specifically criminal in their nature. Debt, almost always arising under a contract, is handled by the civil courts. In certain circumstances, the criminal courts may become involved if there is a question of fraud or such like on the part of the debtor. There are three civil courts of first instance.

### 11.5.2 The courts

#### 11.5.2.1 The District Court

The District Court, which handles claims up to £5,000, is a local court and deals with some criminal work as well as civil. Its procedures are generally simple and relatively efficient. Evidence, except in some restricted specific instances, is always given orally, so that attendance of witnesses is required. While the procedures are efficient, the simplicity, informality and lack of documentary pleadings can create uncertainty where cases are defended, as it is sometimes difficult to know before the court hearing what the nature of the debtor's defence is.

Professional fees and disbursements are generally recoverable by a successful party, and they are set out on a scale approved by the Minister for Justice. It is not usual for barristers to appear in this court, and advocacy is handled almost exclusively by solicitors. Witness expenses are recoverable if the District Judge so decides. An appeal, which would be a complete rehearing, may be made to the Circuit Court. Strict time-limits apply in relation to appeals.

#### 11.5.2.2 The Circuit Court

The Circuit Court handles claims up to £30,000. This court is more formal than the District Court, and extensive documentary pleadings are provided for in its rules. Generally, the court is efficient but is sometimes subject to delays caused by a backlog of cases. It has an equitable jurisdiction and, therefore, can issue injunctions and deal with applications for other remedies.

Advocacy is usually carried out by barristers on the instructions of solicitors, although the latter do sometimes appear on their own. Evidence is usually given orally, but extensive use is made of affidavits in relation to preliminary hearings and applications.

Professional fees and outlays may be awarded to any party to an action at the discretion of the Circuit Court judge hearing the action. Generally, costs follow the event with the successful party being awarded his costs. If the amount of the costs cannot be agreed with the unsuccessful party, the County Registrar, who is the civil servant charged with the administration of the Circuit Court, will decide or 'tax' it.

An appeal on specific issues may be made to the High Court. Strict time-limits apply in relation to appeals.

### 11.5.2.3 The High Court

The High Court has full or plenary jurisdiction in all civil matters. It has full equitable jurisdiction to award injunctions and other relief. It is also the forum for actions relating to constitutional issues.

Like those of the Circuit Court, the rules of the High Court provide for extensive pleadings in advance of trial. Advocacy is carried out almost exclusively by barristers on instructions from solicitors. The amount of time taken to reach trial depends on the type of action. Generally, a commercial case will be tried within six months from setting down, following completion of pleadings. Earlier trials can be sought in urgent cases. Applications for urgent relief, such as certain types of injunction, can be made without notice.

Professional fees and outlays, which can be high, can be awarded at the discretion of the judge. As in the Circuit Court, these almost always are awarded to a successful party. If awarded, the amount will be taxed by a Taxing Master if it cannot be agreed between the parties.

### 11.5.2.4 Small Claims Court

While there is a Small Claims Court, it deals with actions brought by consumers only and does not deal with debt recovery or other commercial matters.

### 11.5.2.5 Summary or debt proceedings

All of the civil courts have a separate summary procedure for pursuing debt cases. These procedures provide a facility for obtaining a default judgment where a debtor does not contest the claim. The application for default judgment can be made a certain period after issue and service of the originating writ. Such applications are based on an affidavit, called an affidavit of debt, which must be sworn or affirmed by the credit controller or other person in the creditor's employ who is familiar with the account.

The affidavit, if being completed outside Ireland, should be sworn or affirmed before an Irish Embassy or consular official if there is one close at hand and, otherwise, before any notary public. It is not usual that the completion of the affidavit before the notary public is officially authenticated; the signature and seal or stamp of the notary is usually sufficient. While these affidavits may usually be sworn or affirmed at any time that is convenient to the plaintiff or the plaintiff's credit controller, once completed, they must be returned immediately, as they must be filed in court within 14 days from the date on which they are completed by the notary.

In all three courts, defended cases require that the plaintiff produce witnesses for the oral hearing. There is no provision for evidence to be given on affidavits except in very unusual circumstances.

### 11.5.3 Jurisdiction

There are in turn two aspects to territorial jurisdiction, that of Irish national rules and that of international conventions, principally the 1968 Brussels Convention.

#### 11.5.3.1 Irish national law

The basic principle of Irish law is that proceedings must be taken in the territorial jurisdiction of the court in which the proposed defendant, if an individual resides or carries on business or, if a company, where its registered office is located. To this is added, in the case of a claim arising under a contract which most debts are, the place where the contract was made. In other cases, other rules can apply. The nationality of the defendant is unimportant, as Irish courts will claim jurisdiction over any person present in Ireland at the time of issue of proceedings.

Parties may agree to a specific court having jurisdiction either at the time of contracting (perhaps in terms or conditions of trade) or by responding to proceedings and thus accepting the validity of a court's jurisdiction.

#### 11.5.3.2 The Brussels Convention

Ireland is a contracting party to the 1968 Brussels Convention. That Convention was ratified and became part of Irish Law in 1988. It applies only to civil and commercial matters. Like Irish law, the basic principle of the Convention is that a defendant should be sued in the courts of the State in which he is domiciled. The Convention provides several exceptions to this rule which are detailed in its article 5. Two of these exceptions may be relevant to debt cases. One relates to the right to sue in the courts of the place of performance of the contract and the second, where the parties agree perhaps in terms of trading, relates to specific jurisdiction of a court or courts of a country.

The Convention now applies to all European Free Trade Association (EFTA) countries. Where the Convention does not apply, Irish national rules will.

#### 11.5.3.3 Status of foreign creditor and security for costs

A foreign creditor is entitled to plead through an Irish solicitor and, if required, a barrister in the Irish courts. He must set out an address in Ireland on which notices relating to the proceedings can be served; this will usually be the offices of his solicitor.

If the creditor is not based in a country to which the 1968 Brussels Convention applies, then if the court requires, it may be subject to an order for security for costs. If such an order is made at the request of the debtor, then the creditor may be required to lodge payment with the court or enter into a bond to ensure that a debtor, if successful in defending his action will not be at a loss for the costs and will not be obliged to pursue the creditor in the creditor's country. If the creditor is based in a country to which the Brussels Convention applies then security for costs should not be an issue.

## 11.6  Representation

### 11.6.1  In general

An individual plaintiff may appear in Irish courts personally or through qualified legal advisors, being either a solicitor or barrister. Solicitors are the professionals who deal with clients and, if appropriate, may retain the more specialised barrister to assist. A creditor's communication with the legal profession, therefore, will be initially with solicitors, who will process most claims, only retaining a barrister for higher value or more complex matters. A company cannot represent itself in court.

Solicitors are registered as officers of court and are controlled and monitored by the Incorporated Law Society of Ireland, which also protects and guarantees money held by solicitors on behalf of clients.

Communications between a solicitor and client are privileged, so that neither the solicitor nor the client can be required to divulge information which passes between them.

Solicitors maintain offices and support staff and practise either as individuals or in partnership firms with other solicitors. Firms vary in size from those of a single solicitor to those with 50 or more solicitors. Traditionally, solicitors were general practitioners, but increasingly they have become specialised, especially in areas relating to commercial law. Smaller practices tend to deal with private client and personal issues, while larger practices offer a broad range of services to commercial clients as well as some private client business.

When instructing solicitors in debt recovery matters, it should be established that the solicitor is fully conversant with debt recovery. Debt recovery work is not regarded as profitable, except by firms which have a specialist section dealing with this type of work.

### 11.6.2  Mode of payment for legal representation

In commercial matters such as debt recovery, a solicitor, once retained, acts on behalf of his client and has an automatic duty of confidentiality and care towards his client. While charges are a matter for agreement, in general the client becomes responsible for the solicitor's charges. Methods of charging vary, depending on the type of work, but it is usual in debt recovery work to have a fixed scale or schedule of charges.

The amount of charge will vary, depending on the amount of the debt and the work done. These charges usually permit the economic processing of cases save where the debt is small or the likelihood of recovery is not great. If a claim becomes complex or is defended, additional charges may be made on a time-cost basis. Time-cost charging would be usual in non-debt recovery cases, unless another form of charging is agreed.

If a barrister is retained by the solicitor or if other outlays are incurred, the client will be responsible for these expenses. It is common for solicitors to seek a retainer or payment on account in respect of fees or disbursements to be incurred.

In debt-recovery cases, it is usual for solicitors to charge a commission on moneys successfully recovered. Normally, such a charge would be a contingency fee and, thus, would be prohibited. However, debt recovery is specifically exempted from this prohibition on contingency fees where the commission to be charged is specified in writing in advance.

## 11.7 Costs and interest

### 11.7.1 Liability of debtor for costs

As a general principle, an unsuccessful party in any legal action is responsible for the successful party's costs. This responsibility is based on the successful party's right to recoup the costs which he has incurred. This right vests in the creditor/successful party and not in his solicitor.

The solicitor, as the servant of the creditor/successful party, is entitled to be paid by the creditor whether or not the creditor recovers from the debtor/unsuccessful party pursuant to his indemnity. These recoverable costs are referred to as 'party/party' costs and may not reflect the creditors full bill, as the solicitor may also charge a 'solicitor/client' bill.

### 11.7.2 Value added tax on charges

A solicitor acting for a client in Ireland is obliged to include a charge for value added tax (VAT) on his account. Where a solicitor is acting for a non-Irish client and the client does not have an establishment within Ireland, then VAT will be chargeable at 0 per cent in most debt-recovery cases.

### 11.7.3 Current fees

A solicitor's charges are subject to agreement with the client. As has been seen, the client is primarily responsible for the solicitor's costs. Most solicitors engaging in debt-recovery work will have a scale of charges immediately available and will work on this basis, departing from it only in special circumstances of high value claims or where there are a large number of cases.

### 11.7.4 Legal aid

There is no legal aid available for commercial creditors seeking to recover debts. Legal aid is only available to individual debtors in limited circumstances and where the debtor's financial situation is very weak. In practice, if the debtor qualifies for legal aid, it is unlikely to be worthwhile pursuing the debt.

### 11.7.5   Recovery of costs

Under the rules of the various courts, certain costs may be claimed from the defendant along with the debt. In most debt-recovery actions, these costs are based on statutory scales and are rarely regarded as sufficient remuneration in themselves. Solicitors will rarely accept that these costs will be sufficient to deal with their charges and will require the creditor to pay in accordance with the solicitor's normal scale.

These recoverable charges often form the base of the solicitor's scale of charging. If the creditor has retained a non-Irish lawyer who has incurred costs, it is not possible, in normal circumstances, for these costs to be included in the claim against the debtor. The debtor's responsibility will be for the statutory scale costs only. A solicitor who recovers the scale costs from the debtor must account to the client for those costs.

## 11.8   Proceedings

### 11.8.1   In general

When instructing Irish solicitors to commence action for debt recovery, only a limited amount of information is required. The solicitor will require:

(1)   the full name and the address of the creditor's registered office or place of business. If there is any other name by which the creditor is known to the debtor, this also should be set out;

(2)   the amount of the debt and how it arose; the amount must be exact and, if interest is to be included, the formula by which interest is to be calculated should be set out. The terms of trading or circumstances under which such interest is claimed must also be provided. A statement of account is useful and, if there are not too many, copies of invoices should be provided. It is not necessary that these be certified. A brief narrative as to how the debt arose is useful.

(3)   the name and address of the debtor;[1] and

(4)   a copy of any contract or terms and conditions which applied to the sale in question. If there is correspondence between the parties relating to the debt, copies of this should be provided if relevant.

From this information, the solicitor should be able to pursue the collection of most debts. If further information is required, he will come back to the creditor and request it.

---

1   While as much information as possible should be given from the creditor's file, the solicitor will be accustomed to making further enquiries should this be necessary.

The creditor should set out clearly what he wishes the solicitor to do and query what the charge will be.

### 11.8.2   Initial action by solicitor

Assuming the above information is supplied and there are no obvious queries, the solicitor will issue an initial demand letter, threatening proceedings if payment is not made in a definite period, usually seven days. At the same time, he will check the instructions and, during the seven days, carry out any public register checks that are necessary. Typically, a Companies Registration Office search will be obtained to confirm the trading status and registered address of a company debtor. For larger debts, annual accounts might also be checked.

If there is no response to the initial demand letter, proceedings will be issued and will be served on the debtor. These will include a claim for recoverable scale costs. These proceedings will allow the debtor a limited time to respond. They will set out what he must do if he wishes to defend the claim, if he wishes to pay, or if he wishes to compromise the debt. They also will state that, if the debtor fails to respond, then he may be deemed to have admitted the debt and have judgment marked against him by default.

If the debtor does respond, it would be usual to advise the client and report what the debtor says. If any proposals are put forward, the client's instructions would be sought. If queries are raised, the solicitor will deal with these with information from his file, if possible, or he will revert to the client. Most solicitors experienced in debt recovery will be familiar with handling debtors' queries, especially in sorting those which are genuine from those which are designed to delay, and in dealing appropriately with them.

Usually, the solicitor will go to some trouble to try to keep a case from being fully defended. A fully defended action is expensive and can be time consuming.

Insofar as possible, the solicitor should be conscious that economic recovery of the debt is the objective and, if this becomes or is likely to become unattainable, the client should be advised. Unfortunately, the solicitor will not always be aware of the position.

## 11.9   Procedure to judgment

### 11.9.1   Debtor pays

If the debtor pays the debt to the solicitor, usually the solicitor will bank the payment and advise the client. He will seek payment of any recoverable costs, if the debtor has not already paid these with the debt.

If payment is made by cheque, he will ensure that it clears. On clearance, he will terminate any proceedings commenced. He will then account to client for money recovered, first deducting his fees.

### 11.9.2   Debtor admits debt

Often, a debtor will admit a debt but plead inability to pay or will seek a deferred payment arrangement. The solicitor will attempt to verify the debtor's position and will discuss the position with the creditor. It may be wise to permit a deferred-payment arrangement only where some security is provided by the debtor, and it may be appropriate to proceed to judgment so that it can be enforced later if necessary.

The solicitor should have a procedure for monitoring the debtor's compliance with the deferred payment arrangement. It must be clear what will happen if the debtor fails to comply. If the debtor pleads total inability to pay, the solicitor should verify this and decide with the client if there is any benefit in continuing with proceedings.

### 11.9.3  Debtor disputes the debt

If the debtor disputes the debt, the solicitor must attempt to establish the nature of the dispute. Many disputes can be resolved by communication. Issues in dispute must be narrowed down so that they can be evaluated and dealt with. Often, of course, a 'dispute' is no more than a ruse to delay payment. These cases must be identified and dealt with appropriately, usually by bringing a preliminary application for judgment or seeking an early trial.

If a claim is genuinely defended, then it is important to identify issues promptly. If the creditor's claim can be justified by communication and supply of documents or statements, so much the better. This is sometimes possible where the debtor's legal advisors are practical and advise their client of his true position, and the debtor genuinely wishes to resolve the dispute or where he has no desire to become involved in litigation which is likely to be expensive for him. Even in these circumstances, it is unlikely that the debtor will pay or compromise until he appreciates that not paying is futile, so settlements often only come shortly before trial.

A real problem arises where a debtor realises that he is unable to deal with his liability but is determined to continue to protract the situation as long as possible. This can turn a success in legal terms into a Pyrrhic victory, a judgment obtained being unenforceable because the debtor has no assets against which to execute. While efforts are made to watch for this situation, success is limited. It is usually wise to consider early settlement in situations where this might apply. There are rules against insolvent trading, but these are difficult to enforce, both in terms of proof and cost. In addition, a debtor who is in serious financial trouble may have nothing to lose.

Where a settlement is proposed, it should be considered and negotiated on. Defended actions can be protracted and expensive.

### 11.9.4  Debt part admitted, part disputed

If a debt is partly admitted and partly disputed, it is usually possible to separate these and pursue the portions individually. If part is admitted, then the debtor will be called on to pay this and be subject to proceedings for the disputed portion. If he fails to pay the admitted portion, this can be the subject of a consent or, more likely, a default judgment application. If the debtor appears to be in difficulty paying the admitted debt, consideration must be given to the value of pursuing the disputed portion.

Sometimes, a debtor will refuse to pay an admitted liability until a dispute, perhaps relating to another liability is resolved. Thus, he will use the liability as a lever to assist him in his negotiating position in the dispute. The creditor will wish to separate the claims. In most cases, separation is possible but, if the debtor's claim amounts to a counterclaim, he may be entitled to effect a set-off.

### 11.9.5 Debtor neither admits nor disputes the debt

If the debtor fails to respond to the proceedings, application can be made for judgment to be entered against him by default. This application is based on an affidavit, called an affidavit of debt, which must be sworn by the creditor or its credit controller. This is a simple affidavit, verifying the amount due.

### 11.9.6 Debtor declared insolvent

There are several ways in which insolvency arises; some are formal, such as liquidation or bankruptcy, while others are de facto, but without the same finality.

#### 11.9.6.1 Liquidation

Liquidation of a company may commence, as far as a creditor is concerned, with receipt of a notice of creditors' meeting or with a notice relating to a petition to the High Court, seeking the winding up of the company appearing in newspapers. The creditor himself, of course, may be the initiator of the court petition.

If a notice of a creditors' meeting is received, it means that the directors of the company have decided that a situation prevails which requires the company to cease trading, usually due to its inability to pay its debts as they fall due. The creditors are invited to appoint a liquidator. Usually, the notice of creditors' meeting encloses a form of proxy to enable the creditor nominate someone to vote on his behalf.

It is rarely in the interest of the creditor that this proxy is given to the chairman of the creditors' meeting. The chairman is often one of the directors and is perhaps partially responsible for the company's failure; he is unlikely to be the appropriate person to represent a creditor. Regrettably, attendance at or involvement in creditors' meetings is often unproductive for unsecured creditors.

If a petition to the court is advertised in newspapers, it usually means a creditor is seeking the winding up of the company and the appointment of a liquidator by the court. The petitioning creditor, in the notice, will request that other creditors notify him or his advisors if they intend to support or oppose the granting of the petition by the court. There can be a great deal of communication between creditors and perhaps the company at this point, and claims are sometimes settled.

Overall, if a liquidator is appointed, he will dispose of the company's assets and pay creditors insofar as he can and, in accordance with specific rules, out of the proceeds of sale of the assets. Creditors will be paid in the order of priority of the liability due to them. Secured creditors will exercise their rights under their mortgages; then the rest of the assets will be used to pay first the liquidator's expenses, then preferential creditors (employees and tax, mainly), and then unsecured creditors. All too often, there is insufficient money available to the liquidator to enable him pay a dividend to the lower-ranking unsecured creditor.

### 11.9.6.2   *Bankruptcy*

An individual may be declared bankrupt. If so, all his assets cease to belong to him and become the property of a court official, the official assignee, who will gather in and sell the bankrupt's assets and pay the proceeds to his creditors. As with a company liquidation, there are rules governing the order of payment to creditors.

A de facto insolvency arises where an individual or company becomes insolvent, but no steps are taken to liquidate or bankrupt. The debtor himself will have no desire or ability to pay for a bankruptcy or liquidation and, if he has no assets, there is little point in a creditor throwing good money after bad by pursuing such a course.

### 11.9.6.3   *Receivership*

Two other forms of quasi-insolvency of companies require consideration, receivership and examinership. In a receivership, a secured creditor appoints a receiver or manager over some or all of the assets belonging to the company under a power given to the creditor by the company in a deed of mortgage, charge, or debenture.

Often, the receiver will be appointed over all the company's assets and undertakings, and he will manage or sell the company for the benefit of his client, the secured creditor. In effect, he replaces the normal company management as far as the assets over which he is appointed are concerned. This often leaves an unsecured creditor in a position of being owed money by a company which has no assets and no business and, therefore, no prospect of being paid.

Sometimes, companies do survive receivership, but this is unusual. Sometimes, a receiver will sell the company as a going concern but, unless he realises sufficient assets to pay the secured creditor in full and have a significant balance over, this is no comfort to an unsecured creditor.

### 11.9.6.4   *Examinership*

In certain circumstances, a company or others can apply to have an examiner appointed. If an appointment is made, the debtor company is referred to as being under the protection of the court. An examiner is typically appointed where a company has become insolvent but might be capable of being rescued and a scheme of arrangement put in place. The company is protected from action by its creditors for three months to enable the examiner to put a rescue package to the court and the creditors for approval.

A creditor who is owed money by a company in examinership is not permitted to sue or execute a judgment during the examinership period. He may, however, be able to exercise retention-of-title claims. A receiver can, and an examiner can with the consent of the court, continue trading. Usually, in either case, personal liability is assumed by the receiver or examiner for goods or services ordered by him but this is not always the case. A creditor dealing with a receiver or examiner should clarify this before allowing a liability to arise.

## 11.10  Registering and enforcing judgment

### 11.10.1  In general

Where the claim is contested and judgment is entered after trial or, where the claim is not contested and judgment is entered by default against the debtor, a judgment is issued in either case and may require to be enforced. Judgments of all courts are enforced in the same ways.

### 11.10.2  Registration of judgments

The registration of the judgment is a process which makes the judgment public. Various trade gazettes inspect the Registrar of Judgments each week and publish new judgments each week. A judgment registered against a business person or trader can have a disastrous effect on his business or trade, as it may cut off all sources of credit to him if his other creditors or perhaps his bankers become aware that a judgment has been entered against him.

The threat of registration of a judgment against a debtor can have a significant impact, but actual registration can be detrimental to the creditor's interests as, by the effect it has on other creditors, it may prevent the debtor from being able to trade further and thus reduce his ability to deal with the judgment creditor.

All registered judgments are recorded on various credit information data-bases and remain for long periods. It is not unusual for debtors who have failed to discharge a debt to contact the creditor after some years to deal with liabilities in order to clear their names.

### 11.10.3  Registration of judgment mortgage

When a judgment has been obtained and the debtor has an interest in land or other immovable property, it may be possible to register the judgment as a mortgage against his interest in that property. Registration of a judgment mortgage should be not be confused with the registration of judgment referred to above.

If a judgment mortgage is registered against the debtor's interest in property, it will prevent him from disposing of the property without dealing with the judgment mortgage. It would also give the creditor the right to apply to the court to seek to have the property sold through the court and the debt paid from the proceeds. When a judgment mortgage is registered, it will rank in priority with other mortgages in the order in which they are registered.

Enquiries can be made through enquiry agents and law searchers to establish the nature of the debtor's interest, if any, in property prior to the registration of a judgment mortgage.

### 11.10.4   Enforcement

There are various ways in which a judgment can be enforced. Enforcement relates to direct action being taken against the debtor on the basis of the judgment so as to produce money to satisfy the judgment.

#### 11.10.4.1   Enforcement by Sheriff

The Sheriff is an official whose function is to enforce judgments by seizure of the debtor's goods. He has no power in relation to seizure of land. After service of necessary notices, he can attend at the debtor's premises and seize certain types of assets belonging to the debtor and sell them in order to satisfy the judgment debt. He can use force to enter and seize if necessary.

There are independent Sheriffs in some counties; in others, the task is carried out by the County Registrar, who is the official who is responsible for the administration of the Circuit Court.

#### 11.10.4.2   Enforcement by examination and instalment proceedings

If the debtor does not have seizable assets, then the debtor may be examined in his local District Court by the District Judge as to his financial circumstances. If the District Judge thinks it appropriate, he can make an instalment order, instructing the debtor to discharge the debt by instalments.

The order will be made on the basis of the debtor's means rather than the amount of the debt. If an instalment order is made and the debtor fails to comply with it, it is possible to seek a committal order from the court at a later stage. The committal order may ultimately lead to the debtor being imprisoned if he fails to satisfy the judge that he had good reason for failing to make payments as ordered by the court.

#### 11.10.4.3   Enforcement in bankruptcy

Where an individual fails to comply with the court order for payment of money and the Sheriff has been unsuccessful in executing against him, it is possible to seek that the debtor be adjudged bankrupt. Once he is bankrupt, all the debtor's assets cease to belong to him and they become the property of a court official, the Official Assignee in Bankruptcy, and he must sell them and distribute the proceeds of sale among creditors. It is a criminal offence for an undischarged bankrupt debtor to obtain goods or services on credit.

### 11.10.4.4   Enforcement by court liquidation

A limited company, once judgment has been obtained and the Sheriff has been unsuccessful executing, can be the subject of a petition to the High Court for the seeking of the compulsory liquidation of the company.

### 11.10.4.5   Enforcement by garnishment

If it is known that a third party is indebted to the judgment debtor, then it may be possible to enforce the judgment against the third party, who is known as a garnishee.

### 11.10.4.6   Enforcement: oral examination of defendant or directors

In certain instances, court rules allow for the oral examination of debtors or directors of companies against whom a judgment has been obtained. This is referred to as examination in aid of execution. It is designed to help identify or locate assets belonging to the debtor. This can be an effective weapon against directors of companies which cease trading but first remove assets from the company.

### 11.10.4.7   Enforcement of non-Irish judgments

Ireland is a contracting party to the 1968 Brussels Convention. The Convention was ratified and became part of Irish Law in 1988. While the Convention has significantly assisted in clarifying the position relating to the jurisdiction of courts and has ensured a uniform approach to the enforcement of judgments of other contracting states, in some ways, it has complicated the process relating to enforcement of foreign judgments.

The basic principle of the Brussels Convention is that a defendant to an action is to be sued in the court area in which he is domiciled. Following this principle, proceedings will be taken against debtors in the jurisdiction in which they reside or carry on business. The Convention provides various exceptions to this rule, and often these exceptions permit the issue of proceedings in the jurisdiction of the creditor.

While a judgment issued by the courts of the country of a creditor, in appropriate cases, can be enforced in Ireland under the provisions of the Convention, the practice of so doing can be tedious and expensive. All enforcement of such judgments is through the High Court. The Irish High Court has jurisdiction which, for practical purposes, commences at £30,000, and its costs can be high. Further, the District Courts and Circuit Courts, which deal with the vast majority of debt recovery cases, are reasonably efficient and, for these reasons, together with the difficulties encountered in relation to the official translations of court documents which are sometimes required, it is recommended that consideration be given to commencing debt recovery proceedings in Ireland where the debtor is based in Ireland.

Where the creditor is from a country which is not a contracting party to the Brussels Convention, the situation is less complicated. Such a creditor has the same status as would a creditor from a Brussels Convention state, save that, in a defended action, security for costs may be required. A judgment obtained by a creditor in his own country's court, in such circumstances, would be enforceable in Ireland through proceedings which would regard the foreign judgment as being a cause of action. As such a judgment is likely to seek the recovery of a specific sum of money, and perhaps costs, it can be the subject of summary proceedings. The opportunities for the defendant to contest the claim are restricted to jurisdictional and certain other limited issues.

It is strongly recommended that the question of jurisdiction be considered carefully before the issue of proceedings which may sought to be enforced in Ireland. The most common difficulties in the enforcement of judgments obtained against Irish debtors in non-Irish courts, whether the Brussels Convention applies or not, result from a failure to identify the debtor correctly and a failure to prove satisfactory service of the proceedings.

## 11.11   Insolvency

### 11.11.1   Winding up of limited companies

A company can be wound up by the court for several reasons, but the principal reason, and that of interest to creditors, is where it is unable to pay its debts. The Companies Acts provide that, where a company is served with a notice requiring it to pay a debt of greater than £1,000 and it fails to respond within 21 days, it is deemed to be unable to pay its debts. In such circumstances, a petition can be issued, advertised, and presented to the High Court, seeking that the company be wound up and a liquidator appointed.

If there are other reasons for believing that it is unable to pay its debts, then there may be no need to wait 21 days. In either case, the debt must not be disputed, as the courts will not allow the winding-up process to be used as a method of pursuing a disputed account.

Issuing a 21-day notice can be an effective method of threatening a slow paying company, but following through to liquidation may not be attractive for smaller debts, as liquidation proceedings can be expensive and should not be embarked on without careful consideration of the costs and likely outcome.

The directors of a company which has traded recklessly or fraudulently can be made liable for the company's debts, but the burden of proof that such trading occurred can make it difficult to succeed. In some circumstances, a court might be prepared to 'lift the veil' of incorporation and allow an action against the directors. If a company goes into liquidation, the court may order the other company to contribute to the insolvent company, if it finds there has been improper trading with another company.

A liquidator will gather in the assets of the company, sell them and pay out to creditors in accordance with their priority. (See also **11.9.6**)

### 11.11.2 Bankruptcy of individual debtors

Bankruptcy can be commenced only after a judgment has been obtained and the Sheriff has been unsuccessful in executing it, ie, he has made a return of 'no goods'. While having a debtor adjudged a bankrupt by the High Court can be slow, the process itself can be very effective in producing settlement proposals. In a bankruptcy, all the assets of the debtor vest in the official assignee in bankruptcy, a court official.

A bankrupt debtor ceases to own anything and is prohibited from running any bank or similar account, and obtaining a loan or goods or services on credit becomes a criminal offence. The procedure itself can be long and drawn out, but it is quite effective. Unfortunately, the initial steps can be expensive so there needs to be a reasonable expectation of early settlement or of there being sufficient assets to realise a satisfactory dividend.

Like a liquidator of a company, the official assignee will gather in the assets of the bankrupt debtor, sell them and pay the proceeds to creditors in order of priority.

### 11.11.3 Insolvency of partnerships or proprietors

Under Irish law, there are no separate rules relating to insolvency of partnerships or firms. Any of these entities will either be individuals or companies or combinations of these. The rules outlined above will apply to the individuals or companies concerned.

## 11.12 Conclusion

Debt recovery in Ireland is pursued either through non-legal approaches to debtors, such as by telephone, letter, or personal calls or, alternatively, through the legal process. At the time of writing, the only restrictions on approaching debtors relate to those prohibiting harassment, but legislation is in preparation which will prohibit certain approaches to consumers.

While collection agencies can contact debtors on a creditor's behalf and can often report on the debtor's circumstances, there is no enforcement action which they can take other than through solicitors. There is no licensing or registration of collection agencies, unlike solicitors. Some solicitors specialise in debt recovery and provide an efficient and responsive service; others do not and, therefore, it is important to ensure the requisite degree of knowledge and speciality when instructing.

The legal system in Ireland is generally efficient and cost effective. This is particularly so in relation to undefended matters which constitute the majority of debt recovery cases. Backlogs do occur from time to time in some courts and procedures. The courts are inclined to ensure that an individual consumer's rights are vindicated but, nevertheless, every person, non-national and national, will receive fair and considerate treatment.

# Chapter 12

# ITALY

Enrico Gilioli
Studio Legale Gilioli
Milan, Italy

## 12.1  Introduction

This chapter provides a survey of debt-collection procedures and the legal environment pertaining in Italy for such process.

## 12.2  Initial considerations

### 12.2.1  Status of the debtor

The need to establish the status of the debtor is important since a collection action will be handled in a manner dependent on the status of such a debtor. The first step is to ascertain the full name and address of the entity involved as the debtor.

Entities which may be pursued by legal action before an Italian court include:

(1)  an individual who has incurred the debt while engaged in a trading activity (ie, a person actively carrying out a commercial business);

(2)  an individual who has incurred the debt in a situation which is not that of a trader (ie, a consumer);

(3)  an enterprise organised in one of the various legal forms contemplated by Italian law, ie, a sole proprietorship, a partnership (with unlimited liability of the partners), or a limited liability company limited by shares (SpA) or by quotas (Srl); and

(4)  a private association (where the representatives of the association may be personally liable).

It should be noted that no executory action may be undertaken against enterprises which are undergoing bankruptcy proceedings.

### 12.2.2  Sources of information

All Italian enterprises must be registered at the Chamber of Commerce having jurisdiction over the area in which they are located. The easiest manner of ascertaining the existence of an enterprise (short of using the telephone or trade directories) is to request issuance by the local Chamber of Commerce of a certificate of registration. The fee is minimal and, as a rule, the certificate is issued on request. The certificate will show all relevant information regarding the formation of the enterprise and its capital and will identify its authorised representatives.

Italian companies must also be registered with the clerk of the local court having jurisdiction over the area in which they are located. Companies are required to file a yearly balance sheet which is available to the public on request. Records from the clerk of the court are usually not up-to-date and are not readily secured. A number of private companies provide computerised information for a fee (ItL 25,000 or more) which is generally, but not exclusively, based on data obtained from the Chamber of Commerce.

### 12.2.3 Is the debt statute-barred?

Various time limitations apply to collection actions depending on different factual situations. A claim for damages is barred five years from the date of occurrence of the event which has generated the damages. The account receivable of a trader for the price of goods sold to consumers is generally barred one year from the date of the sale. Different time limitations apply in other situations.

The creditor, however, may interrupt the running of the period of the limitation by making a formal written demand on the debtor. In this connection, the assistance of an attorney is strongly recommended.

### 12.2.4 Security

#### 12.2.4.1 In general

It may not be easy to obtain appropriate security in a commercial transaction, unless the debtor is financially solid (in which case no security might be needed). International transactions are often secured by irrevocable and confirmed letters of credit issued by primary banks, in which case the risk of non-payment is practically eliminated.

#### 12.2.4.2 Letter of guarantee

Alternatively, in the event of commercial transactions within Italy, the debtor may provide security by way of a letter of guarantee issued by a bank, financial institution, legal entity, or solvent individual.

#### 12.2.4.3 Promissory note

In the event that the debtor is unable to provide an appropriate letter of guarantee, a form of security may be represented by promissory notes executed by the debtor, or by a third party, in the manner prescribed by Italian law. Promissory notes, in fact, facilitate the collection of the debt by allowing immediate executory action in the event of default. In the absence of agreement to the contrary, a creditor may proceed, at its discretion, against the principal debtor and/or the guarantor. The same remedies are available for both actions.

### 12.2.4.4   Retention of title

Retention of title grants some protection to the selling party. It must be agreed between the seller and the buyer at the time of the sale by means of an appropriate contract clause. There are some conditions for the enforceability of the retention-of-title clause, such as the recording of the contract containing such clause with the Recording Office (*Ufficio del Registro*). Such recording establishes conclusively the date of the contract, a factor which may become of paramount importance in the event the debtor becomes insolvent and there are other claims in respect of the same goods.

A further condition is that the goods being sold be clearly identified at the time of the sale. Retention of title entitles the seller to regain possession of the goods, without, however, using force to remove the same, should repossession be opposed. There are legal means to obtain such repossession; a judicial order (*decreto ingiuntivo*), in fact, may be secured in a relatively short period of time, based on which the creditor may legitimately force the delivery of the goods through judicial officers.

## 12.3   Letters before action

### 12.3.1   In general

It is customary and advisable that a formal payment demand be made on the debtor prior to commencing legal action. However, circumstances may be such that the demand letter is not advisable. This is particularly true when it has become urgent for the creditor to take legal action and delay may prejudice the concrete possibilities of the creditor to recover the sums due. The letter before action is not compulsory since legal action itself is the demand of the creditor on the debtor to make the payment.

There is another reason which may make it advisable for the creditor to formally request the payment to the debtor by letter prior to legal action. In fact, under given circumstances, interest may accrue from the date of the formal demand. Thus, a timely demand letter may generate a greater amount of interest for the creditor.

Demand letters should be forwarded by registered mail, return receipt requested, thus avoiding any uncertainty about their having been received and providing evidence of the date of receipt. Under certain circumstances, a payment demand may also be delivered to the debtor by a judicial officer. The creditor should consult an attorney if he wishes to serve the demand on the debtor through a judicial officer.

### 12.3.2   What should the letters say?

The demand by the creditor made by letter should be concise, brief, and to the point. It should contain the following:

(1)  the full name and address of the creditor and of the debtor;
(2)  the amount due and the place where it should be paid;
(3)  all required and useful references regarding the payment (number and dates of the relevant invoices or equivalent documentation); and
(4)  the indication of the time within which the payment should be made.

It is common to grant seven to eight days for payment, depending on circumstances. The letter should also put the debtor on notice that, failing payment within the indicated date, legal action will be instituted for the collection of the account receivable.

### 12.3.3   May the creditor demand interest for late payment?

Interest for late payment may be collected, and should be requested in the demand letter, if a clause providing for interest at a set rate is incorporated into the contract. In the absence of such a clause, the demand letter should contain a request for the payment of interest at the legal rate.

The demand letter should not include threats or remarks of a defamatory nature. In the event that the debt is secured, there are multiple debtors, or the creditor has additional rights depending on circumstances, the rights of the creditor should be reserved with a simple statement to that effect. Of course, if the debtors are jointly and severally liable for the debt, a payment demand may be issued to each of them for the entire amount. In this case, should one of the debtors make payment (in full or in part), the creditor must inform the other debtors of such payment and, if necessary, request payment of the balance.

## 12.4   Pre-action and non-judicial remedies

The creditor may enforce the retention-of-title clause, if such clause has been agreed in a valid manner, as described above. Even in this event, however, legal action may be required if repossession is denied by the debtor. Under certain circumstances, when the payment is to be made in cash and the buyer fails to pay, the seller may regain possession of the goods. If the debtor does not co-operate, a claim may be filed within 15 days from the delivery of the goods, provided that the goods are still in the possession of the buyer.

In the event that security has been granted, the creditor may proceed to satisfy its account receivable by relying on the security. As to the manner of such enforcement, the assistance of an attorney may be necessary.

## 12.5   The court system

### 12.5.1   Structure of courts and rules of jurisdiction

In the event that payment is not made, notwithstanding all efforts (such as, among others, the formal demand letter), the creditor will require the professional assistance of an attorney (unless the account receivable is ItL 1 million or less, in which case, at least theoretically, the creditor can pursue its claim personally before the judicial authority).

The legal action must be filed with the competent judicial authority. The Italian judicial system is organised throughout the territory and is based on different levels of jurisdiction, depending on the subject matter of the litigation and the value of the claim. Generally, the lower level of jurisdiction is the *Pretore* (who also has exclusive jurisdiction in some specific subject matters, such as labour and rent controversies). The *Tribunale* has jurisdiction for cases of higher value and for specific subject matters, such as family matters.

As for the recovery of accounts receivable, consideration must be given to the value of the claim, ie the amount of the claim, plus interest and legal expenses (which value will determine whether the jurisdiction belongs to the *Pretore* or to the *Tribunale*) and to the location of the competent judicial body. In this connection, it will be the responsibility of the attorney to establish which court has jurisdiction, considering various factors (which may include the validity of contract clauses establishing the jurisdiction in a given place). All claims between ItL 1 million and ItL 5 million fall within the jurisdiction of the *Pretore*, while claims of a higher amount are to be decided by the *Tribunale*.

Modifications of the jurisdiction based on new legislation are in the process of being introduced into the legal system. Consult your lawyer in this connection.

### 12.5.2   Appeals

The decision of the first-level judicial body (*Pretore* or *Tribunale*) is subject to appeal to the next higher court. The higher court in respect of the *Pretore* is the *Tribunale*, while the higher court in respect of the *Tribunale* is the Court of Appeal. Courts of Appeal are located in various districts in Italy. It will be the responsibility of the attorney entrusted with the case to select the Court of Appeal having territorial jurisdiction.

Appeals are not infrequent in Italian legal practice, and they will further delay the conclusion of the action. Appeal proceedings may last two or more years.

### 12.5.3   Status of the foreign creditor

A foreign creditor of an Italian debtor is entitled in all respects to exercise the same rights and actions which are exercisable by a domestic creditor. However, this may not be so when the legal system of the non-Italian creditor does not grant reciprocity to an Italian citizen seeking to exercise the same rights and actions within the legal system of the creditor.

A foreign creditor may find that its status as a foreigner may be a prejudicial factor, not in law but from a practical standpoint, in the event that foreign depositions or technical investigations are required (in which case burdensome international investigations may become necessary). Furthermore, all documents filed in court must be translated into Italian, and the translations must be sworn in the prescribed manner. An evaluation of these aspects of the litigation and of the related costs should be made by the creditor and his attorney prior to the filing of the action.

## 12.6  Legal representation

### 12.6.1  Nature of legal representation

A party must be represented in a judicial proceeding by an attorney duly admitted in Italy, unless the case involves the jurisdiction of a justice of the peace (*giudice conciliatore*), having a value not higher than ItL 1 million. In this case, the party may act on his own behalf in the judicial proceeding. Modifications of the value are being introduced.

Generally, the attorney is admitted where the action is to be filed. In the event that the creditor selects an attorney located in a different area, the creditor may grant to him the authority to designate another local attorney as needed. There should be no greater costs if the latter course is chosen.

The appointment of an attorney must be made in writing in the wording usually suggested by the attorney. Usually, the appointment is made by executing a power of attorney in the office of the attorney. If done by mail, the creditor should carefully follow the instructions of the attorney. In fact, the procedure for legislation of the power of attorney by apostille, as prescribed by the Hague Convention, may be required. In some cases, the most practical way is that of executing the power of attorney before a local notary public, if the creditor is located within the European Union (EU), or before the Italian Consul. In any event, a power of attorney granted by a simple letter signed by the creditor will not be sufficient.

When an attorney is entrusted with the case, the creditor should deal exclusively with him. This means that no direct contact should be made with the debtor (which contact would, at best, cause confusion and, at worst, be detrimental to the case). Once the creditor has appointed an attorney, the attorney will be responsible for the case and should keep the creditor informed of all significant developments.

Should the designated attorney fail to keep the creditor informed, or should the creditor for any reason not be satisfied with his professional assistance, the creditor will be entitled to select another attorney at any time. However, the creditor should be aware that the mere fact that no judicial response or decision is forthcoming on a timely basis is, in most cases, not due to the inaction or negligence of the attorney but to a number of other factors related to the slow pace and inefficiency of the court system.

### 12.6.2  Payment of legal fees

When a party requests the professional assistance of an attorney, he becomes responsible for the payment of costs and fees. The creditor may request the attorney to advise the creditor of the costs and fees the creditor may reasonably expect, even though it may be difficult for him to make intelligent estimates. In fact, costs and fees for legal services are strictly related to the activities which may be needed in the course of the proceeding and which may greatly vary depending on the developments of the case.

Italian attorneys cannot accept cases on a contingency basis, ie compensation based on the amount of recovery, if recovery occurs. It is technically mandatory for attorneys to charge fees in accordance with the schedule of fees enacted by law and which provides for minimum and maximum amounts related to each type of action taken by the attorney.

## 12.7   Costs and interest

### 12.7.1   Liability for and recovery of costs

The amount of the fees is related to the value of the case. The creditor may request that his attorney provides a copy of the schedule of fees. Apart from the fact that the schedule is written in Italian, the document will be difficult for the creditor to read, and the creditor might need assistance in this connection. Should the creditor feel that an attorney is overcharging, the creditor may replace him at any time and consult with a new attorney in regard to the propriety of the charges. In extreme cases, the creditor may have the statement of fees verified by the Bar Association with which the attorney is registered.

One peculiar rule is that both litigants, plaintiff and defendant, are jointly liable for the payment of the fees of both attorneys. This means that the creditor may ultimately be called on to pay the fees of the attorney representing his opponent should that attorney not be paid by his client. The rule is seldom applied in practice, and devices have been put into effect to limit its impact, such as that of requesting both attorneys, when a settlement is reached, to include a waiver clause to be signed by both of them.

While primary responsibility for the payment of costs and fees rests with the creditor (the party who is instructing the attorney), a judgment favourable to the creditor may include a provision awarding the creditor a sum to cover part of the creditor's costs and fees. The extent of recoverable fees and costs from the losing litigant may vary widely in respect of the full costs and fees. Recoverable fees and costs are fixed by the schedule of fees enacted by law (ranging between a minimum and maximum at the discretion of the court). In the event that the claim is only partially accepted, the judge may proportionally allocate fees and costs according to each fact situation and to the extent a party may be viewed as prevailing or not prevailing in the case.

The actual collection of fees and costs (as well as of the principal amount and interest) will depend, of course, on the existence of sufficient assets of the debtor. In any event, regardless of the final outcome and of the success or lack of success in collecting, the creditor will be directly responsible for the fees and costs of the attorney he has appointed.

### 12.7.2   Interest

Generally, an amount receivable which is liquid generates interest by effect of law. The rate of interest may be agreed by the parties. If no agreement is reached (in writing) by the parties, the so-called legal rate will apply, equal to 10 per cent per year.

## 12.8   Procedure to judgment

### 12.8.1   In general

Once the creditor has instituted legal action for the collection of the account receivable, the debtor may pay his debt at any time, in which case the cause of action will cease to exist and the proceeding will be concluded. The creditor, however, is entitled to continue the action in the event that payment is not made in full.

In fact, the creditor may be entitled not only to the principal amount but also to interest and the reimbursement of legal costs and fees, in which case the creditor might decide to instruct his attorney to continue to pursue the action unless and until the additional costs also are fully paid.

### 12.8.2   Admission of debt

The debtor, at any time prior to or in the course of the legal action, may admit the debt, in full or in part. The admission will dramatically improve the creditor's position as plaintiff in the proceeding and will entitle the creditor to obtain a judicial payment order which may be immediately executory.

Thus, the creditor will have the right to institute attachment proceedings, under court supervision, and force the sale of the assets of the debtor.

### 12.8.3   Dispute of debt

On the other hand, the debtor may dispute the debt. This may be done by filing a written defence or opposition, supported by documentary evidence or offer of testimony or request for technical investigation, as warranted under the circumstances. If a claim is disputed, the immediate consequence is that a judicial investigation will become necessary. Such investigation may include:

(1)   the review of the documents filed by each party;
(2)   the taking of oral depositions of the witnesses identified by each party;
(3)   the questioning of the parties themselves (through their authorised representatives, if it be the case); and
(4)   the appointment of technical experts, who will assist the judge and who will report to him on the specific technical issues assigned to them.

It is obvious that the carrying out of the judicial activities described above will materially affect the time needed to reduce the case to judgment and the costs and fees of the case. Careful evaluation of the possible occurrence of these delaying developments should be made at the outset of the case.

### 12.8.4   No opposition by debtor

The debtor may not react to the judicial petition of the creditor, ie may fail to file an opposition. This will mean that the debtor neither admits nor disputes the case, but simply ignores it. In this case, as has been seen above, the payment order having been issued and the debtor having failed to pay or to file an opposition to it within 20 days, the order will become final, and the creditor will be entitled to seek execution on the assets of the debtor.

If, on the other hand, the action is an ordinary action, the default by the debtor will not, in and of itself, be viewed by the court as the confession of the existence of the debt (and thus the plaintiff will need to prove its account receivable), but will be evaluated at the discretion of the judge, who may deem it a materially negative factor for the debtor. The allegations of the plaintiff, adequately supported and not contested by the debtor, may be viewed by the court as having been proven.

### 12.8.5   Bankruptcy in the course of the collection proceedings

It may happen that, in the course of the creditor's collection proceedings, the debtor is declared bankrupt. When this occurs, the collection proceedings are interrupted and have no effect. The immediate impact of the declaration of bankruptcy is that of determining the ability of the creditors to enforce individually their rights against the bankrupt debtor, as such rights become exercisable exclusively in accordance with bankruptcy rules.

If, on the other hand, the legal action instituted by the creditor is directed to obtain a judgment regarding the existence (as opposed to the enforcement) of rights which are disputed by his opponent, the creditor, notwithstanding the bankruptcy, may have an interest (although such rights, once judicially recognised, may not be enforceable because of the bankruptcy) to proceed judicially against the bankrupt estate itself, represented by its receiver. The creditor's attorney will give the creditor the appropriate advice in this connection.

## 12.9   Enforcing judgment

### 12.9.1   Payment order

Generally, commercial accounts receivable entitle the creditor to a summary judicial remedy called a payment order (*decreto ingiuntivo*). This is an order issued ex parte by the judge having jurisdiction over the case. The request for a payment order is subject to the condition that the evidence of the account receivable is documentary, within the meaning attributed to the word by the law.

The payment order is issued on the basis of the documents evidencing the existence and the validity of the claim, generally in a matter of days (at the latest, two to three weeks). The order will call on the debtor to pay the amount in question within 20 days (or, in some specified circumstances, immediately) and will advise him of his right to file a written judicial opposition, within the 20-day period and in the manner prescribed by the law. Under given circumstances, the payment order may be immediately executory. In any event, it will become executory if no opposition is filed by the debtor within 20 days, as specified in the order.

If, on the other hand, a written opposition is filed by the debtor within the prescribed term, the filing of an opposition will trigger the institution of the so-called ordinary proceeding. In the course of the first hearing of such ordinary proceeding (usually six to eight weeks from the issuance of the payment order, but sometimes longer), the petitioner may request that the payment order be declared provisionally executory, unless it has been already so declared on its issue.

If the order is declared provisionally executory, the unsatisfied creditor may attach the assets of the debtor and attempt to obtain satisfaction through the sale of said assets under judicial supervision. The creditor should be aware that, while a *decreto ingiuntivo* proceeding may bring results, if not opposed, in a matter of weeks, such proceeding, if opposed, will develop into an ordinary proceeding which may require years before a final judgment is rendered.

### 12.9.2 Execution by attachment of debtor's assets

Once the judgment is obtained, be it a final judgment or a judgment which is declared provisionally executory, the creditor is entitled to enforce it by means of executory action. This is normally accomplished by means of the attachment of the assets of the debtor, ie the physical identification by the clerk of the court of the assets (usually with the active co-operation of the creditor) and the issue of an order by the judicial officer to the debtor not to sell or assign the assets to any third party and to keep them in custody so that they may be disposed in accordance with the law.

The assets are sold at a public auction at a later time (months and sometimes years later), under judicial supervision, and the proceeds are applied first to cover taxes and the administrative fees and costs of the attachment-sale procedure and secondly to satisfy the debt.

The costs of the executory proceeding, although relatively low, should be taken into consideration at the outset. It may happen, in fact, that the proceeds of the sale will be lower than the cost of the sale procedure. Such cost is to be borne by the party who has requested the sale.

### 12.9.3 Attachment of assets located with third parties

Another way to carry out the execution is that of attaching assets belonging to the debtor but located with third parties or attaching sums which are due to the debtor by third parties. Should the creditor know that sums are owed to his debtor, the creditor, by way of execution, may obtain a judicial order directed to the third party (the debtor of the creditor's debtor) to pay to the creditor directly the amount the creditor is entitled to receive. This principle also applies to the wages of the debtor, but only to the extent of one-fifth of the amount of the debtor's wages.

Executory proceedings are subject to the right of other creditors to intervene in the action and attach the same assets already attached by the creditor to protect his account receivable. In this event, the intervening creditors will be entitled to share the proceeds of the sale on a proportional basis. Likewise, the creditor may intervene in other pending executory proceedings against the same debtor and obtain his proportional share of the distribution.

## 12.10  Insolvency

### 12.10.1  Insolvency of the debtor

Insolvency is generally defined as the inability of the debtor to meet regularly his obligations. Failure by the debtor to meet one or more debts is not, in and of itself, tantamount to a state of insolvency, such as would justify the petitioning for the declaration of bankruptcy. This means that petitioning for bankruptcy of the debtor may not always be the appropriate means to obtain collection (even though it often proves to be the most effective one).

In any event, the creditor's attorney will need to direct the creditor. Should the creditor's petition for the declaration of the bankruptcy of the debtor be rejected by the *Tribunale*, the creditor may be required to pay to the debtor the costs and fees of his defence. The creditor also may be exposed to a damage action.

A petition for bankruptcy implies not only a situation of established insolvency of the debtor but also implies the existence of the creditor's undisputed right to be paid (typically evidenced by a judgment). The proceeding for the declaration of bankruptcy requires a hearing before the *Tribunale* having jurisdiction over the location of the debtor, in the course of which the debtor may oppose the request. The decision is issued in the form of a judgment, which is subject to appeal. The judgment will contain a provision appointing a bankruptcy receiver and setting the date of the hearing for the verification of all claims by the creditors.

Once bankruptcy has been declared, all pending executory proceedings are automatically terminated and collection by the creditors may occur only through the distribution which will take place at the closing of the bankruptcy proceeding once the liquidation process has been completed.

Proceedings which are classified, in a general way, as bankruptcy proceedings, however, may be carried out without the mandatory liquidation of the debtor company. This occurs, among other cases, when the insolvency is deemed to be of a temporary nature, in which case the debtor may be legally authorised, subject to the approval of the creditors, to suspend the payment of his obligations for a given period of time (up to 24 months) or to pay only a percentage (the minimum being 40 per cent) of his debt.

### 12.10.2    Personal insolvency

In the event that the debtor is not an enterprise or a businessman who has incurred the debt in connection with his business activities, the creditor may not seek a declaration of bankruptcy but may still institute executory proceedings.

If, on the other hand, the debtor is a commercial enterprise, having a legal form which does not limit the liability of its owners (eg, a partnership), the creditor also may petition for the bankruptcy of the individual owners.

## Chapter 13

# LUXEMBOURG

**René Faltz**
**Faltz & Associés**
**Luxembourg**

## 13.1   Introduction

This chapter provides an overview of the procedures available to the creditor for collection of debts in Luxembourg. Reference also is made to relevant aspects of the legal system.

## 13.2   Initial considerations

### 13.2.1   Legal entities

The following entities can be pursued in Luxembourg courts:

(1)   individuals, trading in their own name or acting as traders;

(2)   commercial companies, such as the *société anonyme*, the *société a responsabilité limitée*, the *société en nom collectif*, the *société en commandite simple*, the *société en commandite par actions*, and the *société cooperative*, all being represented in court by their statutory representatives;

(3)   civil companies, created by agreements between two or more persons willing to do something in common in order to share the profits;[1]

(4)   associations and public utility companies; and

(5)   the Grand-Duchy of Luxembourg.

### 13.2.2   Sources of information

If the debtor is an individual, the creditor can trace him by using telephone books or by contacting the *bureau de la population* of the commune where he lives or used to live.

For registered companies and individuals using a registered trading name, the easiest way to trace a debtor is to contact the trade register (telephone 22 18 83), which can provide information about the existence, form, and registered office of the debtor.

The creditor can also contact the office responsible for the publication of the official journal, the *Memorial C*, (telephone 478 2151) for references to the various official publications concerning a registered company.

---

1   Such companies cannot be sued as a legal entity, but all the associates must be personally sued.

*13.2.2.1   Is the debt statute-barred?*

In Luxembourg, actions for recovery of debts must generally be introduced within 30 years after the date on which the money becomes due for payment. However, the following exceptions must be noted:

(1)   six months for the recovery of teacher's fees;
(2)   six months for the recovery of hotel and restaurant invoices;
(3)   one year for the recovery of bailiff's fees;
(4)   one year for invoices concerning goods sold by tradesmen to non-tradesmen;
(5)   two years for the recovery of lawyer's fees;
(6)   three years for salaries;
(7)   five years for alimony arrears and perpetual and life pensions;
(8)   five years for the recovery of rents; and
(9)   five years for the recovery of interest on loans and generally of any amount due year-after-year.

### 13.2.3   Security

There are various forms of security available in Luxembourg, the most important being guarantees, mortgages, pledges, and charges.

The most common security, especially because of its easy use, is the guarantee. Once the debtor does not pay, the creditor may return against the guarantor, against whom he may use the same means as against the main debtor.

### 13.2.4   Retention of title

Usually, the transfer of property is realised at the moment when the contracting parties have agreed on the object and the price of the contract. However, the parties may agree that the transfer of property be delayed until a certain event occurs, such as payment. This is a retention-of-title clause. In such a case, as long as payment has not occurred, the seller will be the owner of the goods.

The major problem often is the enforcement of the clause. If the goods have been resold by the buyer or if they are no longer identifiable, it will be impossible to enforce the retention-of-title clause. However, as long as the goods are still in the possession of the buyer, there should normally be no problem in enforcement.

The person in possession of the goods should be notified by registered mail that the goods will be removed on a certain date. If the debtor refuses to relinquish the goods, it is advisable to immediately proceed by means of an attachment in order to ensure that the goods will not be removed and will remain available for retention.

## 13.3 Letters before action

It is recommended that a letter before action is sent by a lawyer prior to the issue of proceedings. Letters before action can be considered as the date from which interest runs.

### 13.3.1 What should they say?

The letter must clearly indicate the cause and the amount of the debt. It also must include the bank account to which the money must be transferred. Usually, the debtor is asked to transfer the money to the account of the creditor's lawyer, as that way it is easier for the lawyer in charge of the file to supervise the situation.

The letter before action should also mention a date after which proceedings will be initiated if payment has not occurred. For reasons of proof, such letters must be sent by registered mail.

## 13.4 Pre-action and non-judicial remedies

If it is necessary to prevent the debtor from selling his assets, in order to ensure that payment will be possible by the debtor, the creditor may seek the attachment of the debtor's assets.

The attachment of assets is granted on a decision of the President of the Commercial Section of the District Court. The creditor does not need a legal title proving the debt. However, certain conditions must be fulfilled before assets may be attached.

First, the debtor whose assets will be attached must be a trader. Secondly, the situation must be one of urgency. There must be elements which force the creditor to act rapidly, as otherwise the money due will not be recovered. Thirdly, the debt must be current and identifiable at the moment when the attachment is requested.

Even if a legal title is not compulsory, there must nevertheless be a sufficient appearance of certainty of the debt. The President of the Commercial Section of the District Court will not grant the attachment if the required elements are imprecise and unconvincing.

If the attachment is granted on certain assets, the debtor cannot dispose of them until the judgment is given either to dismiss the debt, in which case the attachment must be withdrawn, or to certify the debt, in which case the execution procedure as developed below can be followed.

## 13.5 The court system

### 13.5.1 The Justice of the Peace

Any recovery of debts of less than LUF 200,000 must be filed before the Justice of the Peace (*Justice de Paix*). There are three Justices of the Peace in Luxembourg (Luxembourg City, Diekirch, and Esch-sur-Alzette).

### 13.5.2 The District Court

Every recovery of a debt worth more than LUF 200,000 must be dealt with before the District Court (*Tribunal d'arrondissement*). There a two District Courts in Luxembourg (Luxembourg City and Diekirch). There are two ways of proceeding before the District Court.

### 13.5.3 Appeals

Appeals of judgments of the Justice of the Peace are lodged before the District Court. Appeals of judgments of the District Court are lodged before the Court of Appeals.

## 13.6  Legal representation

### 13.6.1  Nature of legal representation

Proceedings must be divided into two categories. On the one hand, proceedings before the Justice of the Peace, the judge for summary proceedings, and the Commercial Section of the District Court do not require representation by a lawyer. Individuals may defend themselves without the intervention of a lawyer. Companies may be represented by their legal representatives, or by their employees if they have a special proxy issued by the company.

However, even if representation by a lawyer is not compulsory, it is nevertheless the only authorised way of representation; the intervening parties either appear in person or they are represented by a lawyer, noting, however, the following exceptions:

(1) members of a trade union or any professional organisation may be represented by a delegate of that union or organisation, in their cases before the social security courts; and

(2) anyone having litigation with the tax authorities may be represented by a qualified accountant or an auditor.

For all other proceedings, representation by a lawyer is compulsory.

### 13.6.2  Mode of payment for legal representation

Normally, the costs for legal representation are to be paid by the person hiring the lawyer. However, the judge may decide that it is inequitable to let the plaintiff pay for the entire cost of his representation if it clearly appears that the proceedings are due to the unique fault of the defendant. In such a case, the judge may order the defendant to pay part of the plaintiff's legal representation costs.

The basis of a charge can be determined in various ways. The creditor may arrange a fixed fee with the creditor's lawyer. The creditor also may be charged on an hourly basis, the rates varying among firms. Instructions on a purely contingency fee basis are not allowed.

Usually, lawyers' fees depend on several elements in relationship to the file, including the importance of the case, its difficulty, the result, and the financial situation of the client.

## 13.7  Costs and interest

### 13.7.1  In general

Costs for a judicial action include the bailiff's fees for serving writs of summons and judgments. These must be paid by the losing party. The losing party must pay to the opponent's lawyer costs due in any procedure where representation by a lawyer is compulsory and they are determined by the law (*frais et emoluments*). A part of these costs is fixed, and a part is proportional to the value of the claim.

### 13.7.2  Legal aid

Individuals in a difficult financial situation may ask for legal aid. Persons interested in receiving legal aid must present a request to the Board of Lawyers, together with a certificate from the commune, attesting that that person is not taxable, due to his low income.

If the request is granted, the member of the Board of Lawyers in charge of legal aid appoints a lawyer to defend the interests of the applicant. The appointed lawyer has no right to charge fees to the person who is admitted to legal aid. He must work for free.

However, there is a proposal to introduce a new law in Luxembourg, according to which the State would pay the lawyers' fees for persons qualified for legal aid, based on a tariff determined by a law.

### 13.7.3  Liability for and recovery of costs

Legal costs, with the exception of lawyers' fees, are charged to the person who loses the case. For the recovery of legal costs, the same rules as for the recovery of other debts are applied, with the exception that their charge is already defined by an executory judgment based on the main proceedings.

### 13.7.4  Interest

The creditor may claim two kinds of interest: contractual interest or interest at the legal rate.

#### 13.7.4.1  *Contractual interest*

At the conclusion of an agreement, the creditor may decide that, in case of late payment by the debtor, interest at a conventional rate and a compensatory indemnity for late payment will become due. However, to protect the consumer, such interest is allowed by the courts only if two cumulative conditions are present:

(1) the two parties must have had a continuous trading relationship in the past; and

(2) the debtor must be sufficiently informed of the supplementary charge imposed on him in case of late payment; he may have expressly accepted the provisions or his attention may have been attracted to that particular provision.

However, the existence of those two conditions is very difficult to prove. Luxembourg courts are very reluctant to allow a creditor interest at a contractual rate.

### 13.7.4.2 *Legal interest*

Legal interest is allowed by the judge any time a debtor is ordered to pay his debt. There remains, however, the question of the date from which the legal interest will accrue.

As noted above, letters before action have an important impact in determining the date from which interest will accrue. In the majority of cases, the judge decides that legal interest is due from the date of the letter before action. If such a letter has not been sent before a judicial action, legal interest will accrue from the date of the summons before the court. The legal interest rate in Luxembourg is 7.75 per cent.

## 13.8    Issuing proceedings

### 13.8.1    The Justice of the Peace

There are two kinds of proceedings for the recovery of those debts. For cases without serious dispute, the simplest method of recovery is by the use of the *ordonnance de paiement*.

By a request on a pre-printed form, the creditor may ask the main judge of the Justice of the Peace to give an order (*ordonnance de paiement*) to the debtor to pay the amount due.

Within 15 days of receipt by the debtor of the order, he may oppose (*contredit*) the order by a letter to the clerk's office. In that case, both parties will be called before the Justice of the Peace to present their positions, on which the judge will take his decision in a judgment.

If the debtor does not oppose the payment order within the 15-day period and if he does not pay that period, the creditor may ask the judge to issue an executory title, enabling the creditor to enforce the court order.

The creditor also may proceed by means of a summons to appear before the Justice of the Peace, in which case a bailiff must serve the debtor with the summons. The summons must contain details regarding both the debtor and the creditor and the amount and the basis of the debt plus interest.

The writ of summons must be served on the defendant by a bailiff. The initiative for forwarding the writ to the bailiff must be taken by the lawyer. At the date fixed for appearance in court, the defendant must be present personally or be represented by a lawyer. At the first appearance, the case is normally continued to another date for pleadings.

### 13.8.2   The District Court

Here, a distinction must be made between oral and written procedures. In both procedures, the writ of summons prepared by the lawyer must be served on the defendant by a bailiff. In the written procedure (applicable for all actions where the representation by a lawyer is compulsory), the defendant must engage a lawyer who must inform (*constitution d'avoué*) the plaintiff's lawyer that he will represent the defendant.

The opposing lawyers must then exchange their points of view and any practical and legal arguments by written pleas, which must be notified to the opponent at least five days before the date of the hearing. The oral procedure before the District Court is the same as the procedure before the Justice of the Peace.

If the debt cannot be seriously disputed by the debtor, the creditor may serve a writ to the debtor to appear before the judge for summary proceedings, and the judge may validate the creditor's claim against the debtor. This manner of proceeding is meant to accelerate the debt collection, which normally tends to be quite long.

However, even in summary proceedings, it usually takes several months before a judgment (*ordonnance*) can be taken. It should be noted that a judgment in summary proceedings is only provisional.

If the debt is seriously disputed by the debtor, the creditor must serve a writ to the debtor to appear, either before the Civil Section of the District Court, if the debtor is a non-trader, or before the Commercial Section if the debtor is a trader (individual or company). A trader is defined as being a person (individual or company) whose usual profession is to perform commercial acts. Proceedings in a disputed claim can take up to two years.

## 13.9   Procedure to judgment

### 13.9.1   The debtor pays the debt

If the debtor pays his debt before the hearing in court, the case is simply cancelled and removed from the roll of the court. If the payment does not include costs and interest, the plaintiff may enter a judgment for these.

### 13.9.2   The debtor admits the debt

If the debtor admits the debt, but does not pay, it is advisable to obtain a judgment. After the judgment, it is always possible to allow the debtor delays for payment, by monthly instalments, for instance.

If the debtor does not adhere to the agreement for repayment or if no such agreement had been taken, the creditor may proceed to enforcement of the judgment.

### 13.9.3 The debtor disputes the debt

In the procedure of the *ordonnance de paiement*, the debtor must dispute the debt by the means of the *contredit*, which is done by a written declaration at the clerk's office of the Justice of the Peace. This declaration must mention briefly the reasons why the debtor does not admit the debt. The court then summons the creditor and the debtor, where they must defend their positions before the judge, who then makes a judgment.

The executory title granted by the judge in the procedure by *ordonnance de paiement* has the same effect as a default judgment. If the debtor did not offer a *contredit* at the first step of the procedure but wants to dispute the debt, he still has the possibility to appeal against that executory title within 15 days from the date of the notification of that title to the debtor.

In the procedure by writ of summons, before the Justice of the Peace or before the District Court, the debtor or his lawyer must provide reasons for not admitting the debt before the court. If the debtor does not do so, the creditor may enter a default judgment, from which the debtor, however, may appeal within 15 days.

### 13.9.4 The debtor disputes part of the debt

Where the debtor disputes only part of the debt, the combined procedures discussed at **13.9.2** and **13.9.3** will apply.

### 13.9.5 The debtor neither admits nor disputes the debt

If the debtor does not react to the proceedings instituted against him, the plaintiff may enter a default judgment, followed by execution as described below.

### 13.9.6 The debtor is declared insolvent

If the debtor is declared insolvent and has been declared bankrupt by the court, individual creditors may not seek to collect ahead of other creditors. The curator of the bankruptcy must ensure that any individual action will be stopped. The curator must attempt to realise the assets of the bankrupt's estate in order to proportionally reimburse the creditors. Certain categories of creditors are privileged, in a sense that they will be reimbursed before unsecured creditors.

## 13.10 Enforcing judgment

### 13.10.1 Execution

Before proceeding to the execution of a judgment, an order must be notified to the debtor, at least one day before the execution. During the execution, the bailiff must be assisted by two witnesses.

The bailiff must draft an official report, meeting the required formalities and giving the order to the debtor to pay his debt. The report must also precisely detail the nature of the seized assets. Certain assets, necessary to ensure a decent human life for the debtor, cannot be seized. The report must also indicate the date of the execution sale, which cannot be earlier than eight days after the execution.

### 13.10.2 Garnishment

Garnishment is a remedy which allows a creditor to attach amounts due to the defendant by one of his debtors. The remedy is mostly used against banks which hold deposits of the debtor.

If the creditor has no official title concerning his claim, he must request an authorisation to attach from the President of the District Court. If the creditor has an official title concerning his claim, or the authorisation by the President, a writ concerning the attachment or prohibition to deliver any amount of money to the defendant is served by a bailiff on the garnishee, who must then refrain from delivering money or assets to the defendant.

Within eight days, the plaintiff must notify the attachment to the defendant and to serve on him a writ of summons in order to validate the attachment. Within another eight days, the request for validation must be notified to the garnishee. If validation has not been claimed within the eight-day period, the entire procedure is cancelled.

At the hearing, the court must decide whether the claim is justified. The creditor, in possession of a validated attachment, will receive from the garnishee the total amount of the debt. If the garnishee does not make the payments, he is personally responsible for the reimbursement of the claim.

### 13.10.3 Attachment of earnings

If the debtor is a wage earner, the creditor may request that the earnings of the debtor be attached. If the creditor wants to attach wages, he must determine who the debtor's employer is.

The creditor can obtain this information through the Social Security Institution, which maintains a record of all the wage earners and their employers. However, the Institution is only required to give the creditor information on an order by the Justice of the Peace. Such an order can be issued in response to a simple written request.

Once the identity of the employer is known, the creditor may request a Justice of the Peace to order the attachment of wages. This request may be made by using a pre-printed form. It must indicate the name, address, and status of the creditor and the debtor, the debtor's employer, and the basis and the amount of the debt.

The creditor must include with the request all documents establishing the debt, such as invoices or the judgment confirming the debt.

If the judge considers that the debt is valid, he enjoins the debtor's employer to retain the salary of the debtor up to the amount of the debt. The whole of the salary is not attachable, so it may take a long time before the debt is completely paid.

Once the attachment is granted, the creditor must ask that the clerk's office summon the parties to court in order to validate the attachment. This must be done within six months from the date the attachment has been granted by the judge.

## 13.11   Insolvency

Any merchant, individual, or company which has suspended payments and whose credit standing is disturbed can be subject to a bankruptcy procedure. There are three ways to commence a bankruptcy procedure.

The trader himself may be aware of his desperate situation and make an admission of that situation to the court, which then declares the bankruptcy.

The bankruptcy procedure may also be initiated by one of the trader's creditors. If the creditor has a claim against the debtor and the creditor believes that the debtor will not be able to pay the amount due, the creditor may proceed by an action to declare the debtor bankrupt.

The Commercial Section of the District Court must decide whether the defendant has suspended his payments and whether his credit standing is disturbed. If these two conditions are fulfilled, the court may declare the defendant bankrupt and appoint a curator to effect conduct of the bankruptcy and a judge commissioner to supervise these operations. The curator will normally be a lawyer.

The Commercial Section of the District Court can automatically declare an individual or company bankrupt if there is sufficient evidence that the debtor is insolvent.

After the declaration of bankruptcy, the defendant is no longer allowed to act personally in conducting his affairs. The curator will act in the name of the insolvent debtor and take over the daily administration in order to liquidate the company or to re-establish the financial situation of the individual. The curator will realise the assets in order to be able to reimburse as many creditors as possible.

The creditors must file declarations concerning their claim against the insolvent debtor before a date fixed by the court in the judgment declaring the debtor bankrupt. The declaration is filed at the clerk's office of the competent court, and it must indicate the name of the creditor, the amount of the claim and its basis, and the affirmation that the declaration is genuine and true.

After the realisation of the debtor's assets, the proceeds will be distributed among all the creditors whose claims had been acknowledged by the curator. Certain claims are privileged, such as those relating to salaries, taxes, value added tax, and social security. These claims will be reimbursed before any others.

The reimbursement will be done proportionally. Often, the assets are taken up by the privileged creditors, so that the unsecured creditors will recover, if anything, only a small part of their claim.

*Chapter 14*

# THE NETHERLANDS

**Sandra A In 't Veld**
**Van Schoonhoven In 't Veld**
**Amsterdam, The Netherlands**

## 14.1   Introduction

This chapter deals with the legal aspects of the collection of debts in The Netherlands. As in many countries in continental Europe, The Netherlands has codified its laws, and the Dutch civil legal system is set out in the Dutch Civil Code. The Netherlands has a civil law system, originally based on the French Civil Code. There are significant differences between the Dutch legal system and the Anglo-American common law system. The courts of The Netherlands consist of appointed civil servants, who are completely independent from the government.

Provided that parties to a contract have not agreed on arbitration or agree on arbitration after a conflict arises, judges decide on all cases. The Netherlands does not have a jury system. Legal proceedings are largely conducted in writing. The courts can base their decisions only on the information submitted to them by the parties and which is proven or not disputed or is information of accepted general knowledge. The following survey is limited to civil proceedings and does not deal with criminal or administrative law aspects.

## 14.2   Initial considerations

When confronted with a claim against an individual or a company domiciled or established in The Netherlands, the creditor must consider appropriate measures to recover the debt. Before any action can be taken, all relevant information and documentation must be gathered.

The exact status of the debtor and the contractual relations with the debtor must be established. It should be verified whether the claim is still enforceable and, if so, whether any direct or indirect securities which have been granted may be enforced.

### 14.2.1   Status of the debtor

If the debtor is a private individual, his exact full name and address must be determined. The address can be verified by means of a search with the registry office (*Bevolkingsregister*) of the municipality in which the debtor is believed to live.

If the debtor is an enterprise, whether in the form of a company with limited liability, a partnership, or an individual trading under a trade name, information on domicile, capital, managers, and who is authorised to represent the enterprise towards third parties can be obtained from the Trade Register of the Chamber of Commerce in the area where the enterprise is registered. There are 12 Chambers of Commerce in The Netherlands.

If the debtor is a governmental institution, the Dutch state, which is based in The Hague, must be addressed. If a writ of summons must be served, special rules need to be observed. If a municipality or a province is involved, the municipality or the province itself should be addressed.

Investigation agencies may be requested to provide information on the debtor and its assets. It should be taken into account that minors under 18 years of age do not have the capacity to enter into contracts and, thus, cannot be pursued for their debts unless they have received specific permission from a court to trade. This is also the case with individuals who are mentally disqualified and, consequently, do not have the capacity to enter into contracts.

### 14.2.2 Is the claim statute-barred?

The enforceability of a claim will depend on whether the claim is time-barred. This could follow from a foreign statute of limitation if a foreign substantive law is applicable to the claim.

If Dutch law is applicable, the general period of limitation for recovery of claims is five years, running from the moment the claim is due and payable. For specific subject matters, other limitation periods may apply, varying between three and 20 years.

The period of limitation can be barred by the creditor with a letter of summons. When a letter of summons has been sent to the debtor, a new period of limitation commences and, to prevent the claim from being statute-barred again after a certain period of time, new actions must be taken.

### 14.2.3 Security

Prior to the entering into a contract, but also during the performance of a contract, a creditor can negotiate the granting of security by the debtor in order to obtain comfort that the obligations under the contract will be fulfilled. There are various forms of security. A distinction can be made between real and personal security.

Real security gives the creditor, in case of enforcement, the right to be paid from the proceeds of a particular asset (not necessarily owned by the debtor), with priority over unsecured creditors. Personal security gives the creditor a right to enforce his claim against all assets of the debtor, without priority over unsecured creditors, or it gives the creditor a right to enforce his claim against persons other than the debtor. The latter can be achieved by means of a third-party guarantee or by means of a statement making the debtor and the other person jointly and severally liable. The types of security mostly used in business relations are the following.

### 14.2.3.1  Mortgage

A mortgage (*hypotheek*) is only possible on registered goods, eg, land or buildings, registered vessels, or registered aircraft. Once the mortgage has been registered with the appropriate registry office, it will provide security, regardless of subsequent transfer of title. A debt thus secured will rank prior to virtually all others. The following deals with mortgages on property only.

A mortgage can be created only by means of a Dutch notarial deed between the owner of the property and the creditor asking security, followed by registration of this deed with the Land Registry Office. The civil law notary takes care of this registration. The date of registration determines the priority. The civil law notary will check the title of and the encumbrances on the property to be mortgaged before passing the deed. Notarial and registration fees are related to the amount of the debt secured by a mortgage. Invariably, these costs are for the account of the debtor.

Married persons require the approval of their spouses for dealing with and encumbering a house they jointly use or which is used by one of them. The same applies to the inventory of such house, relevant in the case of a right of pledge, which will be discussed below. If this requirement has not been observed, the other spouse can simply nullify the transaction by addressing a statement to this effect to the party with whom his partner concluded the transaction.

### 14.2.3.2  Right of pledge

A pledge (*pandrecht*) is the right of a creditor to be paid from the proceeds of a debtor's movable asset in his possession, with priority over other creditors. The requirements for creating a right of pledge are:

(1)  a written agreement between the creditor and the debtor, in which the goods which are pledged are specified; and

(2)  possession by the creditor of the goods which are pledged.

A pledge is not possible in regard to a movable asset which remains in the control of the debtor or the pledgor. The asset must be in the custody of the pledgee or his agent or of a third party agreed on by the parties.

Here, also, a married person requires the consent of his spouse for a pledge of the furniture and household effects of the house where the couple are jointly resident or where other spouse is resident.

A pledgee has the right to withhold the asset until the debt secured by the pledge has been fully repaid, including interest and charges, as well as any costs dispersed by the pledgee for the preservation of the asset. However, the pledgor has the right to claim back the asset in the event of the pledgee's abuse of the pledge.

### 14.2.3.3  Non-possessory lien or pledge

A non-possessory lien (*stil pandrecht*) is a right of a creditor to take possession of certain movable assets which are not brought in the possession of the creditor, after the debtor is in default.

The non-possessory lien is converted into a right of pledge, as discussed above, at the moment the creditor takes possession of the assets. A non-possessory lien is quite common in normal business practice. A non-possessory lien can be created only by a Dutch notarial deed or an officially registered written agreement.

### 14.2.3.4 Guarantee

The guarantee is a form of personal security which is often used, making another person or entity a joint and several co-debtor. For business transactions, a bank guarantee is often used. A proper bank guarantee provides that a reputable, recognised bank commit itself to pay the debt to the creditor should the debtor be in default.

The wording of the bank guarantee should be checked carefully, as the obligation of the bank to secure the debt fully depends on such wording.

### 14.2.3.5 Other forms of security

Retention of title (*eigendomsvoorbehoud*) is a person's reservation of the right of ownership with respect to certain property as a security for certain obligations of another party to whom the property's possession has been transferred. Retention of title is most commonly used in connection with the sale and purchase of property, whereby the seller retains the title to the property until the purchaser has fully paid the purchase price and/or has complied with other obligations to the seller.

When the seller is fully paid, an automatic transfer of ownership takes place from the seller to the purchaser. Retention of title can take place by oral or written agreement or, as is often the case, it can be stipulated in general terms and conditions. It should be noted that Dutch law only allows the retention of title as a security for payment of goods which are the object of the purchase agreement. Retention of title as security for obligations not related to the specific transaction, or in favour of third parties (eg, banks or other financiers) is considered to be null and void.

Set-off (*schuldvergelijking, compensatie*) takes place by force of law when two persons are mutually in debt to each other, when both debts are due and payable, and to the extent that they are reciprocally due. The creditor must send a statement to the debtor to the effect that set-off will be applied. Set-off is limited to reciprocal debts in sums of money and to reciprocal obligations to supply consumable goods of the same type. By agreement, parties often limit the possibility of set-off. General conditions of sale frequently contain such a clause, obliging the purchaser to pay the price without set-off.

Right of retention (*retentierecht*) is the right of, eg, a repairman to retain goods given into repair, if he has not been paid for the repair work. The repairman can retain the goods until he is paid and, if not, he can foreclose on the goods. The right of retention is different from retention of title.

Subordination (*achterstelling*) of a claim is outside the scope of this chapter. But briefly, in a subordination, instead of a right to be paid with priority, the creditor consents to be paid after certain, or all other, creditors have been satisfied. However, a creditor's position may improve if another creditor can be persuaded to subordinate his claim. The subordinated creditor, to a certain degree, can be compared with a guarantor with respect to those other creditors.

The inter-company guarantee gives rise to a special form of joint and several liability. It occurs when a parent company, in order to avoid publishing separate annual accounts of a subsidiary, deposits a statement of responsibility with the competent Commercial Register, declaring itself jointly and severally liable for the subsidiary's trade debts. This declaration is known as a '403 *verklaring*', referring to Article 403 of Book 2 of the Dutch Civil Code. Whether such a statement has been filed with the Trade Register of the competent Chamber of Commerce can be verified by telephone.

### 14.2.4   Privileges and the Dutch tax authorities

Within the scope of limiting risks, a debtor can be asked to provide for direct or indirect securities, as mentioned above. When these securities are enforced, a creditor may inadvertently be confronted with the highly privileged position of the Dutch tax authorities. By virtue of the Dutch Civil Code, creditors share, in principle, equal rights regarding the net proceeds of the goods of a debtor (*paritas creditorum*). However, there are exceptions to this rule.

First, the Civil Code provides for certain privileges (*voorrechten*) in case of bankruptcy, eg, the privileges of the tax authorities, employees, and administrative expenses of the bankruptcy petition. Secondly, a preferential position may have been secured by a creditor himself (by holding a security, such as a mortgage or pledge). Claims ensured by mortgage and pledge precede the privileges stipulated by the Civil Code.

These privileges are subdivided according to priority, the rights of the tax authorities having the highest priority in almost all cases. A second factor of enhancement of the tax authorities' position is the so-called *bodemrecht* (a particularly preferential right). This right enables the tax authorities to levy an attachment on *bodemzaken*, goods situated on the 'floor' (*bodem*) of a tax debtor, ie, fixtures and fittings for permanent use. Hence, the attachment does not apply to stock and fleets of cars. The *bodemzaken* may comprise goods that are not fully owned by a debtor, but by a third party.

It should be given due consideration that these goods may also be claimed by the Dutch tax authorities. Only those cases that are not based on some form of financial lease agreement, the so-called *reële eigendomsverhoudingen*, are respected. By virtue of the *bodemrecht*, the following goods can be claimed by the tax authorities:

(1)   goods used by the debtor that are subject to a financial lease agreement; and

(2)   goods used by the debtor with reservation of title.

Furthermore, it should be noted that the tax authorities have preferential claims on *bodemzaken* subject to a non-possessory lien.

## 14.3   Letters before action

### 14.3.1   Are they necessary?

From a strictly legal point of view, letters in which the debtor is summoned to pay are not necessary. By failing to meet the obligations under the contract, the debtor is already in default.

However, especially if an invoice does not state a specific due date and in order to avoid the possibility that a court might rule that a claim is not reasonable or that action was taken without proper notice, it is advisable to remind the debtor of his obligations and to properly document written and telephone communications.

### 14.3.2   What should they say?

Once the creditor's own credit control procedures are exhausted, he should arrange for a letter before action to be sent by his lawyer (*advocaat*).

In choosing an *advocaat* in The Netherlands, the foreign creditor may wish to rely on the advice of his local solicitor. Otherwise, The Netherlands Order of Advocates (*Nederlandse Orde van Advocaten*), established in The Hague, can be of assistance in making the selection. In any case, the demand letter should mention the following:

(1)   full and correct name and domicile of the debtor;
(2)   specific reference to the outstanding invoice, the date thereof, and the due date of payment;
(3)   formal demand for payment;
(4)   formal demand for interest for late payment;
(5)   notification that the debtor will be liable for costs of proceedings;
(6)   notification of final payment term; and
(7)   notice of initiation of court proceedings if the final payment term is not met.

The letter should be sent by registered mail, with receipt confirmed, as well as by regular mail, in order to avoid any possible defence in court proceedings by the debtor that the reminder was not received.

### 14.3.3   May they demand interest for late payment?

In the case of money claims, the court, at the request of the creditor, will grant interest for late payment. The so-called statutory or legal interest is calculated from the day by which the debtor was in default. The interest is due without the creditor having to prove any cost or damages caused by the delay.

## 14.4   Pre-action remedies

When confronted with a reluctant debtor, the creditor may consider the following actions prior to initiating legal proceedings.

### 14.4.1 Attachment

There are several kinds of attachment (*beslag*). A distinction can be made between the attachment to enforce a judgment or an obligation established in a notarial deed, (*executoriaal beslag*) and the attachment to freeze assets, the so-called conservatory attachment (*conservatoir beslag*).

A conservatory attachment is an important and widely used action to prevent a debtor from frustrating recovery by its creditor. Conservatory attachment can be made, for instance, on assets of the debtor in his possession, on assets of the debtor held by another party (the third-party attachment), including part of the salary which must be paid to the debtor, and on shares in a company.

Before a conservatory attachment can be made, a creditor must receive permission from the President of the competent District Court. Usually, the permission is granted at very short notice. The debtor is generally not heard. After the permission has been obtained, a court bailiff must be instructed to make the attachment. The District Court President who grants the permission also determines a period of time in which court proceedings against the debtor should be initiated. This period of time must be a minimum of eight days.

A conservatory attachment can be made only through the services of a lawyer. A debtor who is of the opinion that conservatory attachment is wrongfully made or is unreasonably burdensome may initiate preliminary relief proceedings to obtain a court order to lift the attachment, or he may offer a (bank) guarantee in exchange for such lifting.

### 14.4.2 Repossession

Retention of title has been dealt with above. If a transaction has been entered into under the condition of retention of title, the seller owns the sold property until the secured obligations have been met. Therefore, the seller may repossess such property if the purchaser defaults on any of the secured obligations, eg, by failing to make timely payment of instalments of the purchase price. Under certain circumstances, the creditor may repossess even if the purchaser has been declared bankrupt.

### 14.4.3 Foreclosure

Generally, two conditions must be met in order for a creditor to be in a position to foreclose (*uitwinning, executie*):

(1)  the debt must be due and payable; and
(2)  the creditor must have an enforceable instrument, ie, a court or arbitral judgment or a notarial deed.

A first mortgagee and a pledgee have the right of recourse by way of foreclosure. A first mortgagee may foreclose by means of a public auction of the property on which he has a mortgage. A private sale is possible only with prior permission from the court. Foreclosure of a right of pledge takes place when the debt is due, at the pledgee's option by:

(1) sale on the pledgee's authority, unless the parties have agreed otherwise; the sale must be by public auction in accordance with local customs and conditions;

(2) any other sale authorised by the court; the pledgee may apply to the court to determine the manner of foreclosure; and

(3) a court order that the asset will remain with the pledgee constitute payment in an amount to be determined by the court.

### 14.4.4 Application for bankruptcy

When a debtor is reluctant or unable to pay his debts, bankruptcy can be petitioned (*faillissements-aanvraag*) by one or more of the creditors of the debtor. Bankruptcy can be applied for only when the debtor has at least two creditors.

To avoid bankruptcy, the debtor will often pay the creditor the whole debt or reach a settlement agreement with the creditor. If the debtor has paid the debt or a part of it according to the settlement agreement, the creditor should withdraw the bankruptcy request.

### 14.4.5 Recovery

If a seller does not receive payment for goods delivered, he can demand these goods to be transferred back. This is called the right of recovery (*recht van reclame*). The requirements for invoking the right of recovery are:

(1) there must be a sales agreement with regard to movable property;

(2) the goods must have been delivered to the purchaser;

(3) the goods must be in the same condition as when they were delivered (by finishing and processing the right of recovery lapses);

(4) the requirements of a 'regular' annulment of the contract must have been met, meaning that the purchase price is due and payable, but has not been paid, and that the purchaser is to be declared in default (in writing); in the case of partial payment, the right of recovery can only be executed for a corresponding part of the debt; and

(5) the invocation of the right of recovery should take place at least within either six weeks after the purchase price was due or 60 days after the goods have been stored by the purchaser or another person on the purchaser's authority.

The right of recovery must be executed by means of a written statement by the seller, directed towards the purchaser, in which the seller demands the goods back.

## 14.5 The court system

When considering legal proceedings to collect a claim, it should be established whether Dutch Law is applicable to the claim. In the case of an international contract, ie, where the parties to the contract are domiciled or established in two different countries, a choice of law and jurisdiction clause is often used. Under Dutch law, such clause is generally held to be valid.

Furthermore, it should be established whether the parties did agree to have possible disputes between them settled by means of arbitration. Once it has been established that the Dutch courts are competent, it must be verified which court is to be addressed.

### 14.5.1 Structure of the courts

The Netherlands is divided into 62 cantons. Each canton has a Cantonal Court (*Kantongerecht*). Cantonal Courts have first instance jurisdiction over all claims not exceeding DFl 5,000, as well as over all disputes concerning agency agreements, lease-purchase agreements, labour law, and rental of land and buildings. The Cantonal Courts sit with one judge.

The Netherlands is also divided into 19 districts. Each district has a District Court (*Arrondissementsrechtbank*). The District Courts are the courts of first instance for most matters that do not fall within the jurisdiction of the Cantonal Courts. Furthermore, the District Courts serve as the appellate courts of first instance for decisions of the Cantonal Courts. The District Courts sit with three judges.

Five Courts of Appeal (*Gerechtshof*) hear appeals in the first instance from decisions of the District Courts, and they have first-instance jurisdiction in tax matters. The Courts of Appeal sit with three judges.

The Amsterdam Court of Appeal is the court of first instance for disputes concerning the management of companies and all disputes concerning annual accounts.

The highest court is the Supreme Court (*Hoge Raad*) in The Hague. The Supreme Court may review decisions of a lower court, but only with respect to questions of law. The facts are irrevocably established by the lower court. The main function of the Supreme Court is to ensure that law is applied uniformly. It sits with five judges.

Court decisions are not binding on courts in deciding future cases. There is no rule of precedent. Supreme Court decisions, however, are esteemed particularly highly and are usually followed by the lower courts.

### 14.5.2 Rules of jurisdiction

A distinction should be made between subject matter, or absolute, exclusive jurisdiction, and venue, or relative jurisdiction.

Absolute jurisdiction has been dealt with above under the structure of the courts. Once absolute jurisdiction is established, the proper venue (relative jurisdiction) must be determined. The basic rule is that an action should be brought before the competent court in the place of the defendant's domicile. If there are several defendants, the action may be brought before the competent court of the place of domicile of any one of them, at the election of the plaintiff.

In certain cases, the venue provisions are more specific. If the dispute concerns property, the action should be brought before the court of the site of the property. In the case of bankruptcy claims, the competent court is the court that declared the bankruptcy. In preliminary proceedings, the court of the place where the injunction or measure requested will have its effect is also competent.

Attachment of assets that are located in The Netherlands generally establishes Dutch jurisdiction over the cause of action in which regard the attachment is made, even if one or more of the parties are not domiciled in The Netherlands, provided that no applicable international treaty or choice of jurisdiction clause provides for a different venue. The competent court to hear the claim is the District Court in whose district the attachment was made.

### 14.5.3   Appeals

An appeal is a request to a higher court in the judicial hierarchy to review a judgment of a lower court. Appeal is available on almost all decisions by Cantonal Courts, District Courts, or Courts of Appeal in matters where these courts have first-instance jurisdiction.

Exceptions include decisions by the Cantonal Courts in actions for less than DFl 2,500, but these decisions, under certain circumstances, are nevertheless subject to review by the Supreme Court.

### 14.5.4   Status of the foreign creditor

The Dutch legal system makes no distinction between nationals or foreigners. A foreign creditor is in exactly the same position from a legal point of view as a Dutch creditor.

The only exception to this rule can be found in a provision on Dutch legal proceedings before a court which states that a foreign party (as plaintiff) can be required to guarantee the costs involved with the proceeding it has initiated.

## 14.6   Legal representation

### 14.6.1   Nature of legal representation

By law, representation in court proceedings of both the plaintiff and the defendant by lawyers is compulsory. A lawyer, in this sense, is an attorney-at-law who is admitted to the bar in The Netherlands. There is no distinction between barristers and solicitors. A qualified lawyer may conduct litigation before all courts in The Netherlands, as well as before the European Court of Justice of the European Union (EU). However, in order to file pleadings in proceedings before a District Court other than the one to which he or she is admitted, a lawyer requires the assistance of a so-called procureur with the competent District Court.

Nearly all lawyers act at the same time as procureur with their District

Courts. Lawyers have the legal privilege to refuse the disclosure of information, in any form whatsoever, entrusted to them in their professional capacity. Only in proceedings before the Cantonal Courts and, with respect to the defendant, in summary proceedings (*kort geding*) does the rule of mandatory representation not apply. Moreover, the representation by in-house lawyers is not allowed.

In actions before the Cantonal Courts, a bailiff often assists the plaintiff. The possibilities of self-representation are consequently very limited and, in practice, legal representation by a lawyer is the rule.

### 14.6.2 Mode of payment for legal representation

The Board of The Netherlands Order of Advocates issues to its members (all lawyers in The Netherlands) guidelines which indicate how the fees of lawyers may be calculated. However, such fees are usually based on the amount of time spent on the matter, the importance or the monetary value of the subject matter, and the experience of the lawyer. In cases requiring specific expertise or in urgent matters, a higher hourly rate may be charged.

A bill of costs generally consists of a fee, disbursements, and value added tax (VAT or *BTW*). The disbursements are separated into expenses, including VAT and costs which are exempt from VAT (so-called untaxed disbursements). VAT is charged at a rate of 17.5 per cent on the advisory fee except for services rendered to entrepreneurs abroad and to non-entrepreneurs outside the EU.

Disbursements include such charges as court fees, bailiff costs, and travel and accommodation expenses. For expenses which are difficult to specify, such as general office expenses, the lawyer will generally charge a fixed percentage of the fee, but not more than five per cent. The basic hourly fee for lawyers, as of 1994 was DFl 280. This basic fee is revised annually by The Netherlands Order of Advocates.

There are two possible exceptions to the fee system described above:

(1)   if the collection rate is applied (see below relating to collection rate); or
(2)   if the parties have decided on a different arrangement.

It should be noted, however, that contingency fees are not allowed except for the collection of claims. The fee arrangement should be clearly discussed with the lawyer whose services are retained, and preferably in advance, in order to avoid any possible misunderstandings.

### 14.6.3 Collection rate

Where collection of a debt is involved, instead of calculating his fee on the basis of the hourly rate, a lawyer may agree to charge the so-called collection rate. The collection rate is calculated on the collected amount as follows:

(1)   over the first DFl 6,500: 15 per cent;
(2)   over the amount above that, up to DFl 13,000: 10 per cent;

(3)   over the amount above that, up to DFl 32,500: eight per cent;

(4)   over the amount above that, up to DFl 130,000: five per cent; and

(5)   over the amount exceeding DFl 130,000: three per cent.

The collected amount is considered to be the amount that is paid directly to the client after the lawyer has demanded payment from the creditor.

### 14.6.4   Deduction of value added tax

VAT will be charged by a lawyer on his fee for services to a Dutch client or a non-entrepreneur (for VAT purposes) within the EU.

For entrepreneurs who are registered for VAT in The Netherlands, the VAT included on the fee charged by the *advocaat* can be reclaimed from the Dutch tax authorities.

## 14.7   Costs and interest

### 14.7.1   Court fees

The courts charge an administrative levy (*griffierecht*) to the plaintiff and the defendant, in order to have the case heard. This fee differs, depending on the court involved, ie, the Cantonal Court, the District Court, the Appeal Court, or the Supreme Court. Furthermore, the levy varies depending on the nature of the subject matter brought before the courts. For money claims, the levy varies between the minimum of DFl 85 for claims up to DFl 200 in a Cantonal Court and 1.9 per cent of the claimed amount with a maximum of DFl 6,625 for claims in excess of DFl 25,000 in District Courts. In certain circumstances, when the party involved meets the criteria for legal aid, the court fees are reduced.

When the services of a court bailiff are retained (eg, for the serving of writs of summons and public auctions) certain fixed costs are incurred, which vary depending on the act performed.

### 14.7.2   Availability of legal aid

#### 14.7.2.1   *For the creditor*

If the creditor is an individual, it is possible that he may be eligible for legal aid by the Dutch government. In exceptional circumstances, legal aid is also available for small enterprises.

To be eligible for legal aid, an individual must provide to his lawyer a statement of income, and a company must provide its articles of association, the latest annual accounts, and the declaration and notice of assessment of taxes.

Even if eligible for legal aid, the creditor is required to pay a certain amount of the costs, an amount which varies on the basis of the creditor's income. The creditor will also pay a reduced court fee if the matter is taken to court. The costs of the bailiff are waived.

*14.7.2.2   For the debtor*

A debtor who meets the criteria for legal aid under the applicable laws and regulations may apply for a lawyer to be assigned to his case, or he may request that a lawyer of his choice be paid by the government.

As with the creditor, even if eligible for legal aid, the debtor is required to pay a certain amount of the costs, an amount which varies on the basis of the debtor's income. The debtor will also pay a reduced court fee if the matter is taken to court. The costs of the bailiff are waived.

### 14.7.3   Liability for and recovery of costs

The court determines the amount of the costs of litigation to be paid by, in almost all cases, the losing party. These costs seldom compensate the actual costs and lawyer's fees incurred.

The costs granted by the court are based on certain standard amounts for certain standard activities and on the amount of the claim. There is no possibility of recovering the actual costs of litigation.

### 14.7.4   Interest

Damages due as a result of delay in the payment of a sum of money consist of the statutory interest on that sum calculated over the period that the debtor is in default. The rate of the statutory interest is fixed from time to time by Decree. Parties can agree on an interest rate higher than the statutory rate.

## 14.8   Court proceedings

### 14.8.1   Initiation of proceedings

Most court proceedings are initiated by a writ of summons (*dagvaarding*) served on the defendant by a court bailiff (*deurwaarder*). The particulars of a claim are specified in the writ of summons. The writ of summons is filed with the competent court. Thereafter, at a certain date fixed by the court, both parties may file their written statements on which the court will render its judgment.

After the exchange of the written documents and prior to the judgment, parties may request oral pleadings. Appellate and review proceedings differ slightly from first instance proceedings. Legal proceedings can be initiated against foreign companies with a subsidiary, branch, or other place of business in The Netherlands.

## 14.9   Procedure to judgment

### 14.9.1   The debtor pays the debt

If the debtor pays the debt after court proceedings have been initiated and in a manner satisfactory to the plaintiff, a statement of discontinuance is to be lodged with the court handling the matter. Often, it is advisable to confirm the payment of the debt (with possible additional cost) in correspondence or a settlement agreement.

Should there be doubt that the debtor will comply with the commitments undertaken in such arrangement, the arrangements can be set out in a notarial deed. Such notarial deed is an enforceable instrument which can be executed by a court bailiff in the manner described below.

### 14.9.2 The debtor admits the debt

If the debtor admits the debt, and consequently does not file any statement of defence, the court is to be requested to render judgment at the earliest possible date.

The court will rule in favour of the plaintiff as specified in the writ of summons. On the basis of the judgment of the court, the plaintiff can proceed to enforcement.

### 14.9.3 The debtor disputes the debt

Should the debtor dispute the debt, he has the opportunity to file, at the date fixed by the court, a statement of defence. Thereafter, both plaintiff and defendant are entitled to submit further written pleadings, ie, a statement of reply to the defence by the plaintiff and a statement of rejoinder by the defendant.

Thereafter, the parties may request oral pleadings. Finally, both parties must submit all documents to the court and request the court to render its judgment.

### 14.9.4 The debtor disputes part of the debt

If only a part of the debt is disputed, the proceedings will take the course as set out above, and the court, when rendering a judgment, will take the undisputed part of the debt into account and, as to the undisputed part, rule as set out in the writ of summons.

### 14.9.5 The debtor neither admits nor disputes the debt

If the defendant does not appear in the court, the court will render judgment by default.

## 14.10 Enforcing judgment

### 14.10.1 Dutch judgments

The judgment of a court is an enforceable instrument (*executoriale titel*). The enforcement or execution of court judgments is carried out by a court bailiff who, if necessary, may request assistance from the police. Before proceeding to execution, the judgment must be served on the losing party. Disputes concerning enforcement can be dealt with by the President of the District Court in summary proceedings.

Judgments ordering the losing party to pay an amount of money are usually enforced by a post-judgment attachment of the assets and/or salary of the judgment debtor. This post-judgment attachment is possible with respect to all movable or immovable assets of the debtor, whether in his possession or in the possession of a third party, and it generally leads to a public sale of the charged asset(s).

A solvent debtor often pays what the court has ordered him to pay, if only to avoid additional costs. A judgment by default is enforceable in the same manner as any other judgment. Opposition or appeal prevents the execution of a judgment, unless the judgment is 'enforceable notwithstanding opposition of appeal', as most are.

### 14.10.2   Foreign judgments

The Netherlands is a party to various treaties relating to the recognition and enforcement of foreign judgments. If a creditor has obtained a foreign judgment in a treaty country against a debtor established in, or having assets within The Netherlands, such judgment can be enforced in The Netherlands after having obtained an exequatur.

The exequatur, a request for permission to enforce a foreign judgment, must be applied for with the President of the competent District Court. The President renders his permission after summary investigation of the formalities to be observed, without investigating the merits of the case and generally without hearing the debtor. The ruling in which the permission is granted must be served on the debtor by a court bailiff.

Thereafter, the debtor has one month (two months in the case of a foreign debtor) to lodge an appeal. After the expiry of this period without appeal having been lodged, the foreign judgment can be enforced as set out above.

The exequatur procedure is applicable to judgments obtained in all EU Member States and the European Free Trade Association (EFTA) Member States, which are party to the Lugano Convention. With respect to judgments rendered in countries which are not party to an execution treaty with The Netherlands, court proceedings in The Netherlands must be initiated anew in order to obtain an enforceable judgment as described above.

## 14.11   Insolvency

### 14.11.1   Insolvency proceedings

In the case of insolvency of a debtor, there are two types of proceedings which may be commenced under the Bankruptcy Act:

(1)   creditors and/or the debtor himself may apply for bankruptcy (*faillissement*); and

(2) the debtor may apply for suspension of payments or moratorium (*surseance van betaling*).

### 14.11.1.1 Bankruptcy

Bankruptcy is a general attachment on practically all of the assets of the debtor, imposed by a judgment of the District Court for the benefit of the bankrupt's collective creditors. The purpose of the bankruptcy is to provide for an equitable distribution of the proceeds of the bankrupt's assets among his creditors.

A bankruptcy is pronounced by the court, which also appoints a receiver (*curator*) and a member of the court to supervise and to co-operate with the receiver. The receiver is charged with the administration and liquidation of the bankrupt estate. Only lawyers can be appointed as receivers.

As a result of the bankruptcy, the debtor loses all his rights to administer and dispose of his assets with immediate effect. The receiver manages the bankrupt estate. Creditors must submit their claims to the receiver and indicate whether they have a preferred claim and/or have a claim secured by mortgage, pledge, or by right of retention.

Creditors, unsecured as well as secured, can present their claims in writing to the receiver. A simple letter outlining the claim is sufficient. Even if no payments are to be expected, the presentation of the claim to the receiver may be required in order to reclaim VAT from the tax authorities.

Bankruptcy can be petitioned for by one or more of the creditors of the debtor, by the debtor himself or, in exceptional cases, by the tax authorities and by the public prosecutor if the public interest requires it. The basis for a bankruptcy petition is that the debtor is not paying his debts or is 'in the condition of having ceased to pay his debts'.

Any creditor, domestic or foreign, may file a bankruptcy petition. All debtors, including individuals, companies, other legal entities, associations, and foundations, as well as entities not having a separate legal personality (such as partnerships or a deceased individual's estate) may be declared bankrupt. The filing fee must be paid by the party initiating the bankruptcy proceedings.

The courts require that the debtor have at least two creditors (one of them being the filing creditor if the filing is involuntary) and that at least one of these debts is currently due and payable. The petition must be filed in the court of the district in which the debtor resides or, if the debtor is a company, in the district in which the corporation has its registered office as indicated in its articles of association.

The property of the bankruptcy estate includes all property of the debtor (certain bare necessities excepted) as of the time the petition of bankruptcy is filed as well as all property acquired during the bankruptcy proceedings.

### 14.11.1.2 Moratorium

Moratorium is a court ordered general suspension of a debtor's payment obligations. Its purpose is to give the debtor an opportunity for recovery and thus avoid the debtor's bankruptcy in the interest of both the debtor and his creditors. Only the debtor himself can apply for a moratorium or suspension of payment. An application is filed if the debtor anticipates that he will be unable to continue payments. On such petition the court will grant the moratorium on a provisional basis and appoint one or more trustees (*bewindvoerders*).

The trustee in a moratorium has less powers than a receiver in the bankruptcy. A trustee can act only with the co-operation of the debtor. Thereafter, the court can grant the moratorium definitively for a maximum period of one and a half years. The moratorium ends with a composition (*akkoord*) between all creditors, the bankruptcy of the debtor or the withdrawal of the moratorium.

### 14.11.2   Bankruptcy of individuals

The main difference between the bankruptcy of a company and the bankruptcy of an individual is that a bankrupt company is liquidated after the annulment of the bankruptcy due to lack of assets, whereas an individual will remain in debt.

Consequently, even after the annulment of the bankruptcy due to lack of assets, the individual remains liable for any debts which have not been settled in the bankruptcy proceedings.

## 14.12   Conclusion

There seems to be a general tendency to late payment of foreign debts, and Dutch businesses are no exception. In order to secure one's position as a creditor, it is important to take all appropriate measures, when negotiting a contract and thereafter.

Should a debtor not comply with its payment obligations, timely and effective measures are required. These measures can be summarised as follows:

(1)   summons;
(2)   conservatory measures;
(3)   court proceedings; and
(4)   enforcement.

The specific course of action depends on the nature of the claim, the solvency of the debtor, and the costs related to the measures to be taken.

## Chapter 15

# NORTHERN IRELAND

**Brendan J. Smyth**
**Bigger & Strahan**
**Belfast, Northern Ireland**

## 15.1   Introduction

In this chapter, 'Northern Ireland' is the expression used to identify the six counties in the North East of the island of Ireland. The six counties form part of the political unity known as the United Kingdom of Great Britain and Northern Ireland. Many of the laws of Northern Ireland are similar to those in England and, except as set out in this chapter, it may be assumed that the comments on England and Wales are applicable to Northern Ireland. The similarity in legislation may arise from some laws enacted in England applying to Northern Ireland or from legislation enacted specifically for Northern Ireland. For example, the English Insolvency Act of 1986 is, to a large extent, reproduced in the Insolvency Order (Northern Ireland) 1989. Creditors should note that, currently, legislation in England and Wales is enacted by Parliament sitting at Westminster in London, each piece of legislation being referred to as 'an Act'. Legislation particularly enacted for Northern Ireland is also passed at Westminster, but this is done by a process known as an Order in Council and such enacted legislation is therefore known as 'an Order'.

Northern Ireland is composed of the following six counties: Antrim, Armagh, Down, Fermanagh, Londonderry, Tyrone. The Republic of Ireland (which has 26 counties) is a separate independent sovereign state and none of the laws of Northern Ireland apply to the Republic of Ireland and vice versa. If a creditor wishes to recover a debt from a debtor within the island of Ireland, his first priority is to determine in which of the two jurisdictions his debtor resides or carries on business. To assist in this task, the 26 counties which make up the Republic of Ireland are set out below:

| | | |
|---|---|---|
| Carlow | Kilkenny | Offaly |
| Cavan | Laois | Roscommon |
| Clare | Leitrim | Sligo |
| Cork | Limerick | Tipperary |
| Donegal | Longford | Waterford |
| Dublin | Louth | Westmeath |
| Galway | Meath | Wexford |
| Kerry | Monaghan | Wicklow |
| Kildare | Mayo | |

Should the debtor have a place of business in both the jurisdiction of Northern Ireland and the Republic of Ireland, a creditor may be able to sue him in either jurisdiction but not in both at the same time. The correct jurisdiction to select will be advised by the lawyer, who, in advising on jurisdiction, will consider the residence of the defendant, where the contract was entered into, where the contract was to be performed and where any goods may be located which are to be the subject of any intended litigation.

Although the chapter on England and Wales also applies largely to the collection of debts in Northern Ireland, there are some minor variations and a substantial variation in the system for enforcement of debt judgments in Northern Ireland. The following text notes the variations between England and Wales and Northern Ireland.

### 15.1.1   Sources of information

The comments in the chapter on England and Wales on sources of information at **6.2.3** apply equally to Northern Ireland, but the following exceptions should be noted:

(1) *Land charges*. There is no equivalent in Northern Ireland to the English Land Charges Department. To ascertain if a debtor in Northern Ireland has any mortgage or charge against his property, the creditor's lawyer in Northern Ireland conducts a search in the appropriate Title Registry.

(2) *County court judgments*. In Northern Ireland, there is no equivalent Register of county court judgments. There is a Central Office which registers enforcement of all money judgments and which will issue (upon payment of £3) a certificate setting out details of any application made by a creditor in the previous six years to enforce a judgment against a debtor. The Office is located at Bedford House, 7th Floor, 16/22 Bedford Street, Belfast. A creditor should, of course, furnish full information on his debtor's name, address of residence business, to ensure that the search of the judgments index is sufficiently accurate to identify the debtor.

Generally, these comments apply equally in Northern Ireland but please note that the Judgments Enforcement (Northern Ireland) Order 1981 provides that a person commits an offence if, with the object of coercing another person to pay money claimed from the other, as a debt due under a contract, he:

(1) falsely represents that process of any court or the Enforcement of Judgments Office has been issued, or that any judgment has been obtained, in respect of the money claimed;

(2) falsely represents, in relation to the money claimed, that criminal proceedings may be instituted for failure to pay it;

(3) falsely represents himself to be authorised in some official capacity to claim or enforce payment; or

(4) utters a document falsely represented by him to have some official character or which purports to have, or, by reason of its form or appearance or both, has the appearance of having, some official character which he knows it has not.

There are severe financial penalties on summary conviction for being found guilty of the above offences.

## 15.2 The court system

As in England and Wales, the court system in Northern Ireland is divided into the county court jurisdiction and the High Court jurisdiction.

County court jurisdiction is comprised of the small claims court and the ordinary county court. There are a number of divisions within Northern Ireland and the county court sits, usually quarterly, to hear defended claims in the following divisions:

(1) Division of Londonderry, sitting at Londonderry, Magherafelt, Limavady.
(2) Division of Antrim, sitting at Ballymena and Coleraine.
(3) Division of Armagh & South Down, sitting at Armagh.
(4) Division of Fermanagh & Tyrone, sitting at Omagh, Strabane, Cookstown and Enniskillen.
(5) Division of Craigavon, Co Armagh, sitting at Craigavon and at Lisburn.
(6) Division of Ards, sitting at Newtownards and Downpatrick.
(7) Division of Belfast, sitting at the Recorder's Court, Victoria Street, Belfast.

The High Court is located at Belfast, and for civil purposes all High Court litigation is conducted at the Royal Courts of Justice, Chichester Street, Belfast. Please note that there are no District Registries of the High Court in Northern Ireland for debt recovery litigation.

In Northern Ireland, in the county court, interlocutory applications are dealt with by either the county court judge or the district judge and in the High Court by either a judge or a master.

### 15.2.1 County court

The current jurisdiction of the county court in Northern Ireland is to deal with all claims up to and including £15,000. Any claim for an amount over this sum must be through the High Court of Justice in Northern Ireland.

In Northern Ireland, Sheriffs and bailiffs were abolished in 1969 and were replaced by a Central Office known as the Enforcement of Judgments Office (see below).

There is no summons production centre in Northern Ireland and all summons (whether in the High Court or county court) issued within Northern Ireland, will be prepared and issued by a party's lawyer.

### 15.2.2 High court

There is no equivalent of the Official Referee's Court in Northern Ireland. The High Court commercial list is dealt with by the Commercial List Office at the High Court of Justice, Chicester Street, Belfast.

## 15.3 Legal representation

In Northern Ireland, County Court Rules oblige a company to be legally represented in any litigation.

## 15.4 Issuing proceedings

In the county court, a summons is prepared by the plaintiff's lawyer in Northern Ireland who will arrange to have the summons issued by the county court and the solicitor then issues the summons by sending it for service upon the debtor, either by post or by way of a court-appointed process server.

## 15.5 Procedure to judgment

Where the debtor admits the debt, the summons issued in Northern Ireland does not contain any pre-printed forms permitting the defendant to apply for time to pay. With the county court summons the defendant receives two additional forms (one for completion by the defendant and return to the lawyer and one for completion by the defendant and return to the county court) which enable the debtor to state whether or not he admits the debt and whether or not he has a counterclaim against the plaintiff. Once the lawyer receives this notice from the debtor, he will arrange for the summons to be issued for hearing in the county court defended list. This hearing date is likely to be three or four months after the date of issue of the summons. If the debtor does not return either form, then the plaintiff will be entitled to apply for judgment against him without the necessity of a court hearing. This will require the plaintiff to swear an affidavit averring that the debt is due, which is then returned to the lawyer who will extract the judgment.

No acknowledgement of service forms are issued with High Court writs of summons in Northern Ireland. Once a defendant is served with a writ, he has the period of 14 days within which to file at the High Court and deliver to the plaintiff's lawyer, a memorandum of his appearance to the writ. Where the writ issued by the lawyer is endorsed with a statement of claim the defendant must then, within 21 days from the delivery of memorandum of appearance, deliver a defence to the writ and thereafter the litigation will either proceed to be set down for hearing as defended litigation or the plaintiff's lawyer may advise that the defence is a delaying tactic by the debtor and suggest that the plaintiff apply to court to have the defence struck out and summary judgment entered.

Please note that current county court jurisdiction in Northern Ireland is £15,000 and not £50,000.

All winding up and bankruptcy proceedings in Northern Ireland are dealt with through the appropriate Court Office at the High Court of Justice, Chichester Street, Belfast. The county courts in Northern Ireland have no winding-up nor bankruptcy jurisdiction.

## 15.6   Enforcing judgment

The procedure for enforcement of money judgments is markedly different in Northern Ireland from that prevailing in England and Wales. Prior to 1969, both Northern Ireland and England and Wales had largely identical enforcement procedures. However, in 1969 the Sheriffs and Bailiff system in Northern Ireland was abolished and replaced by a Central Office, known as the Enforcement of Judgments Office (the Office) which is located at 7th Floor, Bedford House, 16/22 Bedford Street, Belfast BT2 7FL. The original 1969 Act (which abolished Sheriffs and Bailiffs and established the Office) has since been replaced by the Judgments Enforcement (Northern Ireland) Order 1981. The Office has a judicial section and an administrative section. The former, being headed up by a Master of the Queen's Bench Division of the High Court of Justice. The task of the Office is to recover a creditor's judgment debt, without creating undue hardship to the debtor. Some important aspects of the enforcement system are noted below.

### 15.6.1   The enforcement system

The recovery of all money judgments in Northern Ireland must be made through the Enforcement of Judgments Office. This includes judgments granted by courts outside Northern Ireland, providing those judgments have been registered with the Supreme Court in Northern Ireland.

Once an application from a creditor for enforcement of a judgment is accepted by the Office, that application is assigned a serial number and each subsequent application from either that creditor or another creditor is assigned a later serial number.

Judgments are enforced in priority, determined by the date of acceptance by the Office of the application from the creditor. Therefore, the first application accepted against a debtor will rank first in priority for satisfaction, the second accepted application will rank second in priority for satisfaction and so on.

In the course of enforcement proceedings, the office will from time to time issue to the plaintiff's lawyer various documents for service upon the debtor, or may make requests for information as to the balance outstanding at any time on the judgment debt, and if the plaintiff or its lawyer fail to deal with the summons or these requests within a reasonable period, the Office may upon notice request that the master issue an order declaring that the application has lost priority by reason of dilatoriness.

Prior to lodging an application at the Office, the plaintiff or his lawyer must prepare, in duplicate, a notice of intent to enforce money judgment. This notice sets out the amount due by the debtor at the date of issue of the notice (and should include interest on the judgment debt to date of issue). The notice, in duplicate with a copy of the court judgment annexed, and a cheque for £15, is lodged at the Office. The Office then posts one copy of the notice to the debtor, warning the debtor that if payment is not made of the judgment debt within 10 days, then the creditor will be free to apply to the Office to enforce the judgment against the debtor. Once the notice is posted by the Office to the debtor, the remaining copy of the notice is returned with a receipt for the £15 paid and an endorsement confirming that the notice had been sent to the debtor. After expiry of the 10 days' notice period, the plaintiff is then free to apply for enforcement.

Applications under the 1981 Order fall into two categories:

(1) Those over £3,000. If a judgment debt exceeds this amount, the plaintiff may lodge an interim application with the Office requesting that it examine the debtor and furnish a detailed report on the debtor's financial circumstances. This application is lodged with the original receipted notice of intention to enforce together with payment in the sum of £100. Once the application is accepted, the plaintiff will be notified of your serial number. In due course, the plaintiff will receive a report from the Enforcements Office on its debtor's financial circumstances and in order to maintain priority the plaintiff must, within the period of 10 days, proceed with an application for full enforcement, should it so wish.

(2) Those under £3,000. If a judgment debt is under this amount, the facility of an interim application for a report on debtor's circumstances is not available and should the plaintiff wish to recover the amount of judgment debt, it must lodge an application for full enforcement (see below).

### 15.6.2  Applications for full enforcement

An application for full enforcement can be made by a creditor at any time within 12 years from the date upon which he obtains his judgment, providing he has issued a notice of intent to enforce that judgment. The notice of intent must have been issued no more than three months prior to the date of the application to enforce. Even if the judgment debt exceeds £3,000 the plaintiff can ignore the procedure by way of initial application for report on debtor's circumstances and can proceed immediately for full enforcement proceedings. An application for full enforcement, when filed at the Office, must be made by:

(1) completing and signing an application for enforcement in the appropriate form;
(2) making payment of the appropriate fee; and
(3) lodging the duplicate notice of intent to enforce which will have previously been issued to the Office.

Once the application is accepted, the Office will allot the serial number which will determine the ranking of the judgment for priority purposes. It is important to note that in recovering the amount due on judgment the Office will, in addition to the judgment debt, recover from the defendant all fees paid to the Enforcement of Judgments Office.

### 15.6.3 Steps taken in the course of enforcement proceedings

It is important that creditors realise that the Office will decide the most appropriate method for the recovery of the judgment debt. Whilst the Office will be appreciative of any information which can be furnished to it as to the debtor's assets or income, the plaintiff has no statutory right to insist that the Office issue any particular enforcement order. The Judgments Enforcement (Northern Ireland) Order 1981 merely provides that the Office *may make various orders* – it does not stipulate that the Office *must* make various orders. However, a plaintiff can assume that if it furnishes to the Office information on the debtor's assets or income and if the debtor should prove to be uncooperative with the Office, then the Office will likely issue an order based upon the information furnished.

Once the enforcement application is accepted by the Office, it immediately issues a custody warrant which the Office will serve upon the debtor. The effect of the service of this custody warrant is that all goods (save any that may be stipulated in the custody warrant) upon all premises occupied by the debtor and in any other place, being goods under the sole control of the debtor or under the joint control of the debtor and his spouse or any of his dependents shall, as from the service of the custody warrant, be deemed to be in the custody and possession of the Office. Shortly after service of custody warrant the debtor will receive notification from the Office obliging the debtor to either attend at the Office or, alternatively, to make arrangements for a member of the Office to call on the debtor, so that the Office may prepare a detailed report on the debtor's assets, income and liabilities. Once this report is compiled the creditor will normally receive a copy and the Office will decide which enforcement order to issue to secure recovery of your judgment debt. Should the debtor fail to attend for examination or fail to make an appointment for a member of the Office to call on him, the plaintiff's lawyer will be issued with a conditional order for the issue of a warrant for the arrest of the debtor. This order will be served by the lawyer upon the debtor personally and should the debtor then fail to appear before the Office for examination as to his means, the warrant for his arrest will be issued and will be placed with the Royal Ulster Constabulary to enable them to arrest the debtor and bring him before the Office to be examined.

### 15.6.4   Enforcement Orders

Having examined the debtor, the Office has within its statutory powers the right to make any of the following Orders.

#### 15.6.4.1   Instalment order

The Office may direct a debtor to make payments by either weekly, monthly or quarterly instalments of the judgment debt until the debt has been discharged.

#### 15.6.4.2   Seizure order

The Office may make an order directing that sufficient goods be seized as to discharge the judgment debt. Goods once seized are normally disposed of by way of public auction. The plaintiff should note that the Office has no authority to seize the following:

(1)   wearing apparel, furniture, bedding and household equipment of the debtor and his spouse, essential for domestic purposes, of the debtor, his spouse and dependents residing with him or any of them;
(2)   the tools and implements of the debtor's trade;
(3)   any property which has been seized under any other statutory provision;
(4)   property held by the debtor in trust for another;
(5)   property in the hands of a receiver appointed by the court;
(6)   any property exempt from seizure under any other statutory provision.

Creditors may also wish to note that in the event of the Office seizing property which is properly the property of a third party, then that third party is entitled to issue an inter-pleader summons which will be heard by the Master at the Office to determine whether or not the goods so seized are the property of the debtor or the third party. If it is found that they are properly the property of the third party, then those goods will be released to that third party.

#### 15.6.4.3   Enforcement against land

The Office may issue an order charging a judgment debt against any interest which the debtor may have in any land situated within Northern Ireland. This is a most important order in that once the order is registered by the lawyer against the debtor's title, the plaintiff becomes a secured creditor for the amount of that debt, enjoying all the privileges and benefits of a person who holds a mortgage or charge for that amount. Furthermore, once registered the order charging land provides for interest to accumulate at a variable rate (currently eight per cent) from the date of registration until date of full payment and interest is charged on not only the original judgment debt but also upon all fees which have been paid to the Office. The registration of the order, against the debtor's title to land, will, of course, be subject to the usual priorities affecting land in Northern Ireland and the plaintiff should note that any mortgages, charges or other orders charging land registered prior in time to the judgment debt, will have priority over that judgment debt. Furthermore, judgments registered by the Department of the Environment in respect of rates (which are a local authority tax on property owners for services provided by the local authority) enjoy a statutory priority, irrespective of their date of registration. Subject to leave being granted by the Office, the plaintiff would have a right to issue proceedings in the High Court of Justice, seeking possession and power of sale over the debtor's lands or premises so charged.

### 15.6.4.4 *Delivery of goods*

Should the judgment against the debtor provide for the specific delivery of goods by the debtor to the plaintiff, the Office may issue an order directing those goods to be delivered to the plaintiff and in the event of the debtor not so doing, the Office may enter the debtor's property for the purposes of enforcing the Order.

### 15.6.4.5 *Enforcement against stocks and shares*

Should the Office become aware that a debtor has a beneficial interest in any government funds or stock or funds or stock of any local authority or public undertaking in Northern Ireland or stocks or shares registered in Northern Ireland of any public company, the Office may make an order charging such funds, stocks or shares with the whole or any part of the amount recoverable on a judgment debt. Once the order is notified to the relevant government department or company, it shall have the effect so as to require that all dividends or interest due on the funds or stock shall be paid to the plaintiff and it shall further have the effect of preventing the owner of the funds or stocks from disposing of them.

### 15.6.4.6 *Enforcement against shares in private companies*

Where a debtor has a beneficial interest in any shares in a private company incorporated in Northern Ireland, the Office may make a restraining order restraining the company from paying to the debtor, or to any other person, any dividends or directors emoluments which would otherwise be payable to the debtor and restraining them from dealing in any way with the shares without the consent of the Office. In tandem with the order, the Office may make an order appointing a receiver or attaching the debts due by way of dividends or directors' emoluments.

### 15.6.4.7 *Order appointing a receiver by way of enforcement*

This order must not be confused with the appointment of a receiver by a debenture holder over the assets of a limited company. The power of the Office to make an order appointing a receiver is an appointment only for the purposes of collection of a judgment debt and for no other purpose. An order appointing a receiver may be made in respect of any monies which might be due to the debtor, from any third party source. The plaintiff should, however, note that the power of appointment of a receiver does not extend to:

(1) earnings or salary (which may be subject to an attachment of earnings order, see below);
(2) future earnings or salary, unless assigned or charged by your debtor;
(3) any income payable at the discretion of trustees;
(4) certain payments accepted under the Crown Proceedings Act 1947.

### 15.6.4.8 *Attachment of debts*

The Office may make an order attaching all debts due or accruing to a debtor from any person within the jurisdiction for the purpose of satisfying the amount recoverable on the judgment debt. If the party owing the debt fails to make payment of the debt within the period specified in the attachment order, then the plaintiff may proceed to enforce the order against that party, just as if it were a judgment. The plaintiff should note that the attachment of debts may extend to monies held for a debtor's benefit by his bankers (including any monies held in a deposit account).

### 15.6.4.9 *Attachment of earnings order*

Where it appears to the Office that the debtor is a person to whom earnings fall to be paid, the Office may make an attachment of earnings order requiring the person to whom the order is directed to make out of those earnings such payments as may be specified in the order. To obtain an attachment of earnings order, the plaintiff's lawyer will file with the Office an application for an attachment of earnings order (no fees are payable on this order) and once the order is issued the employer will be directed to deduct periodic payments from the debtor's earnings and to pay those periodic payments to the Office for the plaintiff's credit. However, a plaintiff should note that in assessing the debtor's means the Office will notify the debtor's employer that the debtor's earnings (after deductions due under the order) must not be allowed to fall below a minimum threshold level to ensure that the debtor is left with sufficient earnings to support himself and his dependants. While an attachment of earnings order is in force, the debtor and his employer must notify the Office in writing of every occasion on which the debtor leaves any employment or becomes re-employed.

### 15.6.4.10 *Administration orders*

Where a debtor is an individual, unable to pay forthwith the amount recoverable on a money judgment for an unsecured debt, and the debtor alleges that all his unsecured debts amount in aggregate to a sum not exceeding £2,000 and furnishes to the Office a list of all his debts, the Office may on the debtor's application make an administration order providing for the administration of the debtor's estate. This is not a frequently used order within this jurisdiction, probably because most debtors are unaware of its existence. The order is made on the application of the debtor and not on the creditor's application. However, should an order be made, it may provide for the payment of the unsecured debts of the debtor by instalments or otherwise and either in full or to such extent as to the Office, in the circumstances of the case, appears practicable and subject to any conditions as to future earnings, income or assets which the Office may think just. So long as an administration order is in force, a creditor who is scheduled to the order shall not, without the leave of the Office, be entitled to present or join in a bankruptcy petition against the debtor, except in certain circumstances. Should the debtor fail to make any payment which he is required to make by virtue of the administration order, the Office may, if it considers it proper, revoke the administration order, leaving it open to the creditor to petition the High Court for the debtor's bankruptcy, if the creditor should so wish.

### 15.6.5   Conclusion

The creditor will note the wide variation of powers available to the Enforcement of Judgments Office and it will be self-evident to a credit controller that it is of assistance to that Office in considering enforcement proceedings, that the Office be furnished with as much information as possible as to the debtor's assets and income.

## Chapter 16

# PORTUGAL

**Amaral Cabral-Advogados**
Lisbon, Portugal

## 16.1   Introduction

This chapter examines various aspects of law and procedure in Portugal relating to the collection of debts, and concerning the rights of commercial and judgment creditors.

## 16.2   Initial considerations

### 16.2.1   Status of the debtor

In accordance with the law, individuals or companies must give to the entities with which they maintain a trading relationship certain information. Accordingly, all companies must have the following elements printed on their letter headings, contracts which are entered into, publications made and publicity:

(1)   the name of the firm;
(2)   the type of incorporation;
(3)   the location of the head office; and
(4)   the commercial registry where the company is registered and its registration number.

Individuals trading and incorporated with a limited liability status must indicate the commercial registry to which they belong, the registry number, and the place of their business.

Individuals who do not trade but take part in the business market, such as a person who renders a certain type of service and works only for himself, must indicate his name, civil status and address.

All debtors must indicate at all times their fiscal and taxpayer number. This is an obligation prescribed by law whereby any supply of goods or services must be accompanied by the respective invoice which is to have the identification of the buyer, including his taxpayer number.

In accordance with Portuguese law, all debtors may be pursued in court, whether companies, individual tradesmen, private and public entities, or the Portuguese state. Members of the Portuguese parliament, government ministers, and the President of the Portuguese Republic are not subject to court actions for acts of a private nature, unless a special authorisation is given by the Portuguese Parliament. In addition, a company subject to insolvency proceedings may be subjected to claims only within those proceedings (see **16.9**, below).

Finally, a company which is wound up may not be pursued in court. Where the debtor is a single person, on his death the creditor has the right to be paid from the debtor's estate. The heirs may be charged up to the amount inherited.

Where the debt is to be recovered from a legal person, such as a company, the death of one of its managers or owners in no way limits the rights and actions which may be used against the company as it remains per se a 'legal person'. General information on companies may be obtained at the Registry for Collective Persons (*Registo Nacional de Pessoas Colectivas*). If more detailed information is required, then this will be available from the Commercial Registry where the company is registered.

Commercial registries require that information on companies be requested in writing, and they have special forms for this purpose. Usually, photocopies of the records kept at the Commercial Registry are provided. These involve a small cost and may take up to a month to be issued. All relevant information regarding a company may be acquired at the commercial registries, such as that relating to share capital, type of company, head office and the identification of owners and managers.

There also are private institutions which provide the same kind of information as the commercial registries. The cost is considerably higher, but the service is speedier. Among these institutions, those regarded as the most reliable are American Appraisal, Dun & Bradstreet, and MOPE.

### 16.2.2 Is the debt statute-barred?

There are a number of factors which may limit the recovery of a debt. Some may be of a formal nature, such as the requirement for payment of stamp duty on foreign documents of credit and the translation into the Portuguese language of foreign documents of credit, both of which are mandatory.

The limitations may also result from the contents of the document of credit, in which case the credit itself may be considered as non-existent. For example, a credit has a certain duration, depending on what has been established by the parties, its nature, and what is prescribed by law. If such time expires, the debtor is immediately released from his obligation to make payment.

### 16.2.3 Security

The non-payment of a debt gives the creditor the right to recover the sum owing through the courts and the debtor's assets. As a rule, all things making up the debtor's assets may be apprehended or seized and used as a means for payment of outstanding debts.

Therefore, a debtor does not have complete liberty in the management of his assets, especially if he diminishes their value without justification. In accordance with Portuguese law and in conformity with what has been described above, the debtor's assets represent the general security for his debts. There are four particular measures to be used through court petition by creditors to protect the debtor's assets:

(1) declaration of null acts – the creditor may petition that certain acts of the debtor be declared void by the court and, therefore, of no effect, when the debtor, whether or not in bad faith, has taken such steps and, as a consequence, lost certain of his assets;

(2) substitution of the debtor's position – the creditor may take the position of the debtor in certain relationships with third parties in order to increase the debtor's assets;

(3) defence of fraud against creditors – the creditor may react against certain acts of the debtor which were only practised by him at the expense of the creditor's interests and chances of recovery of the debts; and

(4) apprehension or seizure of goods – the creditor may request that the court apprehend and hold as a form of security a number of goods making up a part of the debtor's assets to ensure that the debt will be paid. This measure cannot be used against a debtor who has a commercial activity.

The parties at the time an agreement is entered into, may decide on a special guaranty as a form of security for the agreement. Special guaranties include the following:

(1) personal guarantee – a guarantee given by a third party, whereby through his assets the creditor is assured of payment. The third party must be in a situation where he can exercise all his rights as permitted by law. The guarantee should comprise a written declaration in the agreement entered into by the creditor and the debtor;

(2) deposit of income – a guaranty where the debtor's income or a part of the debtor's income is given as a guarantee of the debt;

(3) pawn or pledge of goods or rights – a guaranty which involves the submission of certain movable goods or of a right which may be held by the creditor to recover the debt if it is not voluntarily paid by the debtor;

(4) mortgage – a fixed asset of the debtor;

(5) creditor's privileges – where the law attributes privileges to certain credits, meaning that they will be paid preferentially because of the reason on which the credit is based; and

(6) seizure – where judicial apprehension of goods is made in order that the debt be paid by the sale of the apprehended goods.

### 16.2.4   Retention of title

The seller may restrict the sale of the goods with a clause which establishes retention of title of those goods until such time as the goods are partially or totally paid. This means that the property of the goods sold is not transmitted at the time of the sale but only later when the goods are paid for. Such goods will not be part of the debtor's estate before he pays for them. They cannot serve as a means of guarantee for other creditors. To be effective against third parties, sales under these conditions must be registered whenever the item sold has a mandatory registration.

## 16.3 Letters before action

### 16.3.1 Are they necessary?

It is usual, but not necessary, to send a letter to the debtor in order to demand payment of the debt. At an early stage, the letter may be sent by the creditor himself in an attempt to avoid bringing the matter to court. Only when the creditor is unable to obtain satisfaction of the debt are the documents relating to it sent to a lawyer or a paralegal. Before taking judicial action, the lawyer normally sends a letter to the debtor in the name of his client. However, there may exist situations in which it is inadvisable to send a letter and it is preferable to appeal to court immediately, eg, if it is practically certain that the letter will be unsuccessful or that the loss of time in sending it will increase the risk of the creditor's claim not being satisfied. In almost all cases, however, there are various advantages in sending a letter. These include:

(1) immediate and full satisfaction of the debt is often obtained or an agreement as to its payment made; the client's problem, thus, is solved in a manner faster and less expensive than by an action in court;

(2) where an obligation that is not yet due is concerned, that obligation can be crystallised thus enabling the demand for interest for late payment from that date on; and

(3) normally, it appears convenient to clearly demonstrate to the judge that the appeal to the court was the creditor's last alternative to obtain satisfaction of the debt. Before filing judicial action, all of the creditor's possibilities of reaching an amicable solution, without need to appeal to the courts should be exhausted.

### 16.3.2 What should they say?

There is no standard model for letters before action. Not only does every lawyer and paralegal have his own form but, depending on the particulars of each case, the letter can be altered, with attention to both the identity of the debtor and the origin of the debt. As a general rule, the letter is sent to the debtor's professional address, if he is an individual, or to the administrative office, if the debtor is a corporate body. The letter should be registered with acknowledgement of receipt so that no doubt remains, not only about its receipt, but also about the date of its receipt, which is essential when counting the time allowed for payment. Save for exceptional cases, the letter should contain:

(1) the most precise identification as possible of the creditor and debtor, with inclusion of their respective addresses;

(2)   the subject matter of the claim;

(3)   the amount of the debt;

(4)   the time granted to the debtor to pay the debt or to make a proposal to regularise the situation. Normally, the time allowed varies from 8 to 15 days as from date of receipt of the letter; and

(5)   a warning that judicial proceedings will be filed if the debt is not met within the appointed term or if an acceptable proposal is not made.

The letter should be as clear and concise as possible. As it is addressed to the debtor who, in most cases, is unlikely to be a jurist, complicated arguments of a judicial nature, as well as exhaustive legal explanations, should be avoided.

### 16.3.3   May they demand interest for late payment?

As a rule, in Portuguese law, any obligation that is overdue and remains unfulfilled, starts to bear interest from the expiration of its term. In commercial transactions, Portuguese law requires that the demand for payment be preceded by the making and sending of an invoice that should mention the mode and term of the payment. If the appointed term expires before payment is settled, the debt starts to bear interest immediately.

When an obligation with no term for payment is involved, interest becomes due only after the creditor demands payment. That demand can effectively be made through a letter sent to the debtor by the creditor himself or by his lawyer. In that letter, the capital debt and the interest legally due should be demanded. The interest that is due is counted from the date of expiration of the term, either the date of the receipt of the letter or an earlier date.

Should it become necessary to take judicial action for an overdue debt, the creditor's position will not be harmed if the interest due was not demanded in the letter. No matter what was demanded in the letter, in the judicial process, the creditor may receive both payment of the capital debt and the interest on deferred payment.

## 16.4   Pre-action and non-judicial remedies

### 16.4.1   Injunctions

Prevention proceedings are only put into practice when all the requisites prescribed by law are met. Their objective is to prevent the non-fulfilment of a court decision. They do not solve a disagreement but serve to safeguard court proceedings which are still underway. For this reason, whenever prevention proceedings are filed in court, the petitioner must file in the same court within 30 days his main petition.

Such proceedings are temporary in that the prevention measure will be imposed only while a court decision on the main issue has not been reached. When the final court decision is issued, it will also deal with in definitive terms the object of the prevention proceedings. They have a simple structure to permit the giving of an urgent decision by the court. There are six types of prevention proceedings:

(1) alimony pendent lite where the object of the main petition is the request of alimony;

(2) suspensions of the effects of a shareholders' meeting resolution where the object of the main petition is an illegal or void resolution taken by the shareholders' meeting;

(3) suspension of construction works where the right of property is at risk because of construction works;

(4) preventive apprehension, ie, judicial apprehension of certain goods when it is feared that the goods will be dissipated;

(5) inventory which consists of making a list of certain goods, with their description and value, the goods are then deposited with a person named by the court; and

(6) unspecified prevention measures, the measures described above are those established by law for specific situations, however, a prevention measure of any kind may be petitioned for in court.

It must be noted, however, that preventive apprehension, described at (4) above, may not be used against an individual or company having commercial activities as their objective. A result to the same effect as preventive apprehension may sometimes be achieved through an unspecified prevention measure.

## 16.5    The court system

### 16.5.1    Structure of the courts

The Portuguese legal system has two types of courts: state courts and arbitration courts. State courts comprise various judges, secretaries, and representatives of the district attorney. Arbitration courts are not operated by the state, and they function with non-professional judges. Many of these courts function only on certain occasions. In other words, arbitration courts will usually be established only in order to analyse and decide a single matter. However, there are permanent arbitration courts which are continuously at work with permanent judges and personnel, such as the arbitration courts of the Portuguese Commercial Association, the Portuguese Catholic University, and the Portuguese Bar Association. The recovery of a debt through an arbitration court is dependent on the parties having agreed to submit a possible disagreement between them for decision by an arbitration court.

There are two limitations regarding the agreement made by the parties relating to the arbitration courts. The first relates to the matter which is the object of the dispute as, in accordance with the law, certain matters may be decided only by a state-operated court, such as suits which involve real property. The second is the fact that the arbitration courts cannot execute their own decisions. In other words, if an arbitration court issues a decision which recognises that a debt exists and that it is due, the court is not able to put into force measures to guarantee payment; either the debtor will agree to pay voluntarily, or the creditor will have to file execution proceedings at the appropriate state court.

State courts in which proceedings can be brought for the recovery of debts are judicial courts, of which the Supreme Court of Justice (*Supremo Tribunal de Justiça*) is the highest. There is an exception to this rule when the recovery of debts is to be made by a public entity, such as the state or country services. The competent courts in these cases are the administrative courts. Proceedings for recovery of debts must be filed at the appropriate county court. Jurisdiction is established by law and will depend on a number of factors, such as residence of the debtor, the place where the debt was to be paid, or whether the parties have agreed on the use of a particular county court.

Any of the parties may appeal the decisions given by the county court. There are four courts of appeal situated in Lisbon, Oporto, Coimbra, and Évora. From the courts of appeal, the parties may appeal to the Supreme Court of Justice.

### 16.5.2 Appeals

As a rule, any of the parties may appeal a decision given by a judge of any court until the suit reaches the Supreme Court of Justice. In order to appeal, the appellant must file a petition at the court which gave the decision which is the object of the appeal, requesting appeal within eight days of the judge's decision having been issued. The possibility of appeal is dependent on the monetary value of the suit pending. In debt recovery cases the value of the suit will be the amount owing, plus interest and other related costs.

Accordingly, petition to the Courts of Appeal is possible when the suit has a value of Pte 500,001 or more and to the Supreme Court of Justice when the value of the suit is Pte 2,000,001 or more. There are five different types of appeals, depending on the reason on which the appeal is based. Very often in suits for recovery of debts, the debtor will use appeals with the sole purpose of delaying payment.

### 16.5.3 Status of the foreigner creditor

Portuguese law does not make distinctions between a national and a foreign creditor regarding the implementation of their rights. A foreigner who wishes to have his right to collect a certain debt recognised in Portugal, in accordance with national or foreign law, will not face any barriers other than those based on general principles intended to safeguard international public order.

## 16.6  Legal representation

### 16.6.1 Nature of legal representation

In principle, Portuguese law requires a party to be represented by counsel, both in prosecution and in defence of an action. In disputes involving up to Pte 500,000, the party can exceptionally represent himself in trial, ie, without a lawyer. Otherwise a lawyer should be engaged. For admission to legal practice in Portugal, it is necessary to possess a law licence and to register with the Bar Association. Every lawyer so registered is subject to the professional rules of the Statute of the Bar Association.

Although representation by counsel is obligatory, the parties may personally present petitions in processes that do not raise issues of law. If a party does not employ a lawyer when it is obligatory to do so, the court, at its own discretion or in answer to a petition put by the opposing party, will require that a lawyer be engaged within an appointed period, and in default that the matter be dismissed. If a party is unable to obtain counsel, the court itself will appoint one, normally a trainee, based on a list supplied by the Bar Association. The judicial mandate is given either by a written procuration or by a party's oral declaration in the minutes of a court hearing.

A client who wishes to change lawyers is free to do so. However, according to the Statute of the Bar Association, the lawyer receiving a matter that was previously entrusted to another, must do everything in his power to ensure that the other lawyer is paid his fees and other amounts owing. The new lawyer must indicate orally or by writing to his colleague why he accepted the instructions and what efforts he made to obtain it. Provided he has justifiable grounds, the lawyer may also withdraw from a case or decline instructions. One of the motives considered to justify withdrawal from or declining to accept a case is the non-payment of fees or failure to provide for expenses and fees.

### 16.6.2 Mode of payment for legal representation

A client who employs a lawyer is responsible for the payment of his fees and of the expenses connected with the matter in question. It is usual and advisable for client and lawyer to agree in advance the final amount of the fee or the way it should be calculated. In making the agreement and calculating the fee, the lawyer must observe the following rules that are established by the Statute of the Bar Association:

(1) in fixing the fee, the lawyer shall proceed with moderation, attending to the time spent, the difficulty of the matter in question, the importance of the legal service rendered, the client's financial ability, the results obtained, and the amount customarily charged in the locality where the activity is performed;

(2) the lawyer shall not demand part of the object of the debt; and

(3) the lawyer shall not determine that his right to fees depends on the results of the demand or of the matter in question; it is proper and normal for the lawyer to ask for part of his fees in advance.

In the event of a dispute regarding the amount of the fee, the lawyer, the client, or the court itself may ask the Bar Association to comment on the bill that was presented.

## 16.7 Costs and interest

### 16.7.1 Current fees

The issue between the parties includes costs. The amount charged by the court includes justice tax (which is calculated as a percentage of value of the suit), stamp duty and costs related to various expenses involved in the proceedings. One quarter of the total fees involved must be deposited at the time the petition is filed. With each new phase of the proceedings, a percentage of the total court fees must be deposited by the parties. When the decision is issued, the party who wins will be reimbursed the amounts paid, while the losing party will be responsible for the total court fees.

### 16.7.2   Availability of legal aid

Eligibility for subsidised and free legal aid is dependent on a person's income. Persons with low incomes may be spared payment of court fees and lawyers' fees. A petition for free or subsidised legal aid may be requested by individuals and legal entities, through their lawyers, by the district attorney, or by the interested parties themselves. The request for free legal aid may be opposed by other parties involved in the proceedings and will be finally decided by the presiding judge.

## 16.8   Proceedings and their enforcement

### 16.8.1   Procedure to judgment

Before taking judicial action to collect a debt, it is necessary to determine whether or not the creditor has a document that may be executable. The following are executable documents:

(1)   condemnatory judgments;
(2)   documents that are written or authenticated by a notary public;
(3)   drafts, promissory notes, cheques, invoice extracts, bills, checked invoices, and any other documents signed by the debtor that state an obligation to pay certain amounts or for delivery of consumable items; and
(4)   documents that have been conferred the power to be executed, by a special disposition.

The situations in which the creditor has no executable documents must be handled separately from those in which the creditor has a title that may be executable according to the law.

#### 16.8.1.1   *The creditor does not have executable title*

In these cases, the creditor must take a condemnatory judicial action in court. If he wins the case in that action, he will obtain a condemnatory sentence and will then have an executable title. The condemnatory action is a judicial process during which only the existence and the amount of the debt are discussed. The final judgment may be acquittal, by concluding that the debt is non-existent, or condemnatory, certifying the debtor must pay the amount considered to be in debt, with the addition of the corresponding interest (not only the interest already due but also that which becomes due until effective and full payment is performed). For the continuation of this judicial action commenced on the creditor's initiative, the debtor must be summoned. In practice, this can lead to enormous delays in the process, as it is frequently difficult to summon the debtor, either because he refuses to receive the court's communications or because he has stopped pursuing his commercial activity. In Portuguese law, the legal mechanisms that are meant to overcome these situations are slow and not always easily applicable.

A favourable condemnatory sentence enables the creditor to start the second judicial stage that serves the purpose of effective satisfaction of the debt and that consists of filing a judgment execution.

### 16.8.1.2 *The creditor has an executable title*

In this case, the creditor does not have to take any condemnatory judicial action and can start at the second stage, the filing of a judgment execution. The judgment execution consists of two main stages:

(1)  the seizure of effects; and
(2)  putting up the property for sale at court auction.

In the first stage, all of the debtor's effects that are necessary and sufficient to pay the debt are seized by a court clerk. The seized effects are brought within the custody of the court itself or an appointed body who is entrusted with keeping the effects in custody, at the risk of penal sanctions. If necessary, the second stage of the process starts. The effects are sold to the highest bidder under the court's order and supervision. With the amount obtained, the creditor is paid and, if a balance remains, it is handed over to the debtor.

### 16.8.1.3 *Common aspects to both processes*

Both in the condemnatory action and in the execution, the debtor must decide on one of three ways of proceeding:

(1)  do nothing;
(2)  object against the debt; or
(3)  pay all or part of the debt.

If the debtor does nothing, the facts alleged by the creditor are considered proved, and the remainder of the process follows. If the debtor contests the debt, the process follows its normal procedures until the court's decision. If the debtor pays the whole debt, the process is terminated. If he pays only part of the debt, the process continues only as to the amount not paid.

## 16.8.2  Recovery of small debts

A judicial process has been recently introduced into the Portuguese legal system which may be used for the recovery of small debts. Before this new process was put into force, in order to recover a debt not founded on a document permitting the creditor to file for execution proceedings, the creditor filed proceedings in order to execute the first decision only when a decision of recognition of the debt was obtained through court proceedings.

However, it was general practice that, when the debtor did not want to or could not pay, he would not defend himself in the first proceedings, therefore using recognition proceedings as a simple way of delaying payment, which is very often possible only with the completion of execution proceedings. The new process may be used for debts up to the amount of Pte 250,000. A petition is filed in court against the debtor requesting the payment of the debt, together with all the documents the creditor possesses and on which the debt is founded. The petition will not be given to a judge, which is usual for all other proceedings, but rather a copy will be sent to the debtor by the court clerk. The debtor will have to oppose the petition within seven days of having received it. If an answer is not received from the debtor, the creditor may immediately move to execution. On the other hand, if an answer is received, the proceedings will be presided over by a judge and will follow all the usual phases.

## 16.9   Insolvency

### 16.9.1   In general

Insolvency proceedings may have one of two consequences, either to declare a company insolvent through court proceedings and to proceed with its winding up and liquidation or the controlled administration of the company in order to proceed with its recovery. The latter occurs when, during the insolvency proceedings, it is proven that the company is still viable. In either case, the company's main creditors are given a decisive vote on the fate of the company through the creditors' committee. In each case, the creditors' main objective is to recover the debts owed them. Both proceedings are long and costly, and the chances of recovering money owing are slim as, in most cases of insolvency which reach the courts, the companies have been working in a state of undeclared insolvency for a long time, having therefore no assets to make good outstanding debts.

Legislation which came into force on 23 April 1993 is intended to put an end to the above situation and to make insolvency proceedings an effective way of collecting debts. It is too early to evaluate the impact of the new law.

Once insolvency proceedings are commenced, the company's business comes to a halt, no more transactions will be undertaken and debts will be deemed payable only at the end of the proceedings. Outstanding debts will not accumulate interest from the time the insolvency proceedings are filed and may be recovered only under the terms determined by the insolvency proceedings. In other words, various court actions normally possible for the recovery of debts may not be used while the insolvency proceedings are under way.

In order to file for insolvency proceedings, a company must be in a position whereby it is no longer capable of satisfying its obligations by its own means. A company which has enough assets to meet its obligations but which cannot do so due to liquidity is also understood to be liable to insolvency proceedings.

In other words, it is generally understood that, if a company ceases in a systematic manner to meet its obligations on time, proceedings for insolvency may be filed.

However, and for the purpose of insolvency proceedings, only the most important obligations in terms of value and as relate to the volume of business of the company may be considered. Therefore, the inability to make payments and perform obligations must be analysed in each case. It is usual to compare the percentage of obligations met with that of those not met.

Once insolvency proceedings are filed, the debtor is notified within seven days of the proceedings and may file a petition for the recuperation of the company, should the debtor company consider its deficient financial situation temporary. Under Portuguese law, there are four procedures that envisage the recuperation of a company.

### 16.9.2   Winding up of limited companies

The company subject to insolvency proceedings may petition that the process be changed into proceedings for recuperation of the company. The petition must be duly supported and will be analysed by the creditors and the court. Should the court or the creditors believe that recuperation proceedings are possible, then the insolvency proceedings will be changed to recuperation proceedings.

However, the debtor also may accept that it is insolvent and declare before the court its insolvency, or even passively accept the insolvency proceedings by not defending himself. In either event, the court will declare the company insolvent. The status of insolvency will force the company to meet certain obligations before the court and lead to the appointment of the creditors' committee and a liquidator as administrators of the company during the proceedings.

The declaration of insolvency must be published in the Official Gazette (*Diário da República*) and in one of the main newspapers where the company had its business within seven days of the declaration being given by the court. The court will establish a period of 20 to 60 days within which all the company's creditors may submit claims.

The administration of the assets belonging to the insolvent company is undertaken by the appointed liquidator, who works in collaboration with the creditors' committee and who is directed by the judge in charge of the proceedings. Once the company is declared insolvent, it must immediately cease its business activity and submit its accounts to the court. Acts required in the interest of the insolvent company will be carried out by the liquidator. In addition, all obligations undertaken by the company will become immediately due. However, interest on such obligations will not be deemed payable.

Following the declaration of insolvency, all things making up the estate of the insolvent company will be sold. The process of liquidation of the company must not exceed six months, and it will be carried out by the appointed liquidator in collaboration with and under the supervision of the creditors' committee.

The money acquired from the sale will be deposited in a special bank account to be managed jointly by the liquidator and one of the creditors from the creditors' committee. As mentioned above, all of the insolvent company's creditors will be able to claim their credits through a petition to be filed in court, and such petition must include declarations as to the origin of the debts, their nature and their amount. In the same petition the creditors may also file a statement giving their opinion or defending their position in relation to the insolvency proceedings.

The next phase of the proceedings will be the payment of debts with the money acquired from the sale of the company's physical estate and from actions taken by the liquidator to increase the estate such as the claiming of debts due to the insolvent company.

Some creditors of the insolvent company are considered preferential creditors and will be the first to be paid. Preference is established in terms of the guarantees held by the creditors. Accordingly, creditors who have been guaranteed payment through certain goods or through property will receive the amount of money realised from the sale of those goods or that property. If their credit is not satisfied by the amount received, the creditors will be considered common creditors in relationship to the remainder of their indebtedness. Once the preferential creditors have been paid in the above manner, the other creditors will be paid proportionately as proposed by the liquidator and approved by the judge who is presiding over the insolvency proceedings.

### 16.9.3 Bankruptcy of individuals and insolvency of partnerships and proprietors

Prior to April 1993, there were different proceedings applicable to limited companies, individuals, partnerships, and proprietors. When the new legislation on insolvency proceedings came into force on 23 April 1993 it established a single process for the recovery of all debts, and this procedure is described above in connection with the winding up of limited companies.

*Chapter 17*

# SCOTLAND

**Tony Deutsch**
**Bermans**
**Glasgow, Scotland**

## 17.1   Introduction

This chapter deals with actions commenced in Scotland. Until 1707 Scotland
and England were two separate countries, each with its own separate Parliament and legal system linked by the fact that they shared a single monarch. In
1707 the Scottish Parliament voted itself out of existence and the two countries became one with a single legislature based in London. The Act of Union
gave certain guarantees to Scotland, one of which was the preservation of its
distinct law and legal system. This separation has to a large extent been
preserved up until the present day, although obviously there has been a great
deal of convergence between the two systems.

## 17.2   Initial considerations

### 17.2.1   Status of the debtor

The remarks of Andrew Bogle in his chapter on England and Wales are, in
general, equally applicable to Scotland. There are, however, one or two points
of difference to be emphasised:

(1)   in Scotland a sole trader may only be sued at his residential address;
(2)   it is possible to pursue an action against a firm even if the names of the
      individual partners are not known, eg 'Piggies Dress Hire';
(3)   the Charity Commission does not have jurisdiction in Scotland except
      perhaps in relation to English-based charities which operate in
      Scotland;
(4)   members clubs in Scotland are not required to register with the local
      authority unless they are licensed;
(5)   the equivalent of the local Probate Registry in Scotland would be the
      Commissary Department of the local Sheriff Court;
(6)   Scotland has its own separate Land Registry and its own separate
      Companies' Registry. Searches in either of these are most efficiently
      carried out by firms of private searchers of which there are several.
      These private firms will also carry out searches in the Register of
      Inhibitions and Adjudications, which discloses whether or not a bank-
      ruptcy petition has been commenced or indeed whether an individual
      has been bankrupted. It should be noted that the Scottish term for
      bankruptcy is 'sequestration';

(7) advertisements of winding-up petitions and awards of sequestration, meetings of creditors, etc appear in the *Edinburgh Gazette*, which is published weekly;

(8) there is no central registry for winding-up petitions maintained in Scotland;

(9) limitation periods (known in Scotland as prescriptive periods) also apply in Scotland. For debt recovery cases in Scotland the creditor will generally be required to issue proceedings within five years of the date upon which the money became due for payment;

(10) security. Scotland has a completely separate conveyancing system from England. Traps for the unwary frequently arise where assumptions are made that English forms of security exist equally in Scotland. This is particularly so in relation to securities over moveable property, ie property other than land or buildings. Securities may be taken over land and buildings and limited companies are able to grant floating charges over all types of property. It is not possible to grant a fixed charge over anything other than land or buildings;

(11) in Scotland only the holder of a floating charge granted by a limited company may appoint a receiver;

(12) in Scots property law no such entity as a receiver for rents exists.

(13) Scots law in relation to retention of title has recently been completely assimilated to English law in this respect.

## 17.3    Pre-action remedies

In Scotland, the principal pre-action remedies available in debt recovery cases are arrestment on the dependence and inhibition. In respect of debts of any size they are very much the norm and are widely perceived as relatively inexpensive.

### 17.3.1    Arrestment

Arrestment is a means of freezing moveable assets (ie non-land assets) belonging to the debtor, especially money held by a third party for him. One example of a target for arrestment would be debts due to the debtor in connection with his own trade or business. Another example would be money deposited by the debtor with a bank. Other moveable items, such as shares or sums due under insurance policies are capable of arrestment.

Clearly, those debtors whose business involves a relatively few high-value transactions with a limited, readily identifiable customer base are most vulnerable to arrestment, eg contractors in the building industry.

One self-help measure which creditors can take is to gather intelligence to assist with the targeting of arrestments.

A warrant to arrest on the dependence is usually asked for and granted when the warrant is obtained on the initial writ. Arrestments can then be lodged immediately thereafter, and indeed, even before the actual writ is served on the debtor.

The recipient of the arrestment (the arrestee) is not bound to disclose to the creditor whether any sums have been attached until judgment has been granted by the court. It can be seen that an arrestment which attaches any of the debtor's property is a form of judicial security in favour of the creditor.

Even if the creditor is eventually successful, the cost of lodging the arrestment is not recoverable from the debtor. The cost of each arrestment lodged is variable. A typical cost will be £40 for each arrestment lodged.

It should be noted that an arrestment may only be lodged in the hands of an arrestee located in Scotland. In theory, the pursuer is liable in damages for a wrongful arrestment.

### 17.3.2  Inhibition

An inhibition is the equivalent of an arrestment against land or buildings. It effectively blocks the sale of any land or buildings in Scotland owned by the debtor until the debt is paid. As with arrestment the inhibition can be used at the stage of raising a court action and the cost of obtaining an inhibition is not recoverable from the debtor. Costs vary but a budget figure of £200 is realistic. The pursuer is liable in damages for a wrongful inhibition.

It should be realised that both arrestment and inhibition are freezing remedies and once judgment is obtained further steps need to be taken if the assets frozen are to be used to satisfy the creditor's debt.

## 17.4  The court system

In Scotland, there are two courts in which debt recovery litigation can be undertaken, the Court of Session and the Sheriff Court.

### 17.4.1  Court of Session

The Court of Session is based in Edinburgh and is the supreme Scottish court. Until very recently all appearances in this court had to be undertaken by advocates (barristers). Certain suitably qualified solicitors have recently been granted rights of audience; however, the vast bulk of appearances are undertaken by advocates. The Court of Session is exclusively located in Edinburgh although there are plans for certain commercial causes to be conducted in other locations. The location of the court and the two-tier structure of representation means that the cost of proceedings is high. This means that very little routine debt recovery work is undertaken in the Court of Session.

### 17.4.2  Sheriff Courts

Scotland is divided into six Sheriffdoms and in each Sheriffdom there is a Sheriff Court situated in one or more of the principal towns or cities. There is no upper limit to the value of actions that can be brought in the Sheriff Court, which has a very wide jurisdiction, considerably wider than the English county court. The Sheriff Court is therefore used in almost all recovery work. Solicitors undertake most Sheriff Court work themselves. It is unusual for an advocate to be involved much in the processing of Sheriff Court actions except in complicated cases or for the conduct of lengthy trials.

The reasons which in England cause many lawyers to favour taking action in the High Court rather than the county court do not exist to promote a similar comparison between the Court of Session and the Sheriff Court. Both the Court of Session and the Sheriff Court are administered by civil servants; however, while within the county court system it is civil servants who are responsible for issuing summonses, this work in Scotland is undertaken by solicitors and Sheriff Officers, both private contractors. Similarly, the enforcement of judgments (the Scottish term is 'decree') is undertaken by Sheriff Officers. There is, therefore, no clear comparison to be made between the Court of Session and the Sheriff Court in terms of efficiency. Generally speaking, the choice between the two systems is dictated by considerations of expense and the value and complexity of the costs.

## 17.5   Appeals

Any order or judgment made by the court in an action is subject to appeal. In the Sheriff Court there is an appeal from the Sheriff to the Sheriff Principal. While an appeal to a single judge is relatively unusual, it is a popular system because it is both quick and cheap. The decision of a Sheriff Principal can be appealed and indeed it is possible to miss out entirely an appeal to the Sheriff Principal. Appeal from the Sheriff Court is to the Inner House of the Court of Session. This is the equivalent of the English Court of Appeal. Beyond the Inner House there is the possibility of an appeal to the House of Lords and in appropriate cases to the European Court of Justice. Appeals are generally on points of law although in exceptional cases an appeal on a point of fact is possible. Appeals other than in the Sheriff Courts are costly and, for debt recovery actions, relatively unusual.

## 17.6   Legal representation

In Scotland, the party bringing the action is known as the pursuer and the party who is sued is known as the defender. Where the pursuer or defender is an individual or a firm then that party may represent themselves. The situation is different for companies, which must be represented by a solicitor or advocate except in regard to small claims in the Sheriff Court. Other than in the case of small claims, party litigants are a rarity.

As indicated above, most debt recovery work in Scotland is conducted through the Sheriff Courts and most work in the Sheriff Courts is carried out by solicitors. Advocates tend only to become involved in actions of unusual complexity or in respect of trials or other hearings which are likely to be protracted. Advocates, like English barristers, cannot be instructed directly by lay clients.

## 17.7 Mode of payment for legal representation

The fees which solicitors may charge are, in the absence of prior agreement, regulated by scales of charges issued both by the Law Society of Scotland and by the courts themselves. In Scotland, a limited contingency fee arrangement is permitted. This is on the basis that a solicitor may agree to work only on the basis of payment of outlays where he is unsuccessful. In such circumstances, the solicitor may, by prior agreement, charge up to twice the recoverable costs when he is successful. Recoverable costs are explained below.

## 17.8 Costs and interest

### 17.8.1 Liability for recovery of costs

Unless a party is legally aided then he is responsible for paying the solicitor whom he instructs. The burden of these costs may be reduced where a party is entitled to recover costs from his opponent. The right to recover costs usually follows success in the proceedings. In undefended actions there is a fixed scale of recoverable costs. In many cases these will go a long way to defraying the cost of pursuing. The recoverable costs will not, however, meet the cost of protective measures such as arrestment or inhibition.

The expenses which a successful party can recover from his opponent in a defended action are very precisely regulated by a table of fees issued by the courts. The costs recoverable from an opponent never represent the full cost of the litigation to the successful party. A general rule of thumb is that the successful party can expect to recover between one half and two-thirds of his total costs. Where an advocate is employed then a substantial part of the cost of doing so may be recovered from the unsuccessful party but only if the court certifies the cause as suitable for the employment of counsel. Usually, those actions where it is perceived as desirable to employ counsel are ones to which a court will be likely to grant certification.

In general, where an unsuccessful party is legally aided, that person's liability in expenses to the successful party will be modified by the court to nil. For this reason the grant of a legal aid certificate in favour of a defender is frequently the end of many actions. This is because only those with very limited means are entitled to legal aid. Many creditors will take the view that whatever the merits of their case there is little point in accruing non-recoverable expenses against a person of straw. Pre-litigation expenses are never recoverable, nor, as has already been noted, are the expenses of arrestment and inhibition on the dependence of a court action.

Theoretically, failure to give adequate notice of proceedings could lose the pursuer his right to recover costs in an undefended action. In practice, this tends not to happen. Contractual attempts to provide for a full recovery of costs are probably not enforceable. The special rules in regard to costs in Sheriff Court summary causes and small claim actions are noted below.

### 17.8.2   Interest

Virtually all debt recovery actions raised in Scotland will include a claim for interest. The interest claimed may be either contractual or statutory.

#### 17.8.2.1   Contractual interest

The parties may have contracted for a particular rate of interest or perhaps, more importantly, a particular date from which interest is to be applied. The parties are entitled to stipulate whatever rate of interest they choose. Provided the initial writ narrates clearly the basis upon which a special claim for interest arises, then there will be no difficulty in obtaining judgment for that interest in any undefended action. In practice, the information necessary to plead a unique claim for interest tends only to be available in those actions which proceed upon some document of debt such as, eg, a finance house agreement.

#### 17.8.2.2   Statutory interest

Statutory interest is available in all actions for payment. The rate of interest applying is varied from time to time by Government order. The rate of interest presently applying is 8 per cent per annum. In debt recovery actions the commencement date for the calculation of interest is the date upon which the action is served. The fact that the debt may be of long standing makes no difference.

## 17.9   Issuing proceedings in the Sheriff Court

There are three types of payment action in the Sheriff Court: summary causes, small claims and ordinary actions.

### 17.9.1   Summary causes

Summary causes are actions where the sum involved is more than £750 and less than £1,500. In a summary cause action the solicitor prepares a summary cause summons. This is a statutory form (either pre-printed or computer generated) upon which are inserted the details of the parties and the sum claimed. To this there is added a brief statement setting out how the sum claimed is computed. In actions relating to the supply of goods or services, detailed invoices are normally attached to the summons. In hire purchase or other finance house type cases, a copy of the agreement will be attached. On preparation of the summons the solicitor takes it or sends it to the particular Sheriff Court which has jurisdiction. On payment of the court dues the Sheriff Clerk grants a warrant to serve the summons on the debtor. Typically, the solicitor will serve the summons by recorded delivery post. If this is unsuccessful then service can be effected personally by Sheriff Officer. The cost of service by Sheriff Officer is a recoverable expense. The warrant issued by the Sheriff Clerk provides for a return date and a calling date. The former is a date by which the debtor must give notice to the court that he intends to defend the action. The calling date, which is a week later, is the date upon which judgment is granted if no defence has been entered.

If the action is defended, the defence is normally noted on the summons and a trial (known in Scotland as a proof) is fixed for a date about 4 to 8 weeks after. The Scottish courts rely entirely on oral evidence. Obviously, the economics of proceeding with a defended action are to be carefully considered. Negotiated settlements should be considered at an early stage. The penalty in expenses for abandoning a summary cause action at an early stage is not great.

### 17.9.2 Small claims

Small claims are actions brought for sums of less than £750. Essentially, small claims are a type of summary cause with one or two important differences. The idea of the small claim is to allow ordinary people to bring claims without using solicitors. In a small claim the calling date is known as a preliminary hearing. If the debtor appears at the preliminary hearing, the Sheriff will try to find out what the facts of the case are and what issues the pursuer and defender disagree upon. If the Sheriff, having heard both sides in the claim, is satisfied that the facts are sufficiently admitted, he may decide the small claim at the preliminary hearing. In practice, this never happens. The Sheriff will note the issues of fact in dispute and will then fix a further hearing at which witnesses and evidence may be heard. This further hearing, known as a full hearing, is broadly similar to a proof in a summary cause but the hearing of a small claim is less formal than other court hearings and, in order to avoid hearings becoming too technical, the normal rules of evidence are relaxed. The debtor is entitled to be represented by an official from a Citizens Advice Bureau or any other person whom the Sheriff considers to be suitably qualified.

One important characteristic of small claims is in relation to expenses. If the value of the claim is less than £200 and the action is defended, then there will be no award of expenses against the unsuccessful party. Paradoxically, if a small claim is brought and not defended, then the pursuer is entitled to recover expenses. If the value of the claim is more than £200 but less than £750 then, where the action is defended, the maximum amount of expenses which will normally be awarded by the court to the successful party is £75.

### 17.9.3    Ordinary actions

Ordinary actions are all actions where the sum sued for is in excess of £1,500. The solicitor prepares an initial writ which sets out the amount of the claim and how it is made up. The amount of detail required in an initial writ is not great. The solicitor then obtains a warrant from the Sheriff Clerk in the appropriate Sheriffdom. This warrant entitles the solicitor to effect service of the writ either himself by recorded delivery or by instructing a Sheriff Officer. The warrant also entitles the solicitor to lodge arrestments and to arrange for an inhibition. In an ordinary action, there are no calling dates as with summary causes and small claims. The solicitor simply serves the writ on the debtor, who then has 21 days following service to give notice to the Sheriff Clerk whether he intends to defend the action. If the debtor does not give notice of his intention to defend, the solicitor applies to the Sheriff for decree in absence. This may be issued by the Sheriff Clerk 14 days after the expiry of the 21 days allowed for giving notice to the court. In practice, there will be a delay of a further few weeks before the extract is issued. The extract entitles the solicitor to continue with the various enforcement measures which are described below.

If the action is defended, the Sheriff Clerk writes to both parties' solicitors giving notice of various critical dates. The first date notified is the date by which the defender must lodge written defences. If these are not lodged within the period specified, then the pursuer is entitled to apply for decree by default. The second critical date is the last date upon which the parties may notify adjustments to each other. Adjustment is the process by which each party expands on their original position giving greater specification of the facts and points of law upon which they intend to rely. The next critical date is the options hearing. Prior to the options hearing, a record of the written pleadings to date is made up and the parties lodge notes of any legal arguments upon which they intend to rely. At the options hearing, the Sheriff decides on further procedure. Typically, the Sheriff may order a debate, which is a hearing at which any preliminary legal arguments are disposed of. If there are no preliminary legal arguments, the Sheriff may order a proof or trial at which the parties lead their evidence. If, at the options hearing, the Sheriff and the parties are of the view that there should be further written pleadings, then arrangements exist for the Sheriff to continue the case for this purpose. The policy of the court is to bring the stage of written pleadings to an end as quickly as possible. Some cases may be decided on legal argument but many will be required to proceed to proof. Any proof or debate is very much restricted to consideration of what the parties have said in their written case. It is therefore essential that the solicitor has all the information available to him at an early stage in a defended action to plead the case as fully as possible.

If during the early stages of the action it becomes apparent that the defence is merely a delaying tactic, then it is open to the parties to apply to the court for summary decree. In practice this is seldom granted unless the lack of a defence is absolutely blatant.

# 17.10   Enforcing judgment

Once the court has given judgment, whether it be in an ordinary action, a summary cause or a small claim, and the solicitor for the successful pursuer has obtained an extract decree, various enforcement procedures become available.

## 17.10.1   Charge

Charge is the first stage of enforcement. Sheriff Officers serve a formal notice on the debtor requiring payment within 14 days. The notice makes it clear to the debtor that if he fails to pay within 14 days then the Sheriff Officers may proceed with a 'poinding' or bankruptcy proceedings may follow.

## 17.10.2   Poinding

Poinding is a process whereby Sheriff Officers inventory the debtor's goods with a view to their being sold. If the debtor attempts to remove or sell the poinded goods himself, this is regarded as a serious contempt of court and the creditor can ask the court to have the debtor imprisoned. Many debtors who have the means will pay up either at the stage of charging or at poinding. If, however, no payment is made, then a warrant sale can be arranged at which the goods poinded can be sold. It should be noted that there are strict rules as to what may be poinded. The basic essentials of domestic life cannot be included. It should also be noted that complications may arise in regard to a poinding where there are claims by third parties such as finance companies in respect of hire purchase or other finance type agreements. There may also be complications arising out of claims for rates and taxes which have a preference over the claims of ordinary creditors.

## 17.10.3   Arrestment

Arrestment on the dependence of the action has already been noted. Further arrestments can be carried out once a decree has been obtained. The major difference between an arrestment on the dependence and an arrestment in implement of the decree is that in the latter case the arrestee must disclose whether any sums have been attached. Where arrestment was carried out on the dependence then, upon decree being granted, the arrestee is bound to disclose whether the arrestment on the dependence was effective and what sums were attached.

## 17.10.4   Furthcoming

It has already been noted that an arrestment only freezes the asset in the hands of the third party. Before that asset can be released to the pursuer, the pursuer must either obtain the consent of the debtor or, failing that, must obtain a further order from the court by means of an action of furthcoming. A furthcoming is relatively unusual. Generally speaking, the debtor will wish to avoid the expense of further procedure and will authorise release of the assets.

### 17.10.5   Adjudication

Adjudication is a relatively unusual and quite expensive remedy but one which in the correct circumstances can be very useful. As has already been noted, an inhibition merely blocks the debtor's right to dispose of any land or buildings. Adjudication is the means by which a successful pursuer can acquire rights in land or buildings belonging to the debtor. For an inhibition to be effective it is not necessary to know what land or buildings the debtor owns.

An action of adjudication is taken by the pursuer to acquire rights over specific properties. It follows that the pursuer must search to find out what the debtor owns. This may be an expensive process. The court action itself must be raised in the Court of Session, which again is expensive.

A decree of adjudication against any particular property of the debtor does not immediately transfer ownership to the pursuers. Once a decree of adjudication has been granted then the debtor cannot sell the property without first paying off his indebtedness to the pursuer. If the debtor is bankrupted within a year of the adjudication then the adjudicating creditor's rights will probably be defeated.

If after 10 years the indebtedness has not been repaid then the adjudicating creditor acquires a right of ownership over the property in place of the debtor.

In the intervening years the adjudicating creditor is entitled to evict the debtor from the property and to let it and to recover rents. If the property is already let, the decree of adjudication entitles the adjudicating creditor to recover the rents.

It will be fairly obvious that adjudication is only worthwhile where the debtor has significant assets in land and buildings which are not already affected by secured lending.

In practice, adjudication has most usefully been used against creditors who have left the Scottish jurisdiction whilst still retaining land or buildings there.

A realistic estimate of the cost of adjudicating including searching would be £600.

### 17.10.6   Earnings arrestment

Earnings arrestment may be used in securing payment if the debtor is in employment. The debtor's employer is required by statute to deduct weekly sums fixed by statute from the debtor's wages and thereafter forward this sum to the creditor. This is done without the need for the debtor's consent or further court action as would be necessary for other types of arrestments.

### 17.10.7   Bankruptcy of individuals and partners

Bankruptcy proceedings may be commenced in respect of debts in excess of £1,500 where the debtor fails to pay 14 days after receiving a charge.

Bankruptcy proceedings can also be commenced 14 days after the service of a demand for payment of a debt in excess of £1,500 provided that demand has been served by Sheriff Officers and is in accordance with the statutory form. Such demands do little more than harass a debtor. The statutory form makes it clear that in order to avoid bankruptcy all the debtor must do is serve on the creditor a formal notice stating that he denies the debt. No grounds for denial are necessary.

Bankruptcy proceedings are attractive. Once a decree has been obtained then the further costs of the creditor of commencing bankruptcy proceedings would likely to be in the order of £250–£350. These costs would represent a first charge on the debtor's estate in the event of the bankrupt having any assets.

If there are no assets then the costs incurred after the award of bankruptcy are met out of the public purse.

While bankruptcy has become less of a stigma, the threat of it is still likely to produce payment from debtors who had otherwise appeared to be without means.

Bankruptcy provides an end to the debt recovery process. In Scotland there is no right to oral examination except within the context of a bankruptcy or a liquidation. The trustee in bankruptcy has wide powers to examine and investigate the affairs of the bankrupt and he is better placed to discover whether there has been concealment of assets than any creditor. Obviously, any sums recovered in this way are for the benefit of the general body of creditors.

### 17.10.8 Liquidation

Liquidation may be commenced where a limited company has failed to make payment after expiry of a charge. It is relatively unusual in Scotland for a creditor to resort to liquidation. The explanation for this is that there is no official receiver in Scotland. This means that a petitioning creditor has to be prepared to meet the whole costs of the liquidation, which can run to several thousand pounds. The practice of appointing a provisional liquidator to make a preliminary investigation of a company with a view to determining whether to proceed with a full liquidation or otherwise has to a large extent fallen into disrepute.

*Chapter 18*

# SPAIN

**José A. Rodríguez García and Juan Carlos Castro Rico**
**Castro, Sueiro & Varela**
**Madrid, Spain**

## 18.1    Introduction

The debt maturity deadline approaches, and the prospects for collecting it are extremely limited. What strategies can be adopted against the threat of default? What legal means does Spanish law make available to the creditor to optimise its policy on doubtful debts? What costs do they involve? The reply to these and other similar questions are an essential element in any company's commercial policy, perhaps even more so in times of economic crisis. This chapter examines the solutions to problems common in this area of corporate management.

## 18.2    Initial considerations

### 18.2.1    Status of the debtor

In general, under Spanish law, debts may arise from the will of the parties (eg under a contract) or as a function of the law (eg the debt of a person who is bound to indemnify another). Who can be a debtor? Both individuals and legal entities can be debtors. In the case of the former, the following must be taken into account:

(1)    dependent minors less than 18 years of age are legally represented by their parents;
(2)    those declared incapacitated by a court ruling are represented by a guardian or assisted by a curator; and
(3)    should the debtor die, the debts are not extinguished but continue to encumber the estate.

### 18.2.2    Legal entities

Legal entities may be of the most varied type and form, and all may occupy the position of a debtor in a contractual relation. Without claiming to be exhaustive, the following types of entities are summarised below:

(1)    public administration;
(2)    privately based corporations, such as professional associations and official Chambers of Commerce;

(3)  associations, including trade unions, employers' organisations, political parties, and religious associations;
(4)  foundations;
(5)  civil corporations which answer for their debts with their own assets and, on a subsidiary basis, with those of their members; and
(6)  businesses, whether personally based (general partnerships, *commandités*, and limited partnerships) or capital-based (limited companies); these differ in the way the latter limit the partners' liability for the corporate debts.

One case worthy of reference, albeit briefly, is the corporate group. In principle, such groups lack a single character, so that the debts of each are not transferred to the others; however, the Spanish courts have allowed the linking of liabilities in certain cases (particularly concerning debts to employees) based on the unity of command between the different companies making up such a group.

### 18.2.3  Administration of property

The administration of the property of debtors finally declared bankrupt or insolvent (see **18.11**, below) is assumed in the first instance by the receivers and subsequently by the trustees to whom the creditors must address their claims.

Property the debtor can use to meet its debts may include all properties making up the debtor's assets, now or in the future. However, where an individual debtor is married, account must be taken of:

(1)  the economic basis of the marriage;
(2)  the nature of the debt; and
(3)  the debtor's classification as a trader, in order to define the scope of the property affected in each case.

### 18.2.4  Is the debt statute-barred?

Claims for payment of a debt, whether judicially or otherwise, must take place in a period defined by two specific dates: that of the legal enforceability of such debt, and the statute of limitations. Under civil contracts where the parties agree a deadline, the debt is not enforceable until that date; if there is no such arrangement, it is payable immediately. Debts arising under commercial contracts can be claimed 10 days after they were contracted unless:

(1)  the parties agreed otherwise;
(2)  a special provision applies which fixes some other term; or
(3)  the instrument in which the contract was documented is of executory nature (in which case the debt becomes payable the day after it was contracted).

Claims arising from debts are generally subject to a 15-year statute of limitations following maturity (ie from the time they became enforceable). There are, however, a variety of exceptions to this rule (eg claims on bills of exchange are, as the case may be, subject to a limitation of six months, one year, or three years). However, if the debt is mortgage-guaranteed, the foreclosure claim does not expire until 20 years following the date on which foreclosure became possible. If a creditor files for court proceedings to claim a debt once the statute of limitations has come into effect, such claim is dismissed out of hand, and the creditor must, moreover, pay the costs involved (see **18.7**, below).

### 18.2.5 Security

There are a number of ways in which to enhance the creditor's certainty of collection, of which the following are the most commonly used:

(1) A penalty clause. This involves a sum of money the debtor undertakes to pay its creditor should it default on its obligation or not meet it in full. In such cases, unless specifically agreed, the creditor cannot simultaneously demand that the debtor meet the main liability and the penalty simultaneously: for its part, unless expressly agreed, the debtor cannot be released from fulfilment of the main liability by payment of the penalty. It should be pointed out that the courts may reduce the sum established in the penalty provision of the contract, if it is considered excessive.

(2) A bond. This consists of a money payment made by one party to the contract to the other to provide a guarantee in case of default. It is assumed with such a guarantee that, if the party who paid the sum of money is in default, that party loses it. If the other party is in breach, it must repay the sum paid in, plus a further equal sum. If the contractual liabilities are performed in full, the bond is returned to the party who paid it.

(3) Suretyship. The contract sometimes includes a clause whereby one or more persons undertake to pay or perform the contract for the debtor should the debtor fail to do so. If a simple suretyship, the guarantor from whom the creditor claims payment may demand that the creditor proceed first against the principal debtor. Under a several suretyship, ie, more than one party guarantees, the creditor may claim payment directly from any guarantor without first demanding it from the principal debtor, and that guarantor can do nothing to prevent this. Commercial suretyships (those securing the performance of a commercial contract) are always several.

(4) Pledge. The most common category of pledge security takes the form of the delivery to the creditor of movable property belonging to the debtor or some other person, which the former retain until the debtor pays. If the debtor defaults, the creditor may sell the property by public auction and collect the adjudication price. If the property cannot be sold after two auctions, the creditor may assume ownership of the property in payment of the debt.

(5) Mortgage. In its most common form, this is a guarantee securing the

property belonging to the debtor or a third party for payment of the debt by the debtor. It is constituted by entry in the Property Register where the property is registered. In case of a default, the creditor is authorised to auction the property and so receive its payment.

### 18.2.6  Retention of title

In deferred-payment sales, the seller usually provides, to secure its credit against the buyer, that ownership of the property sold is not transferred to the buyer until the whole price has been paid (the retention-of-title clause). In the case of movables, instalment sales with a retention-of-title clause may, with some exceptions, be entered in the Instalment Sales Register, a public register which has offices in all Spanish provinces (operated by the Territorial Business Register concerned) and a central office in Madrid (telephone, 91/411-2582). Instalment sales of movables intended to be resold by the buyer cannot be registered. Even if the instalment sale contract includes a retention-of-title clause, the creditor's attempt to recover the property in a case of default may be frustrated by a number of factors:

(1)  the debtor refuses to return the property, in which case the creditor must file a legal claim against the debtor;

(2)  where the creditor is unable to identify the property in order to recover it, prior to filing its claim, the creditor may ask the court to order the debtor to produce the property;

(3)  where the creditor seeks to recover the property but sees that it has been used by the debtor in its production process and is now unrecoverable, it must claim the debt from the debtor, plus indemnification for liquidated damages; and

(4)  where the debtor has sold the property to a third party which purchased in good faith.

In this last circumstance, the creditor may claim its property from that third party, provided that the sale contract could be and was entered in the Instalment Sales Register. Where property is sold for resale by the buyer to third parties (such transactions not being registrable, as already pointed out), such property cannot be claimed from the entity which acquired it in premises or stores open to the public, so that the creditor must proceed against the debtor to claim the corresponding indemnification.

### 18.2.7  Sources of information

In debt-collection proceedings, it may be useful and even necessary to have sufficient information on the debtor and its assets. For these purposes, the main public sources of information are as follows:

(1)  General information on companies. The Central Business Register (telephone, 91/564-5253) gathers information from the Territorial

Business Registers, and such information may be requested by individuals in petitions for informative notes. The data available refers to the first entry of companies (address, name, share capital, corporate purpose, administrators, and managing directors), to certain subsequent circumstances (changes of address, alterations to the share capital, and appointment of new administrators, managing directors, or general representatives), and to branches (creation, address, and closure). Further details of particular interest can be obtained on the companies entered in the Territorial Business Registers which, in addition to the data held in the Central Business Register, provide information such as the identity of the founder shareholders and their contributions, the full text of the company bylaws, and reference to judicial or administrative intervention measures. Companies must file their accounts (balance sheet, profit and loss account, and annual report), the management report, and the audit report every year in the Business Register in the place where they are domiciled, and access to this is free. Finally, the *Official Business Register Gazette* provides information on the first entry of companies and certain subsequent circumstances. It also publishes announcements, such as notice of general meetings of shareholders, dissolutions, liquidations, mergers, and the deposit of annual accounts.

(2)   Information on the debtor's property assets. Simple notes and certifications concerning registered land held by individuals or legal entities may be requested from the Property Register where such assets are entered. If that is not known, the Index Service (telephone, 91/564-3715) provides information on Property Registers where assets may be registered (for post-1983 entries only).

(3)   Information on ownership of motor vehicles. This is available from provincial Head Offices of Traffic.

## 18.3   Letters before action

### 18.3.1   Are they necessary?

It is not necessary in general to make an out-of-court claim for payment from the debtor in order to resort to judicial proceedings. However, there are exceptions. In cases of commercial contracts executed by credit organisations in a public deed or in a contract in which a selling agent intervened, it is necessary to notify the debtor or the guarantor of the sum receivable in order to then claim it in court execution procedures.

However, in practice, payment is always claimed out of court prior to the court claim itself, since this may benefit the creditor:

(1)   the creditor may collect the debt without delay or further expense;
(2)   generally, unless otherwise stipulated in the contract, an out-of-court claim for payment has the effect of placing the debtor in a situation of default (if it is not automatically placed in such a situation pursuant to

a commercial contract whose expiration is either contractually or legally pre-established); as a consequence, interest agreed on for such circumstances must be paid (and, if this was not agreed, the debtor must pay interest at the legal money interest rate, which was nine per cent in 1994); and

(3)    in general, an out-of-court claim interrupts the period of the statute of limitation on claims; however, such a claim against the debtor does not interrupt the limitation on its guarantors.

### 18.3.2    What should they say?

An out-of-court claim is usually made by letter, which ought to be sent by registered post and with acknowledgement of receipt, a copy of which must be kept by the creditor. It may be sent by the creditor itself or by its lawyer (which usually has a greater effect on the debtor); it is recommended that, if the letter is sent by a lawyer, he should thereafter act at all times as the intermediary with the debtor. The letter must state the debtor's name and address, the date and the identity of the creditor. It must refer to:

(1)    the amount of the debt;
(2)    the documents stating the debt (ie, invoices, notes, or cheques), copies of which should be included with the letter; and
(3)    the date of maturity of the debt.

If the debtor is already in default, a claim for interest may be included, although the most usual procedure is to offer the possibility of limiting the payment to the principal of the debt, if this is done within a deadline indicated for the purpose (7 to 10 days), with a warning that legal proceedings will otherwise be initiated against the debtor, in which case both principal and interest on arrears will be claimed. Particular care must be taken in drafting such letters; while they usually have scant effect, because the debtor generally ignores them, the negative consequences may be particularly grave. In fact, the debtor may avail itself in court of statements in the letter by the creditor or its representative, eg, to prove that the creditor waived the interest on arrears or part of the price or to support an interpretation of a particular contractual clause which is favourable to the debtor's interests.

### 18.3.3    May they demand interest for late payment?

This is not necessary, but it is highly recommended, since it deprives the debtor of an argument to claim an alleged tacit waiver of the interest on arrears by the creditor. However, as already pointed out, in cases where the debtor is not automatically in default by a given date, interest on arrears normally starts to accrue from the date of the simple demand for payment.

### 18.3.4    Contractual and legal interest on arrears

Standard interest (such as that paid to a bank for a loan) is designed to compensate the creditor because it does not receive payment of the asset it assigns to the debtor until after a given period of time. It is a liability which is ancillary to the principal, the terms of which are agreed by the parties, and it ends when the principal does (eg in the case of a loan, when such loan is repaid). By comparison, interest on arrears is designed as compensation, and it becomes due as a result of default on an obligation. For the debtor to claim interest on arrears, the debt must be due, net (quantified in money terms) and receivable. The amount of such interest is as agreed by the parties or, failing that, the legal rate. In general, the creditor's claim seeks the following:

(1)  the principal debt;
(2)  if agreed, the standard interest accrued until the date of maturity; and
(3)  the interest on arrears from the date of maturity or of the demand for payment until the actual payment date.

Once the first instance court has ruled and until that ruling is enforced in full, the payment ordered accrues annual interest in the creditor's favour at two per cent over the legal interest rate (in 1994, 9 per cent plus 2 per cent to make 11 per cent), unless the interest on arrears agreed between the parties was higher, in which case that higher rate applies. Interest becomes even more complicated when it is remembered that, with civil liabilities, accrued unpaid interest accrues further interest, at the legal rate, from the time the liability was claimed in court. However, under commercial loan agreements, no interest accrues on unpaid interest due unless it was agreed to include this interest in the figure for the principal debt (capitalisation of interest).

Finally, while interest either as compensation or as indemnification may be agreed freely by the parties, both are limited in this respect by Spain's Anti-Usury Act, under which any contract is invalid which fixes interest significantly above the normal money rate and which is manifestly disproportionate to the circumstances of the case (although the courts do not usually declare interest at more than twice the legal rate at the time as usurious) or where the interest was fixed in a situation when, clearly, it was accepted by the debtor because of distress, inexperience, or its mental faculties were limited.

## 18.4   Pre-action and non-judicial remedies

### 18.4.1   Out-of-court settlements

There are possibilities for certain arrangements to be reached between the parties concerning payment of the debt in order to avoid recourse to court proceedings. Such arrangements usually take any of the following forms:

(1)  Out-of-court settlement. The parties sign an agreement which establishes or clarifies the terms of the contract which led to the dispute, offering mutual concessions. Standard arrangements along these lines are remission of part of the debt, or the stipulation of new payment terms. Theoretically, a settlement thus agreed becomes, between the parties, a matter adjudged, meaning that they may no longer resort to

the courts to discuss the question further beyond merely claiming compliance with the terms of the settlement. However, in practice, this sometimes does not occur, and the matter can be debated once more, as a whole, in proceedings.

(2) Submission of the dispute to arbitration. The parties may have agreed in writing, either in the contract where the debt arises or in another agreement, to submit controversies arising in the performance of that contract to the award of one or more arbitrators. If, despite this, one of the parties takes the matter to court, the court cannot hear the matter if the other party invokes the arrangement concerning the arbitration. The parties must decide whether the arbitration award is to be given in legal arbitration or in equity arbitration. The former is preferable, given the greater certainty of the content of the award. If the award handed down is not fulfilled, its enforced execution can be sought in the court in the place where the award was given.

### 18.4.2 Pre-trial settlements

Pre-trial settlements are proceedings concerning the debt prior to a sub-stantive court claim for that debt, designed either to settle the conflict directly or to ensure the successful outcome of a subsequent court claim. The most common procedures along these lines, always implemented with judicial intervention, are as follows.

#### 18.4.2.1 *Conciliation proceedings*

The aim of conciliation proceedings is to reach an understanding with the debtor without embarking on a lawsuit. To do this, the creditor goes to the Justice of the Peace or the First Instance and Preliminary Investigating Court (see **18.5**, below) and submits a conciliation file. Neither a procurator nor lawyer need to be involved (see **18.6**, below), although the presence of a lawyer is advisable (whose services are paid for by the creditor unless the conciliation is held away from its place of residence, in which case these fees are paid by the other party if it is ordered to pay costs; see **18.7**, below). If an understanding is reached, it is documented in a certification. If applicable, the enforcement of the award in the certificate can be sought from the court before which the conciliation proceedings were held, provided that the court has authority according to the amount involved (see **18.5**, below).

#### 18.4.2.2 *Attachment*

Before the claim is filed, the creditor may apply to the First Instance and Preliminary Investigating Court for the attachment of sufficient assets to secure the debt provided that:

(1) a document is filed demonstrating the existence of the debt; and
(2) the debtor is in a situation such that it can be assumed that it will not meet its liabilities (eg if the debtor is a foreigner or has disappeared

without leaving anyone in charge of its business). This is a most effective measure since, on the one hand, it prevents the debtor from seeking a situation of apparent insolvency in order to default while, on the other, it has a clear psychological effect. Because it is urgent, neither a procurator nor a lawyer need intervene (if, despite this, their services are employed, the associated costs are paid by the creditor, with the familiar exception in which the attachment is applied for somewhere other than the place where the creditor is domiciled).

The court may ask the creditor to pay a bond to cover the losses and costs which the attachment may cause to the debtor. The attachment is enforced once the bond is paid unless, when the time comes to proceed, the debtor pays. The procedure for designating the assets to be attached is dealt with in **18.10**, below. For the moment, it is enough to say that, in the case of land and property, a preventive annotation is made of the attachment in the Property Register where it is entered. This does not mean that the debtor may not sell the property, but that a third party acquiring the property knows that, if the attachment is eventually implemented, the property will be auctioned, and that third party will be unable to do anything to prevent this. With regard to attached movable goods, they remain in bond in certain circumstances.

Once attachment is granted, the associated claim must be filed within 20 days (10 days if demanded by the debtor). If the claim is not filed, the attachment is removed, and the creditor will be ordered to pay costs and indemnify the debtor for the liquidated damages caused.

### 18.4.2.3 *Other actions in preparation of proceedings*

The creditor may ask the court to admit a sworn statement from the debtor concerning any matter relating to its character, unknown to the creditor, which is necessary to the filing of the suit. As pointed out above, the creditor may also ask the court to order the debtor to exhibit the asset which is to be the subject of the claim.

When written evidence is submitted in the proceedings clearly revealing the defendant's obligation to give, do, or not to do something (eg delivery notes, receipts for goods, invoices, and quotations signed by the debtor), the plaintiff may ask the court to adopt such measures as, in the circumstances, may be necessary to ensure the efficacy of the future ruling. There is no fixed list of measures which may be sought, but these may include:

(1) attachment or deposit of the debtor's assets;
(2) a court order for the defendant to refrain from a particular course of action;
(3) judicial intervention in its business; and
(4) a preventive annotation prohibiting the sale of a given asset.

Once the court has granted any of these measures, before it is implemented, the plaintiff which requested the measure must pay the associated bond to cover any loss which the implementation thereof may cause to the defendant.

Finally, should ordinary execution proceedings be contemplated (see **18.10**, below) on the basis of a private document, the creditor must ask the court to order the debtor to recognise its signature or acknowledge the debt.

## 18.5 The court system

### 18.5.1 Structure of the courts

According to circumstances, court claims for debts may be prosecuted through civil jurisdiction (eg for a debt arising under a civil or commercial contract), labour jurisdiction (eg as for salary debts), criminal jurisdiction (eg the demand for civil liability arising from crimes), or in contentious-administrative jurisdiction (eg in claims for a debt arising under a contract with the public administration). This chapter focuses on the civil jurisdiction, in which claims are heard for all types of debts arising from civil or commercial contracts. The following are the jurisdictional bodies in this category:

(1) The Courts of Justices of the Peace. These are to be found in municipalities without a First Instance and Preliminary Investigating Court; they are headed by a Justice of the Peace, who is typically not a professional of the judiciary.

(2) The First Instance and Preliminary Investigating Courts. These are single-member bodies headed by a professional judge, and they are located in the main town or capital city of each Judicial District. In the large cities, the First Instance and Preliminary Investigating Courts are independent bodies, the former dealing with civil matters and the latter with criminal cases.

(3) The Provincial Courts (*Audiencias*). These are collective bodies based in each provincial capital city, their jurisdiction extending to that province.

(4) The High Courts of Law. These are also collective bodies, named after the regions in which they are located. Their jurisdiction extends to the territory of that region. In general, they are based in the capital city of their regional community, although there are some exceptions. Each High Court has three divisions, Civil and Criminal, Contentious-Administrative, and Labour.

(5) The Supreme Court. Based in Madrid, this is the highest jurisdictional body in all spheres (except as to constitutional questions) with authority throughout Spain. It consists of Division One, the Civil Division; Division Two, the Criminal Division; Division Three, the Contentious-Administrative Division; Division Four, the Labour Division, and Division Five, the Military Division.

(6) The Constitutional Court. While not a judicial body as such, it is referred to here because, in some cases, the final decision is left to it in a suit (although this is not normal in civil questions).

### 18.5.2 Rules of jurisdiction

The Spanish courts have jurisdiction to hear a case in the following circumstances:

(1)  in any of the fields in which Spanish law itself establishes this juris-diction exclusively (eg rights concerning property in Spain);

(2)  when the parties have expressed their wish to submit the suit to the jurisdiction of Spanish courts, or when the defendant is domiciled in Spain; and

(3)  in the absence of the criteria noted below, in the field of contractual obligations, when the contract was concluded in Spain or the obligations can be fulfilled in this country.

As to item (2) above, the parties' submission to Spanish jurisdiction is possible as long as the business concerned is connected in some way with Spain. The wish to submit may be expressed specifically (in a contractual clause) or tacitly (by the plaintiff filing the claim in a Spanish court, or by the defendant when it appears before it, unless it does so solely to invite the court, which it does not consider has jurisdiction to hear the matter, to abandon the case and deliver it to the court which it considers does have the authority to hear the matter.

With this general configuration of the jurisdiction of Spanish courts in relation to this matter, a creditor planning to litigate must ask what type of jurisdictional body from among those listed above has authority to hear the case. In the first instance, the response to this question depends on the amount involved, so that hearing of the matter is assigned as follows.

The Courts of Justices of the Peace hear conciliation proceedings (irrespec-tive of the amount involved) and suits not involving more than Pts 8,000. The First Instance and Preliminary Investigating Courts hear conciliation pro-ceedings where there is no Justice of the Peace and all suits not assigned to other courts. These are thus the courts which hear most first instance liti-gation. The Provincial Courts, High Courts of Law, and the Supreme Court have no first-instance authority in the matters under consideration here; they hear only ordinary and special appeals (see **18.5**, below).

This initial objective delimitation of jurisdiction must be complemented by a second criteria of jurisdictional allocation, which is geographical in nature. In fact, if in a particular case the conclusion is reached that the First Instance and Preliminary Investigating Courts have jurisdiction over a case in the light of the sum involved, and given that there are one or more courts of this type in each Judicial District (of which there are 482 in all in Spain), the creditor will wonder to which of these courts it must turn. The following criteria are applied in settling this question:

(1)  the body to which the parties have submitted expressly or tacitly has jurisdiction (the form of such submission is described above); however, submission is not admitted in a variety of procedures (eg in ordinary execution proceedings, as described in **18.8**, below, or in mortgage or eviction proceedings);

(2) in the absence of submission, in general, the court with jurisdiction is the one in the place where the obligation must be fulfilled and, failing that, at the plaintiff's discretion that in the place where the defendant is domiciled, or where the contract was concluded, if the defendant is located there; and

(3) in the absence of the above criteria, for particular judicial proceedings, the law fixes special rules on jurisdiction; eg, in applications for attachment, the court with authority is the one in the place where the assets to be attached are located.

Once the creditor has identified the judicial district in which the court with jurisdiction is located, there may prove to be several bodies of the same sort in that district (eg a number of consecutively numbered First Instance and Preliminary Investigating Courts). In this case, the creditor addresses its claim 'to the pertinent court'. In the first notification received from the court (generally to announce that the claim is deemed to have been filed), the creditor can verify the number of the court to which its case has been entrusted, addressing itself to that court in subsequent writs.

### 18.5.3 Appeals

The diversity of courts means that a procedure can be prosecuted in two instances (first instance and, by means of an ordinary appeal, second instance) and allows, in certain cases, exceptional appeals to the Supreme Court and High Courts of Law. These are the so-called special appeals, to quash and for review, the former being, in fact, a third instance. From this functional standpoint, the distribution of jurisdiction among the various types of courts is as follows:

(1) First Instance and Preliminary Investigating Courts hear ordinary appeals against the rulings given by the courts of Justices of the Peace.

(2) The Provincial Courts (*Audiencias*) hear ordinary appeals against first instance orders handed down by the First Instance and Preliminary Investigating Courts.

(3) The High Courts of Justice hear special appeals to quash rulings of the *Audiencias* (and, in certain cases, those of First Instance and Preliminary Investigating Courts) and special appeals for review filed against 'final' rulings from which there are no other types of remedy, provided that the quashing or review is based on the law of the autonomous region concerned.

(4) The Supreme Court hears special appeals to quash and review in the same terms as the High Courts of Law, when based on state law.

(5) The Constitutional Court, although not a strict jurisdictional body, has two channels through which a matter being heard by a given court may reach it. These are the motion for relief and the question of unconstitutionality. Individuals may appeal for relief to the Constitutional Court, once judicial procedures have been exhausted, in cases

of anti-constitutional discrimination or breach of basic rights (which, it should be emphasised, does not include the right of property) and public liberties. In the second case, where the court is hearing a case whose resolution depends on a provision whose constitutionality is in doubt, the question may be taken ex officio or at the instance of a party to the Constitutional Court so that it can rule as to whether the provision is constitutional and whether applicable to the resolution of the suit.

### 18.5.4   Status of the foreign creditor

The capacity of an individual or legal entity to contract and, as applicable, to file claims in court is determined by the law of the state of which they are nationals. However, if a foreigner concludes a contract in Spain without having capacity to do so according to his or her national law, the contract is valid (and such foreigner's obligations claimable) in Spain if the cause of the disqualification has no parallel in Spanish law.

On the other hand, the consequences of breach of contractual obligations are those determined by the law applicable to the contract and which is as follows in the absence of an international treaty or convention:

(1)   the law to which the parties submitted expressly, if connected in some way with the contract;
(2)   failing that, the national law common to the parties;
(3)   failing that, the law of the place of habitual residence of the parties; or
(4)   failing that, the law of the place where the contract was concluded.

In regard to the above, it should be noted that the Convention of Rome of 19 June 1980 on the Law Applicable to Contractual Obligations has been in force in Spain since 1 September 1993.

Finally, it may occur that a foreigner litigating in Spain is required to deposit a sum of money at the court's disposal to secure a hypothetical obligation to pay the procedural costs should that foreigner lose the case. This must be done when demanded by the other party, if that party can show that the same obligation is imposed on Spaniards in the country of the foreign litigant. There are, however, treaties and conventions of both multilateral (the Hague Conventions of 1 March 1954 and 25 October 1980) and bilateral nature (eg the Convention with Italy of 22 May 1973) which release foreigners from this liability.

## 18.6   Legal representation

### 18.6.1   Nature of legal representation

Both individuals and legal entities have the capacity to appear in court proceedings. However, the plaintiff and the defendant must appear through a procurator qualified to practice his profession before the courts in the place where the claim is filed. The procurator thus acts as the litigant's representative before the court, and it is the procurator who submits all types of writs in the litigant's name and, in turn, who receives the copies of those submitted by the other party, and the text of the court's decrees. Apart from the procurators, the parties must entrust the technical management of the case to lawyers qualified to practice their profession before the local courts. The lawyer (*abogado* or *letrado*) has personal contact with the litigant, designs the legal strategy to be pursued in the case, and drafts the writs to be submitted to the court by the procurator.

Thus, there are three clearly differentiated personal elements in operation regarding each litigating party:

(1)  the individual with an interest in the case;
(2)  the lawyer to whom the defence is entrusted (and, thenceforth, the individual's direct intermediary); and
(3)  the procurator to whom the party assigns its representation before the court which hears the case (and with whom, curiously, the client has in general no dealing). Only in particular cases is it possible to do away with the lawyer and/or procurator; the latter is not necessary, eg, in conciliation proceedings or in suits for less than Pts 800,000 (in such case, the litigants may appear in court in person). The law also establishes the cases where it is not necessary for a lawyer to intervene and, without being exhaustive, this includes conciliation proceedings or suits involving less than Pts 80,000.

Usually, the lawyer entrusted by the creditor with the out-of-court claim of the debt is the one who deals with the court claim. Before proceeding, the lawyer usually seeks to ensure that the debtor has assets with which to meet the payment; otherwise, it would be useless to incur the expenses involved in the procedure. Once it is confirmed that such assets do exist, the lawyer contacts a procurator and then asks the client to execute powers of attorney before a notary, granting the chosen procurator its legal representation. Once the powers of attorney are executed, they must be duly accepted and attested. These two administrative procedures are carried out by the procurator before the Bar Association and the corresponding Association of Procurators. They involve the payment of fees which represent significant financial resources for these associations. A more economical alternative is for the litigant to appear in person before the clerk of the court to grant the powers, thereby avoiding payment of acceptance and attestation fees. This is not a common procedure, however, and the Bar Associations and Associations of Procurators frown on it.

The procurator's fees are usually paid through the lawyer. As soon as the claim is received from the lawyer for submission, the procurator will ask for the appropriate 'provision of funds', amounting to between 60 per cent and 100 per cent of the fees it is estimated will accrue for action in the proceedings. In general, the lawyer then contacts the client, asking for the sum requested, which is then passed on at once to the procurator.

If a litigant makes use of the services of a procurator and/or lawyer in a case where this is not legally necessary, the costs of their services are paid by the litigant itself, even if the other party is ordered to pay costs, with the exception already referred to of the case where the litigant is not normally resident in the place where the proceedings are heard.

Either party may change lawyers during the procedure if wished. However, as a general rule, the new lawyer cannot take over the matter until the lawyer being replaced gives authorisation (*venia*) and the client evidences payment of the fees owed to the previous lawyer.

### 18.6.2   Mode of payment for legal representation

#### 18.6.2.1   *Contractual agreement for costs*

Although the legal relation linking lawyer and client is that of a service-lease agreement, it is uncommon for that contract to take the form of a document signed by both parties (the most common exception to this rule being the so-called *igualas*, dealt with below); this being so, the arrangement concerning payment procedure for costs of the lawyer's professional services rendered is usually left as a purely oral understanding. On the other hand, it is not possible to generalise on this question; the arrangement for payment will depend on the size of the firm, the work carried out (legal consultancy or litigation), and the relationship with the client.

For consultancy services, regular clients are usually billed periodically. For occasional clients, it is usual to ask for a provision of funds at the time when the work is commissioned, to cover between 40 per cent and 80 per cent of the expected fees (although, if the client has recognised creditworthiness, it may not be asked to make any such payment). As to the form of charging, most firms bill individual jobs, calculating fees according to the financial scope of the matter and its degree of technical complexity. Only some firms, particularly those specialised in the business field and in international trade, bill according to the time taken in resolving the case.

Litigation services are usually billed apart from other services, with each matter invoiced independently. In general, the minimum rates fixed by each Bar Association are applied. Regular clients may not be asked to make any payment when ordering work done, or they may be asked to pay between 50 per cent and 60 per cent of the expected first instance costs, the remaining being billed following the court ruling or distributed between evidence proceedings and the formalities for conclusion prior to the ruling. Occasional clients are usually asked to provide funds when ordering work of between 60 per cent and 100 per cent of the expected fees for first instance procedures. Similar systems are applied for second instance formalities.

The system of *igualas* is common for small firms. All sorts of legal services are contracted with the client for a given period of time in exchange for a fixed periodic payment (usually monthly). However, the contractual terms of such agreements may vary widely, and they do not usually include business of a major financial scale.

### 18.6.2.2.  *Contingency fee basis*

An arrangement whereby fees are paid according to results is expressly forbidden under Spanish law.

### 18.6.2.3  *Liability of other party*

Regarding the liability of the other party for legal fees, see **18.7**, below.

### 18.6.2.4  *Deduction of value added tax*

Lawyers' services are liable for value added tax (VAT) in Spain, currently at 15 per cent. This may be deducted, in general, where the client has paid such charges in the pursuit of its activity, as employer or professional. If the client paying for a lawyer's services is a foreigner, four possible theoretical situations may be distinguished in deciding whether such services are liable for Spanish VAT.

(1)  A Spanish lawyer rendering services to an employer or professional resident in another European Union (EU) country. The services are considered to be rendered in the country of that employer or professional and liable to VAT there, so that the client must itself pay the sum concerned in its VAT return. It may be entitled then to deduct it (depending on the provisions of its national VAT legislation).

(2)  A Spanish lawyer rendering services to a private individual resident in another EU country. The services are considered to be rendered in Spain, so that the lawyer passes the VAT charge on to the individual, who may not deduct it.

(3)  A Spanish lawyer rendering services to an employer or professional resident in a country not a member of the EU. The services are considered to be rendered in a non-EU country and so are not liable for VAT.

(4)  A Spanish lawyer rendering services to a private individual resident in a country not a member of the EU. As in the previous case, the services are considered to be rendered in the country of the client and so are not liable for VAT.

## 18.7  Costs and interest

### 18.7.1  Current fees

Initially, a distinction must be made between the expenses for proceedings and the costs which are the payments necessary within a procedure or judicial action for the prosecution or defence of a right. In other words, not all expenses are classified as procedural costs, eg a lawyer's fees paid for consultancy prior to proceedings, or sums paid to detective agencies to secure reports on a debtor's solvency. Usually, costs comprise the following:

(1)  the fees of procurators;

(2) the fees of experts and lawyers (if their assistance is mandatory);

(3) the compensation and expenses of witnesses; and

(4) other procedural outlays, such as for legally required publication, register annotations or entries, and notary fees.

It is evident that the costs do not include any charge or fee by the state arising from the use of judicial services. This is because the system of Spanish justice is free. The state does not collect any sum under this heading.

### 18.7.2 Availability of legal aid

Given that the system of Spanish justice is free, ie, there are no charges or fees which must be paid by the public in availing itself of judicial bodies in order to litigate, the term 'benefit of legal aid' must be understood as a right which, when granted, involves:

(1) the release of the beneficiary from the pre-payment of costs during formalities in the proceedings;

(2) the appointment of a lawyer ex officio without having to pay fees or charges; and

(3) the release from the requirement to pay the other party costs incurred by it if ordered to do so.

The benefit may arise from two sources: a legal provision declaring it (as in the case of charitable foundations), or a court order. Moreover, the right to legal aid granted to foreign litigants by the authorities in their country may also be recognised in Spain (pursuant to the Hague Convention of 1 March 1954 or the Brussels Convention of 27 September 1968).

For a plaintiff creditor or defendant debtor to be granted the benefit of legal aid in Spain, the following must be evidenced:

(1) that there are insufficient resources (in general, income less than twice the minimum inter-professional wage in effect at the time of application);

(2) that the party is litigating on its own behalf; and

(3) that the petition is sustainable.

The application for legal aid is filed (prior to or with the claim) in the same court as is hearing or is to hear the case. Legal aid can also be sought once the claim has been filed although, in this case, it must be shown that the conditions necessary for the granting of legal aid have arisen since the claim was filed. A procurator is not necessary in order to file the application, although a lawyer must be hired (application can be made for a lawyer to be appointed ex officio). In practice, the party believing itself entitled to legal aid must ask the Bar Association in the place where it intends to litigate to appoint for it a lawyer ex officio, which the Bar Association does without asking the litigant to show that it meets the financial terms of entitlement to legal aid and without any formalities, and this lawyer deals with the legal aid application.

Foreign litigants may also be granted right to benefit from legal aid in Spain.

This may be done through application for the benefit directly in Spain or through recognition in Spain of the court order which, in the litigant's own country, granted the benefit. Concerning the first procedure, it must be remembered that, under the Strasbourg Agreement of 27 January 1977, anyone normally resident in the territory of one of the states which has ratified the Agreement and who wishes to seek legal aid in another state which has also done so, may file its application in the state where it is normally resident, which will deliver it to the other state. For the acknowledgement in Spain of a foreign court order granting legal aid, account must be taken, in the context of the EU, of the Brussels Convention of 27 December 1968, under which resolutions handed down in a signatory state are recognised in the remaining signatory states merely with the completion of certain formal requisites.

It may be that, even though legal aid was granted, the beneficiary must pay its own costs, within certain limits. This is the case if it wins its suit and as a result is awarded a sum of money and the other party is not ordered to pay the winning party's costs. Moreover, the legal aid beneficiary's economic situation may improve within a given period of time following the termination of the procedure, as a result of which it may be obliged to meet the costs generated in its defence, and those of the other party if it was ordered to pay them.

Finally, if legal aid is not granted, the applicant must pay the costs of the procedure, unless there are exceptional circumstances.

### 18.7.3  Liability for and recovery of costs

The court must decide who pays the costs resulting from the proceedings, and how much must be paid. The party ordered to pay these costs must reimburse the other for the sums pre-paid under this heading. In this connection, the parties' contractual arrangement concerning payment of court costs in an eventual dispute is not binding on the court, which must rule according to a strict application of the legal criteria. The general principle of payment of costs is that the party whose pleas were totally dismissed must pay both its own costs and those of the other party. Only exceptionally is the losing party not ordered to pay costs, when circumstances arise which justify this. If the ruling partly upholds or dismisses the pleas of each party, and in the exceptional cases where the losing party is not ordered to pay costs, each litigant pays its own costs and half each of joint costs, unless there are exceptional reasons justifying an order for one of the parties to pay all costs, for having litigated wilfully.

Should a defendant agree to a claim (ie it accepts the plaintiff's pleas in such claim) before replying, it can only in exceptional circumstances be ordered to pay the other party's costs. For its part, if the plaintiff waives or abandons a claim it had begun, the court will order it to pay the defendant's costs.

There are certain quantitative limits on orders to pay costs. Some items of expense cannot be included, such as costs arising from superfluous actions or the fees of procurators or lawyers whose participation was not mandatory (and unless the party which hired them was not resident in the place where the proceedings were heard). In addition, the party ordered to pay costs is not bound to pay fees for lawyers and experts whose services were used by the other party beyond one-third of the amount involved in the case, unless it acted wilfully. If the party ordered to pay costs does not do so voluntarily, the party benefiting under the order may initiate procedures, known as 'cost appraisal', which define the exact sum payable by the party against which the order was made. These charges are then exacted in executory collection proceedings.

### 18.7.4   Interest

The creditor's entitlement to claim is discussed at **18.3.4**, above.

## 18.8   Proceedings

### 18.8.1   In general

The civil court procedure is fundamentally written. It is basically governed by the parties, who place the facts before the court, submitting evidence and their pleas. The court does not investigate independently. There are a limited number of instruments of evidence, the public document being the most effective. In handing down its decision, the court assesses the evidence submitted by the parties overall. It cannot grant more than they have sought nor rule on matters on which the parties did not seek a resolution.

It must be remembered that the Spanish justice system currently operates slowly. Often a year elapses between the filing of the claim and a ruling. If appealed, at least a further 14 months will be required for a decision. Finally, in the Supreme Court, procedures may be prolonged a minimum of a further 16 months. None of this takes account of the additional time required in obtaining enforcement of a ruling. The slowness of the procedure, plus the costs involved and the greater or lesser uncertainty as to the outcome, stress once more the importance to the creditor, prior to beginning, of making the necessary checks to identify assets belonging to the debtor which might be executed in the future. This is even more advisable insofar as a debtor who loses a suit is not obliged in any way to designate property of its own for realisation, and the court has no obligation in practice to investigate this aspect. For these purposes, the information sources mentioned in **18.2.1**, above can be used. If the creditor is unable to locate and designate sufficient assets, it will not collect its credit, however favourable the ruling is to it.

Once it is decided to proceed with the suit, the creditor's lawyer must prepare the claim, setting out the facts which led to it and the legal principles underlying the creditor's petition. Quotation of judicial precedent is of particular importance in setting out these legal principles, making it necessary to consult previous rulings from which arguments can be extracted in favour of the plaintiff's interests. The main sources of the texts of decisions are:

(1) for rulings of the Supreme Court, the Spanish Legislative Collection (official text) and a variety of private collection (which are the ones most used by lawyers and jurists in general), such as those of the publishing house *Aranzadi*; various publishers also distribute rulings in computer data bases (eg *Aranzadi*, *La Ley*, and *Colex Data*);

(2) for rulings of the Provincial Courts, *Sentencias en Apelación* (published by the Ministry of Justice and the Interior, latest volume being 1991); there are also more easily accessible private collections, such as that of the publishing house *La Ley* (also in a computer data base).

## 18.9 Procedure to judgment

In the first instance, a distinction must be made between the ordinary declaratory procedure, which itself has a variety of categories depending on the amount of the claim, and the different summary civil and special procedures (the former including possessory procedures and ordinary execution proceedings, and the latter procedures for insolvency and mortgage foreclosure). For obvious reasons, review here is limited to the different phases of just two procedures, the ordinary declaratory suit for smaller amounts (Pts 800,000 to Pts 160 million), which is the standard procedure and the most frequent of the declaratory types, and ordinary execution proceedings, which are the most prevalent.

| *Ordinary declaratory procedure for minor amounts* | *Ordinary execution procedure* |
| --- | --- |
| [Conciliation proceedings] | [Conciliation proceedings] |
| [Preliminary proceedings] | [Preparation of execution: recognition of signature and acknowledgement] |
| Claim | Claim |
| | Enforcement order |
| | Attachment |
| [Appearance and reply to claim] | [Defendant's writ opposing the claim] |
| | [Plaintiff's writ replying to the defendant's opposition] |
| [Appearance before the court] | |
| [Phase of evidence] | [Phase of evidence] |
| [Resumé of evidence/hearing] | [Hearing] |
| Ruling | Ruling |

There may be several creditors and/or debtors as parties to the suit. If there are several debtors, the claim must be filed against all the persons who may be affected by the future ruling. Should any necessary parties be omitted, the court will dismiss the claim (since no one may be found liable without having the opportunity to defend), releasing the defendants and ordering the plaintiff to pay costs.

### 18.9.1    The debtor pays the debt

It may occur that the debtor agrees, in the light of the claim filed against it, to pay its debt. Such payment does not in itself end the procedure. The parties must finish the process, to which end they may use a variety of tools. The most correct is a judicial settlement, in which creditor and debtor record their agreement (including, if applicable, reference to the payment made) in a document which, once notified to the court, concludes the procedure. An additional benefit of judicial settlement is that, if the terms of the agreement are breached, either party may file for judicial execution, as if a ruling were involved. This makes it particularly advisable in cases of deferred payments. There are other possibilities, such as the defendant's acceptance of the claim, or relinquishment by the plaintiff. In the former case, the debtor files a submission to the court acknowledging the creditor's claims. This does not, however, oblige the court to find in the plaintiff's favour since, eg, the debt may arise from a contract which is invalid because it is contrary to law. In such a case, the court cannot find in the creditor's favour because, being invalid, the contract is without effect. Relinquishment amounts to a writ filed by the plaintiff declaring to the court that it is abandoning the action begun.

The formula to be employed must be agreed by the parties. Costs are an item to be kept well to the fore in these negotiations; in cases of acceptance, in general, each party pays its own costs, while relinquishment means that the creditor will be ordered to pay both its own costs and those of the defendant. In a judicial settlement the arrangement made in respect of costs is observed.

### 18.9.2    The debtor admits the debt

Should the debtor agree to the plaintiff's claims, acknowledging the debt but not paying it, the procedure must continue until a ruling is handed down. If the court finds for the creditor, and the debtor chooses to default, the plaintiff may file for execution before the body which handed down the ruling (see below). The defendant has no right to defer compliance (unless the plaintiff which won the case consents).

### 18.9.3    The debtor disputes the debt

The debtor may put forward its arguments in the writ of reply or opposition to the claim. The plaintiff may then reply briefly to the defendant's pleas, in the court appearance proceedings or in the corresponding writ, depending on the procedure involved. The evidence proceedings are then initiated, if requested by the parties, after which a petition may be filed for the holding of the hearing. The court will then finally hand down its ruling in the case.

### 18.9.4    The debtor disputes part of the debt

See **18.9.2**, above, concerning the part of the debt that is acknowledged; as to that part of the debt that is challenged, the procedure is as set out at **18.9.3**, above.

### 18.9.5 The debtor neither admits nor disputes the debt

If the defendant does not appear in court, he is declared in contempt. This situation may remain in effect until the end of the procedure or be interrupted by the defendant's appearance. Declaration of contempt does not imply acceptance on the debtor's part, nor does it release the plaintiff from the need to evidence the facts on which its claim is based. However, it does enable the plaintiff to ask the court to order the seizure of chattels and attachment of property of the defendant in contempt which are enough to ensure implementation of a future ruling. Both remain in effect until the case is over.

When the defendant appears but neither replies to nor opposes the claim, he cannot be declared in contempt; nor can the claim be deemed to have been accepted. In principle, it means simply that the defendant loses his opportunity to take a stand against the claim and to introduce new facts.

### 18.9.6 The debtor is declared insolvent

It may occur that, at the same time as the procedure, another creditor or the debtor itself files for a judicial declaration of insolvency. The effects of such a declaration on the debt procedure underway are dealt with in **18.11**, below. It is enough to point out here that the main effect is to suspend the procedures against the debtor declared insolvent as soon as they reach the execution phase, at which point they are all combined into a single procedure, known as a 'universal' procedure.

It may also be that, although there is no judicial declaration of insolvency, the debtor, in fact, is in such a financial situation, without assets to meet the provisions of the court ruling in which it lost its case. Here, there would be no point in seeking execution of the ruling in the absence of property in the debtor's assets with which to meet the winning plaintiff's credits. However, on occasions, the creditor to whom the ruling was favourable and who knows that the debtor is in fact insolvent must nonetheless file for execution as follows:

(1) when it intends then to sue the guarantor, if any;
(2) should the creditor plan to file for the defendant's insolvency in order to secure its judicial declaration (see **18.11**, below); and
(3) in the labour jurisdiction, with the sums involved owed by an insolvent employer to an employee for the employee's work or for compensation arising from the cancellation of the labour relation, where the employee seeks to collect such sums from the state from the Wage Guarantee Fund.

## 18.10 Enforcing judgment

Once a ruling has been handed down and is final (ie no longer appealable), its execution follows. This is always at the creditor's petition. The judicial body with authority to hear the execution proceedings is the one which heard the

case at first instance. For the execution of orders other than rulings, jurisdiction must first be defined in accordance with the criteria established at **18.5**,
above. The grounds which open the way to execution proceedings are, for the
most part, settlements reached in conciliation proceedings in court, final
rulings (provisional execution of appealed rulings also may be filed for,
provided that the appropriate guarantee is provided) and arbitration awards.

Within common execution proceedings, a distinction must be made between generic execution (payment of a sum of money) and the different
specific execution proceedings (where the creditor seeks an order for
something to be done or not to be done, or to provide some specific thing). On
the other hand, there are also a variety of special procedures, along with
common execution proceedings, such as mortgage foreclosure. The following
are the phases of general or monetary execution proceedings on which attention is focused here.

### 18.10.1   Application

The application must be duly signed by the procurator and the lawyer, stating
the sum for which execution is sought. If the ruling whose execution is sought
was limited to a general monetary order, without a precise definition of the
amount, this must now be fixed by the process known as 'integration of title'.
The sum for which execution is filed includes both that granted in the ruling
and the interest accrued between the date of the ruling and actual payment (see
**18.3**, above), plus the sum calculated to meet costs in the execution phase.

Foreign currency debts must be defined in their peseta equivalent, solely to
estimate the value of the assets which will subsequently be attached. The
equivalent value is accredited by means of the official seller's exchange rate
reference on the date on which the liability matured.

### 18.10.2   Attachment

Once the petition for execution is filed, the court 'dispatches' it, or deals with it,
if it considers that the prerequisites are present and the conditions met, issuing
an order for attachment of sufficient of the debtor's assets to cover the sum for
which execution was cleared as well as costs, without the need for a prior
instruction to pay. A commission, consisting of a court clerk and agent, is
entrusted with completing the attachment proceedings, to which end they go
to the address of the debtor against whom the execution was ordered. The
creditor may be present (represented by its procurator who may sometimes be
accompanied by the lawyer). The commission instructs the debtor, if present,
to designate assets for their attachment; if the executing party is present, it
may also indicate assets.

It must be remembered that some assets may not be attached, eg certain
personal rights, publicly used or owned assets, assets owned by the public
administration, the debtor's usual bed and that of the spouse and children,
their necessary clothing, furnishings, books and instruments necessary to the

practice of a profession, salary, daily wage, income, pension, or equivalent earnings received by the debtor not exceeding the minimum inter-professional wage (any excess is declared partially attachable, in increasing proportion to the sum received).

The law classifies the different types of assets, defining an order of preference which, in principle, must be followed when designating assets for attachment. In first priority are assets pledged or mortgaged to the creditor. In the absence of these, the classification of assets is ordered basically according to a criterion of decreasing liquidity (beginning with money and listed securities and ending with commercial and industrial establishments). This order can be altered by convention; in practice, the assets designated are those whose existence was previously known, or which are visible. However, if assets are designated without observing the order indicated, the debtor may offer others included in preferential sequence. The same occurs if the debtor designated the assets: if the creditor is aware of others included in a preferential group and in whose designation it has an interest, that creditor may make this designation.

### 18.10.3 Securing the attachment

The law fixes a number of guarantees intended to keep the attached properties within the debtor's assets:

(1) Deposit of properties. If applicable, a depositary is appointed, which may be the debtor itself.
(2) Withholding of intangible assets. Thus, in the case of the debtor's current accounts held in a bank, the court orders the bank, at the creditor's request, not to withdraw from that account.
(3) Judicial administration. This involves, eg the attachment of shares or companies, and that of some of the debtor's income.
(4) Preventative annotation. The preventative annotation of the attachment involves entry of its notice in public registers (see **18.4**, above).

### 18.10.4 Third-party rights

Assets may be attached which, while in the debtor's hands, are the property of a third party. In this case, the third party may have the attachment lifted which was improperly imposed on those assets by filing a third-party ownership claim which immediately suspends the execution proceedings involving those assets.

Likewise, there may also be another creditor than the one implementing the execution proceedings who considers that it has a preferential right for its claim to be met with the proceeds from the sale of the attached assets. Such a third party does not challenge the validity of the attachment but rather seeks to have the proceeds from the sale of the attached properties used to pay it rather than the execution creditor claiming debts which ought to be collected preferentially over the other. In this case, a third-party preference claim is filed, which does not suspend the execution proceedings. They continue until the attached assets are sold and the proceeds are then placed in bond to pay the creditors according to the preferential order established in the ruling in the third-party preference claim.

### 18.10.5 Auction, adjudication, and payment

Once the attachment is in place on certain of the debtor's assets, they must be converted into cash by sale at public auction, so that the proceeds obtained can be used to pay the creditor prosecuting the execution proceedings ('enforced collection phase'). If money was attached, it is paid directly to the creditor.

### 18.10.6 Subsidiary claims

The debtor's assets may include credit rights which were not realised because it did not claim them from its debtors. The creditor may resort in the light of such passivity to the so-called 'subrogation claim', in which the creditor exercises to its benefit the debtor's rights and claims.

There is a further possibility whereby the creditor's investigations lead it to conclude that the debtor dissipated certain assets, assigning them to third parties in order to defraud its creditors by placing itself in a situation of insolvency. In this case, provided that the intention to defraud is proved, the creditor may file a so-called 'revocation claim' for the reinstatement in the debtor's title to those assets. On the other hand, from a penal law standpoint, the debtor's action may lead to charges of concealment of assets, fraudulent bankruptcy or insolvency and even embezzlement, for which the creditor may file the appropriate charge or complaint.

Both subrogation and revocation claims, in principle, are subsidiary, ie, to employ them, the creditor must have first sought all assets in the debtor's possession. Only when this proves fruitless, and the creditor is sure that the debtor is insolvent, can those claims be prosecuted. However, this requirement has now been tempered and it is sufficient to demonstrate the debtor's insolvency in the same procedure in which the subrogation or revocation claim is filed.

### 18.10.7 Enforcement of foreign orders

For the enforcement of foreign orders in Spain, in the first instance, the provisions of the international treaty or convention applicable to the case must be observed. Failing this, the orders must pass a system of consideration and control by the Supreme Court, which enables rulings as well as other types of judicial orders to be recognised, along with decisions of other bodies (such as arbitration awards), provided that they are final (ie not appealable).

#### 18.10.7.1 Rulings

In the area of admission of rulings and other judicial orders, a variety of bilateral treaties are in effect in Spain (eg, those concluded with Switzerland,

France or Italy), and there are multilateral agreements (of which the most important, in the context of the EU, is the Brussels Convention of 1968, in effect in the version of the San Sebastián Convention of 1989). In the absence of an applicable treaty or convention, authority to recognise foreign orders or rulings is the province of the Supreme Court which, to this end, must analyse the foreign ruling in light of the following criteria.

In the first place, the Supreme Court considers the question of reciprocity; the foreign ruling has the same force in Spain as Spanish rulings do in the country where the foreign ruling was handed down. In the absence of reciprocity, Spanish law establishes a system of supplementary examination which gives effect in Spain to rulings which:

(1)  are the outcome of prosecution of a personal action;
(2)  are handed down in a case in which the party convicted had the opportunity to be present;
(3)  are not contrary to Spanish public order; and
(4)  are duly proved to exist.

### 18.10.7.2  *Arbitration awards*

The enforcement of arbitration awards in Spain is governed by the applicable treaty or convention. Spain has signed and ratified the most important multilateral conventions: the 1923 Geneva Protocol, the 1927 Geneva Convention, the European Convention on International Commercial Arbitration, of Geneva of 1961, and the New York Convention of 1958 (Treaty of Adhesion of 29 April 1977). In the absence of an applicable treaty, the award is implemented according to the rules set out above on implementation of foreign court rulings. Enforcement can be refused only if:

(1)  the award is contrary to Spanish public order;
(2)  the arbitrators resolved questions which may not be submitted under Spanish law to arbitration or, in specific cases; or
(3)  on the initiative of the public prosecutor's office.

If enforcement of an award is denied due to formal defects, it can be sought anew once such defects have been corrected.

## 18.11  Insolvency

### 18.11.1  In general

A threat by the creditor to file for a declaration of the debtor's insolvency may be a last resort to force the debtor to pay its debt. However, it must be remembered that, as a general rule, if the procedure, in fact, is filed and the debtor is declared insolvent, this has the automatic effect of suspending execution of the procedures underway, combining all the creditors' claims in a single procedure, to be governed by the rules on preference and priority of debts established, so making it even more difficult to collect debts which do not enjoy preference.

None the less, it may be beneficial to file the procedure in cases where the debtor continues its operations given that, in order to carry on in business, it may very well be willing to pay if the creditor will then relinquish the insolvency procedure filed.

Among the insolvency procedures regulated in Spanish law, a distinction can be made between those applied to debtors legally classified as traders (including all companies) and those applying to non-trading debtors (whether individuals or legal entities). The former include suspension of payments and bankruptcy, and the latter acquittance and moratorium and insolvency. A further possible classification of the same procedures is that distinguishing insolvency procedures designed in principle for lack of liquidity (non-trader acquittance and moratorium, suspension of payments by a trader) and those for permanent proprietary insolvency (insolvency of non-traders, and traders' bankruptcy).

### 18.11.2   Companies limiting shareholders' liability

These are capital-based companies (mainly limited liability companies, the *Sociedad Anónima*, SA, and the *Sociedad Limitada*, SL) characterised, among other factors by always being legally classified as traders and because the shareholders do not answer for the corporate debts with their own assets. The insolvency proceedings which may affect this type of company are suspension of payments and bankruptcy. As already pointed out, the first is designed for cases where, even though the company's assets exceed the liabilities, particular circumstances have put it in a situation of temporary lack of liquidity. Bankruptcy is applied to cases where the company's liabilities exceed its assets, leading to a situation of permanent insolvency. However, as will be shown, it is also possible to file for suspension of payments in cases of permanent insolvency.

#### 18.11.2.1   *The suspension of payments procedure*

In this procedure, which must be initiated by the company in a resolution passed by its administrators and ratified by the shareholders in a general meeting, the company seeks to establish a new payment schedule and, if applicable, secure a partial release from debts. In practice, suspension of payments is filed on occasions to prevent creditors from filing for bankruptcy; if the former is underway, a bankruptcy declaration cannot be sought simultaneously.

Once the suspension has been requested, the court appoints three auditors to:

(1)   intervene in future operations by the company through its administrators (operations implemented without such intervention are invalid and may lead to criminal liability);

(2)   draft a report on the debtor company's accounts and the causes of the suspension; and

(3)   prepare a final list of creditors.

It must be noted that it is the responsibility of a creditor not included on this list, or which is included for a sum less than due to it, to make the resulting claim in a submission addressed to the court hearing the suspension proceedings.

In the light of the auditors' report, the court will declare the company in suspension of payments, at the same time deciding whether the insolvency is temporary or permanent. While the suspension of payments procedure is intended for situations of temporary lack of liquidity, it is also possible in permanent insolvencies. In such cases where the debtor's liabilities exceed its assets, the court allows it a period during which to provide the difference. If it fails to do so, the creditors can file for bankruptcy. If they do not do this, the procedure continues as a suspension of payments, albeit with some special features.

Once the suspension of payments is declared, the court calls a creditors' meeting to discuss and vote on the settlement proposed by the debtor. The creditors attending this meeting are those initially included by the auditors on the list, plus those which, having challenged the list, were admitted by the court. In suspensions involving more than 200 creditors, the meeting's voting procedure may be substituted by a written vote. Once approved, the settlement affects all creditors whose credits have been acknowledged, except for those entitled not to attend the meeting (eg wage or mortgage creditors) who exercised this right. On the other hand, if the debtor fails to comply with the settlement, any creditor may ask for it to be cancelled and petition the court which heard the suspension procedure for the debtor to be declared bankrupt.

The costs for suspension of payment proceedings are charged to the debtor which filed for suspension. This is the general rule applied to all insolvency proceedings.

### 18.11.2.2   *Bankruptcy procedure*

A company whose liabilities exceed its assets and which no longer pays its current liabilities can file for bankruptcy. For their part, creditors may also file for the debtor company's bankruptcy following an execution procedure in which there were insufficient assets which could be attached to cover payment or, even though there were documented debts, the trader generally ceased paying its liabilities. Authority to hear this procedure is assigned to the First Instance and Preliminary Investigating Court in the place where the debtor is domiciled. If it was the creditors who filed for the bankruptcy, the court with jurisdiction is, where appropriate, the one hearing the execution procedure concerned (and, if there are several, the court also operating in the place where the debtor is domiciled).

The court order declaring bankruptcy has significant legal effects, notably the following:

(1)   it disqualifies the debtor from administering its assets. In the case of a

company, the administrators are prohibited from continuing to exercise their function;

(2)   the bankrupt (in the case of companies, their administrators) is placed under house detention;

(3)   all the debts are deemed due and automatically cease to generate interest;

(4)   the company's assets are all attached and placed in bond, its books and papers are seized and its correspondence withheld. For these purposes the court appoints depositaries (subsequently replaced by the trustees appointed by the creditors).

(5)   as a consequence of the bankruptcy declaration, a legal system is initiated for the reinstatement of assets which may have been removed from the debtor's estates before it was declared bankrupt. There are a number of mechanisms for these purposes, chiefly the establishment of a 'period of retroaction' (a provisional term prior to the bankruptcy declaration) whereby the law orders the invalidity of all the bankrupt's actions during that time.

Given these effects, it is clearly hazardous to conclude mortgages and other real guarantees with companies close to bankruptcy, since the contracts concerned run the risk of being declared invalid in the near future.

Once bankruptcy is declared, the creditors are called to an initial meeting to appoint the trustees whose fundamental role is to dispose of and liquidate the assets of the debtor company to pay pending debts with the proceeds. To this end, a third person appointed by the court to aid it draws up a list of creditors, based on the accounts of the bankrupt company, and they are then personally invited to attend the meeting. Those not invited should notify their claim as soon as they become aware of the proceedings.

It must be remembered that not all the creditors, merely because they are in that situation, will have the opportunity to collect even part of their debt. Nor will all those attending the first meeting, in general, only those whose debts were acknowledged by the other creditors in a second meeting held for the purposes will collect. On the other hand, those whose debts were duly recognised do not collect equally. They are classified or graded according to legal provisions on privilege and preference. To grade the claims, the court calls a third creditors' meeting, which is attended solely by those whose claims were previously recognised.

Once the bankrupt company's assets have been liquidated, the trustees pay the recognised claims according to the grading applied. The essential criteria followed in payment is the legal order of preference, so that payment of one category of creditors does not begin until those in the previous category have been met in full. On the other hand, while the liquidation of assets and payment of creditors is the usual purpose of a bankruptcy procedure, it is accepted that, at any time, the bankrupt company's administrators and creditors may reach an agreement, voted on in a meeting, similar to that of the suspension of payments procedure.

An essential aspect of the bankruptcy procedure concerns investigation of the causes which led to the bankruptcy. As a result of this investigation, the bankruptcy is classified as fortuitous, negligent or fraudulent. In the latter two cases, the associated criminal proceedings are initiated to clarify the potential criminal liability of the administrators of the bankrupt company.

Bankruptcy of capital-based companies does not imply the bankruptcy of their shareholders. From a strictly technical point of view, it does not automatically imply the winding up of the company, unless a general meeting of its shareholders expressly resolves accordingly. However, in the absence of a resolution along these lines or of an agreement with the creditors, the company's assets will be liquidated so that it can no longer continue its activity, eventually leading to its dissolution.

### 18.11.3 Insolvency of individuals

The insolvency of an individual may lead to suspension of payments or bankruptcy proceedings in the case of traders, or acquittance and moratorium or insolvency proceedings in the case of non-traders. Analysis here is limited to standard, non-trader insolvency procedures.

#### 18.11.3.1 *Acquittance and moratorium procedure*

Non-trader debtors may file for acquittance and moratorium proceedings in the First Instance and Preliminary Investigating Court where they are domiciled, should they find themselves in a situation of temporary lack of liquidity. The purpose of this procedure is similar to that of suspension of payments by traders: to reach an understanding whose efficacy is restricted to the creditors designated by the debtor and who have been served notice for this purpose by the court, fixing a new payment schedule and, if applicable, partly releasing pending debts.

The agreement reached affects only the creditors included in the list prepared by the debtor, and excludes those who, legally entitled not to attend the meeting in which that agreement is voted, in fact did not do so. If the debtor does not meet the terms of the settlement, it expires and the creditors it affects recover all the rights they held before the agreement was reached.

#### 18.11.3.2 *Insolvency proceedings*

This is very similar to the trader bankruptcy procedure, both substantively and procedurally. The most significant differences are:

(1) the debt of the creditor wishing to file for the insolvency must have been acknowledged in a final court ruling; and

(2) the retroactive effect characteristic of bankruptcy does not apply here.

### 18.11.4 Companies not limiting partners' liability

These are the so-called 'personal companies' (general partnerships, commandités, and limited partnerships) which, for present purposes, have the following features:

(1)  they may be classified as traders or as non-traders; and
(2)  their collective partners answer with their own assets for the corporate debts, albeit on a subsidiary basis.

Although there is no unanimous agreement among the theorists as to the delimitation between trading and non-trading personal companies, the distinction would appear to be according to the successive application of the following criteria:

(1)  a company whose purpose is typically commercial is classified as a trader; and
(2)  the trader classification applies to companies duly entered in the Territorial Business Register in the place where they are domiciled.

The decision as to whether a personal company is a trader or not is of the very greatest significance for insolvency purposes. The insolvency procedures applicable to a company which is classified as a trader are suspension of payments or bankruptcy, while those applying to companies not so classified are acquittance and moratorium and insolvency.

Finally, it must be pointed out that, unlike capital companies, the insolvency of personal companies involves that of their collective partners and the dissolution of the company itself. From the reverse standpoint, bankruptcy of a collective partner leads to the dissolution of such companies.

*Chapter 19*

# SWITZERLAND

**David Jenny**
**Gloor Schiess & Partner**
**Basel, Switzerland**

## 19.1   Introduction

The Swiss legal system is composed of 27 subsystems: the federal and 26 cantonal legal systems. For the subject matter addressed here, both the federal and the cantonal legal systems are of relevance. The law on contracts and torts, eg, negligence, is codified in the Federal Code of Obligations. The rules regarding debt collection (or enforcement of debts), insolvency, attachment and bankruptcy are found in the Federal Statute on Enforcement of Debts and Bankruptcy (*Bundesgesetz über Schuldbetreibung und Konkurs*), which dates from 1889 and is now being brought up to date by the Federal Parliament. With regard to the organisation of the offices of enforcement of debts and bankruptcy and of the courts handling actions provided for in the Federal Statute, 26 cantonal statutes implementing the Federal Statute on Enforcement of Debts and Bankruptcy must be consulted.

Within guidelines set by federal, constitutional and statutory law, the cantons are free to establish the court system handling civil cases and enact rules of civil procedure. Matters related to the Swiss Supreme Court, the only federal court relevant to the topic discussed here, are regulated by federal law.

It is not possible to deal with the problems discussed in this chapter on a canton-by-canton basis. Where cantonal law matters, the solution chosen by most cantons or by Basel-*Stadt* is described. In any case, procedural questions must be researched for each canton in which they arise.

The revision of the Federal Statute on Enforcement of Debts and Bankruptcy is causing additional problems. The parliament has not yet enacted the new statute, it will probably do so before the end of 1994, and there is still the theoretical possibility that this new statute will be put to a popular vote in a referendum.[1] The provisions of the new statute are examined where they offer solutions other than those of the old statute which is still in force.

A unique feature of Swiss law on debt collection is that debt collection procedures can be initiated by a creditor, before a judgment has been entered into against the debtor, by simply claiming to have a valid claim against a debtor. This peculiarity of Swiss law must be kept in mind while reading this chapter.

---

1   On 19 December 1994, after this chapter was written, the Swiss Parliament has finally adopted the new statute which will come into effect on 1 January 1997.

## 19.2   Initial considerations

### 19.2.1   Status of the debtor

Two questions are of importance when considering the status of the debtor. First, whether a legal entity or an individual can be sued, respectively whether debt-enforcement procedures can be instituted against a legal entity or must it be directed against an individual? Secondly, is an individual or a legal entity subject to involuntary bankruptcy? Under Swiss law, the following legal entities (juristische Personen), created by private law, have the capacity to sue and, therefore, to be sued:

(1)  an association (*Verein*);

(2)  a foundation (*Stiftung*);

(3)  a (share) corporation (*Aktiengesellschaft*, AG);[1]

(4)  a (share) corporation with unlimited partners (*Kommanditaktienge-sellschaft*), of which there are only a few in Switzerland;

(5)  a limited liability company (*Gesellschaft mit begrenzter Haftung*, GmbH); and

(6)  a co-operative (*Genossenschaft*).

Even though they are not *juristische Personen*, the following entities, among others, of private law can be pursued in the courts:

(1)  a general partnership (*Kollektivgesellschaft*), which is composed of two or more individuals;

(2)  a limited partnership (*Kommanditgesellschaft*), which is composed of one or more unlimited partners who must be individuals and of one or more limited partners; and

(3)  a community of owners of condominiums (*Stockwerkeigen-tümergemeinschaft*).

All legal entities created by public law, eg, the Swiss Confederation, the cantons, municipalities, and various types of corporations and institutions (*Anstalten*) can be sued. Public institutions which are not legal entities, the most important examples being the Federal Railways (SBB) and the Federal Post and Telephone Authority (PTT), can be sued if the statute establishing them permits.

After the declaration of bankruptcy, the estate cannot be sued for claims which have arisen before the bankruptcy. Enforcement procedures can be initiated against all individuals and all the legal entities mentioned above.

The following individuals and legal entities registered in the Register of Commerce are subject to involuntary bankruptcy:

(1)  an individual conducting a trading, manufacturing, or other business carried out in a commercial manner (*Inhaber einer Einzelfirma*);

(2)  a partner of a general partnership;

(3)  an unlimited partner of a limited partnership;

---

1 The overwhelming majority of all Swiss legal entities are corporations.

(4) an unlimited partner of a corporation with unlimited partners;
(5) a corporation;
(6) a corporation with unlimited partners;
(7) a general partnership; and
(8) a limited partnership, a co-operative, and an association (and, from 1 January 1997, or a foundation).

### 19.2.2 Sources of information

Information about debtors can be gathered by consulting the privately published *Schweizerisches Ragionenbuch*, which contains information from the Register of Commerce, or a data bank, such as TELEDATA, or by ordering an extract from the competent Register of Commerce about the debtor.

If a legitimate interest can be shown (eg by submitting a copy of a contract or an order), financial information can be obtained by ordering an extract from the Register of Enforcement of Debts (*Auszug aus dem Betreibungsregister*). The extract shows the status of all debt-collection procedures instituted against a debtor, the amounts claimed, and the names of the creditors.

Corporations having bond issues outstanding or having shares listed on a stock exchange are obliged to send to every person requesting it, within one year after approval, a copy of the annual financial statement and the consolidated statement. Other corporations must disclose this information only to creditors who can provide evidence of an interest worthy of being protected.[1]

### 19.2.3 Is the debt statute-barred?

Normally, claims are forfeited 10 years after having become due. Claims arising out of periodic performances and the professional work of attorneys are forfeited after five years. The statute of limitations for claims originating from torts and unjust enrichment is one year from the date the creditor has received knowledge of the damage or the unjust enrichment and, in any event, 10 years from the date the act causing the damage or the unjust enrichment took place. The statute of limitations is interrupted and runs once again if the debtor acknowledges the claim or if a debt-enforcement procedure, a lawsuit or a bankruptcy procedure has been instituted.

Debtors often agree to waive their right to invoke the statute of limitations for a specified period of time. This makes sense if settlement negotiations are taking place. Such waivers should be drafted by attorneys.

### 19.2.4 Security

The debtor or a third party can secure a claim by pledging movable goods or real property or by assigning claims to the creditor. A pledge of movable goods is not valid if the pledge remains in the possession of the pledgor. Pledges

---

1 Code of Obligations, article 697h.

(*Pfänder*) can be realised by instituting a special enforcement of debts procedure (*Betreibung auf Pfandverwertung*). Pledges of movables can also be realised by private sale should the debtor have consented to it. If a pledge is given, then a debtor can insist, by invoking a provision known as the beneficium excussionis realis, that the secured claim is enforced by a *Betreibung of Pfandverwertung*.

The lessor of business space has the legal right of retention over movables located on the rented premises, securing one year's rent already due and the rent of the current half year. The retained movables are realised by way of *Betreibung auf Pfandverwertung*.

Third parties can secure a claim by guarantee of an obligation, by assuming joint liability (*Solidarschuldnerschaft*), and by entering into a suretyship (*Bürgschaft*). Creditors must be aware that Swiss law affords quite strong protection to third parties (especially to individuals), securing obligations of other parties by strictly regulating the suretyship (in English, sometimes called a guarantee), and by declaring guarantee and joint liability obligations null and void if the requirements of the suretyship have not been met. Creditors, therefore, must carefully check whether a proposed security is really valid. The least problematic instrument for a creditor is an irrevocable and unconditional bank guarantee.

### 19.2.5   Retention of title

A retention of title for movable goods (*Eigentumsvorbehalt*) is effective only if registered with the office of enforcements of debts of the domicile of the debtor.

## 19.3   Letters before action

### 19.3.1   Are they necessary?

A letter reminding a debtor of its obligations has the effect of causing default on the debtor's part. Such a reminder (*Mahnung*) is not legally required if a due date for the performance by the debtor has been explicitly or implicitly stipulated. However, in such cases, it is advisable to send reminders to a debtor. Normally, such reminders need not be drafted by attorneys.

### 19.3.2   What should they say?

A first reminder is usually quite friendly, calling to the debtor's attention the fact that a claim has become due, that no payment has been received, and that payment should be effected, usually by transferring the amount due into a designated account and within a specified period. Should a second reminder be necessary, then it should be emphasised that default interest is due and that legal proceedings (debt-collection procedure or court action) will be instituted if the payment has not been made within a specified period. A creditor improves his position in later proceedings considerably if he manages to receive from the debtor an acknowledgement of debt. Reminders written by attorneys, especially on behalf of foreign creditors, are advisable if it is known that the debtor is recalcitrant and might be impressed by the creditor's willingness to retain an attorney.

### 19.3.3 Can they demand interest for late payment?

According to article 104 of the Code of Obligations, a debtor in default regarding the payment of money must pay default interest at five per cent per annum, even if the contract provides for a lower rate. If a higher interest rate has been stipulated in the contract, such an interest rate may be claimed during the period of default. Among merchants, ie, among individuals and legal entities who should be registered in the Register of Commerce, default interest at a rate higher than five per cent may be charged when the usual bank rate at the place of payment is higher than five per cent. It is advisable to state in reminders that default interest at a specified rate is demanded.

## 19.4 Pre-action and non-judicial remedies

### 19.4.1 Enforcement of debts procedure

As indicated above, a creditor may institute a debt-collection procedure by simply filing a form, called the *Betreibungsbegehren*, with the office of enforcement of debts (*Betreibungsamt*) at the domicile of the debtor and by paying a fee which depends on the amount claimed. The form must contain the following information:

(1) name and address of the debtor and the creditor and of the creditor's representative, should he have one;

(2) the amount claimed in Swiss francs and the interest rate claimed on the principal;

(3) an indication of the document on which the claim is based or indication of the grounds of the claim if no such document exists;[1]

(4) should the claim be secured by a pledge, the pledge and its present location and name or address of the pledgor if not the same person as the debtor.

The office of enforcement of debts is not entitled to examine whether the claim is justified. If the formal requirements of the *Betreibungsbegehren* are met, the office will serve on the debtor a so-called payment order (*Zahlungsbefehl*). Creditors must be aware that service of the payment order does not block the debtor's assets. The validity of the *Zahlungsbefehl*, a condition for all other steps of the debt-collection procedure, is limited to one year. Time spent with various court procedures is not regularly taken into consideration.

---

1 The creditor's claim must have become due, except where the debtor has no domicile or where there is danger that the debtor will flee or improperly dispose of his assets.

The debtor must pay the demanded amount within 20 days or declare opposition (*Rechtsvorschlag*) within 10 days after receipt of the payment order. Should he neither pay nor declare opposition, the creditor can continue the debt-collection procedure by filing a demand to continue the procedure (*Fortsetzungsbegehren*). As explained below, the debtor's opposition must be overcome by the creditor in court.

### 19.4.2  Attachment

A petition for attachment must be filed with a judge sitting in a district where the assets to be attached are located. The hearing on the petition is ex parte, and the creditor must demonstrate that there is a valid claim, that there are grounds (*Arrestgründe*) for the attachment, and that specified assets exist.[1] The following are sufficient grounds for attachment:

(1)  the debtor has no domicile;
(2)  the debtor is about to flee or dispose of his assets in order to avoid his debts;
(3)  the debtor is in transit and the claim is one which, by its nature, must be satisfied at once;
(4)  the debtor has no domicile in Switzerland (*Ausländerarrest*); or
(5)  the creditor is in possession of a provisional or definite certificate of loss against the debtor.

The revised Federal Statute on the Enforcement of Debts and Bankruptcy will make it harder to obtain the so-called *Ausländerarrest*.

It is in the judge's discretion to demand that the creditor post a bond securing the debtor's claims in case of an unjustified attachment. In some cantons, the bond is regularly set at 10 per cent of the claim. If not done prior to the attachment, the creditor must initiate within 10 days after receipt of the official attachment document a debt-collection procedure or must file a proper lawsuit. The competent office of enforcement of debts is the one which has executed the attachment order, ie, where the assets are located.

## 19.5  The court system

### 19.5.1  Structure of the courts

The overwhelming majority of cases concerning debt collection will be brought in cantonal courts; cases that can be brought directly in the Swiss Supreme Court are rare. The cantons enjoy considerable autonomy in establishing their own court systems. The civil court system of a Swiss canton may be structured as follows:

(1)  justices of the peace (*Friedensrichter*), each responsible for normally a small district;

---

1 Federal Statute on the Enforcement of Debts and Bankruptcy, article 271.

(2) special conciliation authorities for questions related to the renting of land and property (*Mietschlichtungsstellen*);
(3) district courts (*Bezirksgerichte*), which are courts of first instance;
(4) special labour law courts (*Arbeitsgerichte*), which are courts of first instance;
(5) a commercial court (*Handelsgericht*), from which no appeal to a court of appeal is possible;
(6) a court of appeal (*Obergericht* or *Appellationsgericht*), which is a court of a second instance; and
(7) a court of third instance (*Kassationsgericht*).

The office of the justice of the peace is known in almost all cantons, one exception being Basel-*Stadt*. Only a few cantons, the most important being the cantons of Zurich, Bern and Aargau, have commercial courts. Even fewer cantons, the most important being the canton of Zurich, have a court of third instance.

### 19.5.2 Rules of jurisdiction

#### 19.5.2.1 Local jurisdiction

As a general rule, according to article 59 of the Federal Constitution, debt collection cases against debtors not bankrupt must be brought in the courts of the canton where the debtor has his domicile. This rule has numerous exceptions. Some can be found in Federal Statutes; others, based on cantonal law, have been recognised by the Swiss Supreme Court. In addition, the right to be sued in one's own domicile, subject to some restrictions, can be waived. Creditors must be aware that waivers contained in general business conditions are quite often not valid.

Because of the Lugano Convention between the member states of the European Union (EU) and the European Free Trade Association (EFTA) on jurisdiction and the enforcement of judgments in civil and commercial matters, it is increasingly rare that a lawsuit against a foreign debtor can be taken after an attachment to the court at the place of attachment.

#### 19.5.2.2 Jurisdiction for ordinary civil lawsuits

After determination of the local jurisdiction, the problem is which cantonal court to seize. The first question to ask is whether it is mandatory to have a hearing before a justice of the peace. This question is answered by each canton differently. Generally, the justice of the peace is never involved in cases which will go to labour law courts and the special conciliation authorities for questions related to the renting of property. In cases which fall within the commercial court's jurisdiction, the plaintiff is quite often entitled to proceed without appearing before the justice of the peace.

The next question which must be answered is whether the 'normal' court of first instance, ie, a District Court, is competent or whether the case falls into the jurisdiction of one of the special courts. All claims related to the rental of property must start with the conciliation authorities. The competence of the labour law courts depends on the amount in dispute, eg the upper threshold in Basel-*Stadt* is SFr 20,000. Disputes between parties registered in the Register of Commerce fall within the exclusive jurisdiction of commercial courts. Should only the defendant be registered in the Register of Commerce, then it is up to the plaintiff whether or not to take action in the commercial court or in a District Court. The commercial court offers the faster procedure (with no appeals to a court of second instance possible) and the recruitment of non-professional judges from the ranks of persons familiar with trade and industry.

Whether a case will be judged by a single judge, a panel of three judges or one of more than three judges depends on the amount in dispute. In Basel-*Stadt*, a sole judge will adjudicate cases where the amount in dispute is not more than SFr 3,000, a panel of three judges if the amount in dispute is between SFr 3,001 and SFr 8,000, and a panel of five judges if the amount in dispute is more than SFr 8,000. Cases which fall within the competence of the single judge and the panel of three judges will regularly be decided in an oral procedure, ie without filing of pleadings by the parties. Such jurisdictional rules are in force in all cantons.

### 19.5.3  Appeals

Appeals from courts of first instance to a court of appeal are not restricted to legal questions. Depending on the civil procedure of a canton, it is possible to introduce new facts in the appellate procedure which could have been introduced while the case was still pending in the courts of first instance. However, in cases where the amount in dispute is quite small, there is often no full appeal (*Appellation* or *Berufung*) but only an extraordinary appeal (*Nichtigkeitsbeschwerde*), and the Court of Appeal will determine only whether the judgment of the court of first instance is arbitrary or not. Appeals to a cantonal court of third instance are, with some exceptions, possible only on grounds of arbitrariness.

The appeal from cantonal courts of second instance to the Swiss Supreme Court is limited to questions of Federal civil law and is possible only if the amount in dispute is SFr 8,000 or more. There is also no appeal against decisions granting or denying provisional or definite removal of opposition. Factual questions and questions of procedural law can be submitted to the Swiss Supreme Court by lodging a constitutional complaint (*staatsrechtliche Beschwerde*). A decision attacked by means of a constitutional complaint will be quashed only if it is found to be arbitrary.

It must be pointed out that it is impossible to describe in the space allotted here all the types of appeals possible under federal and cantonal law. It is often difficult to decide which kind of appeal must be filed. Sometimes, it is necessary to simultaneously file, within 30 days after receipt of a decision, an appeal to the Swiss Supreme Court and an appeal to a cantonal court of third instance. Courts must indicate in a judgment if it is possible to file a full appeal.

### 19.5.4 Status of the foreign creditor

Depending on the cantonal procedural law, foreign creditors acting as plaintiffs may be ordered to designate a domicile in Switzerland where service can be effected, a so-called *Zustellungsdomizil*. Should the foreign creditor be represented by an attorney, the attorney will be served by the court.

At the request of the defendant, a foreign creditor may be ordered to deposit with the court the amount of money payable to the defendant as indemnification of the defendant's attorney's fees should the defendant prevail. However, several international treaties, the most important being the Hague Convention on Civil Procedure, prohibit the requirement of a deposit from a foreign plaintiff if the only reason for it is that the plaintiff is a foreigner.

## 19.6　Legal representation

### 19.6.1　Nature of legal representation

No party is obliged to be represented by an attorney in a debt collection procedure in a Swiss court. Except for procedures in the Swiss Supreme Court, parties are entitled to be represented by a third person who is not an attorney and who is not being indemnified for his services. All cantons, with the exception of Solothurn, and the Swiss Confederation reserve the right to represent parties in court professionally to attorneys (and, in some canton, to professors of Swiss faculties of law). An attorney (*Anwalt, Rechtsanwalt, Advokat,* or *Fürsprecher*) admitted by one canton, with some limitations, is entitled to be admitted by all other cantons and, without any special admission, may represent clients in procedures of the Swiss Supreme Court.

Some cantons forbid representation by attorneys in labour law disputes with an amount in dispute less than, eg SFr 20,000 and in procedures of the special conciliation authorities for questions related to the renting of property.

Despite the theoretical possibility to appear in all courts of Switzerland, Swiss attorneys will normally only take cases which will be heard by a court of their home canton or one of the neighbouring cantons. Cantons are barred from restricting professional representation in debt-collection procedures to attorneys. However, cantons may, and most cantons probably do, restrict representation on a professional basis in a summary court procedure to attorneys.

### 19.6.2　Mode of payment for legal representation

Attorney's fees to be charged for representation in courts in civil law cases are regulated by cantonal acts normally emanating from the cantonal court of second instance. The principal criteria for the determination of attorney's fees are the following:

(1)  the amount in dispute;
(2)  the legal and/or factual complexity of the case; and
(3)  the number of procedural steps, eg the number of pleadings and court hearings.

The basis for the calculation of fees is usually a base fee depending on the amount in dispute which will be increased or decreased in consideration of the two other criteria mentioned above.

In Basel-*Stadt*, the base fee for representation in a lawsuit with, eg, SFr 8,000 to SFr 20,000 in dispute is SFr 1,700 to SFr 3,200; with SFr 20,000 to SFr 50,000 in dispute, SFr 2,800 to SFr 5,600; and with SFr 200,000 to SFr 500,000 in dispute, SFr 14,300 to SFr 30,000. Increases are limited in Basel-*Stadt* to 280 per cent of the base fee.

Normally, the actual amount of hours worked is not a legal criterion. However, some cantons set hourly rates depending on the amount in dispute. Some cantonal regulations permit the conclusion of special agreements about the calculation of fees, eg entirely based on a fixed hourly rate. Contingency fees are not permitted.

Attorneys will regularly inform clients before the decision to initiate a lawsuit is taken regarding the estimated attorney's fees, and they will ask clients to make an advance payment covering the fees.

The cantonal regulations do not apply to services rendered by attorneys which are not connected to litigation. Attorneys will charge for services such as representation in a debt-collection procedure or in out-of-court settlement negotiations on the basis of the fee schedules of the cantonal bar associations and, therefore, on the basis of hourly rates.

From 1 January 1995, Switzerland will have value added tax (VAT). Services of attorneys will be subject to VAT. However, there will be no VAT on services for a recipient domiciled outside of Switzerland if these services will be used outside of Switzerland. Whether services in connection with debt collection for foreign creditors will be subject to VAT is still under discussion. A ruling of the federal tax authority should decide this question in the near future.

## 19.7 Costs and interest

### 19.7.1 Court costs

The costs of the cantonal courts for civil lawsuits are regulated by the cantons themselves. There are only a few minor exceptions. According to federal law, procedures of the special conciliation authorities for questions related to the renting of property and of the labour law courts with an amount in dispute of not more than SFr 20,000 are free.

In Basel-*Stadt*, the base fee for court costs in a lawsuit with, eg, SFr 8,000 to SFr 20,000 in dispute is SFr 750 to SFr 1,300; with SFr 20,000 to SFr 50,000 in dispute, SFr 1,300 to SFr 2,200; and with SFr 200,000 to SFr 500,000 in dispute, SFr 5,600 to SFr 10,000. There may be increases of up to 100 per cent should a lawsuit be more complex than normal.

In most cantons, the plaintiff must advance the court costs; in some cantons, the plaintiff and the defendant must make advances for court costs. All costs related to debt-collection procedures, including court costs for the summary procedure, are regulated by federal law. The maximum fee for a summary procedure involving a claim of more than SFr 1 million is SFr 1,500.

A special fee schedule is applicable to procedures of the Swiss Supreme Court. The base fee for an appeal with SFr 20,000 to SFr 50,000 in dispute is SFr 1,000 to SFr 5,000 and with SFr 100,000 to SFr 200,000 in dispute, SFr 2,000 to SFr 8,000.

### 19.7.2 Availability of legal aid

Legal aid for individuals, not for legal entities, is guaranteed by the Swiss Federal Constitution. The extent of this guarantee is quite limited. Individuals on low income (or without private means of some substance), regardless of whether they are creditors or debtors or whether they are domiciled in Switzerland, having reasonable chances of succeess in the lawsuit, need not advance court costs or, should representation by an attorney be necessary, attorney's fees. Most cantons are more generous than required by the Federal Constitution and forego, eg the possibility to recover court costs and attorney's fees from an individual on low income.

In some cantons, an individual on low income also need not pay the other party's attorney's fees should the lawsuit be lost. The prevailing side may be awarded, at its request, a special indemnification for its attorney's fees to be paid by the court. Legal aid is granted, sometimes only partially, or denied by the court which will decide the case. Swiss residents will usually seek to prove that they have insufficient income as defined by the law by introducing as evidence an official certificate issued by municipal authorities.

Until recently, the Swiss Supreme Court held that there was no constitutional right to receive legal aid in debt-collection and bankruptcy procedures. The Supreme Court, however, has overruled this practice and made it possible for debtors to be freed of their obligation to advance the costs of their own voluntary bankruptcy procedure. The consequences of this decision for other procedures related to the enforcement of debts and bankruptcy are still under discussion.

It must be noted that the Supreme Court, in the above decision, denied the debtor assistance by an attorney paid by the state. The revised Federal Statute on the Enforcement of Debts and Bankruptcy may address this problem in a specific provision.

### 19.7.3 Liability for and recovery of costs

Each party is liable to its attorney for its attorney's fees. Usually, the plaintiff is liable for court costs.

The party prevailing in a lawsuit will normally be able to recover court costs and the costs for its attorney from the losing party. Depending on the specific provisions of the applicable cantonal law, courts will order that the losing party must pay a defined amount of indemnification for attorney's fees to the other party or will merely indicate that the losing party must pay for all or part of the attorney's fees. In the second alternative, the attorney of the prevailing party will send his statement to the attorney of the opposing party. Should this statement be contested, then there will be an additional court procedure in which the precise amount to be paid by the losing party will be determined. The cantonal courts will always apply cantonal legislation regarding attorney's fees. The Swiss Supreme Court has enacted a special tariff for the indemnification of the prevailing party for its attorney's fees.

The indemnification for attorney's fees in summary procedure (*Rechtsöffnungsverfahren*) is governed by federal law, and the court will fix the indemnification in consideration of the amount of time spent on the case, the complexity of the case, and the amount in dispute. Attorneys will regularly submit a statement to the court, specifying the amount of time invested in a summary procedure and the hourly rate which should be applied.

### 19.7.4   Interest

Entitlement to claim interest is discussed at **19.3.3**, above.

## 19.8   Proceedings

### 19.8.1   Removal of debtor's opposition

As explained above, a debtor can bring a debt-collection procedure to a temporary halt by simply declaring opposition after receipt of the payment order. The Federal Statute on the Enforcement of Debts and Bankruptcy gives creditors the opportunity to have this obstacle removed and obtain the so-called *Rechtsöffnung* in a summary procedure (*Rechtsöffnungsverfahren*).

Depending on the amount claimed, the creditor's petition will be granted or denied by one judge or a panel of judges of a District Court. The competent court is always the court of the debtor's domicile, regardless of any agreements on jurisdiction. Definite removal of the objection will be granted if the claim is based on an executory judgment entered by a Swiss or a foreign court or a court of arbitration. The kinds of objections that can be raised by the debtor depends on whether the judgment has been entered by a court of the same canton (or by the Swiss Supreme Court), by a court of another canton, by the court of a foreign country with which a relevant treaty has been concluded, or by a court of a foreign country with which no relevant treaty has been concluded.

Should the claim have been acknowledged by the debtor in a notarial deed or in a signed acknowledgement of debt, then the judge will remove the opposition on a provisional basis (*Provisorische Rechtsöffnung*), unless the debtor raises credible objections. It is often quite difficult to determine whether an acknowledgement of debt exists and whether the debtor's objections are credible.

A provisional removal of opposition becomes definite and allows the creditor to continue the debt-collection procedure if the debtor did not initiate a lawsuit (*Aberkennungsklage*) within 10 days (to become 20 days, according to the revised Federal Statute on the Enforcement of Debts and Bankruptcy) of the removal of opposition in order to obtain a declaratory judgment that there is no valid claim.

### 19.8.2   Issuing proceedings

As explained above, each canton regulates its own civil procedure. Even though there is much agreement on the main principles of civil procedure, the variety in detail of the 26 cantonal civil procedures should not be underestimated. There is especially great variety in the rules governing the first step of a civil procedure, the bringing of an action.

As pointed out above, it is quite often mandatory to go to the justice of the peace before involving the court. The justice of the peace summons the parties for a hearing after receipt of a short brief by the plaintiff, most of the time signed by the plaintiff's attorney, stating the claim and asking the justice of the peace to hold a hearing. Should the creditor already have initiated a debt-collection procedure and should this have been stopped by the debtor's declaration of opposition, then the relief demanded by the creditor will include the removal of the opposition (*Beseitigung des Rechtsvorschlages*).

Should the justice of the peace not be able to reconcile the parties (ie to bring about an acknowledgement or a withdrawal of the action or a settlement) or should the defendant not have appeared, then a writ (*Weisung*) is issued, authorising the plaintiff to take his action into court within a certain period of time (eg six months or a year). Should an action not be brought within the time-limit, then it is necessary, once again, to start with the justice of the peace.[1]

In cases where the so-called oral procedure is not possible because the amount in dispute is too high, the brief in which an action is filed with a court should normally contain a statement of the facts supporting the claim and, depending on the complexity of the case, a detailed discussion of the applicable law. In some cantons, the brief discussing the merits of the case need only be introduced after an initial hearing has been held.

## 19.9   Procedure to judgment

### 19.9.1   The debtor admits the debt

Should the debtor admit the claim in his reply brief, then the court will enter a judgment in favour of the creditor based on this acknowledgement. Should a debtor not defend himself, then the court will enter a default judgment based on the statements of the creditors, if they are prima facie plausible.

### 19.9.2   The debtor disputes all or part of the debt

Should the debtor dispute all or part of the claim in his reply brief, then the creditor usually has the opportunity to rebut the debtor's allegations in a

---

1 Federal Statute on the Enforcement of Debts and Bankruptcy, article 207.

second brief. The codes of civil procedure of most cantons permit the introduction in the second brief of evidence which could have been offered in the first brief. In some cantons, the judge in charge of handling the case might summon the parties after the brief stating the action and the reply brief have been filed for a hearing reserved to settlement discussions on the basis of the judge's provisional understanding of the merits of the case.

After the exchange of briefs has been declared closed by the court, there usually will be a main hearing in which witnesses and the representations of the attorneys are heard. In some cantons, the court has much discretion to decide that no main hearing is necessary because all relevant questions have been addressed in the briefs and can be dealt with on the basis of the documents filed as evidence by the parties.

### 19.9.3 The debtor is declared insolvent

Should the debtor be declared insolvent, ie should the competent court declare the debtor's bankruptcy, then all pending lawsuits in which the debtor is a party, except for urgent matters, will be stayed by law and can be continued only at a later stage of the bankruptcy procedure. Often, the bankruptcy estate will not continue a pending lawsuit and will assign the right to do so to creditors.

A creditor whose lawsuit against the bankrupt debtor's estate is stayed will file his claim in the bankruptcy proceedings. Such a claim will be listed in the list of claims with the remark that a lawsuit is pending. Should such a lawsuit not be continued by the estate or by creditors, then the claim is deemed by law to have been acknowledged.

## 19.10 Enforcing judgment

### 19.10.1 In general

As explained above, a debt-collection procedure may be started even though the creditor is not in possession of a Swiss or foreign judgment in his favour.

Should no debt-collection procedure have been started prior to the court procedure, then the creditor will normally start such a procedure should the debtor not make the payment voluntarily.

After removal of the debtor's opposition, should this have been necessary, the creditor asks for the continuation of the debt-collection procedure. Should the object of the debt-collection procedure not be the realisation of a pledge, then the office of enforcement of debts determines whether the debtor is subject to involuntary bankruptcy.

### 19.10.2 *Konkursbetreibung*

Should the debtor be subject to involuntary bankruptcy, then the so-called *Konkursbetreibung* applies. The debtor will be notified that the creditor is entitled to request that the debtor be declared bankrupt 20 days after the notification. The details of the bankruptcy procedures are explained below.


### 19.10.3  *Betreibung auf Pfändung*

Should the debtor not be subject to involuntary bankruptcy, then the office of enforcement of debts proceeds by way of *Betreibung auf Pfändung*. After notification, seizure is made of the debtor's assets necessary to satisfy the claim of the creditor. Assets which are indispensable for the continuation of the private and professional existence of the debtor are not subject to seizure. Such assets are not subject to seizure in a bankruptcy procedure. To the extent that the debtor's income exceeds the subsistence minimum, future income may be seized for one year.

Realisation of the seized assets must be requested by the creditor. The realisation of movable property and claims may be requested not before one month and not later than six months (one year according to the new statute) after the seizure; the realisation of land and property may be requested not prior to six months and not later than two years after the seizure.

The proceeds will be distributed among creditors who have asked for the seizure of the debtor's assets within a certain period of time and according to their status: four classes of privileged creditors must be satisfied ahead of the ordinary creditors. To the extent that a claim has not been satisfied, a definite certificate of loss (*Definitiver Verlustschein*) is issued. Its main effects are described below.

It is, by law, an acknowledgement of debt which makes it possible to undertake in the future debt-collection procedures (*Provisorische Rechtsöffnung*). A creditor, within six months after the date of the certificate of loss may reinstitute the debt-collection procedure without a new payment order. It also serves as a ground for attachment. Finally, the claim, at least against the debtor himself, is not subject to the statute of limitations. Should the debtor die, then a statute of limitations of one year starts to run. The revised Federal Statute on the Enforcement of Debts and Bankruptcy imposes a statute of limitations of 20 years, starting with the issue of the certificate of loss.


### 19.10.4  *Betreibung auf Pfandverwertung*

In the event of a *Betreibung auf Pfandverwertung*, the creditor may request the realisation of the pledge, not earlier than one month after the receipt of the payment order by the debtor if movable property is pledged or not earlier than six months if immovable property is pledged. Should the proceeds not fully satisfy the creditor's claim, then a special certificate of loss (*Pfandausfallschein*) is issued. Its main effect is that the creditor, within one month after the receipt of this certificate, may request a continuation of the debt-collection procedure by way of *Betreibung auf Pfändung* or *Konkursbetreibung*.

# 19.11 Insolvency (bankruptcy and judicial arrangement)

## 19.11.1 Types of insolvency procedures

The Federal Statute on the Enforcement of Debts and Bankruptcy distinguishes between two types of insolvency proceedings, namely bankruptcy proceedings (*Konkursverfahren*) and proceedings for a judicial arrangement (*Nachlassvertrag*) accompanied by a moratorium. The revised Federal Statute on the Enforcement of Debts and Bankruptcy provides a third type, allowing individuals who are not subject to involuntary bankruptcy to ask the competent court to permit a private debt-settlement procedure (*Einvernehmliche privat Schuldenbereinigung*), which will be conducted by a court-appointed trustee.

In addition, banks and similar financial institutions are governed by the Banking Code. The Code contains specific rules with respect to insolvency proceedings dealing with the assets of such institutions.

## 19.11.2 Bankruptcy

### 19.11.2.1 Declaration of bankruptcy

Bankruptcy is declared by the competent court at the request (*Konkursbegehren*) of a creditor who has successfully completed the preliminary stages of the debt-collection procedure and whose claim is not fully satisfied at the time of the court hearing. The creditor requesting bankruptcy is liable for the costs of the bankruptcy procedure up to the first assembly of creditors and must make an advance payment at the request of the bankruptcy court.

Without a prior debt-collection procedure, bankruptcy is declared at the request of a creditor whose claim, which need not be due, is credible and who shows that one of the following requirements is met:

(1) the debtor's whereabouts are unknown;
(2) the debtor has fled in order to avoid to be forced to meet his obligations;
(3) the debtor defrauded his creditors;
(4) the debtor concealed a part of his assets in a *Betreibung auf Pfändung*;
(5) the debtor has ceased to make payments and will not resume them in the near future; or
(6) an arrangement has been rejected or revoked.

Should one of the requirements indicated in items (1) to (4), above, be shown, then even a debtor who is otherwise not subject to involuntary bankruptcy will be declared bankrupt.

Bankruptcy is declared at the debtor's request in two instances:

(1) if a debtor, whether or not he is subject to involuntary bankruptcy, files with the court a declaration of insolvency; and
(2) if a corporation, a corporation with unlimited partners, or a co-operative notifies the judge of its over-indebtedness.

Adjudication of bankruptcy is postponed where there is a prospect of a financial reorganisation.[1]

### 19.11.2.2 *Effects of bankruptcy*

Adjudication of bankruptcy has the following effects on the legal relationship between a solvent and an insolvent party:

(1) all seized assets of the bankrupt debtor are attached for satisfying the bankrupt's obligations;

(2) all claims, save the ones secured by immovable property, against the debtor become due;

(3) the rights to administer and dispose of the assets passes from the bankrupt debtor to the trustee in bankruptcy (*Konkursverwalter*); and

(4) individual measures to enforce claims against the bankrupt debtor are prohibited.

### 19.11.2.3 *Filing claims and realising and distributing assets*

A bankruptcy will be published in the official publications. Creditors will be given a deadline for filing their claims and the documents supporting them. Secured creditors must hand over pledges to the trustee in bankruptcy.

In most bankruptcies, a trustee in bankruptcy, a functionary of the office of bankruptcy (*Konkursamt*), is in charge of the bankruptcy procedure. His decisions are subject to appeal. Should the assets of the estate be substantial or should a creditor advance the necessary funds, then the so-called ordinary procedure allows the creditors to participate in the decision-making process; creditors' assemblies will be held, a committee of creditors may be formed, and a private person may be designated as trustee in bankruptcy.

The trustee in bankruptcy lists all claims in the so-called *Kollokationsplan* and decides which claims to admit or reject. A creditor not accepting the rejection of his claim must initiate a lawsuit against the bankruptcy estate within 10 days of the publication of the *Kollokationsplan*.

The proceeds resulting from the realisation of the assets of the bankrupt debtor will be distributed among the creditors of admitted claims. Ordinary creditors receive a bankruptcy dividend only if the claims of the four (in the future perhaps only two) classes of privileged creditors have been fully satisfied. Disputed claims of the debtor and claims arising out of directors' liability are assigned to creditors willing to enforce them at their own risk in most bankruptcy procedures.

To the extent a claim has not been satisfied, a certificate of loss (*Konkursverlustschein*) is issued, and this is of significance only if the debtor is an individual. The most important effects are the following:

(1) the claim on which interest is no longer charged is not subject to the statute of limitations, at least against the debtor himself, but can be

---

1 Code of Obligations, articles 725 *et seq.*

enforced only if the debtor acquires other assets, eg, by inheritance; and

(2)  the certificate of loss constitutes a ground for attachment.

### 19.11.3  Arrangement

In order to avoid being adjudicated bankrupt, many insolvent persons or legal entities submit a petition for a moratorium. By granting such a moratorium, the court institutes judicial arrangement proceedings. This so-called arrangement moratorium (*Nachlasstundung*) has the following effects on the legal relationship between a solvent and an insolvent party:

(1)  the debtor may delay his due payments for several months;
(2)  a person appointed by the court supervises all actions taken by a debtor, but the debtor effectively continues to administer and dispose of the assets; and
(3)  individual measures to enforce claims are prohibited.

The arrangement moratorium has the purpose of establishing an arrangement (*Nachlassvertrag*) between the insolvent debtor and the creditors. Such an arrangement is binding on all creditors if the majority of the creditors, representing two-thirds of the total value of all claims, consent to it and the court approves it. Should the creditors or the court reject it (or revoke the moratorium), then the creditors, within 10 days, may request the declaration of bankruptcy should the debtor be subject to involuntary bankruptcy.

Such arrangements will either provide for payment of a certain percentage of the debts to each creditor or assign all debtor's assets to the creditors.

An assignment of all assets to the creditors has similar consequences as the adjudication of bankruptcy. Therefore, it is universally accepted that the rules of the Federal Statute on the Enforcement of Debts and Bankruptcy dealing with the effects of bankruptcy proceedings are applicable by analogy to an arrangement assigning all debtor's assets to the creditor.[1]

## 19.12   Conclusion

Collecting debts in Switzerland is, in some respects, quite simple (mostly thanks to the unified debt-collection procedure which can be initiated without a judgment) and in other respects, quite complicated (mostly due to the cantonal autonomy in the fields of court organisation and civil procedure).

A creditor's position in the debt-collection procedure is especially strong if the debtor has been successfully induced to acknowledge the debt; then it is most likely that the summary *Rechtsöffnung* procedure (see **19.8.1**, above) will be granted, and the debtor will have to take the initiative and assume the position of the plaintiff in the main procedure. Knowledge of Swiss assets of

---

1  Federal Statute on the Enforcement of Debts and Bankruptcy, articles 208 *et seq*.

debtors not domiciled in Switzerland is a pre-condition to a successful attachment procedure, the consequence of which is still quite often that the non-Swiss (and non-EU and non-EFTA) debtor becomes subject to the jurisdiction of a Swiss court.